THE BATTLE
FOR BURMA
1943–1945

DESPATCHES FROM THE FRONT

*The Commanding Officers' Reports from
the Field and at Sea*

THE BATTLE
FOR BURMA
1943–1945

From Kohima and Imphal
through to Victory

Introduced and compiled by
John Grehan and Martin Mace
with additional research by
Sara Mitchell

Pen & Sword
MILITARY

First published in Great Britain in 2015 by
PEN & SWORD MILITARY
An imprint of
Pen & Sword Books Ltd
47 Church Street
Barnsley
South Yorkshire
S70 2AS

ISBN 978-1-78346-199-8

Typeset by Concept, Huddersfield, West Yorkshire HD4 5JL.
Printed and bound in England by CPI Group (UK) Ltd, Croydon CR0 4YY.

Pen & Sword Books Ltd incorporates the imprints of Pen & Sword Archaeology, Atlas, Aviation, Battleground, Discovery, Family History, History, Maritime, Military, Naval, Politics, Railways, Select, Social History, Transport, True Crime, and Claymore Press, Frontline Books, Leo Cooper, Praetorian Press, Remember When, Seaforth Publishing and Wharncliffe.

For a complete list of Pen & Sword titles please contact
PEN & SWORD BOOKS LIMITED
47 Church Street, Barnsley, South Yorkshire, S70 2AS, England
E-mail: enquiries@pen-and-sword.co.uk
Website: www.pen-and-sword.co.uk

Contents

Introduction

The achievements of the Allied forces in Burma in 1944 and 1945 have always been overshadowed by the great battles in Europe during that period. It is easy to understand why. The countries of Europe are close by and easily accessible. They are places a great many of people in Britain and the United States have visited; their geography is familiar to us, their languages taught in schools. How different it is with Burma, remote and, until recently, a difficult place to travel to and across.

Yet the war in the Far East was a fascinating one. Not only were the Japanese suicidally courageous, but the Allied troops faced conditions that were completely alien to them and terrain that was almost impassable. That they succeeded is a testament to the planning and training that was undertaken after the British and Commonwealth forces had been driven out of Burma in 1942, as well as the determination of those troops to battle on through the jungle and the monsoons, and overcome the animals and insects and the silent foe which killed and incapacitated so many – disease.

It was on 16 November 1943 that the South-East Asia Command was formed to encompass all the military formations in the region. The Army formation within South-East Asia Command was 11 Army Group, whose principal body was the Fourteenth Army. The 11 Army Group was commanded by General Sir George J. Giffard, whose first despatch paints a very clear picture of the country and conditions in which his men had to fight. He also provides an interesting appraisal of the enemy:

> The Japanese soldier is fanatically brave when ordered to succeed or die, yet he is liable to panic when surprised or in doubt. His planning is bold yet he is at a loss if plans go wrong. Although most secretive and careful, he will go into action carrying diaries and military papers. He takes infinite pains to conceal his positions and then nullifies the result by talking in them at night. An expert in the use of ground and in silent movement, yet his patrol work is frequently bad. Although bold at infiltrating into, and then rushing a position from an unexpected direction, he becomes easily nonplussed by determined resistance. He is good at laying fixed lines of fire and skilful in the use of snipers, yet he is a bad shot.

As Giffard then explains, whilst the Japanese were still willing to die for the Emperor, this policy of holding their ground regardless of the sacrifice was already, by June 1944, proving to be a poor tactic in many instances where retreat would have been a more sensible option. Slowly the ordinary Japanese were becoming aware of this and some were actually running away or surrendering, something that would have been considered impossible just a few months earlier. The tide was beginning to turn.

Like most conflicts, the fighting in Burma was not conducted in isolation. The Allied offensive that was mounted in South-East Asia in 1944 and 1945 was undertaken with two strategic goals, both of which were beyond the frontiers of Burma. These were, as spelt out by Giffard, the security and improvement of the air ferry route to China and the establishment of land communications with China; and the close and continuous engagement of Japanese land and air forces, so as to cause attrition and diversion from the Pacific Theatre.

Because of the nature of the high mountains and dense jungles, the movement of large bodies of men was always slow. This would make any large-scale deployment of forces difficult and would allow the Japanese the opportunity to block any advance. Before any major operations could be conducted, therefore, a good road, wide enough for two-way traffic had to be built. Giffard provides a highly detailed report on the actions of the Allied forces up to 22 June 1944. The significance of this date is that it marked the end of one of the most decisive battles of the Burma campaign, Kohima. Another battle of even greater significance, the Battle of Imphal, was still raging, though its end was in sight. With these two victories the last attempt by the Japanese to invade India was defeated.

Giffard's second despatch continues the story of the Burma campaign up to November 1944. It was a period of almost continuous success as the back of the Japanese Army in Burma had been broken at Kohima and Imphal, particularly in the latter where they had lost more than 50,000 men.

Giffard, understandably, writes his despatch with a triumphal air: 'The Japanese retreat [from western Burma] began as a well-planned and orderly withdrawal. Gradually, as our pressure grew, the pace of the withdrawal increased until the enemy forces were split up into small, disorganised parties. Hungry, harassed, beaten; abandoning their wounded, their guns and their transport, and even deserting in small, but increasing numbers; the Japanese were driven in defeat over the border, down the far side of the mountain wall, and back over the Chindwin, which they had crossed in triumph and with such high hopes less than five months earlier.'

Such observations, however, must not disguise or minimise the experiences of the Allied troops, in effect the Fourteenth Army, fighting their way into central Burma. 'Battles were fought at 5,000 feet and over, often in almost impenetrable jungle,' Giffard wrote, 'and troops, loaded with full equipment, struggled up from nullahs [steep, narrow valleys] 2,000 feet below in the face of heavy small arms, grenade and mortar fire.'

It may be surprising to note that Giffard states that, despite the nature of the ground, it was tanks that often proved the decisive factor, 'fighting up and down these mountain ranges, where they climbed almost precipitous slopes to blast Japanese bunkers at a range of 10 yards'. The Allies continued their advance through the monsoon seasons (two in Burma) that 'turned tracks into leech-laden streams and chaungs [streams] into treacherous torrents; rain that washed away our already exiguous roads, turned rivers into raging floods'.

This despatch is similar in length to Giffard's previous one, and together, amounting to almost 50,000 words, they form one of the most detailed accounts of the Burma campaign from the strategic level. One of the subsidiary campaigns undertaken during this period forms the third despatch in this collection. This is the attack upon Ramree Island in January and February 1945, by Vice-Admiral Arthur Power. Once again, the terrain was so inhospitable that Power, like Giffard, was moved to describe it in his despatch: 'Dark during the day as well as during the night, acres of thick impenetrable forest; miles of deep black mud, mosquitoes, scorpions, flies and weird insects by the billion and – worst of all – crocodiles.'

It is the crocodiles which have made the Ramree operation so infamous. The retreating Japanese were urged to surrender but instead tried to escape through the mangrove swamps where some were savagely attacked and eaten by the crocodiles.

The final despatch reproduced in this book was written by Lieutenant General Sir Oliver Leese who became Commander-in-Chief, Allied Land Forces, South-East Asia in November 1944. In this move the American and Chinese troops in South-East Asia were placed under Leese's control along with 11 Army Group.

Predictably, Leese devotes space to describing the Burmese countryside which, as those before him had seen, 'exercised a preponderating influence on all operations'. Leese also makes a point in highlighting the part played by the medial services and the suppressive drugs available without which, he claims, the campaign simply could not have been fought.

Operations undertaken during 1945 focused on the capture of Mandalay and Rangoon with the ultimate aim of crushing the enemy forces. This involved a huge logistical effort with the Fourteenth Army alone requiring 2,000 tons of supplies every day. As the long and difficult overland routes only enabled 700 tons a day to be transported, the rest of General Slim's requirement was delivered by air. This air supply was the largest in any theatre of the war and was one of the key features of the campaign.

It was not until July 1945 that victory was finally achieved in Burma. The country, already poor, had been devastated by the fighting, and Leese found that with each territory that was recaptured from the Japanese an enormous civil program had to be undertaken. Thousands of tons of aid had to be shipped in to help the Burmese who had seen their country ravaged by war twice in just four years.

*   *   *

The objective of this book is to reproduce the despatches from Giffard, Power and Leese as they first appeared to the general public some seventy years ago. They have not been modified, edited or interpreted in any way and are therefore the original and unique words of the commanding officers as they saw things at the time they were written. The only changes that we have made are with the footnotes which are placed at the end of each despatch rather than at the foot of the respective page.

Any grammatical or spelling errors have been left uncorrected to retain the authenticity of the documents. Much has changed in Burma, or the Republic of the Union of Myanmar as it is now known, including many place names and some of the places referred to in the despatches are difficult to find on a modern map of the country.

Martin Mace and John Grehan
Storrington, 2015

Abbreviations

A and MT	Animal & Motor Transport
AA	Anti-Aircraft
AATO	Army Air Transport Organisation
ADC	Aide-De-Camp
ALFSEA	Allied Land Forces South-East Asia
AOC	Air Officer Commanding
Bde	Brigade
Bn, Btn	Battalion
BYMS	British Yacht Minesweeper
CAATO	Combined Army Air Transport Organisation
CAB	Civil Affairs Burma
CAI	Chinese Army in India
CASB	Civil Affairs Service Burma
CB	Companion of the Order of Bath
CBE	Commander of the Most Excellent Order of the British Empire
Cdr	Commander
C-in-C	Commander-in-Chief
CCAO	Chief Civil Affairs Officer
CEF	Chinese Expeditionary Force
CIE	Companion of the Most Eminent Order of the Indian Empire
CMG	Companion of the Most Distinguished Order of Saint Michael and Saint George
COS	Chiefs of Staff
CRE	Commander Royal Engineers
CSI	Companion of the Order of the Star of India
CVO	Commander of the Royal Victorian Order
DDT	Dichlorodiphenyltrichloroethane
DSC	Distinguished Service Cross
DSO	Distinguished Service Order
ENSA	Entertainments National Service Association
FAMO	Forward Airfield Maintenance Organization
FOB	Forward Observer, Bombardment
FOO	Forward Observer Officer
CB	Companion of the Most Honourable Order of the Bath
CBE	Commander of the Order of the British Empire

GCB	Knight Grand Cross of The Most Honourable Order of the Bath
GCIE	Knight Grand Commander of The Most Eminent Order of the Indian Empire
GCSI	Knight Grand Commander of The Most Exalted Order of the Star of India
GCVO	Knight Grand Cross of The Royal Victorian Order
GHQ	General Headquarters
GOC	General Officer Commanding
GOC-in-C	General Officer Commanding-in-Chief
GSO	General Staff Officer
GSOI	General Staff Officer, Intelligence
HE	High Explosive
HMAS	His Majesty's Australian Ship
HMIS	His Majesty's Indian Ship
HMS	His Majesty's Ship
HQ	Headquarters
HQALF	Headquarters Allied Land Forces
IEME	Indian Electrical and Mechanical Engineers
INA	Indian National Army
IWT	Inland Water Transport
JIF	Japanese Indian Fifth Column
KBE	Knight Commander of the Most Excellent Order of the British Empire
KCB	Knight Commander of the Most Honourable Order of the Bath
KOYLI	King's Own Yorkshire Light Infantry
L of C	Lines of Communication
LCA	Landing Craft Assault
LCI	Landing Craft Infantry
LCI(L)	Landing Craft Infantry (Large)
LCS	Landing Craft Support
LCS(M)	Landing Craft Support (Medium)
LGOC	London General Omnibus Company
LRP	Long-Range Penetration
Ls of C	Lines of Communication
MC	Military Cross
MGA	Major-General in charge of Administration
MGGS	Major-General General Staff
ML	Motor Launch
MT	Motor Transport
MVO	Member of the Royal Victorian Order
NAAFI	Navy, Army and Air Force Institutes
NCAC	Northern Combat Area Command

NCO	Non Commissioned Officer
OBE	Officer of the Most Excellent Order of the British Empire
OP	Operation(s)/Observation Post
PC	Patrol Craft
PCO	Principal Commercial Officer
POL	Petrol, Oil, Lubricants
RA	Royal Artillery
RAAF	Royal Australian Air Force
RAC	Royal Armoured Corps
RAF	Royal Air Force
RAMC	Royal Army Medical Corps
RAMO	Rear Airfield Maintenance Organisation
RAN	Royal Australian Navy
RAOC	Royal Army Ordnance Corps
RAP	Regimental Aid Post
RAPC	Royal Army Pay Corps
RASC	Royal Army Service Corps
RAVC	Royal Army Veterinary Corps
RCAF	Royal Canadian Air Force
RE	Royal Engineers
REME	Royal Electrical and Mechanical Engineers
RIASC	Royal Indian Army Service Corps
RN	Royal Navy
RNVR	Royal Navy Volunteer Reserve
RT, R/T	Receiver-Transmitter/Radio Transmitter/Radio Telephony
SAF	Strategic Air Force
SEAC	South-East Asia Command
USAAF	United States Army Air Force
VCP	Visual/Vehicle Control Post
VHF	Very High Frequency
WD	War Department
YMCA	Young Men's Christian Association
YWCA	Young Women's Christian Association

1

GENERAL SIR GEORGE J. GIFFARD'S DESPATCH ON OPERATIONS IN BURMA AND NORTH-EAST INDIA, 16 NOVEMBER 1943 TO 22 JUNE 1944

MONDAY, 19 MARCH, 1951

The following Despatch was submitted to the Secretary of State for War on the 19th *June,* 1945, *by GENERAL SIR GEORGE J. GIFFARD, G.C.B., D.S.O., A.D.C., Commander-in-Chief,* 11 *Army Group, South-East Asia Command.*

PART I. – INTRODUCTION.

1. This Despatch covers the operations in Burma and North-East India between the 16th November, 1943, the date on which the Supreme Allied Commander,[1] South-East Asia, assumed responsibility from the India Command, and the 22nd June, 1944, the date on which our lines of communication from Manipur Road (Dimapur) to Imphal were re-opened, after the defeat of the Japanese forces at Kohima. By this date, also, the enemy had been cleared from the area north of Kamaing, Mogaung and Myitkyina by the Chinese-American forces under General Stilwell,[2] and a re-adjustment of our dispositions to meet monsoon conditions had been made in Arakan. Thus a definite phase of the campaign may be said to have ended. The Despatch also gives an account of the administrative situation and certain major changes in our organization during the period.

Forces allotted and assigned to South-East Asia Command (S.E.A.C.).
2. The formation of the South-East Asia Command necessitated a reorganization of the system of command of the land forces. Until then, the Eastern Army had been under the command of the Commander-in-Chief, India,[3] who was responsible for the conduct of operations in Burma and Assam. The assumption of command by the Supreme Allied Commander entailed the formation of 11 Army Group Headquarters and of Fourteenth Army Headquarters, which then assumed command of the operations which had, up to then, been directed by me as G.O.C.-in-C., Eastern Army.

I was appointed to command 11 Army Group and Lieut.-General W.J. Slim,[4] was selected for command of Fourteenth Army.

The undermentioned formations, etc., previously under India Command, were allotted to South-East Asia Command:-

FOURTEENTH ARMY.

4 *Corps.*

   Lieut.-General G.A.P. Scoones.[5]

      17 Indian Light Division.

      20 Indian Division (less 32 Brigade – joined end of November).

      23 Indian Division.

15 *Indian Corps.*

   Lieut.-General A.F.P. Christison.[6]

      5 Indian Division (less 9 Brigade – joined in December).

      7 Indian Division.

      26 Indian Division (less 4 Brigade – joined in February, 1944).

      81 (West African) Division (less 3 Brigade, allotted to Special Force).

CEYLON ARMY COMMAND.

   Lieut-General H.E. de R. Wetherall.[7]

      11 (East African) Division.

      99 Indian Infantry Brigade.

      Royal Marine Group, Mobile Naval Base Defence Organization
         (less one A.A. Brigade assigned to S.E.A.C. in Southern India).

INDIAN OCEAN BASES.

   Addu Atoll   } Containing

   Diego Garcia } small

   Cocos Islands } garrisons.

In addition, the following troops in India were assigned to South-East Asia Command, being allotted later:-

Headquarters 33 Indian Corps (Lieut.-General M.G.N. Stopford).[8]

2 British Division.

19 Indian Division (Did not arrive until October, 1944; in the interim 25 Indian Division was substituted for it).

36 Indian Division (This consisted of two British brigades, and of divisional troops, some of which were Indian; but it was called "Indian" for deception purposes. It was renamed 36 British Division in July, 1944, and I shall refer to it as such throughout this Despatch).

3 Indian Division (Cover name of Major-General Wingate's[9] "Special Force": consisting of six Long-Range Penetration Brigades; 14, 16 and 23 British Infantry Brigades; 77 and 111 Indian Infantry Brigades and 3 (West African) Infantry Brigade. It contained Gurkha but no Indian units. I shall refer to it hereafter as "Special Force").

50 Indian Tank Brigade.

3 Special Service Brigade (consisting of No. 5 Commando and No. 44 Royal Marine Commando).

Details showing when these "assigned" formations were actually transferred to my command, and allotted to Fourteenth Army, will be given later in this

Despatch. In November, 1943, 15 Corps, consisting of 7 Indian Division and 36 Brigade of 26 Indian Division and 81 (West African) Division (which was just moving in), was holding a line in Arakan approximately from Teknaf to Taung Bazaar facing 55 Japanese Division. The enemy Division had its Headquarters in Akyab, its 143 Regiment was on a line from Maungdaw to Buthidaung, with 112 and 213 Regiments disposed in depth behind this line, in reserve.

4 Corps, composed of 17 Indian Light Division and 20 and 23 Indian Divisions, was responsible for the defence of the Imphal and Tiddim areas of the Central front. The Light Division (48 and 63 Indian Infantry Brigades) was holding the Fort White – Tiddim area against 214 and 215 Regiments of 33 Japanese Division, which was disposed generally along the line of the Chindwin River as far north as Mawlaik. 23 Indian Division was in the Imphal Plain, and had under command 80 Indian Infantry Brigade of 20 Indian Division which was coming forward in relief of 23 Indian Division.

In the north of Burma (designated Northern Combat Area Command – N.C.A.C.) the American-trained and equipped Chinese 22 and 38 Divisions under the command of General Stilwell were in the general area between Ledo and Maingkwan towards which they were advancing. They were opposed by 18 Japanese Division, with 114 Regiment between Myitkyina and Sumprabum, 56 Regiment around Katha and Rail Indaw, and 55 Regiment between Wuntho and Shwebo.

In no sector was there close contact but we, and the Japanese, were patrolling to gain contact; and in Arakan we were preparing for an offensive. The Headquarters of Fourteenth Army was at Barrackpore (later at Comilla) and of 15 Japanese Army at Maymyo.

Geography and Topography.
3. Before discussing the numerous plans which were made and discarded for various reasons and describing the operations which actually took place, it is essential to appreciate the extent to which all operations for the capture of Burma are affected by peculiar topographical and climatic conditions such as exist in few other parts of the world.

4. The Indo-Burmese frontier, from where it leaves the sea in Arakan, near Maungdaw, until it joins the Sino – Thibetan frontier on the Salween River north of Myitkyina, follows a series of mountain ranges, the general axes of which run from north to south. The main features of these mountain ranges are their precipitous sides and the fast flowing rivers in the deep valleys. These mountains are at their maximum heights at the north-east end of the frontier, where they rise to heights of ten to twelve thousand feet and more. Their height gradually declines as the ranges run southwards, though in the Naga and Chin Hills there are many peaks of 9,000 feet, until they reach the lesser ranges in Arakan where the maximum heights are seldom over 2,000 feet. The main spine, however, of this range continues southwards, parallel to the coast, towards the mouth of the Irrawaddy and finally disappears just north of the town of Bassein. Throughout

these ranges the hillsides are for the most part covered with jungle so dense that it is not possible to move without cutting paths. In the whole length of this mountain system there are only three roads, none of them of good quality, over which wheels can pass. These are the Ledo – Myitkyina road, the Dimapur – Imphal – Tamu road and the Taungup – Prome road, none of which has been completed to a standard which will carry heavy traffic all the year round.

5. East and south of this great mountain system lies the main river basin of the Irrawaddy with its principal tributary the Chindwin to the west and almost parallel to it until it joins the Irrawaddy at Myingyan. The Irrawaddy forms a delta which begins just north of Henzada, but the main mouth reaches the sea just south of Rangoon. The Irrawaddy is navigable by various craft, according to the time of the year, as far north as Myitkyina; and the Chindwin can be navigated up to Tamanthi. These two great rivers provide, therefore, first class lines of communication throughout the year. The valley of the Irrawaddy and other tributary valleys provide access for a system of railways which, starting at Rangoon, pass through Mandalay to Myitkyina. There are various branches such as that from Rangoon to Prome and from Sagaing to Ye-U. The road system in Burma is reasonably good, especially from Ye-U southwards. Communications, therefore, in Burma, may be said to be adequate for the maintenance and movement of large forces. It is clear, therefore, that it should always be possible for the Japanese with these communications to concentrate superior forces to meet any advance by us over the three indifferent roads over the mountains.

6. In Arakan the "chaungs" (or waterways) with which the coastal strip is intersected are almost as great an obstacle as the hills and the jungle. In dry weather they can be forded by infantry at low water, but at other times a six-foot tide makes them difficult to cross. In the rains of the South-West monsoon they are swollen by flood water which makes them greater obstacles. The banks are usually muddy and crumbling. Bridging presents considerable difficulties and special arrangements have to be made at each for the passage of tanks and mechanical transport.

7. There are other difficulties also for our forces operating southwards in Arakan. The two main rivers, the Mayu and the Kaladan, with their tributaries, converge on the main Japanese base at Akyab. By his command of the entrance to these two waterways, the enemy was able to make use of excellent water communications which were denied to us.

Climatic Conditions.
8. The climate of Burma is affected by the two monsoons, the North-East in the winter and the South-West in the summer. The influence of the former produces fine dry weather with little cloud and conditions are good for operations both on land and in the air. The South-West monsoon on the other hand, blowing as it does across the Bay of Bengal, is heavily charged with moisture which it discharges over Burma and Eastern Bengal during the months of May to October.

Precipitation of rain, especially on the Arakan coast, is extremely high, reaching in places as much as 200 inches. The climate varies too, according to the altitude, the temperatures above 3,000 feet being reasonably low and above 5,000 feet cool and invigorating. In the lowlands along the coast, the temperatures are high, with a high humidity which makes campaigning in those areas exhausting.

9. Malaria is endemic throughout the country below 3,000 feet but it is worse in some areas than others; for instance, the Kabaw Valley is reputed to be one of the worst malarial valleys in the world. There are two seasonal increases in the rate of infection, one at the beginning of the monsoon in May, and the other at the end of the monsoon in October and November. Much has been done to reduce the casualties from malaria during the past two years and the ineffective rate amongst all troops has fallen very considerably. This is due to much improved personal discipline, efficient draining of bad areas on the lines of communication, training and various medical prophylactic measures which have been introduced. In such a climate there are other diseases which are products of the conditions; dysentery, the worst effects of which have been reduced by discipline and good hygiene measures, skin diseases of various types, especially during the rainy season, and scrub typhus which is endemic in various areas.

10. While the South-West monsoon has a bad effect upon the health of troops and causes them also acute discomfort from wet, its really worst effect is upon the communications in the country. The heavy rain turns Arakan, a rice growing area, into a muddy swamp quite impassable to wheeled vehicles unless the roads have proper foundations and surfaces capable of withstanding heavy rain. In Assam and Burma there is very little stone, most of the hills, which are clothed in forest or bamboo, being composed of a soft shale quite useless for road making. The making of roads is, therefore, very difficult as they have to be built to a high standard in order to stand up to the torrential rains which fall between May and October. The heavy rains also make the ordinary native tracks very nearly impassable as they get so slippery on the steep hillsides that neither man nor beast can stand up on them. Finally, as can be imagined, these heavy rains make the rivers and streams into very formidable obstacles, all of which have to be bridged to allow the passage of troops and transport.

Indeed, campaigning in the monsoon in Burma may be said to be one of the most arduous operations anywhere in the world today.

The Japanese Soldier.
11. The Japanese soldier is fanatically brave when ordered to succeed or die, yet he is liable to panic when surprised or in doubt. His planning is bold yet he is at a loss if plans go wrong. Although most secretive and careful, he will go into action carrying diaries and military papers. He takes infinite pains to conceal his positions and then nullifies the result by talking in them at night. An expert in the use of ground and in silent movement, yet his patrol work is frequently bad. Although bold at infiltrating into, and then rushing a position from an unexpected

direction, he becomes easily nonplussed by determined resistance. He is good at laying fixed lines of fire and skilful in the use of snipers, yet he is a bad shot.

12. Our successes in the fighting have, in no small measure, been due to the fact that we have taken full advantage of the enemy's weak points. The results have been gratifying, not only tactically, but also psychologically: signs are not lacking that the blind obedience, fanatical courage and determination to die rather than surrender, which the Japanese soldier has hitherto displayed, may not withstand the continuous reverses which he is now suffering and will suffer in the future. That this fact has been recognised by the Japanese High Command, and is causing some misgiving, has been seen in captured orders.

This must not be taken to mean, however, that the Japanese soldier now surrenders easily. His whole up-bringing and outlook make him regard capture as the worst disgrace. Consequently, even when cornered, he not only sells his life dearly, but will frequently commit suicide rather than surrender. The mopping-up of captured enemy positions is, therefore, a slow process, as every Japanese officer and man has usually to be ferreted out and killed. Since the crushing defeat inflicted on the enemy in the Imphal battle, and the failure of his lines of communication, there have been a few surrenders of unwounded men, but they are still rare.

13. To sum up, I would say that, although his discipline and training are good, the Japanese soldier has shown himself lacking in initiative and self-reliance when his leaders have been killed and he is faced with the unexpected. The very fact that surrender has now made its appearance, though on a very small scale, in an army where such a thing was undreamt of, is not without significance.

The Outlook in November, 1943.

14. Strategically, Burma is important for three reasons:-

(*a*) The only way in which we can, either now or in the immediate future, send help to China is through or over Burma.

(*b*) Burma is the principal area in which we can contain and destroy considerable Japanese forces.

(*c*) In our hands Burma provides a stepping stone for operations further east or south. In Japanese hands it is a base for operations against the eastern frontier of India.

15. As a result of decisions reached at the Quebec Conference, the Chiefs of Staff directed the Supreme Allied Commander to undertake operations in Burma with two objects:-

(*a*) The security and improvement of the air ferry route to China and the establishment of land communications with China.

(*b*) The close and continuous engagement of Japanese land and air forces, so as to cause attrition and diversion from the Pacific Theatre.

To execute these orders meant, of course, offensive operations whenever and wherever possible; but it was obvious that the main operations to secure Northern Burma, without which complete security of the China air route could not be ensured, would have to be launched from Imphal, Yunnan and Ledo.

16. As our resources were limited, it was essential to decide on the southern limits of such an offensive. Examination showed that only the capture of the Shwebo – Mandalay area would fulfil the instructions of the Chiefs of Staff but this was beyond our resources, either in troops or transport aircraft. Plans of a less ambitious nature which would obey the spirit of the instructions to the Supreme Allied Commander had, therefore, to be considered.

17. The plan generally approved at Quebec was:-

(*a*) The capture by Long-Range Penetration Forces of the Katha – Indaw area which would be then held by a division, flown in or moved overland across the Chindwin with light equipment.
(*b*) The capture of Mogaung – Myitkyina by Chinese-American forces from Ledo with possible exploitation southwards.
(*c*) An advance on Bhamo – Lashio by Chinese forces from Yunnan.

The plan which I had thought gave the best chance of success was made in September 1943, when the Commander-in-Chief, India, was still in command of the operations and I was G.O.C.-in-C., Eastern Army. This plan aimed at forcing a crossing of the Chindwin on the Imphal Front, and the introduction with the aid of airborne troops of a force of all arms, including tanks and medium artillery, into the Central Burma plain in the Ye-U area. A detailed examination of the many problems which such a plan created, among them the capacity of the Assam lines of communication, and the delays in the concentration programme caused by the breaching of the main railway line to Calcutta from the west by the Damodar River, showed that the launching of such an offensive before early March was not possible.

This plan was submitted to the British Chiefs of Staff, who preferred an airborne operation against Katha – Indaw because there would be closer support and co-operation with Chinese forces advancing south from Ledo and across the Salween. This plan, approved at the Cairo conference in November 1943, had eventually to be abandoned as the necessary transport aircraft were not forthcoming. It became necessary, therefore, to make a less ambitious plan.

18. It was not easy, within the means at our disposal, even partially to achieve the objects given by the Chiefs of Staff. After several alternatives had been examined and rejected, I submitted to the Supreme Allied Commander, in December, the following plan.

(*a*) An advance down the Kabaw Valley towards Kalewa – Kalemyo; the construction of an all-weather road, via Tamu, as far as possible towards Yuwa and Kalewa on the Chindwin.

(*b*) The use (initially) of three Long-Range Penetration Brigades in the Katha – Indaw area.

The objects I had in mind were:-

(i) To achieve a greater, though not complete measure of security for the China air route, by forcing the enemy further south.

(ii) To obtain greater freedom of action for offensive operations in 1944–45, when more resources might be expected.

(iii) To destroy the maximum possible number of Japanese land and air forces.

(iv) To gain some control of Upper Burma by the employment, in conjunction with our main forces and those of the Chinese Army in India (C.A.I.), of Long-Range Penetration Troops to confuse the enemy and inflict casualties.

19. This plan was approved by the Supreme Allied Commander and was referred by him to the Chiefs of Staff early in December. It depended for success not only on overcoming strong enemy defences in the Tiddim area, but also on progress in road construction. At the end of January, the Chiefs of Staff were told that we did not anticipate reaching the Kalewa – Kalemyo area before the monsoon. Actually the all-weather road of a two-way standard had only reached a point ten miles south of Palel, though it was all-weather one-way for a good many miles south of that point, when the enemy launched their March offensive.

20. Concurrently with planning for operations on the Imphal Front, planning for operations in Arakan was, of course, in progress. Several plans, which included amphibious operations against Akyab in conjunction with an advance down the Mayu Peninsula, were examined, but all were eventually abandoned either for lack of resources or for other reasons, and I was thrown back on a plan for an advance with the limited objective of the Maungdaw – Buthidaung road, and the mouth of the Naf River. Once the latter was captured, supplies could be brought in by sea, not only to Maungdaw but also to Teknaf.

21. Other plans for amphibious operations, among them one for the capture of the Andamans, were also examined, but all were in the end rejected as the resources for them were needed for more important operations in other theatres of war.

I was finally compelled, therefore, to limit the operations of the Army to a short advance in Arakan and advances down the Tiddim road and Kabaw Valley with the object of capturing the Kalewa – Kalemyo area.

PART II – OPERATIONS.

Operations by 15 *Indian Corps in Arakan.*

22. In November, 1943, we were in contact with the Japanese in Arakan, the Imphal Front and in North Burma (N.C.A.C.).

The situation in Arakan at the end of the monsoon of 1943, was that we held positions covering Cox's Bazaar with 26 Indian Division on the general line

Teknaf – Taung Bazaar, while the enemy held the Maungdaw – Buthidaung road. The advance to close contact started in the middle of October.

23. Between October and the end of December other changes were made in our dispositions:-

(*a*) 26 Indian Division was relieved by 7 and 5 Indian Divisions.

(*b*) 7 Indian Division moved across the Mayu Range, complete with all its guns and lorries. A fair-weather road was built over the Ngakyedauk Pass, which lies north-west of the village of that name, to provide the necessary communications.

(*c*) 5 Indian Division took over the western sector of the front.

(*d*) Our rear areas were readjusted.

(*e*) Finally we drove in the enemy's out-post line.

At the end of December, 5 Indian Division held from the sea to the crest of the Mayu Range, while 7 Indian Division, had moved over complete into the Kalapanzin Valley. The stage was set for an attack on the main enemy position.

24. Early in January, I issued an Operational Instruction to the Commander, Fourteenth Army, Lieut.-General W.J. Slim, directing him to secure the mouth of the Naf River; Maungdaw – Buthidaung; and exploit success to the maximum. These instructions were based on an Operational Directive issued by the Supreme Allied Commander. My objects were, first, to improve our general situation in Arakan, and, second, to contain and destroy Japanese forces.

25. A period during which certain subsidiary operations were undertaken to secure the necessary jumping-off places for our offensive then followed. The enemy defended these positions stubbornly.

On the 15th January, the dispositions of the forward elements of 15 Indian Corps (Lieut.-General A.F.P. Christison), were as follows:-

5 Indian Division: Maungdaw – Magyi Chaung – Rehkat Chaung – Point 1619, with a brigade in reserve west of the Mayu Range.

7 Indian Division: One brigade in the hills north and north-east of Htindaw. One brigade Tatmakhali to Sinohbyin, with forward troops on the Letwedet Chaung. One brigade Kyaukit *massif* – Pyinshe – Windwin, with a detachment on the Saingdin Chaung.

81 (West African) Division: Daletme – Satpaung area, in the Kaladan Valley.

Tanks: One regiment, in support of 5 Indian Division.

Medium Artillery: One battery in support of each division.

26. The enemy had turned the area about the Tunnels, through which the road runs in its passage through the highest portion of the Mayu Range between Maungdaw and Buthidaung, into a fortress with two strong buttresses – Razabil on the west and Letwedet on the east.

The general plan of attack was framed to capture these two buttresses in turn and surround the garrison of the Tunnels fortress. 5 Indian Division was to take

Razabil and 7 Indian Division Buthidaung, thus cutting in behind the Letwedet buttress. 81 (West African) Division was to advance down the Kaladan River to capture Kyauktaw, with the ultimate object of cutting the Kanzauk – Htizwe road, which was the enemy's main lateral line of communication between the Kaladan and Kalapanzin Valleys.

27. The main offensive was launched on the 19th January, and, despite strong opposition, our preliminary operations against the enemy's outposts were very successful. The original plan had included a sea landing by 2 British Division further south down the Mayu Peninsula. As we did not wish to drive the Japanese into the toe of the Peninsula until 2 British Division had effected a firm lodgement, our attack on the main enemy positions was deferred to synchronize with the sea landing, the date of which could not be put forward as it was governed by the state of the tide and moon. Unfortunately, the craft required for the amphibious operation were taken away and, therefore, this "right hook" had to be cancelled. Thus our land offensive had been held up to no purpose. By the 4th February, however, the attack on Razabil had achieved a measure of success, but the main position still held out. Progress elsewhere had been steady, but slow.

28. It was at this moment that the enemy launched his counter-attack and our offensive had to be delayed until the enemy attack had been defeated. This took some four weeks, but when it was finished the attack on our original objectives was continued.

29. This Japanese counter-attack merits attention, both on account of the boldness of its conception and also on account of the firm stand made by 7 Indian Division which was surrounded and attacked from all sides. The Division was supplied by air and thus did not have to retire when its lines of communication were cut. This was the main cause of the defeat of the Japanese counter-attack.

30. In the last week of January, identification of a fresh enemy regiment was obtained. On the 1st February, documents ordering the J.I.Fs. (Indians fighting for the Japanese) to concentrate east of the Mayu Range at once for an operation were captured. I was in Fourteenth Army area at that time and discussed the position with the Army Commander. We concluded that these moves indicated a counter-attack by the Japanese, but were unable to decide upon the exact form it was likely to take, though it seemed probable that an attempt to outflank 15 Indian Corps was the most probable. We agreed that if 5 and 7 Indian Divisions held their positions against a frontal attack, while at the same time preparing an all-round defence to meet attacks from the flank or rear, it would be possible to destroy any Japanese outflanking detachment with the reserves. I placed 36 British Division, which had arrived at Chittagong for another operation, at General Slim's disposal and he ordered one brigade of this Division, together with 26 Indian Division, which was in Fourteenth Army reserve in the Comilla area, to move south at once. He ordered all formations in the forward

areas to hold their ground. He made arrangements for the packing for air transport of three days' rations, ammunition and medical stores and with the R.A.F. for their delivery by air to 7 Indian Division, if called for. These preparations had a far reaching effect on the battle.

31. When the enemy's blow actually fell on the 4th February, it so happened that preparations for transferring our offensive from the west to the east of the Mayu Range were in progress. One infantry brigade of 5 Indian Division had moved over to the east of the range to free one brigade of 7 Indian Division for this operation; thus 15 Indian Corps had available at that time a reserve infantry brigade and a tank regiment east of the range, which was the flank menaced by the Japanese threat.

32. The Japanese plan, captured early in the battle, was to pass through and round the left flank of 7 Indian Division, take Taung Bazaar from the east, and cut the Bawli Bazaar – Razabil road. This move completed, the Japanese intended to attack 7 Indian Division from the rear and drive it through the Ngakyedauk Pass. This would isolate 5 Indian Division which would in turn be mopped up and the remnants driven over the Naf River. So certain were they of success, that the Tokyo radio announced victories at the appropriate times, according to their pre-arranged timetable, regardless that this time-table bore no relation to the facts.

33. The attack against 7 Indian Division began with the appearance in rear of its left flank at Taung Bazaar of an enemy regiment, with elements from two others, which had passed partly round our left flank through the jungle and partly through the positions held by 114 Brigade. Almost simultaneously, strong frontal attacks were made by two regiments in the area north and north-west of Buthidaung. A brigade of 7 Indian Division, which had been relieved by 5 Indian Division, but had not yet been committed to their new task, was sent north to check the enemy advance southwards from Taung Bazaar. In this it partially succeeded, but, owing to the closeness of the country and the enemy's numerical superiority, was outflanked by a party of the enemy which overran the Headquarters of 7 Indian Division in the early morning. The Divisional Commander, however, regained control of the operations that evening. Brigades and divisional troops had been ordered to prepare positions capable of all round defence as soon as the enemy's presence in Taung Bazaar had been discovered. 9, 33 and 114 Brigades, therefore, dug in on their positions, while another defended area which contained Divisional H.Q., part of 89 Brigade and Divisional Troops was hastily prepared in the area of Awlanbyin and Sinzweya. These areas were called "boxes" during the battle.

34. The enemy cut the Ngakyedauk Pass and closely invested these boxes. One Japanese battalion also crossed by the Maunghnama Pass further north and began to harass 15 Indian Corps Headquarters and the rear of 5 Indian Division from a

position in the hills on the east of the road. But they made no further headway, although on the 9th February the situation in 7 Indian Division's defended area (Sinzweya) was difficult and continued so for several days. 26 Indian Division, which had been moved up to Bawli Bazaar by 15 Indian Corps, now began to make its presence felt, but it was evident that its operations, in conjunction with those of 5 Indian Division from the west to clear the Ngakyedauk Pass, would take time.

35. Supply dropping to the various boxes began on the 9th February, and an airstrip for the evacuation of casualties was ready by the 12th at Taung Bazaar, which had by then been cleared of the enemy.

36. In spite of continuous attacks, supported by the fire of 150-mm guns and by fighter bombers, the enemy were unable to reduce any of our strongholds. On the 12th the Commander, 7 Indian Division issued orders to take the offensive to prevent any further hostile infiltration and the escape of any enemy already in his rear. The enemy was now "in the bag" and it was the task of 7 Indian Division to keep him there until destroyed.

37. Severe fighting continued with the Japanese trying to stem the advance of 26 and 5 Indian Divisions and overcome what their orders described as "the hysterical defence" of the areas of 7 Indian Division. Hysterical or not, it may one day be called historical as it was the first successful reply to Japanese large-scale infiltration tactics in jungle country. The bitterness of the fighting is illustrated by the remark made by a veteran of Dunkirk, who spent two days on the beaches; he stated he would willingly have spent a fortnight at Dunkirk if he could have been let off with two days in 7 Indian Divisional defended area.

38. On the 16th February, 36 British Division began to relieve 26 Indian Division to enable it to concentrate east of the Mayu Range.

39. By the 20th February, the shortage of food and ammunition, severe casualties and lack of any tactical success began to have their effect upon the Japanese forces, and they began to try to escape, at first in driblets and then in larger parties. Many of them failed to run the gauntlet and were wiped out. By the 24th February the Ngakyedauk Pass had been re-opened and the Japanese offensive, heralded as the beginning of the march on Delhi, had been defeated.

40. It is convenient at this stage to examine the enemy's plan and analyse the cause of its failure.

The Japanese have always supported the doctrine that the best defence is the attack. They proved it to their satisfaction in Arakan in the Spring of 1943 and they confidently expected to prove it again in 1944. Their attacks have usually taken the form of an enveloping movement combined with infiltration and frontal attacks.

These tactics achieved success in 1943, partly owing to the lack of training of our forces and partly owing to the fact that it was not possible, for lack of supplies, for forward troops to hold out when their lines of communication were cut.

41. The Japanese plan was bold, typical of their readiness to take risks, and its execution went smoothly for the first thirty-six hours. It then began to fail, at first slowly but with increasing momentum until disaster overtook it. The main reasons for this failure were:-

(*a*) The Japanese conviction that we should retire if our rear was threatened, as we had done in 1943. His whole plan was based on this assumption. A captured directive, by the Commander of 55 Divisional Infantry Group, ended with this significant phrase- "As they have previously suffered defeat, should a portion of the enemy waver the whole of them will at once get confused and victory is thus certain".

(*b*) The fine fighting spirit of all ranks who, in this the first large encounter with the Japanese this year, showed their superiority in jungle-fighting when well trained and adequately equipped.

(*c*) The ability to supply forward troops by air.

Contributory factors to its failure were our successful use of tanks over ground much of which was regarded as "untankable", the use of medium artillery, and our continual harassing from the air of the enemy's water-borne and road communications. The Japanese under-estimation of their enemy and their conviction that they would capture large quantities of supplies in the first few days, led them to neglect their arrangements for the supply of food and ammunition and their troops carried only five days' food. We defeated all their attempts to bring food or ammunition forward. In consequence, their troops soon began to suffer from hunger and starvation and shortage of ammunition. Their casualties amounted to 4,500 killed and wounded out of a total of 7,000 men.

The basic reason for our victory was, however, the refusal of our troops, or any portion of them, to waver, and their unflinching courage in exceptionally trying circumstances.

42. Mopping up in the thick mountainous jungle was a difficult and necessarily slow operation, and it was not until the 5th March that we were able to resume the interrupted course of our offensive. Razabil was captured by 5 Indian Division on the 12th March. It was found to be a position of great strength, complete with underground rooms, etc. The Tunnels position was surrounded by the 19th March, and was finally captured by 36 British Division some days later. Meanwhile, 7 Indian Division had taken Buthidaung and had also captured the outer ring of the Kyaukit defences. These defences were evacuated by the enemy on the 23rd March and considerable equipment fell into our hands. On the 25th, about 500 enemy again infiltrated to the Ngakyedauk area, but were dealt with expeditiously.

43. At the end of March, 25 Indian Division began to take over from 5 Indian Division and the latter was transferred by air to 4 Corps' front.

44. Fighting to improve our positions continued throughout April against strong opposition. As a result of successful actions by 26 Indian Division in the Buthidaung area in the first week in May, we withdrew from Buthidaung, as planned, to positions more suitable for the monsoon; forward brigades of 15 Indian Corps taking up positions on the general line Godusara – Tunnels Area – Taung Bazaar.

45. 36 British Division was withdrawn to Shillong in Assam to rest and refit, with a view to its being transferred to General Stilwell's command in North Burma at a later date. 7 Indian Division, two brigades moving by air, also left Arakan in April for 4 Corps' front.

By the end of May, therefore, we were holding Arakan with 15 Indian Corps, comprising three divisions. Our monsoon dispositions being:-

25 *Indian Division:* In the Tunnels Area, covering the Maungdaw – Buthidaung road, up to and including, the East Tunnel.

26 *Indian Division:* One brigade in the Bawli – Goppe – Taung Bazaars area. One brigade at Taungbro and the third at Cox's Bazaar.

81 *(West African) Division:* Concentrating at Chiringa.

We also had detachments on the Sangu River as flank protection against a small Japanese force which had infiltrated into that area.

46. The term "monsoon dispositions" does not imply static defence. We occupied positions of our own choice, selected for their strength and to preserve the health of our troops by avoiding the worst malarial areas. The necessity, during the monsoon in Arakan, to evacuate certain flooded districts and take up positions which are defensively strong and accessible for supplies, did not mean that every opportunity for local offensive action was not taken.

Results of the Arakan Campaign.
47. As already mentioned (paragraph 24), the objects of the Arakan campaign were to improve our general situation and engage and destroy Japanese forces. Our success had led me to hope that we could clear the whole of the Mayu Peninsula, but the need for providing reinforcements (5 and 7 Indian Divisions) for the Imphal Front frustrated this.

Although this further advance was not possible, the objects of the campaign had been generally achieved. Maungdaw had been firmly established as a base; the Mayu Range, including the important Tunnels area, together with the eastern foothills, was firmly in our hands; and the lateral road was in daily use.

55 Japanese Division, despite reinforcements, had been outfought and was weak and tired. In spite of the reduction in the strength of 15 Indian Corps by three divisions (the 5th, 7th and 36th), operations after their withdrawal went

according to plan. To sum up, the Japanese offensive, from which they confidently expected great results, had been defeated, and we had captured our objectives. Last, but not least, we had established a moral ascendency over the enemy which promised well for the future.

Operations in the Kaladan Valley.
48. The Japanese threatened our left flank during the previous year's operations by advancing up the Kaladan River, and I was determined that this should not happen again. 81 (West African) Division was, in consequence, moved across into the Kaladan Valley to protect the left flank of 15 Indian Corps.

Our ability to supply troops by air made it possible for a division to operate down this valley, but the physical difficulties of moving into the valley were great. A jeep track 73 miles long had to be built from Chiringa to Daletme across four mountain ranges. It was begun on the 18th November and finished on the 17th January – an engineering feat which reflected the greatest credit on all ranks.

49. 81 (West African) Division concentrated in the Satpaung – Daletme area in January and started its move down the Kaladan at the end of that month. They captured Kyauktaw by the 3rd March and were then advancing on Apaukwa when a strong Japanese counter-attack developed from the south-east. The advance had to be stopped in order to meet it. The enemy captured our position near Kyauktaw and the Division withdrew to positions south of Kaladan Village. Thereafter, it continued its rôle of flank protection in the Paletwa area.

50. In April, this Division (less one battalion left at Paletwa, where it was joined by two battalions of Indian troops, one of which was withdrawn later) was moved westwards across the Arakan Yomas to the east of the Kalapanzin River, to provide closer protection to the left flank of 15 Indian Corps. Subsequently, it was withdrawn via Buthidaung – Taung Bazaar to the neighbourhood of Chiringa.

51. The battalion left in the Kaladan was later reinforced by Headquarters 6 (West African) Brigade and another battalion. One Indian battalion also remained in the area. The rôle of this force was to frustrate attempts which the Japanese were making to infiltrate across the hills into the Sangu Valley. It was later withdrawn into this valley and, in June, was providing detachments along the Sangu River, which were successful in driving back, with considerable losses, small enemy forces which had penetrated this area.

The Chin Hills.
52. The link between Arakan and the Imphal Front is the Chin Hills; the strategic importance of which lies in the fact that it covers the approaches to Chittagong and Aijal, via Lungleh. It also flanks the Japanese lines of communication through Gangaw to Kalemyo.

53. The Chin Hills and the Lushai Hills lying west of them, were garrisoned by two detachments of Levies, each with a stiffening of one regular battalion; Headquarters being at Aijal. The rôle of these detachments was to interrupt the

enemy's communications and to hamper his movements in the area Aijal – Champai – Falam – Haka. Early in November 1943, however, just before the assumption of command by Admiral The Lord Louis Mountbatten, the enemy advancing in some strength, had, though they suffered severe casualties in gaining these minor successes, driven our Irregulars out of Falam and Haka and caused our regular troops to withdraw from Fort White.

54. Early in April, another battalion was added to the Chin Hills detachment, which then became the Lushai Brigade. This force has performed its task very satisfactorily, laying ambushes, obtaining information, and inflicting considerable losses. It was reinforced by an additional battalion in June, and ordered to interfere with the Japanese communications along the Imphal – Tiddim road.

The Chindwin.
55. 4 Corps (Lieut.-General G.A.P. Scoones), with Headquarters at Imphal, had been responsible for the defence of the Indian frontier east and south of Manipur since 1942. The area for which the Corps was responsible extended from its boundary with Northern Combat Area Command (N.C.A.C.) on the line Mawlu – Taro – Wakching (40 miles east of Jorhat) down to and inclusive of the Chin Hills. In November 1943, 23 Indian Division had its Headquarters at Tamu, and 17 Indian Light Division with its Headquarters was on the Imphal – Tiddim road at Milestone 102. 20 Indian Division, with its Headquarters at Shenam, about 10 miles south-east of Palel, was engaged in patrolling across the Chindwin. At the end of December the whole of this Division had been concentrated in the Tamu area, its Headquarters having moved forward to Sibong. This Division relieved 23 Indian Division which was withdrawn from the Imphal Plain for rest and training; having been in the forward area without relief since June 1942.

56. The task which I had allotted Fourteenth Army on this sector of the front was to carry out offensive operations with the objects of:-
(*a*) Clearing the Chin Hills as far as the foothills south-east of Tiddim.
(*b*) Dominating the area between the Yu and Chindwin Rivers, south of the Tamu – Sittaung road.
(*c*) Containing and killing Japanese in the Kabaw Valley and Atwin Yomas.
(*d*) Pushing forces across the Chindwin, if the Long-Range Penetration Brigades created a favourable situation.

57. On the 13th January, patrols reported considerable enemy activity east of the Chindwin, between Sittaung and Paungbyin, and also east of Homalin, some forty miles further up the river. This information, which supplemented previous air reconnaissance reports, indicated that the enemy might be preparing for an offensive.

58. On the 17th January, we attacked enemy positions at Kyaukchaw, eighteen miles southeast of Tamu in the Atwin Yomas, and there were other small operations in the same area during the month.

59. Throughout January and February, 17 Indian Light Division was continually engaged with the enemy in the Tiddim area; attack and counter-attack following each other in quick succession.

The Japanese Offensive against Imphal and Kohima.
60. During February, it became steadily more evident that the Japanese were preparing for an offensive across the Chindwin and from the area about Fort White against 17 Indian Light Division. The general situation remained unchanged until the 8th March, when the anticipated Japanese offensive was launched. This began with two main advances, one up the west bank of the Manipur River, the other northwards up the Kabaw Valley, from which Japanese columns moved westwards to cut the Imphal – Tiddim road. It was also apparent, from the enemy's dispositions, that he would probably launch an offensive farther north from the Thaungdut – Homalin area against Tamu, Ukhrul and Kohima.

61. Our dispositions at the beginning of March were:-

50 *Indian Parachute Brigade:* Kohima. This Brigade (less one battalion) had been flown in from India as a reinforcement to 4 Corps early in March.
23 *Indian Division:* One brigade in the Ukhrul area; the remainder south and southeast of Imphal.
20 *Indian Division:* On the Tamu road and in the Kabaw Valley.
17 *Indian Light Division* (two brigades only): Tiddim area.

62. On the 7th March, I had sent an instruction to the Commander, Fourteenth Army, of which the following were the main points:-

(*a*) A warning that the impending Japanese offensive against 4 Corps' area would probably be on a considerably larger scale than anything the enemy had yet attempted in Burma.
(*b*) An indication of the tactical difficulties of the situation, due to the fundamental weakness of our line of communication being parallel to the enemy's front along the Chindwin River.
(*c*) The strategical importance of the Imphal Plain: (i) as a base for the maintenance and operation of our air and land forces, and (ii) its value to the Japanese as a base for attacks against the Surma Valley in Eastern Bengal and our Assam lines of communication. Attacks against Bengal would have an adverse and widespread moral effect; while interruption of the Assam lines of communication would seriously jeopardise both the Sino-American operations based on Ledo and the air ferry route to China. I pointed out that the enemy's effort without control of the Imphal Plain, would probably have to be confined to raids, owing to the indifferent communications and the paucity of food supplies in the hill tracts.
(*d*) The security of the Imphal Plain was his primary task.
(*e*) A confirmation of the authority I had recently given General Slim verbally that he might, if necessary, give ground in the Chin Hills and the Kabaw Valley. In this event, I stated he would be justified in using Long-Range

Penetration forces to operate boldly against the enemy's flanks and communications.

(f) I stated that, apart from 25 Indian Division, Long-Range Penetration Brigades, and 50 Indian Parachute Brigade, immediate reinforcements for 4 Corps must come from Fourteenth Army sources, and that, therefore, preparations should be made for the quickest possible moves of troops to reinforce 4 Corps, although this might (i) limit the depth of our advance in Arakan, (ii) cause troops to be retained in Arakan longer than desirable and (iii) interfere with intended reliefs. 77 and 111 Long-Range Penetration Brigades were already in the Fourteenth Army area; 16 Long-Range Penetration Brigade was marching into North Burma, 14 and 23 Long-Range Penetration Brigades, and 3 (West African) Long-Range Penetration Brigade, were about to move into Fourteenth Army's area from India. I promised to investigate whether the projected moves of 14 and 23 Long-Range Penetration Brigades could be accelerated.

63. The relative dispositions of our own troops and those of the enemy and the topography of the country all combined to facilitate infiltration, which is the basis of Japanese tactics in fighting in close country. General Slim, therefore, decided very rightly, that to leave 17 Indian Light Division at Tiddim, and 20 Indian Division east and south of Tamu would not only give the Japanese excellent opportunities of cutting off these two Divisions, but would imperil the defence of the Imphal Plain which was his primary task.

He also appreciated that, if he could engage the Japanese forces in the neighbourhood of the Imphal Plain, he would impose upon them all the difficulties and disadvantages of a long line of communication over difficult country and preserve to himself the advantages of a short line of communication.

64. The G.O.C-in-C. 4 Corps gave instructions to Commander, 17 Indian Light Division, that he was to withdraw if his line of communication was seriously threatened. The Commander, 17 Indian Light Division, not finding himself unduly pressed frontally, and not realising the extent to which the enemy were infiltrating behind him, postponed his retirement somewhat too long. 17 Indian Light Division, therefore, became so closely involved that the Commander, 4 Corps had to make use of the greater portion of 23 Indian Division, his only reserve, to assist in extricating it. This had serious results as the forces defending Ukhrul were so reduced that the enemy was able to capture the place.

65. I had for many months been anxious to increase the strength of 4 Corps by another division; but the low capacity of the line of communication had prevented its maintenance in that area and I had to be content, therefore, with one extra brigade, 50 Indian Parachute Brigade, which was brought in early in March.

66. With the start of the Japanese offensive, administrative risks had to be taken and General Slim decided to move 5 Indian Division from Arakan to the Imphal – Kohima area. Its move by train and air began on the 19th March. Divisional H.Q.,

9 and 123 Indian Infantry Brigades, were moved to Imphal and 161 Indian Infantry Brigade was moved to Dimapur. The move was finished on the 12th April.

The Army Commander also transferred 3 Commando Brigade from Arakan to Silchar early in April, with the rôle of operating along the track to Bishenpur.

Shortly after this, General Slim moved 7 Indian Division from Arakan (two brigades by air and one by rail): one brigade joining 4 Corps by the 18th April, whilst the Division less this brigade was allotted to 33 Corps, the Headquarters of which had been flown from India to the Dimapur area. 2 British Division was moved by air and train from Bombay to Dimapur, the move being completed between the 25th April and the 2nd May. 33 Corps then comprised 2 British Division, 7 Indian Division (less one brigade), one brigade of 5 Indian Division, 23 Long-Range Penetration Brigade, which had been brought forward from India by that time, and the equivalent of a regiment of tanks. It was later reinforced by a lorried infantry brigade.

67. The situation caused me some anxiety during this time and I was very grateful for the valuable assistance which was given me both by the Commander-in-Chief, India, and by General Stilwell. The former, with that unfailing readiness to help which he has always displayed, had put H.Q. 33 Corps, 2 British Division, H.Q. 21 Indian Division (late H.Q. 44 Indian Armoured Division), 268 Indian Lorried Infantry Brigade, two regiment of tanks and other troops at my disposal. General Stilwell undertook the defence of aerodromes and communications in an area agreed on between him and General Slim, deflecting Chinese troops for this purpose.

68. 17 Indian Light Division pulled out of Tiddim on the 17th March and, after hard fighting, in which the enemy suffered heavy losses, succeeded in cutting its way through to Imphal early in April. This Division in spite of many difficulties had succeeded in bringing through most of its transport and vital stores, together with its wounded during the withdrawal up the Tiddim road. The Silchar – Bishenpur track was cut by the enemy's advance.

On the 15th March, 15 Japanese Division crossed the Chindwin at Thaungdut and their 31 Division at Homalin and Tamanthi. 20 Indian Division was withdrawn to better positions north-west of Tamu, astride the road leading to Imphal.

A few days later, the enemy attacked 50 Indian Parachute Brigade at Ukhrul in force and after heavy fighting it was forced to withdraw fighting towards Imphal.

69. Early in April, we were forced to evacuate Kanglatongbi, astride the Dimapur road, about 15 miles north of Imphal, and thus lost the use of our lines of communication between the railhead at Dimapur and Imphal.

4 Corps Operations on the Imphal Front.

70. The plan of the Commander, 4 Corps on the 10th April was as follows:-

(*a*) To prevent the enemy gaining access to the Imphal Plain by either the Palel – Imphal or Tiddim – Imphal roads.

(*b*) To re-establish a force in the Ukhrul area and cut the enemy's line of communication from the east.

(*c*) To use the largest possible force offensively against either 15 or 33 Japanese Divisions in succession.

71. The successful withdrawal of 17 Indian Light Division and 20 Indian Division in the face of heavy pressure has already been mentioned. 20 Indian Division was now holding positions in depth along the Palel – Tamu road. The gallant delaying action of 50 Indian Parachute Brigade near Ukhrul had proved most useful, as it held up the Japanese advance down the Ukhrul – Imphal road for several days and thus gave time for the recently arrived 5 Indian Division to concentrate in this area.

20 Indian Division was now still further withdrawn in order to release troops for a counter-attack against the Japanese 15 Division, north-east of Imphal.

72. Determined enemy attempts against Imphal from the south and south-east continued, but were successfully withstood by 20 Indian Division. At the end of April, 23 Indian Division on the right, 5 Indian Division (less one brigade) in the centre, and a brigade of 17 Indian Light Division on the left were advancing north and north-east from Imphal, and had moved twenty-three miles up the track running north-east to Ukhrul and ten miles up the main road north to Kohima. (Imphal to Ukhrul is sixty-seven miles as the track goes and Imphal to Kohima is eighty-four miles.)

73. It was apparent from the enemy's efforts that he considered the capture of Imphal to be essential before the monsoon set in. By the first week in May, however, his advance had not only been checked, but forced back in all sectors, except in that of 20 Indian Division. This division had had to give ground slightly in the face of heavy attacks by the Japanese Yamamoto Force, composed of parts of 33 and 15 Japanese Divisions, up the Palel road.

74. Heavy fighting had been in progress in the area of Bishenpur, south-west of Imphal, for some time, and 33 Japanese Division had been pressing strongly against 17 Indian Light Division. It was decided that the situation must be cleared up, as any further Japanese advance here would endanger not only Imphal itself but the neighbouring aerodromes upon which the air supply of 4 Corps entirely depended.

The Commander, 17 Indian Light Division decided, therefore, to engage the enemy closely south of Bishenpur, and simultaneously to make a flank movement with two battalions west of the Imphal – Tiddim road. These battalion's cut the road behind the enemy positions which they then attacked from the rear. This attack, coming as it did simultaneously from the north and the south, took 33 Japanese Division by surprise and inflicted heavy casualties, though the nature of the country, lack of sufficient reserves and maintenance difficulties prevented decisive results.

75. While these actions were in progress 23 Indian Division had relieved 20 Indian Division on the Palel – Tamu road, south-east of Imphal, and had thrown back continuous enemy attacks. 20 Indian Division was transferred to the area east and north-east of Imphal, whence operating in two columns it continued the advance on Ukhrul. 5 Indian Division made slow progress northwards, astride the main road, and by the first week in June, had cleared the strong enemy position at Kanglatongbi, fifteen miles north of Imphal. During the succeeding fortnight, this Division advanced slowly in the face of strong opposition in difficult country and under most adverse weather conditions.

Operations by 33 Corps in the Kohima Sector.
76. Early in April, my main preoccupation had been the Japanese advance on Kohima which, if successful, would have threatened the Assam Railway, our main line communication with North-Eastern Assam, upon which General Stilwell's forces operating in North Burma and the air ferry route to China were both based.

77. When the scale of the Japanese offensive was disclosed and it was apparent that there was a threat to Kohima and that the road to Imphal was likely to be cut, it was clear that 4 Corps could no longer control operations in this area in addition to those to the south and north of Imphal. As a temporary measure, therefore, Kohima was placed under the Commander, 202 Line of Communication Area[10], and an extemporised headquarters was set up at Kohima under Colonel Richards[11], who had formerly commanded an infantry brigade in 81 (West African) Division. Headquarters 33 Corps was meanwhile flown to Jorhat from India and moved forward from there to Manipur Road, where it arrived on the 8th April.

The Siege of Kohima.
78. The strength of the Japanese advancing on Kohima was originally estimated at three battalions, with possibly one more in reserve, and the orders given to Colonel Richards were to hold Kohima and to deny the area Jessami – Kharasom – Kohima to the enemy. It was thought unlikely that the Japanese could move a force greater than this through the Naga Hills, whose tracks were narrow, steep and scarce.

On the 29th March, however, it had become evident that 31 Japanese Division was moving against the Kohima area.

79. Jessami and Kharasom cover the tracks leading to Kohima and Tuphema, the latter is on the main road some fifteen miles due south of Kohima. The enemy attacked Kharasom on the 27th March and Jessami the next day. The garrisons of these two posts, found by 1 Assam Regiment, put up a most spirited defence for several days and then made a gallant fighting withdrawal, which gained valuable time for the preparation of the defences of Kohima.

80. 161 Brigade of 5 Indian Division had concentrated at Manipur Road on the 30th March, and was sent to reinforce the Kohima garrison, but it was withdrawn

to meet a reported enemy threat further north which menaced the Dimapur base. As the enemy closed in on Kohima, however, the Commander, 202 Line of Communication Area, sent back the 4th Battalion, The Queen's Own Royal West Kent Regiment of that brigade to assist in its defence, and it arrived on the day on which the Japanese opened their attack. When it became apparent that the threat to Manipur Road from the east was not serious, and that, moreover, the enemy were making no attempt to cut the railway, although it would have been easy for them to do so by sending forward small demolition parties by forest tracks, the remainder of 161 Brigade less one battalion already in Kohima was again ordered forward towards Kohima. It advanced into the hills to within four miles of Kohima on the west, but, being itself engaged, was unable to reach the garrison, although two companies actually succeeded in fighting their way in on the 18th and proved a welcome reinforcement in the bitter fighting which occurred on that date.

81. The Japanese launched their attack on Kohima itself on the night 4th–5th April, using two regiments (the equivalent of two of our brigade groups) and pressed it incessantly for fourteen days. It was gallantly held by the garrison consisting of the 4th Battalion, The Queen's Own Royal West Kent Regiment, the Assam Regiment, the Shere Regiment of the Maharaja of Nepal's Troops and a number of administrative units and men collected from the convalescent camp.

82. Ammunition and food were adequate, but the water ration had to be reduced to half-a-pint a man for some days as the enemy got astride the water pipeline on the 5th April and it was not till the 13th that a new source of water was fortunately discovered.

83. On the 11th, the Air Force was asked to drop water and mortar ammunition. Boxes of three-inch mortar bombs were dropped, some of which were delivered in error to the enemy. When the Japanese used them against the garrison it was reported that they had started using a new and most effective type of bomb.

84. On the 15th, and again on the 18th, the enemy made determined assaults, but were ejected from the footings they gained; the air support given to the defenders on these dates by bombing and cannon fire proving most helpful.

85. Kohima was relieved by 6 Brigade of 2 British Division on the 20th April. This Division had hard fighting before it was able to break through the defences which the enemy held astride the Dimapur – Kohima road and gain touch with the garrison which by that time had been driven on to one small hill called Summer Hill in the centre of the area.

86. I have dealt with this comparatively small operation in some detail, not only in justice to a gallant defence, but because the holding of Kohima was of great importance, and its successful defence proved to be the turning point in the campaign.

The Relief of Imphal.

87. H.Q. 33 Corps reached Dimapur on the 8th April. The general outline of the Commander's plan was as follows:-

(*a*) Cover the Manipur Road base.

(*b*) Capture Kohima area as a starting point for offensive operations.

(*c*) Operate offensively on the general axis of the Dimapur – Imphal road, as soon as the concentration of his forces permitted.

88. The Japanese held the Kohima area in strength except for Summer Hill. Their strong points were nearly, although as it proved not quite, inaccessible to our tanks: but Kohima was cleared of the enemy by the 2nd June by 2 British and 7 Indian Divisions, after some weeks of severe hand-to-hand fighting in which the Japanese lost heavily. Our casualties were not light. By the 6th June, we had captured the Aradura Spur, which covered the road some two miles south of Kohima.

89. While these operations were in progress, columns of 23 Long-Range Penetration Brigade of Special Force were clearing the country north-east and east of Kohima, and moving southwards by the jungle tracks on Jessami.

90. The capture of Kohima and the clearing of the difficult and hilly country which lies immediately to the east and south of it, marked the first step in our counter-offensive. The Japanese offensive against our base at Manipur Road had been driven back with very heavy losses to the enemy, and the threat to our road and rail communications in North-East Assam had been removed. There remained the urgent task of re-opening the road to Imphal.

91. Our dispositions at this time were:-

268 *Indian Lorried Infantry Brigade* (*33 Corps*): Holding Kohima.

23 *Long-Range Penetration Brigade*: Clearing Jessami area and moving southwards parallel to the Kohima – Imphal road.

2 *British Division*: Advancing south down the Imphal road from Kohima in pursuit of the retreating enemy.

7 *Indian Division*: Less 89 Brigade (still under 4 Corps), but with 161 Brigade (5 Indian Division) under command, operating on the left flank of 2 British Division.

92. The advance south from the Aradura Spur entailed severe fighting and our progress, especially that of our tanks, was hindered by minefields covered by Japanese artillery; but, by the 21st June, the leading elements of 2 British Division had reached Milestone 102. As forward troops of 5 Indian Division from 4 Corps at this time were in the vicinity of Milestone 111, the gap between the two Corps had been reduced to nine miles.

93. 7 Indian Division, which had been operating through very difficult country east of the road, had naturally been unable to keep level with 2 British Division

astride the road; but they had contributed greatly to its advance by capturing several enemy positions on the Japanese lines of communication leading east from the Imphal road, and had thus compelled the enemy to retire.

23 Long-Range Penetration Brigade operating further east, wide on the left flank of 7 Indian Division, caused further interference with the enemy's communications by cutting the Kharasom – Ukhrul track and other tracks to the southward.

94. At about 1245 hours on the 22nd June, 2 British and 5 Indian Divisions met at Milestone 109 from Dimapur (twenty-nine miles from Imphal) and the road to Imphal was open. 31 Japanese Division, which had been allotted the task of capturing Kohima and the base at Dimapur had been severely defeated, and was shortly to meet with virtual annihilation.

95. I think the somewhat confused fighting may be more easily followed if I here briefly summarise the phases of the battle for the Imphal Plain. The main stages were:-

(*a*) The fighting withdrawal of 17 Indian Light Division and 20 Indian Division.
(*b*) The Japanese attack on Kohima.
(*c*) The rearguard action by 50 Indian Parachute Brigade from Ukhrul, and the making of a defensive position north-east of Imphal by 5 Indian Division.
(*d*) The further withdrawal by 20 Indian Division to shortern the southern front and thus enable troops to be released for the attack on 15 Japanese Division north-east of Imphal.
(*e*) The transfer of effort to the south to deal with 33 Japanese Division, and thus to clear the threat to Imphal from that quarter before launching a major offensive northwards, in co-ordination with the drive south by 33 Corps, to clear the Imphal – Kohima road.
(*f*) The operations to open the road, combined with the subsidiary operations to capture Ukhrul, which was the vital point on the lines of communication of 15 and 31 Japanese Divisions.

96. The elimination of the threat to our lines of communication in North-East Assam and the opening of the road from Kohima to Imphal ended a definite phase of the campaign. 31 Japanese Division had been so roughly handled that it had practically lost all fighting value. Similarly, the offensive value of the enemy's 15 and 33 Divisions had been greatly reduced by the very heavy losses they had incurred. A conservative estimate of the enemy's casualties in killed alone amounted to 13,500, which excluded losses by our air action. To this, of course, must be added their wounded and the toll taken by disease, from which, on their own admission, they suffered severely. The total Japanese casualties on this front, after they crossed the Chindwin in March up till the middle of June, may safely be put at not less than 30,000. Against this, our own losses in killed, wounded and missing, from the 4th March to the 17th June totalled 12,525, of whom only

2,669 were killed. We captured a large amount of equipment, including nearly 100 guns.

97. The results achieved had been due to the determination and skill shown by all Commanders in surmounting difficulties and the fine fighting spirit displayed by the troops who had shown a marked superiority over the Japanese. 4 Corps was entirely dependent on supplies brought in by air and in spite of the splendid work of Air Transport Command, which is mentioned later in this Despatch, there were occasions when our stocks of ammunition ran dangerously low. Rations too had to be cut although the numbers of mouths to be fed had been greatly reduced by the movement out of Imphal, by road, before the Japanese cut it, and subsequently by air, of every man whose presence was unnecessary. In spite of these handicaps the spirit of 4 Corps remained as high as ever and officers and men fought splendidly throughout the long battle. This, coupled with the determination and vigour displayed by 33 Corps, led, in the words of the Supreme Allied Commander, to the Japanese Army suffering a defeat greater than ever before in its history.

Fort Hertz.
98. This isolated outpost, in the extreme north of Burma, was originally occupied by a small detachment in September 1942, in order to protect the landing ground and to raise and support Kachin Levies to operate towards Myitkyina. These Levies have carried out many very successful operations and, indeed, at one time, became such a thorn in the side of the enemy that the Japanese made a direct threat against Fort Hertz. To counter this, the 4th Battalion, The Burma Regiment was flown there from India at the end of November 1943.

99. In November 1943, the Americans agreed to maintain the Fort Hertz garrison by air, as there was no road link with India. Command of this detachment was transferred to General Stilwell in February 1944.

100. These troops, including the Levies, after many skirmishes, subsequently made a steady advance down the Mali Hka Valley (which constitutes the headwaters of the Irrawaddy), in conjunction with General Stilwell's forces moving south from Ledo. They did most useful work, inflicting many casualties on small enemy parties, and by the 19th March they had occupied Sumprabum. From the beginning of June they co-operated with the Chinese-American troops in the Myitkyina area.

Northern Burma – Ledo – Myitkyina.
101. The rôle allotted to the Chinese troops which were under the command of General Stilwell in India, in January, was to advance on Mogaung and Myitkyina with the object of covering the construction of an overland route to China via Ledo and Myitkyina and of securing the air route from Assam to China.

   This force, known originally as the Chinese Army in India (C.A.I.), which had been trained with the help of American officers and equipped with American material, comprised initially 22 and 38 Chinese Divisions, and was joined later by 30 Chinese Division. These three divisions were subsequently reinforced by 50 and 14 Chinese Divisions, which were flown from China in April and May respectively. The force was completed by the addition of U.S. 5307 Provisional Regiment, consisting of three battalions of Long-Range Penetration troops which had trained with Major-General Wingate's Special Force in India and were now being used as medium-range penetration battalions. Known officially by the code name "Galahad Force", they were more usually referred to – after the name of their commander – as Merrill's Marauders.

102. General Stilwell, the Deputy Supreme Allied Commander, South-East Asia Command, personally assumed command of these troops in the Field. They never formed part of my Army Group, but General Stilwell agreed, until C.A.I. forces had captured Kamaing, to accept instructions from General Slim, who was, of course, under my command.

103. On the 17th May, C.A.I. had reached the outskirts of Myitkyina and captured the airfield, Galahad Force having contributed much to this very notable advance. Kamaing was captured on the 16th June and Mogaung invested. The situation in the Mogaung Valley on the 22nd June was that the Japanese in the Kamaing area were being forced into the southern end of the valley; while Special Force was attacking their supply lines in the area north of Indaw. Special Force also had a detachment, known as "Morrisforce", blocking the Myitkyina – Bhamo road.

104. Supply of all forces was largely by air, as owing to the weather the construction of the Ledo Road did not keep pace with the advance of the troops.

Special Force.
105. I have already mentioned Special Force. This Force consisted of six Long-Range Penetration Brigades, which were specially selected, trained, organised and equipped by the late Major-General Wingate to give them the maximum mobility in jungle fighting. The plan was to concentrate this Force within a circle of forty miles radius from Indaw, with the objects of:-

(*a*) Assisting the advance of the Chinese-American forces on Myitkyina by drawing off and harassing the Japanese forces opposing them, and by preventing reinforcements reaching them.

(*b*) Creating a situation which would enable the Chinese forces to advance from Yunnan.

(*c*) Causing confusion, damage and loss to the enemy forces in North Burma.

I hoped that General Wingate's operations might also interfere with the Japanese advance against Imphal.

106. The operations of both Special Force and the Sino-American forces moving south from Ledo were co-ordinated by the Commander, Fourteenth Army.

107. The operations of Special Force began on the night of the 5th–6th March, and between then and the night of the 10th–11th March nearly six hundred Dakota and one hundred glider sorties carried 77 and 111 L.R.P. Brigades, totalling 9,500 troops and 1,100 animals, into the heart of Japanese-occupied Burma. The initial rôle of these glider-borne forces was to secure sites for and to prepare landing strips west of the Irrawaddy. Last minute air reconnaissance disclosed that one of the two potential strips selected, thirty-five miles north-east of Katha (called "Piccadilly") had been deliberately obstructed. General Sim, who was present at the starting point when this news was received, was faced with the difficult decision whether to launch the operation, since it appeared that the enemy had got wind of it, or to postpone it until fresh plans could be made. He decided to let the operation go forward and on the first night the landings were confined to one strip only, called "Broadway", which was some twenty-seven miles southeast of Hopin on the Myitkyina – Mandalay railway.

108. The landings at Broadway, and subsequently on another strip ("Chowringhee") some twenty miles south-south-east of Katha, achieved complete surprise and until the 12th March no ground opposition was met. Air attacks did not begin until the 10th and were directed against the Chowringhee strip which, by that time, had fulfilled its purpose and had been abandoned. The Broadway strip was not attacked until the 13th March, when our fighters were present and A.A. defences had been established. The Japanese lost about 50 per cent. of their attacking aircraft.

109. Our losses during the initial fly-in amounted to only one per cent. of the total personnel transported. The only animal casualty was one mule. The smallness of these losses is remarkable in view of the fact that, at the peak period of the fly-in, double the planned effort was achieved, and aircraft were coming in and taking off at the rate of one "landing" and one "take-off" every three minutes.

110. A special American air force, called No. 1 Air Commando, had been formed to co-operate both tactically and administratively with Special Force. It was a composite force comprising some 250 aircraft – long and short-range fighters, light bombers, Dakotas and gliders. This force carried out the hazardous and difficult glider-borne operations, flying fully laden gliders, some in double tow, over 9,000 foot mountains by night, a distance of 300 miles to the selected area. Equally important was the action of the fighters and bombers of this force, before, during, and after the actual landings, against targets which it was vital to attack. No. 221 Group, R.A.F., also did splendid work in these operations. I wish to express my appreciation of the work carried out by these air forces, without whose assistance Special Force could not have operated.

111. 77 and 111 L.R.P. Brigades were followed by 14 L.R.P. Brigade, whose fly-in was completed by the 4th April. 3 (West African) Brigade, which formed part of Special Force, was to have operated in the same way as the other brigades of the Force. But before the operations actually started, it was decided to split up

the brigade and attach one battalion to each of the 77, 111 and 14 Brigades, to act as a garrison for the stronghold which was to form the base of each of the three above-mentioned brigades. 3 (West African) Brigade completed its fly-in by the 12th April. These formations used airstrips established near Manhton ("Aberdeen"), twenty-seven miles north-north-west of Indaw; Mawlu ("White City"), twenty miles north of Katha, and in the Hopin area. During this second phase some 6,000 troops, 850 animals and 550,000 lbs. of stores were transported with the very slight casualties of 15 killed (all in one aircraft) and six injured.

112. General Wingate originally estimated that about twelve weeks would be the maximum period which troops would be able to withstand the rigorous conditions under which they would be called upon to operate. His original plan, therefore, was (i) to march in 16 L.R.P. Brigade from Ledo, because the route was known to be practicable and this formation would be able to co-operate more closely with General Stilwell's forces advancing in the same area, and (ii) later to fly in 77 and 111 L.R.P. Brigades, retaining the other brigades as a "second wave" which might, or might not, be used to operate during the monsoon, in relief of the three brigades sent in initially. This plan was later modified, however, as General Slim decided to fly in 14 and 3 (West African) Brigades early in April. On the 5th February 16 Brigade marched in from Ledo as planned, via Singkaling Hkamti, after a long march during which it had a few minor engagements, and began operations in the Indaw area in March. 23 L.R.P. Brigade was sent into Burma, but was subsequently employed by the Army Commander in the Naga Hills and Manipur area in co-operation with 33 Corps.

113. It is impossible, in a report of this nature, to give a detailed summary of the varied activities of the five brigades of Special Force which operated independently in North Burma. The damage they inflicted on the enemy, both human and material, was considerable, comprising, as it did, the laying of many ambushes, the destruction or blocking of rail and road communications, and the destruction of supply dumps and other military installations. The operations carried out by these columns, combined with the story of how American aircraft released their gliders, filled with British troops and American engineers, to make their landings in jungle clearings in pitch darkness, forms one of the outstanding episodes of the war, but an account of the operations will not be given until a subsequent Despatch.

114. I have nothing but praise for the organization of the initial landings, and the gallantry and endurance displayed by all ranks in the operations which followed. Events have shown, however, that these operations had less effect upon the enemy than I hoped for. The enemy did not divert troops from his forward areas, nor did he alter his main strategical plan. In fact, the results achieved did not prove to be commensurate with the expenditure in manpower and material which had been employed.

These operations:-

(*a*) Did not affect the launching of the Japanese offensive against Assam.

(*b*) Had but little effect on the enemy's lines of communication, to Assam. They delayed for one month up to three battalions of 15 Japanese Division, which might otherwise have reached the Imphal Front earlier.

(*c*) Although they severed the rail communications of 18 Japanese Division for about three months, only one battalion (from the 18 Divisional Reserve) was actually diverted from the front of General Stilwell's forces and that only for about a month.

(*d*) On the other hand, the Japanese were compelled to collect troops to meet the threat but they did not amount to more than twelve battalions at any one time, although the number of enemy battalions which were employed at one time or another added up to sixteen. The concentration of twelve battalions was not complete until two months after the original landings.

115. 16 L.R.P. Brigade, which had originally marched in from Ledo, was evacuated by air early in May. On the 17th May, the three remaining brigades of Special Force came under the command of General Stilwell in the Northern Combat Area Command and subsequently operated, in a normal infantry rôle, in the Kamaing – Mogaung – Myitkyina sector. "Dahforce", which was composed of Kachin Levies, was flown in with Special Force and later amalgamated with three columns of 111 Brigade, the whole being re-named "Morris-force" (already briefly mentioned in paragraph 103).

Before leaving the subject of Special Force, I wish to pay tribute to its gallant commander, Major-General Wingate, whose death occurred in a flying accident late in March. He was that rare combination of the dreamer and the man of action and his example and spirit will remain an inspiration to the men he trained. He was succeeded by his Second-in-Command, Major-General W.D.A. Lentaigne, C.B., C.B.E., D.S.O.

Lessons of the Campaign.

116. The following important facts emerge from a study of the operations undertaken during the first six months of 1944:-

(*a*) The reinforcements received were well trained, thanks to the training arrangements made by the Commander-in-Chief, India, and our troops, both individually and collectively, were able to engage the Japanese with confidence.

(*b*) Our ability to make full use of air supply by virtue of our air superiority has fundamentally altered the tactical picture, and enabled our troops not only to operate in country hitherto considered impassable and so attack the enemy, but also to hold positions when the enemy has cut their lines of communication.

(*c*) The operations have shown that ordinary formations can be transported quickly by air. They have also shown the need, for fighting under Far Eastern conditions, of a "Standard Infantry Division" which can be readily transported by rail, sea, M.T. or air.

(*d*) The urgent need for plenty of infantry in this theatre of war has again been emphasised. All divisions, except 19 Indian Division which was the only reserve at the disposal of the Commander-in-Chief, India, were engaged in the course of the fighting and no proper relief of formations was possible. The relief of tired troops is most important and it was not solved satisfactorily owing to shortage of troops.

Some of my divisions had, by last June, been in the forward areas for twenty-eight months. I need not stress the mental and physical strain which jungle warfare, under adverse climatic conditions, imposes on the soldier.

Naval Operations.

117. I wish to acknowledge the assistance given by coastal forces in the Arakan operations, which carried out valuable raids against vulnerable points on the coast, and were protection against possible small sea-borne raids by the enemy.

In March, 3 Commando Brigade (No. 5 Commando and No. 44 Royal Marine Commando) carried out successfully a small amphibious operation in the Alethangyaw area from St. Martin's Island, with the object of containing the enemy in that area and preventing the movement north of reinforcements during our main attack on the Maungdaw – Buthidaung road.

Although there was no large-scale naval activity in conjunction with land forces during the period under review, it was the ever present threat of amphibious operations which tied nearly two Japanese divisions to coastal areas.

Air Co-operation.

118. *Tasks.* The general tasks performed by Eastern Air Command during the first six months of the year were as follows:-

(*a*) Strategic air offensive to destroy enemy forces, transportation, and maintenance installations.

(*b*) Support of Fourteenth Army operations.

(*c*) Air defence of Calcutta and the adjacent industrial areas and, also, of the airfields used by the American Air Transport Command in North-East Assam for the China ferry service.

(*d*) Air transportation for airborne and air transit forces.

(*e*) Photographic reconnaissance.

119. *Strategic Air Force.* I am, of course, chiefly concerned with the air transport and tactical support given to Fourteenth Army, but I wish to acknowledge the assistance rendered by the Strategic Air Force. Their attacks on Rangoon and Bangkok, and, also, those on Saigon by 14 U.S.A.A.F. from China, have greatly impeded the flow of Japanese reinforcements and material into Burma. In fact, up till the time when monsoon conditions reduced air activity, Rangoon was practically denied to the enemy as a port. Operations against enemy held ports have been supplemented by constant attacks against coastal shipping and, most important from my point of view, against rail communications and military installations. On several occasions, also, elements of the Strategic Air Force have acted in

a tactical rôle and furnished most valuable close support both by bombing and by ferrying supplies.

120. *Tactical Air Force.* The successful provision of ground support in this Theatre, although facilitated by our complete air supremacy, is faced by two difficulties:-

(*a*) the problem of target recognition in dense jungle (enhanced, as it is, by the enemy's skill in camouflaging his positions and dumps), and

(*b*) the Japanese skill in building field defences which require direct hits from heavy bombs to neutralise them.

The difficulty of target recognition was, to a great extent, overcome by use of smoke and wireless.

121. The occasions when air support has been called for and most effectively provided are too numerous to mention but it has not always been easy to assess the results achieved. I have no hesitation in stating, however, that neither in offence nor defence could the Army have achieved the success it did, had it not been for the casualties inflicted on the enemy, and the disruption in forward areas of both their land and water communications by Eastern Air Command. Further, the effect produced on the morale of our troops by the obvious evidence of our air superiority has been most inspiring. Conversely, its disheartening effect on the enemy is evidenced by the statements of prisoners and from captured documents.

122. *Air Transport Operations.* In November 1943, only one R.A.F. Transport Squadron was available for operations with Fourteenth Army, but two Troop Carrier Squadrons, U.S.A.A.F., were working with General Stilwell's forces in the Northern Sector, and other squadrons, both British and American, were on their way as reinforcements. Other reinforcements were sent subsequently from the Mediterranean and elsewhere.

Unified operational control of these forces was effected in December by the formation of Troop Carrier Command, Eastern Air Command, under Brigadier-General W.D. Old of the U.S.A.A.F., with Headquarters at Comilla, where were situated the Headquarters of both Fourteenth Army and 3 Tactical Air Force, as well as the main supply bases. On the 1st May, in order further to integrate air transport with army operations, Troop Carrier Command was placed under the control of the Air Commander, 3 Tactical Air Force, until it was dissolved on the 4th June – a measure rendered necessary by the increasing dispersal of the operational areas and the growing intensity of General Stilwell's operations in North Burma.

123. It is only possible for me here briefly to mention the major air transport operations carried out during this period. These were, in chronological order:-

(*a*) The routine supply-dropping missions to our detachments in the Chin Hills, which I mention because of the hazardous flying conditions.

(*b*) The maintenance of 81 (West African) Division in the Kaladan, which was entirely dependent on air supply.

(*c*) The maintenance of the Chinese divisions advancing south-east from Ledo, which included supplies for our Fort Hertz garrison and the Levies operating in that area.

(*d*) The delivery by air of some 2,000 tons of supplies of all kinds to 7 Indian Division during the fighting between the 8th February and the 6th March.

(*e*) The fly-in of the Brigades of Special Force to the centre of Burma.

(*f*) The move by air of 50 Indian Parachute Brigade from Northern India to the Imphal area, followed by the transfer of the personnel of 5 Indian Division, two brigades of 7 Indian Division, together with a proportion of their heavy equipment, including artillery, from Arakan to the same area. An infantry brigade of 2 British Division was flown from the Calcutta area to Jorhat in North-Eastern Assam.

(*g*) The air supply, on an unprecedented scale, of 4 Corps during the period that the line of communication to Imphal was cut.

(*h*) The evacuation by air of 16 Brigade of Special Force from the Hopin area to India.

(*i*) Concurrently with all the above, the evacuation of casualties from Arakan, North Burma and Imphal, which had a most beneficial effect on the morale of the troops engaged.

124. It is not within the scope of this Despatch to give a detailed account of the operations, but I wish to comment on two of them: the maintenance by air of 7 Indian Division, when cut off in the Arakan, and that of 4 Corps when surrounded in Imphal. The former was the first occasion, in this theatre of war, when a large formation was supplied by air, and was thus able to maintain its positions after its land communications had been severed. This allowed us to inflict a crushing defeat on the enemy. The latter – the air supply of 4 Corps – deserves a more detailed account:

The magnitude of the effort involved in keeping an Army Corps of four divisions and the air forces based at Imphal supplied, was enormous, when it is regarded in relation to the number of aircraft available.

Calculations showed that the Army required 323 tons *per diem*, and the supporting R.A.F. squadrons 75 tons, if we were to hold Imphal. This target figure was, generally speaking, maintained, though we had anxious periods when a shortage of aircraft seemed probable and when bad weather restricted flying. There is no doubt that, if we had not had air supply, we should have lost the Imphal Plain and the position on the eastern frontier of India would have been grave.

125. It is with gratitude and admiration that I acknowledge the immense debt which the Army owes to the Air. No one who, like myself, has watched them, is likely to forget the courage, determination and skill of pilots and crews who have flown through some of the worst weather in the world, and over appalling country in performing their allotted tasks.

Enemy Strengths and Dispositions.

126. To trace the Japanese build-up in Burma, it is necessary to go back to July, 1943, when their total strength consisted of four divisions, disposed as follows: – Arakan, 55 Division; Kale and Kabaw Valleys and Lower Chindwin, 33 Division; Upper Chindwin and Hukawng Valley, 18 Division; Salween River, 56 Division. By November, 31 Division, a new one raised from formations in Central China and elsewhere, and, also, 24 Independent Mixed Brigade (four battalions) had arrived. 54 Division from Java followed in February. Reinforcements during February and early March amounted to two more divisions, the 15th coming from Central China, and the 2nd, originally destroyed in Guadalcanal, but re-formed in the Philippines in June 1943. In February, also, a second Army Head-quarters, the 28th, was created to control the forces in South Burma.

127. The strength of the Japanese army in Burma at the beginning of March was, therefore, eight divisions and one independent mixed brigade, giving a total of seventy-six infantry battalions. These forces were under the control of two Army Headquarters: the Southern (Twenty-Eighth) Army containing thirty-two battalions and the Northern (Fifteenth) Army forty-four.

128. In May, a fresh division made its appearance: the 53rd, coming from Japan, via Malaya. It was located in the Mogaung area. Thus the total Japanese strength in Burma had gradually been augmented from four divisions to nine in the twelve months ending June 1944.

Japanese Subversive Agencies.

129. There are certain non-Japanese forces which the enemy raised to oppose us in Burma, the most prominent being:-

(*a*) The Japanese-inspired Indian Fifth Column.
(*b*) The so-called Indian National Army (I.N.A.).
(*c*) Forces of disaffected Burmans.

The first-named are known as J.I.Fs., a term which, strictly speaking, should only be applied to Indians working for the enemy, who are not members of the I.N.A. These J.I.Fs. have been used in an intelligence offensive against India and the Indian Army since the outbreak of the Japanese war, mainly on propaganda and espionage tasks. Some have been landed in India by submarine or parachute, and considerable numbers have infiltrated across the Indo-Burman border. This movement, which has been in the main a matter for India Command to counter, was largely defeated. Its effects on the troops under my command have been negligible.

130. The I.N.A. is principally composed of Indian prisoners of war taken in Singapore, though civilians are now also being recruited. This army, which had a rather ill-starred beginning in 1942 – at the end of which year it was disbanded by the Japanese – was re-formed by Subhas Chandra Bose, the Bengali revolu-tionary, soon after his arrival in the East from Germany in 1943. It is now

organised in three divisions, of which two are alleged to be fit to take the field. Its headquarters was at Maymyo, with a rear headquarters at Singapore. A strength of 13,000, including No. 1 Division, has been moved up into Burma since last November, while No. 2 Division (approximately 7,000) is prepared to follow.

131. Elements of the I.N.A. first appeared in a fighting rôle in the Arakan operations in February, but the main body was concentrated on the Chindwin front, and was generally employed on foraging and fatigue duties. They did no fighting on either front beyond occasional company actions, in which their morale was not high. Special parties, attached to Japanese units, have been used to try to suborn our Indian troops, but all attempts have been met with fire. Reports show that the Japanese have been disillusioned regarding the value of these troops, the great majority of whom are not really traitors; most of them only accepted service under the Japanese to escape inhuman treatment and in the hope of getting back to India.

132. The activities of the J.I.Fs. and the I.N.A. are directed by an organization composed of Japanese officers and men, under a lieutenant-general, which has its headquarters in Burma and is known as the Hikari Kikan (Rising Sun Organization). Liaison between I.N.A. brigades and the Japanese Army is carried out by Hikari personnel. This organization also controls Bose's "Provisional Government" and the "Indian Independence League" into which Indians in the Far East have been enrolled.

In addition to the Hikari Kikan, there is the Japanese Nishi Kikan (Western Organization) which is trying to organize the peoples of Northern and Western Burma into units somewhat analogous to our own Chin and Kachin Levies.

133. It is difficult to estimate the strength and fighting value of the force of disaffected Burmans. It has done little fighting, and has, up to date, been employed chiefly on lines of communication duties. It contains some definitely anti-British elements who, when the Japanese are being evicted from Burma, maybe expected to try to interfere with our pacification of the country. Other elements have, however, probably been forced into the organization by "voluntary compulsion" methods and will leave it as soon as they can.

134. I wish to pay a tribute to the tribesmen of the Naga, Chin and Kachin Hills, who have remained staunchly loyal to us, in spite of all the enemy's efforts to suborn them.

135. *Casualties.* The following table shows the battle casualties inflicted on the enemy between November, 1943, and June, 1944, both months inclusive:-

	By Fourteenth Army	By C.A.I.
Killed	26,203	13,232
Wounded	39,305	19,848
Prisoners	288	57
Total	98,933	

This proportion of killed to wounded is calculated from captured returns and may be assumed to be reasonably accurate.

This estimate does not include the losses the enemy has suffered from our sustained air attacks or from disease, the incidence of which captured documents have shown to be high. There is of course, always a tendency to over-estimate enemy casualties but I think it would be no exaggeration to assume that the total Japanese losses, on all counts, during the eight months under review amounted to at least one hundred thousand.

PART III – ORGANIZATION.

136. I have already given a summary of the land forces transferred to me from India Command with effect from midnight on the 15th–16th November 1943 when the Supreme Allied Commander assumed command. In addition, the following formations passed to my command between November 1943 and June 1944:-

9 Indian Infantry Brigade (5 Indian Division). (December.)

32 Indian Infantry Brigade (20 Indian Division). (Late November.)

254 Indian Tank Brigade (less 45th Cavalry, but plus 3 Dragoon Guards). (December.)

25 Indian Division. (February and March.)

14 and 16 L.R.P. Brigades. (In March and January respectively.)

77 and 111 L.R.P. Brigades. (January.)

36 British Division. (Between late January and early March.)

23 L.R.P. Brigade. (Early April.)

Advance H.Q., 3 Special Service Brigade (with No. 5 Commando and No. 44 Royal Marine Commando). (February.)

50 Indian Parachute Brigade. (Early March.)

2 British Division, which moved to Assam as follows:-

5 Brigade. (End of March.)

H.Q., 2 British Division and 6 Brigade. (Early April.)

4 Brigade. (Mid-April.)

Also a cavalry regiment, a medium regiment R.A., and two Indian battalions.

28 (East African) Brigade arrived in February and replaced 99 Infantry Brigade in Ceylon, which reverted to India Command.

Headquarters, 21 Indian Division, consisting of a proportion of the H.Q. Staff and a few ancillary units of the late 44 Indian Armoured Division, arrived in Jorhat (Assam) on the 5th March.

268 Indian Lorried Infantry Brigade was lent by India Command early in May (*vide* paragraph 67).

137. A skeleton Order of Battle of the undermentioned formations will be found in the appendices:-

Appendix "A" – Skeleton Order of Battle of 15 Indian Corps on the 1st January 1944, at the commencement of our offensive in the Arakan.

Appendix "B" – Skeleton Order of Battle of 4 Corps on the 8th March 1944, the date the Japanese launched their offensive across the Chindwin.

Appendix "C" – Skeleton Order of Battle 33 Indian Corps on the 31st May 1944, when that formation was engaged in driving the enemy from the Kohima area.

Appendix "D" – Skeleton Order of Battle 11 Army Group on the 22nd June 1944, the date on which this Despatch closes.

138. The major re-organizations, which were finished, or which were begun; during the period covered by this Despatch were:-

11 (East African) Division.
81 and 82 (West African) Divisions.
Standard Organizations for:-
A Corps Headquarters.
An Infantry Division.
Armoured Formations (re-organization of Tank Brigades).
Organization for the movement and maintenance of Air Transported Formations.
Assumption of full contol by 11 Army Group of Fourteenth Army and Land Forces, Ceylon.

The principal changes involved, together with my reasons for effecting them, are summarized in the succeeding paragraphs:-

139. 11 *(East African) Division.* At a conference held in Ceylon in January, at which the G.O.C.-in-C., East African Command was present, I decided to increase the artillery of this formation up to the scale of that in an Animal and Motor Transport (A. and M.T.) Division on the Indian Establishment.

I also decided to reduce the scale of both unit and 2nd line motor transport, and to provide an element within the infantry battalions for carrying fighting equipment under conditions when M.T. could not operate.

140. 81 *and* 82 *(West African) Divisions.* In May, at a conference attended by the G.O.C.-in-C., West Africa, I considered the advisability of amalgamating these two divisions; for 81 Division, which had given up one of its brigades to Special Force, consisted only of two brigades. Owing, however, to the shortage of formations with which to carry out reliefs, I decided to retain both divisions, but to effect certain changes in their organization. These included:-

(*a*) The divisional artillery to consist of one light regiment (three batteries of 3.7-inch howitzers and one battery of 3-inch mortars) and one anti-tank regiment (three batteries, each of twelve six-pounder guns). Field regiments could not be formed, but would be attached when required.

(*b*) A reconnaissance battalion to be included in each division.

(*c*) A proportion (25 per cent.) of the unarmed soldiers, who act as porters, to be armed.

West African resources did not, unfortunately, admit of certain other desirable increases, such as the inclusion of a Divisional Headquarters battalion.

I also decided that 3 (West African) Brigade of 81 (West African) Division should continue to be employed with Special Force.

I intended to bring these two West African divisions and the East African division, into line with the standard divisional organization (*vide* paragraph 142) in due course.

141. *Corps Headquarters and Corps Troops.*
In order to secure uniformity, a standardised War Establishment for a Corps Headquarters and, also, a standard Order of Battle for Corps Troops, is to be adopted.

142. *Standard Organization for Infantry Divisions.*
I have already briefly referred to the desirability of having one standard organization for all infantry divisions operating in this theatre of war, and for some time past I had been examining the possibility of this. Experience had shown that, with our limited resources, it was not practical to have a number of specialised formations such as Airborne, Assault, Armoured, Light, M.T., and Animal and M.T. Divisions. Such a policy was not only uneconomical, but circumstances inevitably forced their use sooner or later in rôles for which they had not been trained or organized.

Early in May, I recommended to the Supreme Allied Commander that the policy of having a Standard Division should be accepted, such a division to be capable of fulfilling all the rôles which it might be called upon to perform within South-East Asia Command, *viz.*:-

(*a*) Normal jungle fighting.

(*b*) Operations involving transportation by air.

(*c*) Amphibious operations (though, for this rôle, special training and the attachment of certain special units such as beach groups, would of course be necessary).

The Supreme Allied Commander gave his approval to my proposals and they have since been accepted by the War Office and General Headquarters, India. In addition the formation of an airborne division has been agreed to.

Action to put this new policy into force is being taken in order to bring the maximum number of divisions on to the standard organization before the end of 1944. This organization will include three infantry battalions per brigade (to be increased to four when practicable, as is the case in the War Office Light-Scale Division for Far Eastern Theatres), two artillery regiments of 25-pounders (in place of the existing one 25-pounder and one jungle field regiment in A. and M.T. divisions), one 3.7-inch howitzer mountain regiment of three batteries (instead of the present four battery regiment), and one anti-tank regiment having an alternative armament of 3-inch mortars (instead of the existing anti-aircraft cum anti-tank regiment). The division will also include a reconnaissance battalion organized on similar lines to the normal infantry battalion, but with extra signal equipment, and, as soon as the manpower situation permits, a medium machine gun battalion.

A major feature of the new Standard Division is the reduction in the number of lorries, both in unit 1st line transport and in 2nd line M.T. companies, and the introduction of a large number of jeeps. Eventually it is hoped to have two types of vehicles only; the jeep and the 3-ton four-wheel-drive lorry (apart, of course, from a limited number of specialist vehicles).

143. *Re-organization of Armoured Formations.*
A review of the role required of tank brigades operating in this Theatre led me to the conclusion that certain major changes in their organization were necessary. I considered that the value of these brigades would be greatly enhanced if (*a*) all regiments were re-equipped with medium tanks, (*b*) a troop of flame-thrower tanks was included in each squadron, and (*c*) an infantry battalion was included in each brigade. By making certain reductions in the existing establishment, it would, I decided, be possible to adopt this re-organization of the armoured units, while at the same tune, effecting a saving in manpower.

This matter is still being discussed with the Commander-in-Chief, India, and will be referred to again in my next Despatch.[12]

144. *Organization for the Movement and Maintenance of Air Transported Formations.*
Recent experience has shown that there is an urgent need for a permanent organization to handle the movement and maintenance of forces by air, instead of the improvisation that has hitherto existed.

Such an organization must, obviously, be designed to ensure the closest co-operation between the staffs at the headquarters of the air force and the army concerned and, also, the staffs at the airfields affected. To achieve this, four elements are required:-

(*a*) An Army Link with the R.A.F. Headquarters dealing with air transport.

(*b*) Joint Army and R.A.F. Air Despatch and Delivery Units at airfields.

(*c*) An Airfield Maintenance Organization to ensure that maintenance require-ments at airfields are met.

(*d*) Air Supply and Maintenance Companies to deal with the packing, loading and ejection of supplies.

My proposals for an organization, which will produce the necessary continuity and flexibility, are under consideration by Headquarters, Air Command, S.E.A.C., and General Headquarters, India.

145. *Assumption of Full Control by 11 Army Group.*
As I have already stated in the opening paragraphs of this Despatch, Fourteenth Army, together with Ceylon Army Command and the Indian Ocean bases of Addu Atoll, Diego Garcia and Cocos, came under my command from the 16th November 1943, but certain administrative matters continued to be dealt with by General Headquarters, India, until more staff became available for 11 Army

Group. My Headquarters, however, assumed full control with effect from the 1st May, 1944, with the exception of some administrative matters which were more conveniently handled by G.H.Q. India.

PART IV – ADMINISTRATION.

146. In order to view the administrative problem which confronted us in this Theatre in its correct perspective, it is necessary to understand the background against which the present organization developed. Eastern Army, the forerunner of Fourteenth Army, came into being at a time of reverses in Burma and un-preparedness in Eastern India. The whole of that rear organization, on which the success or failure of an army depends, had therefore to be built up from nothing, under the most difficult conditions. While the early stages of this build-up have already been described in Despatches from the India Command, a brief re-capitulation of the facts maybe opportune here.

147. Our strategy, in 1942, was defensive and our advanced bases were selected accordingly. The area of operations was, and still is, divided administratively into two fronts – Arakan and Assam – each of which is served by a separate line of communication, connected by poor lateral communications (though air supply is now an important factor which can be, and has been, used to unite these separate lines). The natural advanced base for the Arakan front is Chittagong. This port was prepared for demolition in 1942 and many "denial" measures were actually carried out. It only narrowly escaped being occupied by the Japanese in the summer of that year; and in fact, our subsequent advance in October 1942, when we passed from the defensive to the offensive, began while Chittagong was still under sentence of death. Both the port and advanced base at Chittagong had then to be developed while active operations were in progress, and while they were both having to perform their administrative functions to the forces in the field. These forces rose to a strength of two divisions, and, incidentally, had a sick rate of over 6 per 1,000 *per diem*. Not only was there no all-weather road in Arakan, but no road at all worthy of the name. We were, therefore, compelled to rely largely on coastal shipping and inland water transport and, for many months, there was a serious shortage of both types of vessels. The difficulty was eventually overcome to some extent by the construction of a road which had to be surfaced with bricks, the coal for which had to be imported from India. Ordinary metalling was impossible, owing to the absence of stone.

148. While we were on the defensive, Mymensingh was being prepared as an advanced base, but was only about half finished when our strategy changed. We were not sufficiently certain of success to discontinue construction and, in the light of subsequent events, it is fortunate that we continued to build.

149. On the Imphal Front, we had to construct a large advanced base in virgin jungle, under the most adverse climatic and weather conditions. This base at Manipur Road, or Dimapur as it is sometimes called, had to start work while its construction was yet incomplete.

As a site for a base, Dimapur possessed almost every conceivable disadvantage: heavy rainfall; unhealthy climate; and uneven ground (which did not become apparent until the dense jungle had been cleared). Moreover, it lies on a narrow tongue of land between two rivers, both of which are liable to overflow during the monsoon. To these local topographical disadvantages must be added the further one of the liability to interruption of the railway to Assam by the rivers and streams which pour down from the huge catchment area of the Himalayas, the foothills of which the railway skirts. In 1942, the railway was cut by floods from the 24th June till the 30th November.

150. The railway system, which is metre gauge, had never previously had to tackle more than a moderately heavy seasonal load of cereals and tea. It now had to undertake a much increased load of civil traffic and had to be further pressed to meet the needs not only of the large Imperial forces operating on the Northern and Southern Fronts, but also of the Sino-American forces based on Ledo and, last but not least, the air ferry service to China. Concurrently, road and river transportation had been developed to take some of the strain.

151. The Northern and Southern Lines of Communication areas are divided by the Garo and Jaintia Hills and the only lateral communication connecting them is the hill section of the Bengal and Assam Railway.

152. The whole area was without airfields and so low-lying as to render airfield construction difficult. It entailed, not only the transportation of heavy tonnages of engineer stores, but also of coal, since much surfacing had to be done with burnt brick.

The move and maintenance of forces by air, as well as our probable future commitments, have necessitated a large increase in airfield construction, but I shall deal with this subject in greater detail later on.

153. I propose to deal with the work of my Administrative Services under the following main headings:-

(*a*) Adjutant-General questions.
(*b*) The Lines of Communication.
(*c*) Supply and Maintenance.
(*d*) The Engineering Effort.
(*e*) The Civil Affairs Service, Burma.

Adjutant-General Questions.
154. *Manpower.* The "divisional slice" in this Theatre has averaged 56,000, excluding civil labour, and 70,000 including it, whereas, I believe, the "divisional slice" in Normandy is 40,000. The high figure in the Burma campaign is mainly due to the large administrative "tail", comprising numerous engineer and labour units, which are needed to overcome the physical difficulties on our lines of communication.

155. *Reinforcements.* The demand for reinforcements is heavy, owing to the high sick rate which is, however, much lower than anticipated, and to the time lag between demand and arrival, due to the distances which reinforcements have to cover over a long and indifferent transportation system.

Reinforcement has been below wastage; but, apart from British infantry, in which the shortage is most acute, it has not been so serious as to impair fighting efficiency. Broadly speaking, the numbers available have been in excess of battle casualties, but they have not been sufficient to meet the total wastage and thus keep reinforcement camps full.

156. British reinforcements for Fourteenth Army are provided by General Headquarters, India, from (*a*) the British Base Reinforcement Camp at Deolali, (*b*) personnel freed by the disbandment of units, e.g. A.A. Brigades, and (*c*) returning sick from hospitals in India. Except for (*c*), who go direct to reinforcement camps in the Fourteenth Army area, drafts pass through 52 Training Brigade, where they carry out a two months course of hardening and jungle training. Indian reinforcements, from Regimental Centres and Depots, pass through either 14 or 39 Indian Training Divisions to Fourteenth Army reinforcement camps. There are twelve such camps in the Army area, consisting each of two British and eight Indian Sections. Each Section is 300 strong, and the total capacity of each camp is thus 3,000. Training staffs are available in each camp to keep reinforcements at a proper state of efficiency.

157. *The Medical Aspect – A. Organization,*
(*a*) The medical organization in Fourteenth Army was originally based on the assumption that the main operations would be forward of Imphal. Hospitals were consequently, largely concentrated in the north and, in order to avoid evacuation down a long line of communication, they were sited well forward. The Japanese thrust against Imphal however, necessitated their removal, and a situation arose in which about twenty-five percent. of our hospitals became temporarily non-effective. This would have been serious had it not been for two saving factors: firstly, air transport provided a link between our northern and southern lines of communication, enabling casualties to be rapidly cleared to hospitals serving the Arakan Front; and secondly, the sick rate on both fronts fell far short of the estimate for which provision had been made.

(*b*) In the south, where extensive operations had not been originally contemplated, and where the forces engaged were smaller, our hospitals had not been concentrated so far forward.

Considerable discussion took place early in the year between 11 Army Group and General Headquarters, India, regarding the adequacy or otherwise of the hospitals.

The decisions then taken proved to be sound on the whole, in spite of our forecasts being wrong and of radical alterations in the lines of evacuation. Although there is still a decided shortage of medical officers, and a serious shortage of nurses and nursing personnel, there has been no general shortage of hospital accommodation, but anxiety is always present in an unhealthy tropical theatre of war.

158. At the beginning of the year, facilities for evacuation were reviewed, and as a result of representations made by me to the Supreme Allied Commander, six hospital ships were allotted to Fourteenth Army.

Further, a co-ordinating committee, invested with executive authority, which includes representatives of 11 Army Group and General Headquarters, India, and of the many services affected, has been set up to deal in detail with the complicated problem of medical evacuation. Its measures have so far proved effective, notwithstanding the many problems which have arisen.

159. One interesting feature of the recent fighting is that the medical units have found themselves on occasions called upon to undertake part of the responsibility for their own defence. That medical personnel had to fight proved to be a necessity – it was not a question as to whether they should defend themselves, but how best they could do so.

160. (*a*) The complicated problem of medical evacuation from Arakan involved the use of almost every conceivable form of transport. Hand carriages, mules, jeeps, ambulances, D.U.K.Ws., sampans, flats, paddle steamers, hospital ships, ambulance trains, and light and heavy aircraft have all had to be employed over one stage or another of the journey.

(*b*) To and from 81 (West African) Division operating in the Kaladan Valley, medical supply and evacuation has had to be entirely by air. That the arrangements worked smoothly is due both to the medical officers concerned and to the skilful co-operation of the R.A.F.

(*c*) I have already mentioned how the evacuation of casualties by air from the Imphal Front prevented a serious situation developing when certain hospitals had to be closed down. This air evacuation continued throughout the operations about Imphal and was instrumental in saving many lives. In addition to casualties, two large General Hospitals were flown out with all their valuable equipment.

(*d*) The total number of casualties evacuated by air during the first half of 1944, from all fronts, was over 24,000. Rapid and adequate air transport facilities abolish at one stroke the unsatisfactory and difficult clearance of casualties down long surface lines of communication, with all their attendant disadvantages. This method of moving the wounded has a most beneficial effect on the morale of the fighting soldier.

161. *The Medical Aspect – B. Sick Rate.*

The most satisfactory feature on the medical side has been the surprisingly low sick rate during the first six months of the year. The expected rise to 5 or 6 per 1,000 *per diem* has not happened and the rate in May was as low as 3.1 per 1,000 including battle casualties. This is an almost incredibly low figure compared with that for 1943, which was 6 per 1,000 *per diem*; and, in spite of the seasonal increase of malaria, it has since dropped to 2.9.

Since November 1943, food supply greatly improved, and more fresh meat, fruit and vegetables became available. It is probable that this improvement in rations has been a major cause in keeping down the sick rate.

162. The most serious menace we have to face, where disease is concerned, is of course malaria, and this can only be overcome by unremitting effort and vigilance. The malaria rate, up till the end of June, has remained consistently low compared with last year. This is remarkable, since operations have been carried out on a greatly extended scale, and many more troops have been exposed to the risk of infection. If the same rate had obtained in Arakan and at Imphal from March to June as in the same months of 1943, the effect on operations would have been serious.

I attribute this satisfactory state of affairs to four factors – firstly, better anti-malarial discipline; secondly, the improved anti-malarial organization which, under medical control and aided by the engineers, has freed certain areas from the mosquito; thirdly, the ample flow of anti-malarial supplies of all kinds; and last, but not least, improved morale, since troops in good fettle look after themselves better in every way than when they are depressed.

The efficacy of D.D.T. as an anti-mosquito spray is shortly being tested in the Kabaw Valley.

163. *The Medical Aspect – C. Miscellaneous Medical Points.*
(*a*) There has been no noticeable change in the physical standard of British reinforcements, which can only be classed as average.
(*b*) The physical standard of young soldiers in the Indian Army has improved during the period under review, particularly in combatant units.

164. The Army Pathological Service suffers, in this Theatre, from the lack of laboratories. The importance of accurate laboratory diagnosis requires no stressing.

165. Dental facilities are altogether inadequate. The accepted ratio of dental officers to troops is one per 1,000 for British and one per 10,000 for Indian. The present ratio is one per 7,000 and 30,000 respectively.

166. The present standard of training of medical personnel in this Theatre does not compare altogether favourably with that in others, but, taking into consideration the expansion which the Medical Services have undergone, and the acute shortage of medical officers in India, it is, I am sure, as good as can be expected. Training is, I know, continuous and intensive in the India Command and the situation is improving.

167. The supply of medical stores, including drugs, has been most satisfactory. The consumption of mepacrine in Fourteenth Army as a malaria suppressive has reached twelve million tablets a month.

168. The problem of providing adequate medical supervision for the large amount of civilian labour employed in the Fourteenth Army area is being met at

present, but it may become more difficult when civilian labour forces have to be moved into re-conquered territory as our troops advance.

169. The thirteen convalescent depots in 11 Army Group have proved their value as an essential link between hospital and reinforcement camp. The "patients" in the British Depot at Kohima played a notable part in the defence of that place during the siege, though such strenuous work had hardly been recommended as part of their convalescence.

Miscellaneous A.G. Points.

170. *Legal and Judicial*, (*a*) As a result of the Supreme Allied Commander's Proclamation No. 1 of 1944, under which he assumed control of re-occupied territory, British Military Administration Courts have been set up in Burma.

(*b*) Arrangements have been made with General Headquarters, India, for assistance to be given to Fourteenth Army in the prosecution of those suspected to be military traitors who fall into our hands. More detailed interrogation is now to be carried out at Forward Interrogation Centres and the majority of prisoners will be dealt with in forward areas.

171. *Leave*, (*a*) All British personnel have had to be restricted to fourteen days leave during 1944, owing to the lack of accommodation in suitable areas, and to transportation difficulties which can only be solved by the provision of more aircraft.

(*b*) Representations were made that British Service officers, both with British units and those seconded to the Indian Army, who were willing, should be granted home leave in lieu of repatriation. Many such officers have valuable experience in jungle warfare and their retention is most desirable.

(*c*) Transportation difficulties originally precluded the achievement of the target of twenty-eight days leave per annum for Indian ranks, but these have since been overcome.

172. *Morale and Welfare.* The large number of troops who have taken part in operations have gained confidence from their contact with the enemy. It is universally felt that the Japanese soldier, although a good infantryman, is no match for our well-trained and well-equipped troops, supported by a powerful air force.

173. The still inadequate but increased and, I may add, well deserved publicity now being given to this theatre of war, coupled with the introduction of more amenities such as mobile canteens, cinemas, wireless sets, sports equipment, a daily newspaper ("SEAC"), and also visits from "Ensa", have all contributed to the improvement in morale. Men are beginning to feel that they do not belong to "The Forgotten Army".

In all my efforts to improve the lot of the British rank and file, I am closely in touch with the Commander-in-Chief, India, whose troops share with mine in the severe handicaps of climate, homesickness, and the feeling that the Burma Border is not, at present, the decisive Theatre. In spite of all the steps that have been, and are being taken, the undercurrent of feeling against service in the East still persists, and many "grouses" are still in evidence, though the spirit of the troops in forward units is magnificent.

Among British troops, the most burning question has been, and is, that of repatriation. In particular, the disparity in the terms of overseas service between the Army and the R.A.F. is a continual source of grievance. The measures recently taken to improve this will, it is hoped, allay some of the feeling that has undoubtedly existed.

174. The chief anxiety of Indian troops, as always, is the welfare during their absence of their families, but the leave situation is now satisfactory. The effect of enemy propaganda on the Indian soldier has been negligible.

175. The work of philanthropic bodies such as the Red Cross, the Y.M.C.A. and Toc H has been most valuable and I am very grateful indeed to the large body of voluntary workers who have contributed so much to the welfare of the troops, both British and Indian.

The Lines of Communication.
176. I have already referred to the Northern and Southern Lines of Communication Areas, but there are in fact three lines of communication supplying Fourteenth Army:-

(*a*) *The Assam Line of Communication*, which has three railheads: that at Manipur Road, also called Dimapur, supplying the Imphal Front; and those at Ledo and Chabua which supply the Chinese-American forces operating in Northern Burma, and the air ferry route to China.

(*b*) *The Eastern Bengal Line of Communication*, which serves our bases in Eastern Bengal and the airfields in the Surma Valley, which are extensively used for air supply.

Some flexibility between the Eastern Bengal and Assam lines of communication is provided by the rail link between Lumding and Badarpur, but the capacity of this link is limited owing to the gradients.

(*c*) *The Arakan Line of Communication*, which supplies 15 Indian Corps southwards from Chittagong.

The following paragraphs give a brief general description of these lines of communication, the difficulties which have been encountered and the measures taken to overcome them.

177. *The Assam Line of Communication.*
This line of communication has four main routes:-

(*a*) The metre gauge rail route from Mokameh Ghat[13] to Amingaon, across the Brahmaputra by wagon ferry, and onwards to Dimapur and the American bases in the Ledo area. Stores arrive at Mokameh Ghat by broad gauge railway from depots in Northern and Central India.

(*b*) The broad gauge route from Calcutta to river ghats on the lower Brahmaputra and to transhipment stations of the metre gauge route. The stores carried come from the Calcutta Base Area and from Southern and Western India.

(*c*) The river route. This includes an all water route up the Brahmaputra from Calcutta and, also, lifts between intermediate rail-served ghats on the Ganges and Brahmaputra.

(*d*) A road, known as the Assam access road, from Siliguri where it connects with the broad gauge railway, to Bongaigaon on the metre gauge route.

The control of the Assam line of communication rests with General Headquarters, India.

178. Communications in Assam are complicated and rendered unreliable, by both operating and physical difficulties. The operating difficulties are due to the fact that a far greater load has been imposed on the railway than could be handled by the normal civil organization. The physical difficulties are due to the seasonal liability of both road and rail communications to serious flooding, and also to the vagaries of the Brahmaputra. At some places, sudden rises in the river will wash away ghats, with all their connected installations, completely; while at others, sand banks will form and render them unapproachable by river craft.

The operating difficulties have been overcome to a great extent by the employment of military transportation units to assist the civil staff. The control of a considerable section of the metre gauge main line has been taken over by the United States Transportation Corps which has resulted in a great increase in traffic. The physical difficulties are being met by the provision, where possible, of alternative means of communication.

179. Very extensive measures have been, and are being, taken to improve the capacity of this line of communication. They include the doubling of certain sections on both the broad and metre gauge lines, the conversion of one section from narrow gauge to metre gauge, the construction of additional ghats and ferries, the improvement of existing facilities, and the provision of more river craft.

A proposal to erect a railway bridge across the Brahmaputra at Amingaon was rejected on the grounds that it would take too long to build. The alternative was to increase the capacity of the Amingaon – Pandu ferry, and this has been done.

180. *The Eastern Bengal Line of Communication.* This line consists of three main routes:-

(*a*) The sea route from Calcutta and Vizagapatam to Chittagong.

(*b*) From the Calcutta area to the Eastern Bengal metre gauge railway system, either by rail (via the Tistamukh wagon ferry), or by inland water transport, or by a combination of both. This railway system converges on Akhaura, and from there divides into two branches. The northern branch serves the Surma Valley airfields joining up with the Assam line of communication across the hill section of the railway between Badarpur and Lumding, and the southern supplies the Chittagong area.

(*c*) The road running south from the Assam trunk road, through Shillong, Sylhet and Comilla, to Chittagong.

181. The difficulties encountered on this line of communication are, as regards the railways:-

(*a*) The Eastern Bengal system is unable adequately to cope with the increased lift to airfields used for air supply.

(*b*) The capacity of the hill rail link between Badarpur and Lumding, which is limited to only nine trains a day each way, with a nett load of 140 tons each.

182. The principal developments of the railways in Eastern Bengal have been made with a view to providing a supplementary rail route for the Assam line of communication.

These include:-

(i) The provision of additional crossing stations between the wagon ferry terminal at Bahadurabad and Badapur.

(ii) Re-laying the hill section between Badarpur and Lumding to permit of the use of more powerful locomotives and longer trains.

In June, an investigation was carried out by representatives of 11 Army Group; General Headquarters, India; Headquarters, Supreme Allied Commander, South-East Asia Command; and the United States forces. Their recommendations, which are already being adopted, will increase line and terminal capacity throughout the whole system.

183. *Chittagong Port.* The limited capacity of this port originally restricted the use of the direct sea route, but steady increase has been obtained by improving the railway serving the wharves, providing additional moorings and jetties, building more storage accommodation, re-erecting equipment dismantled and removed under the denial scheme and by the supply of more lighters.

The working of the port has also improved as a result of its reorganization when Fourteenth Army assumed control on the 1st February.

The stores imported have increased by 150 per cent. since November 1943.

Further development is still going on and by March 1945, the port will have been expanded to the maximum practicable extent.

184. *The Arakan Line of Communication.*
This line supplies the area to the south of Chittagong, and the lack of all-weather roads causes the burden to fall mainly on sea and river transport. There are two main routes:-

(*a*) By road, from Chittagong, via Ramu, to Tumbru at the head of the Naf River, and thence on to Bawli Bazaar and Maungdaw. The road is all-weather up to Tumbru, with the exception of the section between Chittagong and Dohazari.

(*b*) By water, from Chittagong to Cox's Bazaar and Utakhali; from Chittagong to Maungdaw direct; and by the Naf River from Tumbru to Maungdaw.

In addition to the above, there were two subsidiary sections of the line of communication:-

(i) On the Sangu and Kaladan Rivers, to support 81 (West African) Division.

(ii) On the Mayu River, to support the left flank of 15 Indian Corps.

185. The main difficulties met with on this line of communication are the physical difficulties of road contraction in an area which is either mountainous or liable to inundation in the monsoons and where no stone exists; the limited capacity of Chittagong and the very restricted capacities of Cox's Bazaar, Utakhali and Maungdaw; and the shortage of craft on rivers, the mouths of which are under enemy control.

The diversity in the types of rivercraft employed is another factor which causes added difficulties; small coasters, ordinary tugs, "D" type diesel driven tugs of wooden construction, cargo flats, ramped cargo lighters, Eureka tow boats, Higgins barges, a variety of country craft fitted with outboard motors (with a horse-power ranging from 9.8 to 22), and last, but not least, the sampan.

186. As on the other lines of communication, very considerable development has taken place in Arakan. The road southwards from Dohazari has been converted to a fair weather two-way road as far as Maungdaw and an all-weather one-way one as far as Tumbru. The development of the road to Tumbru to two-way all-weather standard is in progress.

Our water communications have been improved by increasing the capacity of the ports in the Cox's Bazaar area from 400 to 1,000 tons a day. Tumbru Ghat is also now capable of handling 1,000 tons daily; and as soon as Maungdaw was captured, Transportation Construction Units raised its daily capacity to 600 tons.

Perhaps the most creditable feat, however, was the way in which much needed reinforcements of rivercraft were sailed into the Naf River. In spite of the fact that the mouth of the river was held by the enemy, Inland Water Transportation units, during the early stages of the winter operations, ran craft down the coast and up into the river – air cover being provided – to supplement the water transport which had been used the previous season. The river fleet in the Naf was thus increased until it was capable of handling 1,000 tons a day between Tumbru and the numerous jetties which have been constructed between this ghat and Maungdaw.

187. *Oil Pipelines.* Oil pipelines are under construction which will, of course, relieve the load on other forms of transport. An American 6-inch pipeline has been completed from Calcutta to North Assam and work on a similar line from Chittagong to the same area has been started. We are laying 4-inch pipeline from Chittagong to Imphal, via Manipur Road, which is nearly finished. The American line from Ledo to the Myitkyina area is being extended, and a British line from Imphal to Kalewa will probably be built.

188. *Summary of Developments on our Lines of Communication.* The main features have been:-

(*a*) The increase in the capacity of the Assam line of communication.

(*b*) The increase in the capacity of Chittagong.

(*c*) The development of the capacity of the sea and river line of communication southwards from Chittagong, from 400 tons to 1,000 tons a day.

(*d*) The increase in air supply due to the development of the airfields in the Surma Valley and the lines of communication leading to them.

(*e*) The construction of oil pipelines.

Supply and Maintenance.

189. The base for our operations in Burma is, of course, India, and all imported or indigenous stores pass through the Indian Reserve Base Depots.

The stocks of stores which we intended to hold on both the northern and southern lines were sixty days' working stock plus thirty days' reserve.

Stores from the Indian Reserve Bases are delivered to Advanced Bases in the Fourteenth Army area, which, for Arakan, are located about Chittagong and Mymensingh, and, for the northern line, at Gauhati and Manipur Road.

190. Arakan Front: During the last six months, an average of some 64,000 tons monthly has been moved through the port of Chittagong. A further 4,600 tons is shipped direct from Calcutta to the small ports south of Chittagong. The railway "lift" in this area, *ex* India, has averaged, over the same period, 19,000 tons monthly.

The northern part of East Bengal is served by Mymensingh from which the requirements of the air force, reserve formations in the district, and the air supply base airfields are met.

The Chittagong depots supply the Arakan, using road, sea and inland water transport.

191. Assam Front: For the first three months of the year, the line of communication on this front was unable to meet in full the heavy demands of both the British and United States forces. From the beginning of April 1944, however, its capacity has been notably improved and it can now lift the full requirements of the Allies; the tonnage having risen, in the last six months, from some 3,800 tons *per diem* to 5,200.

From our railhead at Dimapur, a long road line of communication leads up to and beyond, Imphal. Before the Japanese advance in March, a division was fighting beyond Tamu, which is 195 miles from railhead, and another was engaged south of Tiddim, 300 miles from railhead. Imphal is 135 miles from Dimapur.

192. The maintenance of Special Force was entirely by air. For this purpose, bases at airfields in East Bengal were originally organized and stocked, but at a later stage in the planning, the base was transferred to the Surma Valley, and

from the airfields there maintenance by supply-dropping and landing has been carried out throughout the operations.

193. The building up of stocks on both the northern and southern lines was a matter of some anxiety during the earlier part of the period. On the southern line, the capacity of the port of Chittagong, in spite of progressive expansion, barely kept pace with the needs of the forces, while on the northern line of communication, the total capacity available until April was only just sufficient for maintenance. Reserve stocks of many commodities, especially petrol, fell to dangerously low levels.

194. A supply difficulty which exists in both Assam and Arakan is that, with the exception of the rice crop which barely meets the needs of the civil population, no foodstuffs are obtainable in either area. In Bengal last year, this caused famine; and in parts of Assam the local inhabitants can barely support themselves. This imposed on the Army the need for importing fresh meat, vegetables, fruit, etc., from distant areas over difficult lines of communication; and of having to supply large quantities of tinned and dehydrated substitutes to rectify deficiencies in the fresh ration.

195. I have already mentioned the extent to which air supply has developed, but the subject is of such outstanding importance that the following figures are of interest. From the 8th to the 21st February, when the Japanese attack severed the communications of 7 Indian Division, a total of 923 tons of supplies of all types was dropped on the surrounded elements of that division. The month's total for February of air-dropped supplies in Arakan was 2,710 tons. In April, the total tonnage dropped was:-

Arakan, 1,316 (for 81 (West African) Division in the Kaladan Valley).
Special Force, 1,073.

From the 16th April to the 22nd June (the date of the re-opening of the Kohima – Imphal road), the amount flown into Imphal for 4 Corps was 13,155 tons. Nearly 10,000 casualties were evacuated by air from Imphal between these dates.

196. The operation of road transport between railhead (Dimapur) and Imphal, and forward thereof, is also of interest. A "round the clock" or L.G.O.C.[14] system has been adopted which works throughout the twenty-four hours. Vehicles run independently, drivers being changed at intervals which give them adequate rest. The following figures cover the month of January:-

Number of task vehicles	1,321
Tonnage delivered	47,304
Total mileage run	4,463,454
Average daily mileage per vehicle	110
Casualties:	
(*a*) Miles per accident	19,239
(*b*) Vehicles evacuated	103

At this time, as already mentioned, divisions had to be supplied up to 300 miles from railhead. Much of this is narrow and dangerous mountain road and I think the above figures demonstrate the efficiency of Indian lorry drivers.

197. The importance of labour in an undeveloped Eastern Theatre cannot be overstated. The construction of hundreds of miles of railways, roads, and pipelines; the preparation of new airfields and the expansion of existing ones; transportation works on the lines of communication, including port development; the expansion of hospitals, depots and camps in rear areas, etc., all mean an unending demand for more and more labour.

On the 1st May, the figure of organized labour employed by Fourteenth Army was over 178,000, while demands for a further 18,600 were under examination. In addition to this, some 200,000 civilian (contractor) labour was employed on Army projects. These figures include labour supplied to the United States forces. In spite of this total of nearly 400,000, the deficit on this date was 31,400.

198. As regards supplies, the two most pressing problems have been the provision of fresh foodstuffs, and of petrol.

I have already mentioned that dehydrated meat and vegetables were being supplied to meet the inadequacy of fresh supplies. I may add that every encouragement and assistance is given to units to grow their own vegetables where this is practicable.

A Local Resources branch of the staff, assisted by an agricultural expert borrowed from the Government of Assam, which is bringing some 18,000 acres under vegetable cultivation, was established. Pig breeding, goat rearing, and chicken farming have also been planned on an extensive scale.

199. The supply of petrol and lubricants, including those for aviation, has caused some anxiety. The monthly quantities, to be supplied through Army channels, were estimated last May to exceed eleven and a quarter million gallons, of which nearly half was high grade aviation spirit.

In spite of the progressive improvement in the capacity of our lines of communication, which has been more than doubled since December 1943, it has not been found possible as yet to do more than provide the quantities for maintenance. The ever increasing demands of our Allies in Upper Assam have continued to tax our oil resources. I do not foresee much improvement in the situation until more pipelines have been finished.

200. Before leaving the subject of supply and maintenance, there are two matters which deserve notice.

The first is the projected reorganization of mechanical transport in the Royal Indian Army Service Corps. At present, there are no less than eight types of M.T. units – an organization which is both wasteful in manpower, and insufficiently flexible, as well as possessing other disadvantages. My recommendation to General Headquarters, India, that the existing eight types should be reduced to three, has been accepted, and the new reorganization is being adopted.

The second point of interest affects the Veterinary Service. In order that animals with Special Force should not betray the position of our troops in operations behind the enemy's lines, a muting operation was performed. This has achieved its object and there has been no loss of efficiency.

The Engineering Effort.

201. I have already described (with one exception – the Ledo Road) development of the railways, roads and pipelines and I have also mentioned airfield construction. The latter, however, merits more detailed description. I propose, too, to touch on bridging, which is so important in this Theatre, and, also, to discuss briefly the general problem of rapid road construction across mountain barriers or through thick jungle tracts, for on its solution the success of future operations will largely depend.

202. *The Ledo Road.* This road, which, in conjunction with air supply, is the line of communication of General Stilwell's Chinese-American forces operating in Northern Burma, has not been described because it does not form part of Fourteenth Army's northern line of communication. It is, of course, entirely under American control and, begun by British, is being built by American engineers.

It is now "all-weather two-way" to just north of Shaduzup and the intention is to complete it through to Myitkyina in another three months. Roadhead and railhead are to be at Namti, six miles north-east of Mogaung.

203. *Airfields.* Airfield construction in the area under my control can be divided into three categories: construction in the Fourteenth Army area; construction in North-East Assam for the United States Army Air Force, which is primarily in connection with the airlift to China; and construction in Ceylon.

There were eighteen main airfields in the Fourteenth Army area last November. Since that date, three more large fields have been begun and the others have been made up to an all-weather standard.

For future operations, as outlined by the Chiefs of Staff at the end of March, it became necessary to build airfields adequate to allow additional transport to operate during the monsoon. In consultation with Air Command, South-East Asia, it was decided to increase the capacity of fifteen of the existing twenty-one airfields and to raise the standard to admit of their use by Dakotas and certain types of bombers.

204. On the 1st April 1944, the responsibility for the completion and upkeep of the American airfields in North-East Assam was transferred from General Headquarters, India, to 11 Army Group. There are eleven main airfields in this area, all of which have now been completed to all-weather standard, with the exception of two which have been allotted a low priority by the Commanding General, United States Air Forces, China – Burma – India Theatre.

205. Airfields in Ceylon are built by the Air Ministry Works Department, but they remain the responsibility of the Chief Engineer, Ceylon Army Command.

There are nine main airfields on the island, work on the improvement and extension of which continues.

206. It would have been quite impossible to attain the target dates fixed for the completion of this large-scale expansion by using normal materials such as concrete. Use has, therefore, been made of the new (and hitherto untried) bitumenized hessian ("Bithess") process for the provision of all-weather standings and runways. This material prevents water penetrating the ground which accordingly retains its full bearing capacity in wet weather. The experiment has already proved a success and may be of great value in future operations in a Theatre where monsoon rainfall is so heavy.

The magnitude of the engineering effort involved in airfield construction may be judged from the fact that, for the American airfields in North-East Assam alone, some 16,000 British military officers and men and 45,000 civil labour under British military supervision, are employed.

207. *River Crossings, (a)* The problem in this Theatre is complicated by the width of obstacles (the Chindwin and Myittha Rivers at Kalewa are some 330 yards and 200 yards across respectively in the dry season); the speed of current; the great seasonal variation in water levels; and the presence of floating debris. Wide rivers can, of course, only be bridged quickly by using floating equipment, as the construction of piers is a major engineering task, but the factors mentioned above, especially fast currents, render the anchoring of floating bridges precarious.

To overcome these difficulties, a bridge (known as the Falls bridge) has recently been designed and satisfactorily tested. It is composed of steel pontoons – widely spaced to admit of the passage of debris – with a Bailey superstructure, and with a large gantry at each end to control the landing bay during the marked variations which occur in water level.

Other measures, which are under investigation, include a proposal that only assault equipment should be carried in divisions, bridging companies to be Army or Corps Troops. Experiments are also being undertaken to produce a standard type of vehicle capable of carrying all bridging loads.

(*b*) The alternative method of crossing rivers by ferry assumes a special significance in this Theatre owing, not only to the width of gaps, but to the fact that the water level is liable to such sudden changes.

Ferrying is largely resorted to on the lines of communication, especially on the Brahmaputra.

Speeding-up Communications.
208. The rate of building all-weather roads in mountainous or thick jungle country has never amounted to more than one third of a mile a day. This is not fast enough to support a major land operation. The methods by which movement can be accelerated, particularly across physical barriers, are:-

(*a*) By the carriage of formations with weapons and M.T. in aircraft and gliders.

(*b*) By cutting jeep tracks in advance of the all-weather main road axis.

(*c*) By the deployment of the maximum possible engineer force and equipment, with the aid of aircraft, along the proposed alignment.

Both (*a*) and (*b*) restrict the size of modern transport. The only way in which larger vehicles can be transported by air is by so designing them that they can be broken down for air transport and re-assembled quickly on landing.

As regards (*c*), the deployment of an engineer force along a road alignment can only be done if no interference by the enemy is likely.

209. This presupposes the extensive use of airborne troops in an initial operation, to secure focal areas on the line of advance from which engineers and their machines can work in several directions simultaneously and thus rapidly provide a road artery. Without such an artery, operations for permanent occupation will be seriously hampered.

Assuming that aircraft and landing fields for gliders are available for such operations, there remains the necessity for designing types of mechanical equipment which can be broken down for transportation by air and re-assembled quickly after landing. The mechanical equipment at present transportable by air is either too small or, in the larger types, takes too long to assemble.

210. The crossing of mountain and jungle barriers can be accelerated by the use of airborne engineers, and airborne engineer machinery and bridging equipment.

The emplacing of engineer detachments along a proposed alignment is a tactical operation.

The provision of engineer equipment for air travel designed for rapid break-down and reassembly, is essential.

Research has reached an advanced stage. Steps are also being taken to strengthen the allotment of engineer units under Corps control, to facilitate reinforcement of forward divisions or, alternatively, to reduce the divisional task.

The Civil Affairs Service, Burma.
211. The Civil Affairs Service (Burma) (C.A.S.B.) came into being in February 1943, with the appointment of a Chief Civil Affairs Officer (C.C.A.O.). Originally under the control of the Commander-in-Chief, India, it was transferred to the South-East Asia Command, as part of 11 Army Group, on the 1st January 1944.

On the 1st January 1944, the Supreme Allied Commander, South-East Asia Command, assumed full judicial, legislative, executive and administrative responsibility for all the territories of Burma which were then occupied, or might at any future time be occupied, by the forces under his command, and he delegated to the Chief Civil Affairs Officer full authority to conduct on his behalf the military administration of the civil population in these territories.

212. *Administration*, (*a*) In the Fort Hertz and Sumprabum Sub-Divisions of the Myitkyina District, the zone of military administration began to expand in March 1944, Sumprabum itself being re-occupied on the 19th March. By the end of that

month, the number of freed inhabitants had reached 80,000 and the administration was in charge of a Senior Civil Affairs Officer, responsible to the Deputy C.C.A.O. at Headquarters, Fourteenth Army.

(*b*) In the Kamaing Sub-Division the whole Hukawng Valley had been liberated by the 31st March, and was similarly in charge of a Senior Civil Affairs Officer.

The number of inhabitants under administration was 9,000.

(*c*) The Japanese offensive in March only left some 25,000 tribesmen of the Chin and Naga Hills and Upper Chindwin under the British Military Administration, but the situation since that date has changed and the figure has risen to 186,000.

(*d*) In Arakan, the line has fluctuated during the past six months. At the end of March, the administered civil population was 100,000.

213. *Supplies.* The replacement of the Government of Burma Directorate of Supply by a C.A.S.B. Lines of Communication organization became effective in November 1943. Only in exceptional cases is this organization allowed to purchase locally in the open market; normally, it obtains its requirements from Army depots.

214. *Police.* Early in 1944, the Inspector General of Police, Burma, joined the C.A.S.B. as Chief of Police, bringing with him a large part of the organization he had built up since the evacuation. The Intelligence Bureau, established for the collection of information concerning civilians on conditions in enemy-occupied territory, was absorbed into the C.A.S.B., but the Burma Police Depot (in India) remains for the time being under the Government of Burma.

215. *Public Health.* A controller of Medical Services was appointed to the C.A.S.B. in February, from the Government of Burma.

The frontier fringes are served by small hospitals and dispensaries.

216. *Welfare.* The C.A.S.B. Welfare Organization, under a Staff Officer, Civil Affairs, began work in January, when the recruitment of field staff began.

Plans for this organization to work in the Hukawng Valley, and in 4 Corps' area (Naga Hills, Upper Chindwin and Chin Hills), were not put into effect. The Commanding General of the Sino-American forces operating in the Hukawng Valley decided that he did not require its services, and the Japanese offensive nullified plans for 4 Corps' area. These plans have not been prepared in vain.

In Arakan, there was the problem of villagers rendered homeless by military operations, and, at present some 50,000 civilians are being accommodated, supervised, and supplied under the auspices of the welfare organization.

217. *Representation in China.* In November 1943, an officer of the C.A.S.B. was, with the approval of the War Office, attached to the staff of our Assistant Military Attaché at Kunming (China) to advise on Civil Affairs matters generally and, in

particular, on political questions arising out of the operations of the Chinese forces over the Burma border from Yunnan.

218. *Future Commitments.* While administering the relatively small area of Burma which is at present under our control, we have also to look forward to the future, when the whole of Burma is re-occupied and returns under British Military Administration.

With this in view, it has recently been decided to combine into a single team the C.A.S.B. planning team and the Government of Burma planning team, for the preparation of a two-year plan covering, from every aspect, the re-establishment of the administrative and economic life of Burma. This will, I hope, ensure continuity, and a fair start for the Administration when conditions permit of the Government of Burma taking over the country from the C.A.S.B.

Tribute.
219. I referred in my introductory remarks on administration to the well known fact that the success or failure of an army is largely dependent on the efficiency of rear organization. It follows, therefore, that the successes which the Fourteenth Army has achieved are attributable, in no small measure, to the magnificent work of the rearward services. I have given some indication of the size and complexity of the problems which have had to be tackled. That they have been, or are being, solved, is due to the skill and determination displayed both by the Administrative Staff and Services of 11 Army Group and its subordinate formations, and the Commander-in-Chief, India, and his staff who not only laid the foundations on which we have built, but on whose administrative support we continue to depend.

Location of Headquarters.
220. I cannot finish this Despatch without referring to the difficulties by which I was continually hampered in commanding and administering 11 Army Group by the decision of the Supreme Allied Commander to move his H.Q. to Kandy in Ceylon in April 1944.[15] Before South-East Asia Command was set up in October 1943, the Commander-in-Chief, India, commanded the land forces operating against the Japanese and the roots of the Army, which was predominantly Indian, were deeply embedded in India. It was obvious that, even after the transfer of command to the Supreme Allied Commander, very close administrative connection between the two Commands would be necessary and indeed orders were issued by the Chiefs of Staff that the forces of S.E.A.C. would be based upon India. It was clear that the relationship between G.H.Q. India and 11 Army Group which was formed to command and administer the British land forces of S.E.A.C. would have to be very intimate.

The formation of H.Q. 11 Army Group was slow, for while it was possible for the Commander-in-Chief, India, to provide some of the officers and clerks required, it was clear that the majority of both would have to come from outside India; and as the needs of other theatres of war were urgent many months elapsed before these officers and men could be sent. It was, in consequence, impossible for H.Q. 11 Army Group to move with H.Q. S.E.A.C. in April owing to shortage of staff, much of whose work had still to be done by G.H.Q., India.

The decision of the Supreme Allied Commander to move his H.Q. in April, therefore, entailed the splitting – difficult for any staff however efficient – of H.Q. 11 Army Group before it was fully formed, because it was necessary for me to be represented at Kandy. I had to send my M.G. G.S., the most senior officer on my staff, as I had no other officer of adequate experience. This was a grave handicap to the efficient formation and training of the staff and to me. I had in addition to send with him some 40 officers and the necessary clerks. As no telephone communications existed – the highest priority telegrams took several hours and letters not less than 3 days – consultation between my main H.Q. at Delhi and the Advanced H.Q. at Kandy was slow and difficult.

In addition to the work at Delhi, I had of course continually to visit the forward troops and the Commander, Fourteenth Army, to control operations. I could only make occasional visits to Kandy, a journey to which from Delhi or Calcutta took more than 12 hours, except in the fastest aircraft. I was compelled to do much unnecessary travelling.

I pointed out on several occasions the very serious disadvantages of trying to control operations in Assam and Arakan from a H.Q. more than 1,500 miles from either area, without telephones, with slow telegraphic and long, and at certain times of the year unreliable air communication; further that the Air Commander responsible for the support of the Army would not be at Kandy. I continued to press for the establishment of H.Q. 11 Army Group at Calcutta. In August it was at last agreed that H.Q. 11 Army Group should move to the Calcutta area but much time had been lost and the move could not be completed until the beginning of December, at which moment operations would be in progress.

Acknowledgements.
221. My thanks are due to many officers for their ungrudging assistance, but it is not possible to mention more than a few of them.

To General Sir Claude Auchinleck my principal thanks are due, because without his wholehearted and generous support and wise advice, 11 Army Group could not have achieved success. I can never adequately express my gratitude for all he has done.

I should also like to include in my thanks to him my gratitude to his staff for their unselfish help during many months.

I wish also to thank Air Chief Marshal Sir Richard Peirse, and the R.A.F. and the U.S.A.A.F. for their magnificent support during the fighting in Arakan, Assam and in Central and Northern Burma.

Admiral Sir James Somerville gave every assistance possible to the Army, though resources did not permit of a major combined operation.

Upon Lieut.-General Slim, Commander, Fourteenth Army, felt the brunt of operations and well and truly did he stand up to the strain of the continuous and heavy fighting which began in February and ended in August. He remained unshaken during the Japanese offensive and was quick to take advantage of opportunities to counter-attack. To him is due the resounding victory achieved by Fourteenth Army this year.

Lieut.-General Scoones greatly distinguished himself in command of 4 Corps upon which the principal strain of the fighting fell during the operations round Imphal between February and June. Lieut.-General Christison in command of 15 Indian Corps in Arakan first defeated the Japanese in Burma. He has shown fine qualities of leadership.

Lieut.-General Stopford, Commander, 33 Corps, showed great staying power, professional knowledge and dash in the operations which resulted finally in opening the Kohima – Imphal road.

To my own staff, officers, N.C.Os. and men; I owe the greatest debt of gratitude for their splendid support and their fine team work. Always shorthanded, split into two with one detachment 1,500 miles from the other, they have never failed to do the work which has continued steadily to increase.

It is difficult to single out from so many first-rate officers and men, many individuals for special praise, but I must mention particularly my two principal Staff Officers upon whom fell special responsibility.

Major-General I.S.O. Playfair, M.G., G.S., has been the greatest help to me throughout, but especially after the staff was split in April when he went to Kandy as my representative. There, the whole responsibility for representing my point of view to the Supreme Allied Commander fell upon him. I relied entirely upon his unfailing judgment, strength of character and tact and he never failed me.

Major-General E.N. Goddard, M.G.A., 11 Army Group, must have carried one of the heaviest administrative loads in any theatre of war. No man could have discharged his duties with more unsparing devotion and no operations could have succeeded if his work had not been of the highest standard.

APPENDIX "A"
Skeleton Order of Battle, 15 Indian Corps,
1st January 1944.

5 *Indian Division.*
  9 Indian Infantry Brigade.
  123 Indian Infantry Brigade.
  161 Indian Infantry Brigade.
  7 *Indian Division.*
  33 Indian Infantry Brigade.
  89 Indian Infantry Brigade.
  114 Indian Infantry Brigade.
26 *Indian Division.*
  4 Indian Infantry Brigade.
  36 Indian Infantry Brigade.
  71 Indian Infantry Brigade.

81 (*West African*) *Division.*
  5 (West African) Infantry Brigade.
  6 (West African) Infantry Brigade.
Note: 3 (West African) Brigade formed part of Special Force.

APPENDIX "B"
Skeleton Order of Battle, 4 Corps,
8th March 1944.

17 *Indian Light Division.*
  48 Indian Infantry Brigade.
  63 Indian Infantry Brigade.
Note: This formation comprised only two brigades, but it included a Divisional Headquarters Battalion, a Divisional Signals Battalion, and a Divisional Reconnaissance Battalion.
20 *Indian Division.*
  32 Indian Infantry Brigade.
  80 Indian Infantry Brigade.
  100 Indian Infantry Brigade.
23 *Indian Division.*
  1 Indian Infantry Brigade.
  37 Indian Infantry Brigade.
  49 Indian Infantry Brigade.
50 *Indian Parachute Brigade (less one Battalion).*
254 *Indian Tank Brigade.*
Note: For comparison with the Order of Battle of 33 Corps at the end of May (*vide* Appendix "C"), the following formations must be added to those shown above:-
  5 Indian Division (less 161 Brigade).
  89 Indian Infantry Brigade (7 Indian Division).

APPENDIX "C"
Skeleton Order of Battle, 33 Indian Corps,
31st May 1944.

2 *British Division.*
  4 Infantry Brigade.
  5 Infantry Brigade.
  6 Infantry Brigade.
7 *Indian Division.*
  33 Indian Infantry Brigade.
  161 Indian Infantry Brigade (from 5 Indian Division).
Note: 89 Brigade was under 4 Corps, and 114 Brigade *en route* from the Arakan Front.
268 *Indian Infantry Brigade (Lorried).*
Lushai Brigade.
3 *Special Service Brigade (two Commandos).*

Corps Troops:
  149 Regiment, R.A.C.
  7 K.O.Y.L.I. (less one squadron).
  11 Cavalry.
Headquarters 21 *Indian Division.*
  (late H.Q., 44 Indian Armoured Division).
Note: This Headquarters, which had become available on the disbandment of 44 Indian Armoured Division in India, assumed operational control of the lines of communication of 33 Corps.

APPENDIX "D"
Skeleton Order of Battle, 11 Army Group, South-East Asia Command, 22nd June 1944.

FOURTEENTH ARMY.
  Special Force.
  36 British Division.
4 *Corps.*
  5 Indian Division (less 161 Brigade).
  7 Indian Division (less 33 Brigade).
  17 Indian Light Division.
  20 Indian Division.
  23 Indian Division.
  50 Indian Parachute Brigade.
33 *Corps.*
  2 British Division.
  21 Indian Division.
  161 Brigade, 5 Indian Division.
  33 Brigade. 7 Indian Division.
15 *Indian Corps.*
  25 Indian Division.
  26 Indian Division.
  81 (West African) Division.
CEYLON ARMY COMMAND.
  11 (East African) Division.
  Garrisons of the Indian Ocean bases at Addu Atoll, Diego Garcia and Cocos Islands.
Note: i. 82 (West African) Division was about to arrive.
Note: ii. The strength of forces in Northern Burma not under the operational control of 11 Army Group was:-

Fort Hertz area	2,012
American forces	65,784
Chinese forces	147,396

Notes

1. Now Vice-Admiral The Earl Mountbatten of Burma, K.G., P.C., G.C.S.I., G.C.I.E., G.C.V.O., K.C.B., D.S.O.
2. The late Lieut.-General Joseph W. Stilwell, United States Army.
3. General (now Field-Marshal) Sir Claude J.E. Auchinleck, G.C.B., G.C.I.E., C.S.I., D.S.O., O.B.E.
4. Now Field-Marshal Sir William J. Slim, G.B.E., K.C.B., D.S.O., M.C.
5. Now General Sir Geoffry A.P. Scoones, K.C.B., K.B.E., C.S.I., D.S.O., M.C.
6. Now General Sir A.F. Philip Christison, Bart., G.B.E., C.B., D.S.O., M.C.
7. Now Lieut.-General Sir H. Edward de R. Wetherall, K.B.E., C.B., D.S.O., M.C.

8. Now General Sir Montagu G.N. Stopford, G.C.B., K.B.E., D.S.O., M.C.
9. The late Major-General O.C. Wingate.
10. Major-General R.P.L. Ranking, C.B., C.B.E., M.C.
11. Now Brigadier H.U. Richards, C.B.E., D.S.O.
12. Operations in Assam and Burma from 23rd June, 1944 to 12th November, 1944.
13. "Ghat" means a landing stage.
14. L.G.O.C. = London General Omnibus Company (which was absorbed into the London Passenger Transport Board).
15. *War Office footnote* – The views of the Supreme Allied Commander and his reasons for the move to Ceylon are set out in Part A., paragraphs 12–14 of his Report, "South-East Asia, 1943–1945."

2

GENERAL SIR GEORGE J. GIFFARD'S DESPATCH ON OPERATIONS IN ASSAM AND BURMA, 23 JUNE TO 12 NOVEMBER 1944

MONDAY, 2 APRIL, 1951

The following Despatch was submitted to the Secretary of State for War on the 14th August, 1945, by GENERAL SIR GEORGE J. GIFFARD, G.C.B., D.S.O., A.D.C., Commander-in-Chief, 11 Army Group, South-East Asia Command.

PART I. – OPERATIONS.

Introduction.

1. My first Despatch[1] covered the period from the formation of 11 Army Group, 16th November, 1943, to the re-opening of the Kohima – Imphal road on the 22nd June, 1944, when at 1245 hours, at Milestone 109, the leading troops of the 2 British Division (33 Corps) met the forward troops of 5 Indian Division (4 Corps), and thus shattered the Japanese dream of conquering India. This Despatch describes the operations from the 23rd June, 1944, to the 12th November, 1944, when I handed over command of 11 Army Group to Lieut.-General Sir Oliver Leese.

2. The re-establishment of our communications with Imphal opened a new phase in the campaign. The Japanese invasion of India had been stopped; it remained to throw the enemy back whence he had come. In the words of the Prime Minister, the defence of the Imphal Plain and our subsequent successful offensive "constituted the greatest collision which had yet taken place on land with Japan and has resulted in the slaughter of between 50,000 and 60,000 Japanese. The climax was the final eviction of the Japanese from India with the almost total loss of five of his best divisions." My earlier Despatch dealt with "The defence of the Imphal Plain"; this Despatch deals with "Our subsequent successful offensive" which drove the enemy back, not merely across the Indo-Burmese frontier, but across the Chindwin River, and opened the way for the re-conquest of Central Burma.

3. In the operations I am about to describe, the Japanese retreat began as a well-planned and orderly withdrawal. Gradually, as our pressure grew, the pace of the withdrawal increased until the enemy forces were split up into small, disorganised parties. Hungry, harassed, beaten; abandoning their wounded, their guns and their transport, and even deserting in small, but increasing numbers; the Japanese

were driven in defeat over the border, down the far side of the mountain wall, and back over the Chindwin, which they had crossed in triumph and with such high hopes less than five months earlier.

Topography and Climate.
4. The formidable nature of the terrain was one of the features of this campaign. Battles were fought at 5,000 feet and over, often in almost impenetrable jungle; and troops, loaded with full equipment, struggled up from nullahs 2,000 feet below in the face of heavy small arms, grenade and mortar fire. Yet, hazardous and difficult as the nature of the country made every movement or operation, tanks often proved the decisive factor in the fighting up and down these mountain ranges, where they climbed almost precipitous slopes to blast Japanese bunkers at a range of ten yards.

5. As if still further to test the magnificent fighting spirit of the troops, another enemy was advancing steadily upon us: the torrential monsoon rain that turned tracks into leech-laden streams and chaungs into treacherous torrents; rain that washed away our already exiguous roads, turned rivers into raging floods and grounded our supporting air forces. "The Economist," in its issue of the 15th April, 1944, wrote "The monsoons are on their way, and it would be turning a new page in military history if either side campaigned through the rain-sodden and malaria-ridden months ahead." That "new page in military history" has been turned.

Instructions for Monsoon Operations.
6. On the 8th June, the Supreme Allied Commander[2] issued a Directive which included the following:-

(*a*) The broad mission of South-East Asia Command (S.E.A.C.) in Burma was:-
"To develop, maintain, broaden, and protect the air link to China in order to provide a maximum and timely stock of P.O.L. to China in support of Pacific operations; so far as is consistent with the above, to press advantages against the enemy by exerting maximum ground and air effort, particularly during the current monsoon season, and in pressing such advantages to be prepared to exploit the development of overland communications to China. All these operations must be dictated by the forces at present available or firmly allocated to S.E.A.C."
(*b*) The general tasks allotted to me were:-
(i) To secure Eastern Bengal and Assam up to my boundary with Northern Combat Area Command (N.C.A.C.) (General Stilwell's forces).
(ii) Provide the necessary ground forces for the defence of Ceylon.
(*c*) My specific tasks during the monsoon were as follows:-
(i) *Arakan.*
Maintain an active defence on the general line Maungdawm – Tunnels Area – Taung Bazaar during the monsoon. Prepare to capture Akyab by an advance starting as early as possible in the next dry season.

(ii) *Chindwin.*

First Priority. Re-establish communications on the road Dimapur – Kohima – Imphal not later than mid-July.

Second Priority. Clear Japanese forces from the area Dimapur – Kohima – Imphal Plain – Yuma – Tamanthi.

Third Priority. Prepare to exploit across the Chindwin in the Yuwa – Tamanthi area after the monsoon.

(*d*) Northern Combat Area Command would come under the direct command of the Supreme Allied Commander from the 20th June, and the boundary between Northern Combat Area Command and Fourteenth Army would be Wakching – Kaiyaw Naukkon (both exclusive Northern Combat Area Command) – Taro – Lonkin – Indawgyi Lake – Lake Indaw (all inclusive Northern Combat Area Command).

(*e*) The following reinforcements and withdrawals were to be made:-

(i) 82 (West African) Division would be concentrated in India during August.

(ii) 22 (East African) Brigade would arrive in Ceylon during July.

(NOTE: This is an independent brigade; 11 (East African) Division and 28 (East African) Brigade (independent) were already in Ceylon in June.)

(iii) 19 Indian Division would be available as a relief when one British or Indian division returned to India for rest.

(iv) The first brigade group of 36 British Division to be ready to move under the command of Northern Combat Area Command by the 1st July (the remainder by the 20th July), in relief of Special Force.

(v) 3 Commando Brigade would be withdrawn from Imphal as soon after the 1st July as operations permitted, but might again be made available at a later date for operations in Arakan.

7. In accordance with this Directive, I issued operation instructions to the Commander, Fourteenth Army, Lieut.-General W.J. Slim[3],for operations during the monsoon and the move of 36 British Division which was to go by road and rail to Ledo and thence by road to the Myitkyina area.

To complete the picture, the rôle allotted by the Supreme Allied Commander to General Stilwell's forces in North Burma (Northern Combat Area Command) was to protect the Mogaung – Myitkyina area by establishing an outpost line; Lonkin – Talawgyi – Kazu – Fort Harrison – Seniku.

The Chinese Expeditionary Force (C.E.F.) had orders from the Generalissimo to cross the Salween River and join General Stilwell's forces in the Myitkyina area.

8. Such were our tasks: but before continuing the narrative, a word about communication and roads is necessary. I shall give an account of road construction in a later section, when discussing engineering work, but the tracks which did duty for roads in the forward area may conveniently be described here, as they will be frequently referred to in subsequent paragraphs:

(*a*) A road from Palel to Tamu existed, but it rapidly deteriorated when the monsoon started, and to quote from my Chief Engineer's report "The mud had to be seen to be believed". In these conditions, only 4 × 4 lorries[4] were permitted to run south of Palel, though the rule had to be relaxed occasionally for specialist vehicles.

(*b*) The road south from Tamu down the Kabaw Valley can only euphemistically be called a road – it was a sea of mud varying in depth from six to eighteen inches. In the worst places corduroy roads, over which jeeps and 30-cwt. 6 × 6 lorries[4] could pass, had to be built.

(*c*) The Sittaung track from Palel to the Chindwin was not a road at all. It was passable for jeeps and 4 × 4 vehicles as far as the Yu River. There a ferry, beyond which only pack or porter transport could be used, was established. Owing to the amount of blasting which would have been necessary, it was not possible to clear a track with bulldozers.

(*d*) The road to Tiddim was worse, if possible, than the Kabaw Valley road. It was commanded on either side by scrub-covered hills up to 8,000 feet, and some of the more mountainous sections resembled toboggan runs down which vehicles slid on mud instead of snow.

These conditions must be remembered when judging the speed of our advances along the Tiddim road and the Kabaw Valley. We had to overcome not only a determined enemy, but Napoleon's fourth element.

Situation on the 22nd June and subsequent operations.

9. (*a*) *Arakan.* 15 *Indian Corps* (*Lieut.-General A.F.P. Christison*[5]).
   (i) 25 Indian Division: Maungdaw – Tunnels Area.
   (ii) 26 Indian Division:
   One Brigade – Bawli Bazaar – Goppe Bazaar – Taung Bazaar.
   One Brigade – Taungbro – Tumbru.
   One Brigade – Cox's Bazaar.
   (iii) 81 (West African) Division:
   Divisional H.Q. and one brigade – Chiringa.
   One brigade taking up new positions to protect the eastern approaches of the Chiringa – Singpa track, with detachments on the Sangu River to block enemy attempts to pentrate into that area.

(*b*) *Imphal Front* (4 *and* 33 *Corps*). 4 *Corps* (*Lieut.-General G.A.P. Scoones*[6]).
   (i) 17 Indian Light Division, with one brigade of 20 Indian Division under command, was engaged in attacking 33 Japanese Division in the Bishenpur area. Two battalions and one mountain battery had cut the enemy's line of communication about Milestone 33 on the Imphal – Tiddim road by making a wide turning movement from the east, and had then driven north to positions four miles south of Bishenpur. This bold attack on the enemy's rear had thrown them into considerable confusion and inflicted heavy casualties.
   (ii) While these operations were in progress south of Imphal, 5 Indian Division, which had taken over the area north of Imphal from 17 Indian Light

Division, was attacking the enemy on the road to Kohima. After clearing Kanglatongbi it reached Milestone 109, where it made contact with 2 British Division of 33 Corps driving down from the north.

(iii) 20 Indian Division was engaging the enemy in the Ukhrul sector, with one brigade in the area 16 miles west of the village astride the Japanese communications, and one brigade on the Imphal – Ukhrul road clearing enemy positions about Milestone 17. The third brigade of this Division was with the 17 Indian Light Division. 50 Indian Parachute Brigade (two battalions) was in action south of the Imphal – Ukhrul road, east of Wangjing.

(iv) 23 Indian Division was engaged with the enemy in an area some three miles east and south-east of Palel.

(c) 33 *Corps* (*Lieut.-General M.G.N. Stopford*[7]).

(i) 7 Indian Division, which had been on the left flank of 2 British Division, was, after the junction of 33 and 4 Corps, ordered to move east on Ukhrul.

(ii) 2 British Division and 268 Indian Lorried Infantry Brigade were responsible for the protection of the Kohima – Imphal road south and north of Milestone 79 respectively.

(iii) 23 L.R.P. Brigade (Long-Range Penetration Group) was clearing the tracks leading down to Ukhrul from the north, and cutting the enemy's routes to the east.

10. Although the picture at the end of June was one of Japanese retreat on all sectors of the Imphal front, I must emphasize that our success had only been achieved after hard fighting and severe losses on both sides. Indeed, the Army Commander described it as the bitterest fighting he had seen in this or any other war. Even when it must have been obvious to the Japanese High Command that our communications to Imphal were about to be re-established, they issued orders to their 33 and 15 Divisions that Imphal was to be taken at all costs. We captured the orders in which the Commander, 33 Japanese Division, informed his troops "The fate of the Empire depends on this battle. You will capture Imphal but you will be annihilated". 33 Japanese Division made a series of heavy attacks, but they were met with steady valour by our 17 Indian Division who saw to it that the "annihilation" of the enemy commander's prophecy was fulfilled.

What was left of the enemy's 33 and 15 Divisions was driven into the inhospitable country south of Bishenpur and south-east of Palel. Elements of 15 Japanese Division, however, had reinforced 31 Japanese Division which then attacked in the area between Ukhrul and Imphal. This attack failed.

The Situation at the End of June.

11. *North Burma.* 22 Chinese Division, which had captured Kamaing on the 16th June, was continuing its advance southwards in the face of opposition by part of 18 Japanese Division between Kamaing and Mogaung.

77 L.R.P. Brigade (Special Force), assisted by a Chinese regiment, captured Mogaung on the 26th June, the enemy losing severely in men and material, which included some medium artillery. This was a particularly fine action by 77 L.R.P.

Brigade against most stubborn resistance by units of 53 Japanese Division. The capture of Mogaung was important, as it opened the way for further operations southward.

Myitkyina was still holding out against Chinese and American troops and Morris-force (part of Special Force), which were heavily engaged.

The brigades of Special Force were much scattered and were operating in widely separated areas. 14 L.R.P. Brigade was in the area 28 miles west-south-west of Mogaung, 111 and 3 (West African) Brigades in contact with 38 Chinese Division were 20 miles west-north-west of the same place. This Force, which comprised the Long-Range Penetration Brigades flown into North Burma in the Spring, had come under General Stilwell's command on the 20th June, when General Stilwell was transferred from the command of General Slim to that of the Supreme Allied Commander.

On the Salween front, the Chinese Expeditionary Force was engaged 12 miles south-south-west of Lungling.

12. *Arakan.* During the month, 25 and 26 Indian Divisions and 81 (West African) Division had completed their moves to their monsoon positions with little interference from the enemy. Since then, operations in this area had been confined to active patrolling.

13. *Imphal Front.* The opening of the Kohima – Imphal road on the 22nd June completed the first task set by the Supreme Allied Commander in his instructions of the 8th June.

14. Though the opening of the road solved many of our administrative difficulties, it also created a new set of problems. 2 British Division, though its morale was high, had suffered severe casualties and was tired. It was clear that the Division could not continue to fight without reinforcements and the necessary time and facilities to train them. All expedients to bring units up to strength were temporarily exhausted. The Corps Commander considered that the Division should be withdrawn from active operations until the Autumn. A rest area was therefore prepared but, as will be seen, 4 Brigade had to be used temporarily to relieve 20 Indian Division and, later, 5 Brigade was called upon to support 23 Indian Division.

5 and 7 Indian Divisions had to resume their proper compositions, which had been upset when reinforcements had to be flown in during the early stages of the battle. 161 Brigade, which belonged to 5 Indian Division, had been under command of 7 Indian Division, and 89 Brigade of 7 Indian Division had worked with 5 Indian Division. These two Brigades had to return to their own Divisions.

15. The operations against Ukhrul consisted of cross-country advances eastwards by 33 and 89 Brigades of 7 Indian Division, from the Kohima – Imphal road, in co-operation with an advance north-east by 20 Indian Division along the main Imphal – Ukhrul road. This was complicated initially because 20 Indian Division and 89 Brigade were under command of 4 Corps, while 33 Brigade was under

33 Corps. However, as soon as the advance got under way, the Commander, 33 Corps assumed control of the whole operation.

16. By the end of June, 20 Indian Division had reached a point eight miles west of Ukhrul and 7 Indian Division, further north, were clearing the area four miles south-east of Karong.

23 L.R.P. Brigade, advancing southwards, had driven the enemy back to a line eight miles south of Kharasom.

South of Imphal, 17 and 23 Indian Divisions were still engaged in bitter fighting in the Bishenpur and Palel areas respectively. The monsoon had broken, and the troops had to work under very arduous conditions of rain and mud in the mountains and jungle.

17. On the 30th June, the institution of a new boundary between 4 and 33 Corps, and the consequent transfer of 20 Indian Division (less 32 Brigade) from 4 Corps to 33 Corps, marked the beginning of a new phase of operations. This boundary gave the area between Imphal and Ukhrul inclusive to 33 Corps, and left 4 Corps with Imphal and the areas of 5 Indian Division (Imphal – Bishenpur), 17 Indian Light Division (Bishenpur) and 23 Indian Division (Palel).

The Situation in early July.
18. *Chin Hills and Chindwin.* As a result of our continuous pressure in the Imphal Plain, there were signs at the beginning of July that the Japanese forces in Manipur were giving up their plan for a final attack on Imphal.

19. On the 3rd July a brigade of 7 Indian Division captured Ukhrul from the west, while a column of 23 L.R.P. Brigade entered the village almost simultaneously from the east. The fall of Ukhrul was important since it was the focal point of all communications in that area; its capture removed all threats to Imphal from the north and north-east.

20. On the 29th June, I had wired to General Slim that 31 Japanese Division would probably be withdrawn to the south of Ukhrul, but that the enemy might make a final desperate attempt to capture Imphal from the general direction of the Tiddim and Tamu roads. Although we had sufficient strength to defeat any such attempt, our task of clearing the enemy west of the Chindwin would be facilitated if we could develop a real threat to his communications. I therefore directed him to consider whether the advance on Ukhrul could be continued south-south-east to Humine and Myothit at the head of the Kabaw Valley. This would give 31 Japanese Division no chance to recover and would threaten the communications of 15 Japanese Division at Thaungdut and Tamu.

21. On the fall of Ukhrul, General Slim issued an Operation Instruction, dated the 5th July, directing 4 and 33 Corps to destroy the Japanese forces west of the Chindwin River. 4 Corps, with 5 and 17 Indian Divisions and one brigade of 20 Indian Division under command, were to clear the area west of the general line Imphal – Shuganu. 33 Corps, with 2 British, 7, 20 and 23 Indian Divisions,

268 Indian Lorried Infantry Brigade, 23 L.R.P. Brigade and 50 Indian Parachute Brigade under command, were to clear the area east of this line.

22. By the 10th July, it had become clear that the Japanese had begun a general withdrawal from their three main concentration areas about Bishenpur, Palel, and Ukhrul. They had not captured Bishenpur or Palel.

23. *North Burma.* Although General Stilwell was now no longer under General Slim's command, I must review the operations as a whole, as they had, of course, to be co-ordinated. I shall, therefore, throughout this Despatch briefly describe the Allied progress in North Burma.

24. Early in July, after the successful clearing of the Kamaing – Mogaung road, there were signs that the enemy intended to fight successive delaying actions in Taungni and Pinbaw, and then make a determined stand at Hopin. The Myitkyina garrison seemed likely to fight it out, but no major reinforcements were being sent to its assistance. As I have already said, the task allotted to Northern Combat Area Command was to capture the Mogaung – Myitkyina area and to establish an outpost line to cover it.

25. Concurrently with General Slim's Operation Instruction, General Stilwell issued orders to the Mogaung and Myitkyina Task Forces. The former, composed of 22 and 38 Chinese Divisions, with parts of 50 Chinese Division and Special Force, subsequently joined by 36 British Division, was to capture the area from Lonkin to Taungni. The latter, comprising parts of 30 and 14 Chinese Divisions, a United States regiment, and a small detachment of Special Force, was to capture the area from Talawgyi to Seniku.

Operations in July.
26. 15 *Indian Corps.* Operations in Arakan during the month were confined to active patrolling in which several very successful small actions were fought. Some idea of the difficult conditions on this front can be gathered from the fact that the weekly rainfall sometimes exceeded 20 inches.

27. 4 *Corps – Bishenpur Area.* By the end of June, 5 Indian Division had finished mopping up on both sides of the southern sector of the Kohima – Imphal road and had concentrated at Imphal, except for one brigade which had been sent to join 17 Indian Light Division in its operations in the Bishenpur area. During the first week in July these two Divisions cleared the area north of the Silchar – Bishenpur track. To the south, enemy resistance showed signs of weakening – many positions being evacuated in the face of our continued frontal pressure and attacks against his flanks. 33 Japanese Division was, however, reinforced by tanks and a composite regiment drawn from their 53 and 54 Divisions and made a determined stand between the 12th and the 16th July on hills overlooking the track from the south. After sharp fighting, 5 Indian Division pressed southwards through these hills and reached an area three miles west of Ningthoukhong. By

the 18th, one brigade had established itself three miles west of Milestone 24 on the Tiddim road.

28. In the meantime, 17 Indian Light Division was attacking strongly held Japanese positions about Ningthoukhong. The enemy held these till the 16th, when, assisted by the operations of 5 Indian Division, 17 Indian Light Division captured the village. The enemy were closely pursued and we captured much equipment, including 12 tanks. By the 18th, we were following a retreating enemy, having regained four miles of the Tiddim road. On this date, 5 Indian Division assumed responsibility for operations on the Tiddim road with one brigade of 17 Indian Light Division under command. The remainder of 17 Indian Division was withdrawn into reserve.

29. The Japanese withdrawal down the Tiddim road was steadily and successfully pressed. By the 25th July the enemy had been driven out of the Imphal Plain and, by the 1st August, a flanking movement to the west reached the road at Milestone 44.

   Thus, by the end of July, 20 miles of the Tiddim road had been recovered, with considerable loss to the enemy in men and material: captured equipment included 21 tanks. The advance had been made in spite of the destruction of bridges and the laying of minefields and booby traps. The enemy was much helped by continual heavy rain, which turned every stream into a serious obstacle and greatly increased the difficulties of movement off the road.

30. *33 Corps – Ukhrul Sector.* During the first few days of July responsibilities for the protection of the line of communication, the defence of Imphal, the mopping up of enemy parties and operations for the capture of Ukhrul were redistributed between 4 and 33 Corps. 33 Corps had already taken over from 4 Corps the responsibility for operations against Ukhrul on the 30th June, and 20 Indian Division came under its command.

31. Until the 4th July 2 British Division continued to mop up the remaining parties of the enemy who were still resisting fiercely in certain areas to the east and west of the main road. With the eastward advance on Ukhrul in full swing, however, operations on the Kohima – Imphal road ceased, and 2 British Division, less one brigade which was operating in the Palel – Tamu sector under 23 Indian Division, was disposed for the protection of the main road.

32. At the beginning of July, the two brigades of 7 Indian Division, which were advancing towards Ukhrul from the west, made good progress in spite of bad weather, which greatly handicapped not only the marching men but also the air supply on which they depended. It was said at the time that for every two feet a man climbed up the muddy slippery tracks he slid back one. On the 2nd July, they made contact with 23 L.R.P. Brigade, which was advancing from the north to attack Ukhrul and block the enemy's escape to the east. The third brigade of 7 Indian Division moved back to Kohima, which was to be its rest area.

33. Ukhrul was captured on the 3rd July, but opposition in the area was by no means at an end, as the Japanese continued to hold out in strongly entrenched positions, north, south and west of the village. On the 6th one brigade of 7 Indian Division captured the highest hill feature north of Ukhrul while the other moved south and south-east to block all exits. The other enemy positions were assaulted successively and, by the 10th July, all resistance had been overcome.

34. 7 Indian Division continued its advance along the Ukhrul – Humine track, enemy road blocks being passed and left for troops in rear to remove. By the 17th, our leading troops had reached Milestone 22, four miles south of Maoku. The Division was then withdrawn to rest at Kohima and was relieved by 4 Brigade of 2 British Division.

35. The second phase of these operations, which took place concurrently with the first phase which I have already described, was the advance of 20 Indian Division along the Imphal – Ukhrul road to join the forces about Ukhrul and sever all possible lines of escape of the enemy. Like the first phase, the period was one of great activity, and much fierce fighting. A Japanese force some 2,000 strong had been isolated and was trying to escape to the south-west. Bitter fighting developed between a desperate enemy trying to fight his way out of the net thrown round him and troops equally determined to hold him. Very heavy casualties were inflicted, but our losses were not light. The enemy's forces were gradually compressed into a small area and 20 Indian Division made contact with 7 Indian Division on the 11th July.

36. On the 17th July, 20 Indian Division was withdrawn from the Ukhrul sector after destroying the remnant, about 300 strong, of this Japanese force and capturing all its guns and transport. The Division was now concentrated to rest and refit about Wanjing, 16 miles south-east of Imphal, where it could, if necessary, easily move in either direction and act as a reserve to 23 Indian Division on the Tamu road or to 5 and 17 Indian Divisions about Bishenpur. 50 Indian Parachute Brigade (two battalions) which had been operating most successfully on the flank of 20 Indian Division across the tracks running south from the Imphal – Ukhrul road, was similarly withdrawn for rest and re-organization in India.

37. The operations of 23 L.R.P. Brigade, which belonged to Special Force (Long-Range Penetration troops), but which had not been flown into North Burma with that formation in March, deserve special mention. In their advance south from Kharasom to the Ukhrul area, they operated in eight small columns across exceptionally difficult country and inflicted severe casualties on 31 Japanese Division retreating from Kohima. Four of these columns, advancing from the north, co-ordinated their movements with those of 7 Indian Division on Ukhrul from the west. The other four columns moved to the east and south-east of Ukhrul to cut the enemy's communications.

By the 11th July, all tracks leading east towards Homalin on the Chindwin had been blocked and many enemy destroyed, our own casualties being negligible. In the third week in July, 23 L.R.P. Brigade was concentrated at Ukhrul before being withdrawn to India.

38. 23 *Indian Division – Tamu Sector.* By the middle of July, the enemy had been driven from the Ukhrul area, and the operations ended with the complete rout of the Japanese, who retreated down the tracks to Humaine and Tamu abandoning guns and lorries and leaving many dead. With the withdrawal of 20 Indian Division and 23 L.R.P. Brigade, interest switched to the Tamu sector where 23 Indian Division was engaged in driving the enemy from his strongly prepared positions east and south-east of Palel.

For some time past, the enemy had been active in this sector, but his counter-attack failed to make any headway. His only success was early in the month when a small raiding party reached the Palel airstrip at night and damaged three aircraft. By the middle of July, however, he had lost the initiative and was being driven back. The fact that over 100 Japanese were taken prisoner in one week was some evidence of decreasing morale.

39. The opening of 23 Indian Division's offensive down the Tamu road in the middle of July began another phase of the campaign to drive the Japanese forces across the Chindwin. The situation on the 24th July was that one brigade, after making a wide turning movement via the Sibong track, had outflanked the enemy's positions, established blocks on the Tamu road south of Sibong and in the Lokchao bridge area, and achieved complete surprise. The enemy was thus caught between these blocks and the two brigades advancing on them from the north which, on that date, had captured the strong Japanese positions at Tengnoupal after severe fighting. The enemy's defence in this area disintegrated and they withdrew, abandoning much heavy equipment, including some guns. By the 25th, we had cleared an enemy block at Milestone 49 and were exploiting to the south-east.

40. 23 Indian Division continued its advance down the Palel – Tamu road supported by tanks, over-running successive enemy positions and capturing nine guns. 268 Indian Lorried Infantry Brigade, an independent formation, operating north of the road, protected the left flank of 23 Indian Division. Enemy casualties in the last week of July had been heavy and his stubborn resistance had been fruitless.

41. On the 31st July, 33 Corps assumed command of 5 and 17 Indian Divisions and took over responsibility for the Tiddim road sector. On the 1st August, Headquarters, 4 Corps, was withdrawn to India for rest and training in mobile operations.

Summary of Operations in July.
42. *Arakan.* Apart from local patrolling in typical monsoon weather, there was no activity on either side.

43. *Chin Hills and Chindwin.* Our troops continued to press the Japanese withdrawal:-

In the Ukhrul sector, the enemy were driven back to a point 18 miles south of Ukhrul.

In the Palel area, 23 Indian Division reached a point five miles north-west of Tamu.

On the Imphal – Tiddim road, 5 Indian Division reached the area 21 miles south of Bishenpur, capturing a number of guns, tanks and armoured cars in this advance.

44. The general situation at the end of July was that the Japanese were still retiring and it seemed likely they might decide to hold the line Tiddim – Kalewa and northwards, along the Chindwin River, for the rest of the monsoon. Rain continued to hamper our operations, floods and continual landslides impeding our progress and breaking our communications.

45. *North Burma.* Operations against Myitkyina had continued. 77 L.R.P. Brigade (Special Force) which had been operating under General Stilwell's command in the Mogaung area, and some columns of 111 L.R.P. Brigade, had been withdrawn to India by air. On the 19th July, 14 L.R.P. Brigade captured Ngusharaung, an important 2,000-foot height seven miles north-west of Taungni (20 miles south-west of Mogaung). One brigade of 36 British Division had been flown into North Burma and was concentrating in the Mogaung area.

Planning for Operations – Winter 1944–45.
46. In accordance with instructions received from the Supreme Allied Commander, I issued an Operation Instruction on the 29th July to the Commander, Fourteenth Army, directing that plans be made for the following post-monsoon operations:-

(*a*) *Arakan:* An offensive/defence to secure with minimum forces our present forward positions in the Maungdaw – Tunnels Area and to prevent enemy penetration in the Kaladan Valley, which might endanger the operations of our Air Forces and our line of communication west of the Mayu Range.

(*b*) *Imphal Front:* A phased plan (which contemplated certain airborne operations) with the following objectives:-

(i) Seizure of Kalemyo – Kalewa.

(ii) An airborne assault against the Ye-U area, to gain a quick exit into the Mandalay Plain, to be followed by ground operations to open the Kalewa – Ye-U road so that heavy equipment, including tanks, could be brought forward for an advance on Mandalay.

(iii) Capture of Mandalay – Pakokku.

(iv) Consolidation along the general line Pakokku – Mandalay – Maymyo – Kyaukme – Lashio (in conjunction with Northern Combat Area Command).

(*c*) I informed the Commander, Fourteenth Army, that the Northern Combat Area Command forces would advance to capture the Katha – Bhamo area and later Lashio, and that the Chinese Yunnan Force would advance along the old Burma Road to capture Hsenwi and Lashio.

(*d*) *South Burma*. A plan which did not affect the operations covered by this Despatch.

Operation Instructions affecting Operations in August.
47. On the 6th August, the Commander, Fourteenth Army, gave 33 Corps the following tasks:-

(*a*) To pursue the enemy on the lines:
 Imphal – Tiddim – Kalemyo – Kalewa.
 Tamu – Indainggyi – Kalewa.
 Tamu – Sittaung.

(*b*) To occupy Sittaung in order to deny the use of the Chindwin River to the enemy.

(*c*) If opportunity offered, to capture Kalewa and establish a bridgehead in that area.

He was told that air supply could be provided for a maximum of five brigades.
Operations in August.

48. *Tiddim Road Sector*. 5 Indian Division maintained the impetus of its advance down the Tiddim road during the month, in spite of stubborn resistance by Japanese rearguards; the 75th milestone, which marks the Indo-Burmese frontier, was passed; and successive enemy positions – many of them of great natural strength – were overcome by a combination of frontal assaults, and wide turning movements through the jungle-clad mountains. By the 4th August, the number of captured tanks had risen to 32, and by the end of the month a further 10 tanks, 200 M.T. and 12 guns had fallen into our hands. On the 31st August, our troops were engaged with the enemy about Milestone 96.

These operations were distinguished by the highly successful co-operation of air, tanks, artillery and infantry, which inflicted severe casualties on the enemy and maintained the speed of the advance.

49. *Lushai Brigade*. This independent Brigade of three battalions had been given the task of raiding the Japanese flanks and rear during their withdrawal down the Tiddim road. It had been ordered by 33 Corps at the end of July to intensify its operations southwards from Milestone 60 almost to Tiddim. The operation was most arduous as the Brigade had to advance eastwards by bad tracks across steep hills and deep valleys in the height of the monsoon. During August, assisted by detachments of Chin Levies, it was actively engaged with the enemy and caused him much damage.

Some idea of the damage inflicted can be gauged from the fact that, in one week alone, one battalion killed 92 of the enemy, wounded many more, and destroyed a large number of lorries. The operations undoubtedly assisted the advance of 5 Indian Division.

To facilitate co-operation, the Lushai Brigade was placed under 5 Indian Division for operations from the 15th July. It continued to be dependent on air supply.

50. *Tamu – Sittaung Track and Kabaw Valley.* Operations to clear the enemy from the Palel – Tamu road were very successful, and our forces occupied Tamu on the 4th August. This village fell to 5 Brigade, of 2 British Division, which had been placed under command of 23 Indian Division and held in reserve in the Palel area. The village was found in an indescribable state as wounded, sick, dying and unburied dead Japanese officers and men abandoned by the enemy were lying in confusion in the houses and the streets. The large quantity of abandoned equipment included six guns and seventeen 3-ton lorries in good condition. The capture of Tamu was important as it is at the entrance of the Kabaw Valley and lies at the junction of the tracks leading east to Sittaung on the Chindwin, and south to Kalemyo.

51. On the 7th August, 11 (East African) Division, which had been concentrating in the Palel area since the end of July, took over from 23 Indian Division, which was gradually pulled out to rest in Shillong. 25 (East African) Brigade advanced along the track to Sittaung meeting little resistance to start with; 26 (East African) Brigade started down the Kabaw Valley.

The advance continued and, by the end of the month, 25 (East African) Brigade had reached Milestone 28 on the Sittaung track having destroyed the enemy. 26 (East African) Brigade also made good progress, and successfully overcame many difficulties, particularly at the crossing of the Yu River which was in full flood. By the end of August they had reached the Sunle – Htinzin area, though their concentration was hindered by swollen streams. The third brigade (the 21st) of the Division was protecting the road in the rear.

52. *Ukhrul Area.* At the end of July, command of the Ukhrul area had passed from 20 Indian Division to 4 Brigade of 2 British Division.

6 Brigade of this Division was responsible for a sector of the main Kohima – Imphal road, and 5 Brigade was operating in the Tamu sector under 23 Indian Division. 4 Brigade was operating in the Ukhrul area with patrols as far as Humine.

In the middle of August columns were directed on Homalin to destroy what was left of the enemy between the Angouching Range and the Chindwin. At the end of August these columns were actively engaged in clearing this area despite rising streams. The other two brigades of 2 British Division were withdrawn to Kohima.

53. *Myothit – Thaungdut Area.* On the 10th August "Tarcol", a special force of two battalions and a detachment of engineers, was formed from troops of 20 Indian Division to drive the enemy from the Myothit – Thaungdut area.

In the third week of August, "Tarcol" was increased by an additional battalion. Having successfully crossed the difficult Yu River, this force was, at the end of the month, advancing on Tonhe, after destroying weak enemy parties which they met.

Patrols from an Indian battalion of this column reached the Chindwin River on the 30th August, the first troops to do so since the Japanese crossed it at the opening of their offensive in March.

Summary of Operations in August.
54. *Arakan.* Activity limited to patrolling.

55. *Chin Hills and Chindwin.* During the month, the advance along the Imphal – Tiddim road had continued. By the end of the month our troops had crossed the Assam-Burma frontier and reached a point 21 miles south of the border. Numbers of tanks, guns and vehicles had been captured. The Japanese were constructing defences in the Tiddim area and appeared likely to make a stand.

Further east, British and Indian troops advancing to the south-east had capured the village of Tamu on the 4th August. 11 (East African) Division, which then took over from them, had begun operations east and south of Tamu and, by the end of the month, were within four miles of Sittaung. To the south they had reached Htinzin.

56. At the end of August, the Japanese were holding positions astride the Tamu – Sittaung track, the track Tamu – Yuwa, in the hills to the east of the Tamu – Kalemyo road, and astride the road at Yazagyo.

57. North of Tamu, "Tarcol" had captured the village of Thanan, 12 miles north-west of Thaungdut, and were advancing on Tonhe.

58. *North Burma.* Myitkyina was captured on the 3rd August after a siege lasting 78 days. The greater part of the garrison of 6,000 was annihilated, although some troops escaped down the Irrawaddy on rafts.

Chinese forces crossed the Irrawaddy east of Myitkyina and moved down the Myitkyina – Bhamo road to Kazu where, at the end of August, they were consolidating.

About 20 miles west of Kazu, detachments of Kachin Levies were in contact with the enemy along the east bank of the Irrawaddy.

36 British Division was advancing down the railway south-west of Mogaung and had captured the village of Pinbon.

50 Chinese Division had completed its concentration in the Mogaung area.
Events in September.

59. *Tasks allotted to* 15 *Indian Corps – Early September.* On the 4th September, General Slim in an Operation Instruction warned the Commander, 15 Indian Corps, that Fourteenth Army would launch large-scale offensive operations across the Chindwin into Central Burma about December and that his rôle would be:-

(*a*) To secure his present positions in Arakan, including Maungdaw.

(*b*) To keep open the sea line of communication through the entrance to the River Naf.

(*c*) To destroy any Japanese force which might launch an offensive in the Arakan.

(It was possible that the enemy might attack in Arakan as a counter to our offensive across the Chindwin.)

(*d*) To exploit any withdrawal or excessive thinning out of the Japanese forces opposing him.

These orders amplified the Operation Instruction which I had issued on the 29th July regarding our post-monsoon operations. It became necessary, however, to amend these orders at the end of September, but I shall deal with this in a later paragraph.

Operations in September.

60. *Arakan Front* – 15 *Indian Corps*. In pursuance of the Corps policy of anticipating the enemy on important tactical features, and with the object of securing bases for operations directly the monsoon was over, moves were made by 25 Indian Division during September. As events proved, it was not always possible to anticipate the enemy, and sharp fighting on a small scale was frequently necessary to evict him. By the middle of September units of 25 Indian Division were firmly established along the main spine of the Mayu Range. Small but violent enemy counter-attacks on the nights 14th/15th and 15th/16th were heavily repulsed, as was another determined attack at the end of the month. The situation then was:

> 25 Indian Division – patrolling to the east and south-east down the Kalapanzin River, after having advanced well south of the Tunnels Area.
>
> 26 Indian Division – one brigade in the Taung Bazaar and Goppe Bazaar areas respectively, with one brigade in reserve.
>
> 81 (West African) Division – continuing its concentration which had begun some three weeks previously in the Singpa area (five miles west-north-west of Mowdok).

61. *Chindwin Front* – 33 *Corps*: (*a*) 5 *Indian Division* (*Imphal – Tiddim Road*). The advance down the Tiddim road continued. On the 7th September, the enemy, in greater strength than before, were met in the area of Milestone 114. This position was captured on the 8th, after air and artillery bombardment.

62. The Manipur River, which was in full flood, was reached on the 15th September. This was expected to be a serious obstacle to our advance. The Divisional Commander had, however, anticipated an opposed crossing, and had sent a brigade back to Imphal to move round the enemy's flank via the Shuganu track and turn his defences. The operation was brilliantly successful and the enemy were forced to abandon their strongly prepared positions covering the river. A combination of clever tactics, air supply and hard "foot slogging" had deprived the Japanese of their opportunity to check our advance.

63. Tuitum was occupied on the 17th September. Heavy rainfull, with consequent deterioration of the roads, delayed the arrival of bridging equipment, but

ferrying began on the 18th. The enemy's opposition was reduced to the shelling of the main crossings.

64. By the 20th September, we were attacking strong enemy positions about Tonzang, the first town of any size after leaving the Imphal Plain. By the 22nd, a double advance from the north and south made the Japanese evacuate this place without opposition, but severe punishment was inflicted on their retreating columns. Tonzang was full of enemy dead and much equipment was captured.

65. By the end of the month, the leading brigade of 5 Indian Division was south of Milestone 147, after overcoming hostile rearguards.

66. 33 *Corps: (b)* 11 *(East African) Division (Kabaw Valley).* During the first three weeks of September, this Division (less one brigade) advanced down the Kabaw Valley, in very bad weather.

67. One brigade, capturing successive enemy positions, fought its way down the Tamu – Sittaung track, and reached Sittaung on the 4th September. Bases from which extensive patrolling was carried out were established across the flooded Chindwin River. At the end of the month, this brigade was relieved by units of 268 Indian Lorried Infantry Brigade and concentrated in readiness for future operations.

68. By the end of September, 11 (East African) Division (less one brigade) had successfully attacked and captured strongly constructed and well stocked enemy positions three miles north of Yazagyo and was engaged in clearing the area.

The progress made during the month was remarkable in view of the destruction of communications by the continuous rain which strained our administration to the utmost. It was found necessary to employ the infantry and other combatant troops on roadmaking and similar works.

69. The situation at the end of September was:-

One brigade had captured an enemy position one mile north of Yazagyo, and was engaged in clearing the area.

One brigade, some 25 miles to the northeast, was pushing forward against opposition three miles west-north-west of Mawlaik on the Chindwin side of the Mawku Range which separates the Kabaw and Chindwin Valleys.

One brigade, concentrated in the Sittaung area.

70. *Lushai Brigade.* Throughout the month, the Brigade continued its successful raids and ambushes on the Japanese line of communication, and in one week one battalion killed 111 Japanese, wounded 56, destroyed 29 vehicles and damaged 20 others; during the same period, a detachment of Levies destroyed 50,000 gallons of petrol.

71. On the 17th September, Japanese positions west of Haka were attacked, but there was strong opposition and the arrival of enemy reinforcements forced us to

withdraw; not, however, before an enemy supply column had been successfully ambushed and a bridge over the Manipur River, near Falam, destroyed.

72. 268 *Indian Lorried Infantry Brigade.* This Independent Brigade, consisting of four – later five – battalions, was reorganized early in September to provide a screen west of the Chindwin to protect divisions which were resting in the Imphal area. Its rôle also included the protection of the rear and flank of our formations operating south and south-east of Imphal.

It operated under command of 33 Corps in the general area Tamanthi – Sittaung – Ukhrul, but confined its operations across the Chindwin to patrolling. A battalion of this force relieved 25 (East African) Brigade in the Sittaung area at the end of September.

73. *Tarcol.* This small composite force, to which I have already referred, was withdrawn during the month. The Homalin – Thaungdut area had been cleared of the enemy and a battalion left in Thaungdut. A conservative estimate of the Japanese/J.I.F. (Japanese inspired Indian Fifth Column) dead found in the area in which "Tarcol" had been operating was over 1,000 – mainly from starvation. Many abandoned lorries also were discovered near Humine.

Summary of Operations in September.
74. *Arakan.* Certain moves were carried out directly the monsoon slackened to secure areas of tactical importance, and small but determined enemy counter-attacks were repulsed.

Part of 55 Japanese Division, formerly opposed to our forces in the Maungdaw area, was withdrawn during the month.

75. *Chin Hills and Chindwin.* the advance of our troops down the Imphal – Tiddim road and, further east, down the Kabaw Valley continued. 5 Indian Division after crossing the Manipur River was entirely, and 11 (East African) Division in the Kabaw Valley was partly, dependent on air supply.

On the Tiddim road, the village of Tuitum was occupied on the 17th September, and by the end of the month our leading troops were only seven miles from Tiddim. Thus a distance of 62 miles had been covered in one month against determined opposition and under severe weather conditions. The Japanese suffered heavy casualties during their retreat, and the withdrawal of the Headquarters of 33 Japanese Division across the Chindwin indicated that they were not likely to put up a very serious resistance, though it was expected that they might make some stand in the Tiddim area. If they did so, their forces would be threatened by the advance of our troops down the Kabaw Valley.

76. The East Africans had advanced a further 15 miles down the Kabaw Valley towards Kalemyo, and had reached a point 26 miles south of Htinzin. Bad weather was a greater obstacle to their advance than the enemy.

Other East African troops had occupied Sittaung on the Chindwin on the 4th September and established a bridgehead on the eastern bank of the river. They were relieved in this area by an Indian formation at the end of the month.

77. *North Burma.* 36 British Division, moving down the Myitkyina – Mandalay railway, had entered Hopin unopposed on the 7th September. They found 500 Japanese bodies in the precincts of the village. By the end of September, patrols had reached Mohnyin.

Chinese troops in the Kazu area had advanced eleven miles south of the village.

78. *Order of Battle (Moves).* The last of the Long-Range Penetration Brigades of Special Force was withdrawn from Burma into India during the month.

17 Indian Light Division left 33 Corps for India.

2 British Division and 20 Indian Division were resting at Imphal; 7 Indian Division was at Kohima and 23 Indian Division at Shillong.

79. *Record of 33 Corps.* In the six months ending September, 33 Corps, which first took the field at Dimapur in April, had done sterling work. During an advance of nearly 300 miles to the Tiddim area and about 270 to Yazago in the Kabaw Valley, 9,746 of the enemy were killed and 459 Japanese and 331 J.I.F. prisoners taken. 81 guns and 1,284 vehicles had been captured.

80. *Revised Task for 15 Indian Corps.* On the 28th September, the Commander, Fourteenth Army, in view of the re-grouping of the Japanese forces in Arakan, issued a fresh Operation Instruction to 15 Indian Corps. The bulk of 55 Japanese Division had been transferred from North Arakan into the lower Irrawaddy Valley, leaving a force of approximately four battalions in the forward area. Three more enemy battalions belonging to 54 Japanese Division were on Akyab Island and in the lower Kaladan Delta, and five battalions were in the coastal area between the Barongas and Cheduba Island. Thus the enemy was in no position to launch a serious attack. The tasks allotted to 15 Indian Corps on the 4th September were, therefore, changed and the Commander was ordered-

(*a*) To secure the area Chittagong – Cox's Bazaar to prevent the enemy's interference with our preparations for a future airborne offensive.

(*b*) To secure the estuary of the Naf as a base for light coastal forces and landing craft.

(*c*) To carry out reconnaissance, bombardments and raids from the sea along the whole Arakan coast to force the enemy to lock up troops in this area.

(d) To exploit any withdrawal or thinning out of the Japanese forces in Arakan.

Operation Instructions issued during October.
81. On the 1st October, the Army Commander issued an Instruction to 33 Corps which stated that:-

(*a*) His intention was to concentrate Fourteenth Army eastwards in the Shwebo – Mandalay Plain, to bring the enemy to battle and destroy him.

(*b*) The tasks of 33 Corps were:-

(i) To capture the area Kalemyo – Kalewa.

(ii) To establish a bridgehead over the Chindwin at Kalewa.

(iii) To advance eastwards as quickly as possible and capture the Ye-U area with the object of establishing air strips.

(c) 4 Corps was concentrating in the Imphal area and would be flown into the Ye-U – Shwebo area at a later date.

The troops allotted to 33 Corps were 2 British Division, 5 and 20 Indian Divisions, 11 (East African) Division, and the Lushai Brigade, but 5 Indian Division would be withdrawn into Army reserve when Kalemyo had been captured.

221 Group R.A.F. would be responsible for air support, and air supply would increase progressively from 244 tons per day on the 1st October to 364 tons from the 1st November onwards.

82. On the 6th October, I told the Commander, Fourteenth Army, that 3 Commando Brigade (four Commandos) would be placed under his command from mid-October, and that they were to be employed to encourage the enemy to believe that amphibious operations were imminent on the Arakan coast.

83. I issued an important Instruction to the Commander, Fourteenth Army, on the 11th October, regarding Allied operations in Burma, 1944–45. In this, I repeated a Directive received from the Supreme Allied Commander, which stated that:-

"Allied Forces in South-East Asia Command will conduct concerted offensive operations with the object of destroying or expelling all Japanese forces in Burma at the earliest date. Operations to achieve this object must *not*, however, prejudice the security of the existing air supply route to China, including the air staging port at Myitkyina, and the opening of overland communications."

I confirmed in more detail the objectives for which I had ordered plans to be prepared in my Instruction of the 29th July.

The Fourteenth Army Order of Battle was:-

33 Corps – 2 British Division, 5 Indian Division initially, 11 (East African) Division, 20 Indian Division, 254 Indian Tank Brigade, Lushai Brigade, 268 Indian Lorried Infantry Brigade (subsequently transferred to 4 Corps). 4 Corps – 7 and 19 Indian Divisions, 50 Indian Parachute Brigade for a specific airborne operation. 255 Indian Tank Brigade, which was to move to Imphal in October. 28 (East African) Brigade, due to move to Imphal in November.

I have given the composition of each Corps, but the allotment of divisions to Corps was, of course, left to the Commander, Fourteenth Army.

I include, for information, the composition of Northern Combat Area Command.

36 British Division.

5332 Brigade (two U.S. regiments, one Chinese regiment).

Chinese Army in India.

Chinese Expeditionary Force (when released by the Generalissimo).

Fort Hertz Kachin Levies (re-enlisted for service under Northern Combat Area Command).
Chinese-American airborne units.

84. I issued the following administrative orders:-

(*a*) The Tamu – Indainggyi – Kalewa – Ye-U road to be improved to a capacity of 300 tons daily and to an all-weather standard.
(*b*) The construction of the Manipur Road – Imphal pipeline to be continued as rapidly as resources permitted.
(*c*) Inland Water Transport on the Chindwin to be used to the maximum extent possible.
(*d*) Before the outbreak of the monsoon in 1945, reserve stocks to be built up forward of Kalewa for 45 days, plus 15 days' working stocks.

Operations in October.
85. *Arakan – 15 Indian Corps.* On the front of 25 Indian Division, there was no renewal of the fighting which occurred at the end of September, and activity in the coastal sector and east of the Mayu Range was reduced to vigorous patrolling and artillery fire.

On 26 Indian Division's front, however, the Japanese attempted a reconnaissance in force of our left flank. A raiding force drawn from all three regiments of 55 Japanese Division penetrated into the Goppe Bazaar area and between the 6th and the 8th October we repelled attacks at Panzai and in the vicinity of Goppe. Our counter-attack was quick and strong and by the end of the week the enemy had been dispersed into the hills, losing two-thirds of his strength killed and much equipment.

Our patrols were active in the area during the rest of the month.

86. 3 *Commando Brigade* arrived at the end of October and assumed responsibility for the Teknaf Peninsula south of 26 Indian Division's boundary.

87. 81 (*West African*) *Division.* Early in the month, the Japanese based on Daletme and Paletwa showed considerable activity, but 81 (West African) Division continued its advance eastward to the Kaladan. They occupied Mowdok and drove the enemy out of Labawa, six miles to the north-east. After this, resistanc became sporadic and by the 25th October units of both brigades had reached and crossed the Kaladan and were in contact with the enemy on the east bank. At the end of the month one brigade had begun to advance down the Kaladan River, while the other was moving south down the Pi Chaung.

88. *Situation in Arakan at the End of the Monsoon.* Although the monsoon prevented major operations by either side, we had before it ended seized the initiative and occupied several important positions beyond our frontline in the Mayu Peninsula. At the same time, 81 (West African) Division had moved across to the Kaladan Valley and captured Mowdok, thereby controlling the routes from the Kaladan into the Sangu Valley, and removing a threat to our airfields and base.

89. *Chindwin Front – 33 Corps: (a) 5 Indian Division (Tiddim – Kalemyo Road)*. Enemy resistance in scattered pockets both east and west of the road continued, and by the 4th October the battle for Tiddim was developing. Tiddim lies some 5,600 feet above sea-level, 162 miles from Imphal. At about Milestone 149, the road leaves the Manipur River and climbs 3,700 feet in the next ten miles, the first six of which consist of a series of steep hairpin bends. The Japanese were holding strongly dug-in positions about Milestone 158, with a forward position at Milestone 152. They were also entrenched at Valvum (6,000 feet) and Sialam Vum (8,000 feet), which are strong natural features about three miles and seven miles east of Tiddim respectively.

90. By the 10th October enemy resistance at Milestone 152 had been broken and operations, which, in spite of bad weather, were receiving strong air support, were in progress against stubborn and fierce opposition in the Milestone 158, Valvum and Sialam Vum areas. A wide turning movement, by an infantry brigade, found the enemy also strongly entrenched at Tuibal, thirteen miles east of Tiddim.

91. We pressed our attack with great vigour throughout the following week. The final assault on the positions at Milestone 158 covering Tiddim was supported by a co-ordinated attack by tanks and Hurribombers. A thick mist hid the advancing tanks, while the noise of their engines was drowned by the roar of low-flying aircraft. Complete surprise was achieved and the position was captured. Tiddim was occupied on the 18th October, by which date the Valvum, Sialam Vum and Tuibal positions had also been captured.

92. After the occupation of Tiddim, one brigade continued the advance along the Tiddim – Kalemyo road, strong resistance at Milestone 7 being turned by a detachment from Valvum. The Japanese, however, again made a determined stand at Milestone 11 and to the north of it.

93. Meanwhile another brigade, west of Tuibal, was attacking positions on the Dolluang – Kennedy Peak track, in conjunction with detachments of the Lushai Brigade which had come up behind the enemy from the southwest. Successful air strikes were a feature of these operations.

94. By the end of the month, good progress had been made against the main enemy positions in the Vital Corner – Fort White area, "Vital Corner" being the name given to the bend, about Milestone 13, where the road, after running due east and west, turns sharp south. One brigade had successively captured enemy positions from Sialam Vum, through Milestone 11, to Khum Vum, a 7,000 foot mountain about four miles south of the road, and had established a block at Milestone 14. A second brigade was making a shallow right hook to the south of the road, while the remaining brigade of the Division was engaged in a deeper turning movement farther south to cut off the enemy in the Fort White area.

Vital Corner was thus virtually surrounded and the reduction of its defences with maximum air and artillery support was in progress.

95. 33 *Corps:* (*b*) 11 (*East African*) *Division* (*Kabaw Valley and Chindwin*). During the first fortnight of October, the brigade which had been operating in the Sittaung area on the east of the Chindwin was moving into and down the Kabaw Valley. The brigade already in the valley entered Yazagyo on the 4th October and then cleared the tracks, which lead from the Tamu – Kalemyo road across to the Chindwin, of small enemy detachments. To the north-east, the third brigade of 11 (East African) Division had unsuccessfully attacked strong enemy positions north-west of Mawku, on the Chindwin River six miles north of Mawlaik.

96. In the third week of October, two brigades were moving forward against opposition, one brigade south of Yazagyo and one to the north-east of it. The third brigade had launched an attack against the enemy positions on the ridge north-west of Mawku and, after confused fighting, had captured all but one position, which was subsequently surrounded and the enemy in it destroyed. The stores and ammunition captured indicated that the Japanese had intended a prolonged stand in this area.

97. At the end of October, two brigades were continuing their advance south to Inbaung, after destroying enemy positions on the hills to the east of the road. The third brigade was fighting in and around Mawku Village.

98. *Lushai Brigade.* Early in October, the brigade regrouped in order to stop the southern exits from the Tiddim and Kennedy Peak areas, and at the same time continued its operations against the enemy's Falam and Haka lines of communication. These operations ended in the occupation of Falam on the 18th October, Haka falling four days later. These two places had been captured by the Japanese just a year before.

Summary of Operations in October.
99. *Arakan* – 15 *Indian Corps.* During the early part of the month, there was considerable fighting in the Taung Bazaar and Goppe Bazaar areas with a strong hostile detachment of all arms. It was severely defeated by 26 Indian Division. The Japanese object had probably been either to cross the Goppe Pass to Bawli and thus prevent our tanks from entering the Mayu Valley, or else to establish a firm base at Goppe from which raiding parties could operate.

100. The enemy in Paletwa and Daletme had also displayed increased activity in the Mowdok area, probably in an attempt to mislead us as to their strength in the Kaladan. They had not, however, succeeded in delaying the advance of 81 (West African) Division which, by the end of the month, had occupied Daletme and was pushing southwards down the Kaladan Valley towards Paletwa.

101. Activity in the coastal sector was confined during October to extensive patrolling by both sides.

102. *Chindwin Front – 33 Corps.* The advance of 5 Indian Division down the Tiddim road ended with their entry into Tiddim on the 18th October, after strong enemy positions had been captured north and east of the village. The advance then continued in a south-easterly direction towards Fort White and Kalemyo. By the end of the month, strong defences in the Kennedy Peak area were attacked and a turning movement to cut off Fort White was in progress.

103. Falam and Haka had been occupied during the month by elements of the Lushai Brigade, the small Japanese garrisons withdrawing southwards under pressure.

104. In the Kabaw Valley, troops of 11 (East African) Division entered Yazagyo on the 4th October. The advance southwards was held up during the middle of the month by heavy rains, but subsequently continued. By the end of October, the Division, less one brigade, was fighting in the area thirteen miles north of Kalemyo. The brigade operating down the Chindwin Valley, after capturing strong enemy positions north-west of Mawku, was engaged in the vicinity of the village itself. The situation at the end of October was that the Japanese had withdrawn from the Chindwin River, north of Paungbyin, and were occupying positions in the Atwin Yomas, north-west of Mawlaik. It appeared possible that, when driven from these, they might try to hold the escarpment which divides the Chindwin from the Mu River.

105. *North Burma.* Rapid progress was made during the month in our southward advance down the railway. On the 21st October, 36 British Division occupied Mohnyin, the Japanese apparently being taken by surprise as large quantities of stores, ammunition and supplies fell into our hands. After overcoming slight opposition at Mawhun, Mawlu was captured on the 31st October. The enemy abandoned large trenched areas in Mawhun without fighting, but put up a stiffer resistance at Mawlu, which incidentally had been the stronghold of one of our Long-Range Penetration Brigades during the Spring.

38 Chinese Division, advancing down the road towards Bhamo from the Kazu area, was only twenty-four miles north-north-east of Bhamo by the 31st October.

Operation Instructions issued prior to the 12th November.
106. On the 6th November, the Commander, Fourteenth Army, instructed 4 Corps to employ one brigade group with the object of :-

(*a*) Capturing Pinlebu by an overland advance.

(*b*) Patrolling in the direction of Indaw – Katha and establishing contact with Northern Combat Area Command.

(*c*) Patrolling to the rail/road in the area Wuntho – Indaw.

(*d*) Gaining information as to the practicability of routes from the Chindwin River to the line of the rail/road for the passage of large forces, including medium tanks.

Leading units of this brigade group were to cross the Chindwin not later than the 20th November and the roads Tamu – Tonhe and Tamu – Sittaung were to be improved to the standard of "Fair-weather class 5, one-way" by the 15th December and the 15th January respectively.

107. Before relinquishing command, I issued three Operation Instructions:

The first, dated the 6th November, directed that 15 Indian Corps, formerly under Fourteenth Army, would come under command of 11 Army Group from midnight 15th–16th November. 15 Indian Corps' Order of Battle would be:-

25 Indian Division.
26 Indian Division.
81 (West African) Division. (Provision of a third brigade under consideration.)
82 (West African) Division. (On arrival in Arakan.)
50 Indian Tank Brigade.
3 Commando Brigade.
Corps Troops.

The reason for this change was to free the Commander, Fourteenth Army, from responsibility for Arakan, in view of the important operations he was about to undertake in Burma.

108. On the 9th November, I issued orders for the formation of a command and staff for the lines of communication, to centralise the lines of communication under a separate Commander and thus relieve the Commander, Fourteenth Army, and Commander, 15 Indian Corps, of responsibilities for their rear areas. The new Line of Communication Command was to comprise the existing 202 and 404 Lines of Communication Areas and the Fort Hertz Area. The rear boundaries of Fourteenth Army and 15 Indian Corps were to be adjusted as the progress of operations dictated, in order to relieve the forward Commander of administrative responsibilities.

109. My third Operation Instruction dated the 9th November, was addressed to the Commander of 15 Indian Corps.

The general objects I gave to him were:-

(*a*) To clear Arakan to the line (inclusive) Akyab – Minbya as early as possible, in order to release troops for other purposes.
(*b*) To secure the area Chittagong – Cox's Bazaar.

The specific tasks were:-

(*a*) A land advance in Arakan down the Mayu Peninsula, the Kalapanzin Valley and the Kaladan Valley, to destroy or expel the Japanese within the area north of the general line Foul Point – Kudaung Island – Minbya. This advance was to start as soon as possible.
(*b*) An amphibious assault on Akyab Island about the 15th January, supported by the maximum sea and air bombardment.
(*c*) Consolidation to secure firmly the area north of the general line Akyab – Minbya.

110. My object in issuing the above Instruction was twofold:-

(*a*) To tie down and destroy in Arakan Japanese forces which might otherwise be used against Fourteenth Army.

(*b*) By destroying the Japanese forces in Arakan it would be possible to release forces for other operations which the Supreme Allied Commander was anxious to undertake.

Operations from the 1st to the 12th November.

111. *Arakan* – 15 *Indian Corps.* 25 and 26 Indian Divisions continued their active patrolling and other minor operations with steady success. The leading brigade of 82 (West African) Division arrived to relieve troops in the Kalapanzin area.

81 (West African) Division continued its advance down the Kaladan in spite of considerable enemy resistance and reached the outskirts of Paletwa.

112. *Chindwin Front* – 33 *Corps:* (*a*) 5 *Indian Division (Tiddim – Kalemyo Road).* It will be recalled that, at the end of October, 5 Indian Division having cut in behind the Japanese and launched a converging attack, was assaulting their positions at Vital Corner, while one brigade was carrying out a wide turning movement against Fort White. The beginning of November saw the capture of Vital Corner and the final breakdown of all enemy resistance northwards from Milestone 14 to Sialam Vum inclusive, the enemy suffering heavy casualties. We resumed our advance down the road and finally stormed Kennedy Peak, the 9,000 foot mountain just south of Milestone 15, on the 4th November after two attacks had failed. A sharp action was then fought for the positions dominating the road between Milestones 22 and 23. Point 8225 was successfully assaulted on the 7th November and Fort White occupied without further opposition. In spite of the mountainous country, tanks were able to play an important part in the fighting.

113. The brigade moving to outflank Fort White had, in the meantime, cleared the enemy from a 7,000 foot feature three miles down the Fort White – Falam track (Point 7480). Then, after an initial failure, they gained the main road and established a road-block near Milestone 25, where later they gained touch with the brigade advancing along the road itself. Stiff resistance was met at Vownalu Mual (Milestone 29), and again at Milestone 31 where we were held up for two days. However, on the 11th November the advance was resumed, Numbers 2 and 3 Stockades falling without opposition. Forward elements pressed on to Milestone 40, but the main body was delayed by stiff resistance east of Number 2 Stockade.

The third brigade of the Division was engaged during this period in blocking tracks, and a heavy toll was taken of the Japanese trying to escape by these routes.

114. 33 *Corps:* (*b*) 11 (*East African*) *Division (Kabaw Valley and Chindwin).* Early in the month, the leading brigade, with tank support, cleared the enemy from all his positions south of Yazagyo and then inflicted further heavy casualties as he was

successively driven out of positions further to south. The enemy next stood three miles north of Indainggyi (six miles north-east of Kalemyo) where his positions were only captured after all the defenders had been killed.

The brigade in support was following up closely, having sent detachments (*a*) to clear the track leading from the Kabaw Valley to Mawlaik and (*b*) to block the tracks from the west and thus destroy enemy parties escaping from 5 Indian Division in the Dolluang area. Meanwhile the brigade pushing down the Chindwin had overcome strong resistance in the vicinity of Mawku and, on the 11th November, occupied Mawlaik. It then advanced astride the river.

11 (East African) Division reached Kalemyo on the 15th November, and thus ended this phase of the operations.

115. *4 Corps.* The leading division (19 Indian) of 4 Corps entered the forward zone early in November, and concentrated in the area of the Tamu – Sittaung track. 268 Indian Lorried Infantry Brigade was transferred from 33 to 4 Corps. The order not to operate east of the Chindwin was cancelled and part of the Brigade was disposed on the east bank of the river.

Summary of Operations, 1st to the 12th November.
116. *Arakan – 15 Indian Corps.* There was no fighting on an important scale. 81 (West African) Division reached the outskirts of Paletwa in its advance down the Kaladan. The leading brigade of 82 (West African) Division had arrived in Arakan.

117. *Chin Hills and Chindwin – 33 Corps.* On the 4th November, a brigade of 5 Indian Division had captured Kennedy Peak, much equipment falling into our hands. Troops of this Division had then encircled Fort White, and forced the enemy to evacuate his positions on the 8th November. No. 2 and 3 Stockades were taken without opposition on 11th November.

118. Troops of 11 (East African) Division, which had been advancing down the Kabaw Valley, linked up with those of 5 Indian Division on the 13th November and Kalemyo fell on the 15th.

119. *North Burma.* After consolidating their positions at Mawlu, 36 British Division had almost reached Pinwe, six miles north of the important junction of Naba, by the 12th November. Meanwhile, 38 Chinese Division had occupied Myothit, sixteen miles north-east of Bhamo, meeting only slight opposition.

120. On the 3rd November, Lungling fell to troops of the Chinese Expeditionary Force, having changed hands at least four times during prolonged fighting over many months. It is important to note that, when the Bhamo area was finally cleared, we should have a potential fair-weather route from Burma to China, through Myothit, Tengchung and Lungling, although an all-weather road would not be open to us until Namhkam was taken. Thus we were already within measurable distance of achieving one of our objects – the re-opening of land communications with China.

Naval and Air Co-operation.

121. (*a*) Light coastal forces, comprising for the most part heavy draught motor launches, resumed operations off the Arakan coast in October, in support of 15 Indian Corps. The main operational base was Chittagong, but an advanced base was also established in the Naf River, 115 miles south of Chittagong. There were several successful guerilla operations, and several enemy aircraft which attempted to intervene were destroyed.

These small craft harassed the Japanese lines of communication and made successful attacks on the enemy's supply ships.

Flotillas of landing craft, whose crews had been trained by the Royal Indian Navy, were employed off the Arakan coast early in November in landing small raiding parties.

(*b*) As air operations have been described in detail in the Despatches of the Air Commander-in-Chief, I have said little of what was done by the Air Forces during the period covered by this Despatch. This Despatch would, however, be incomplete without some special remarks on the co-operation between the Army and the R.A.F.

The outstanding feature of the operations has been the closeness of the co-operation between the Army and the R.A.F., and the battle may well be described as a true combined operation in which neither Service could have succeeded without the other.

These combined operations may be considered under the following headings:-

(*a*) Strategical.

(*b*) Tactical.

(*c*) Administrative.

Strategically the sustained and very successful attacks on the enemy's air forces, aerodromes and communications combined to destroy his air forces and to restrict the power of his ground forces. These successes gave our own forces freedom of manoeuvre and hampered those of the Japanese so severely that he was short of ammunition, stores and equipment during the battle. The long flights in bad weather over difficult country were splendid achievements by all ranks of the R.A.F.

Tactically, co-operation grew ever closer as the battle continued and the R.A.F. assumed the rôle of mobile heavy artillery which could not be got forward over the roads of Burma. There is no doubt that the low-level attacks with bombs and machine guns on the hostile defences were decisive in enabling the infantry to close with the Japanese. As time went on communication between the forces on the ground and the supporting aircraft improved until it was possible for commanders on the ground to direct them on to small targets entirely concealed by the jungle from the air.

Finally, the Army did not feel happy in attacking Japanese defensive positions unless they had the co-operation of the fighter bomber.

Close as was the co-operation in the actual fighting, success could not have been achieved without the transport of troops, the continued supply from the air and the evacuation of casualties.

Apart from the fly-in of Special Force there were many noteworthy movements of troops, especially those of 5 and 7 Indian Divisions and 2 British Division, large parts of which were flown to Imphal and Dimapur.

These large-scale movements by air defeated the Japanese plan which counted on containing our troops in Arakan when they began their offensive across the Chindwin.

I have written in my earlier Despatch of the magnificent work done in supplying 4 Corps by air. The pursuit of the Japanese by 11 (East African) Division down the Kabaw Valley was likewise made possible by air supply. There were numerous other smaller supply operations.

The greatly increased evacuation of casualties by air gave a great fillip to the morale of the troops. The figures of 56,800 sick and wounded casualties flown back during the year November 1943-November 1944 speak for themselves.

The Army, as can be seen, has great cause to be grateful to the R.A.F., and once again I want on behalf of 11 Army Group to thank all ranks of the R.A.F. from the Commander-in-Chief, Air Chief Marshal Sir Richard Peirse, to the latest joined airman for their magnificent support and co-operation.

Lessons of the Campaign.
122. (*a*) The operations which I have described in this Despatch have emphasised the lessons which I mentioned in my first Despatch, particularly the need for first-class basic training of the junior leaders and the rank and file, physical fitness and good discipline.

(*b*) They have also shown that it is possible for troops to operate in the monsoon if air supply is possible.

I should like, however, to add a word of warning about the possibility of campaigning at full scale in the monsoon. In the operations for which I was responsible, we were compelled by the Japanese offensive to fight in the monsoon.[8] We did so successfully, and drove the Japanese back from the positions they reached in and about Imphal. The cost was high, all divisions, especially 2 British Division, were much reduced in strength by sickness and both officers and men were much exhausted.

The pursuit which continued until the end of November was, with the exception of 5 Indian Division, made by fresh troops, who then had to be withdrawn to rest.

The time limit for troops operating in the monsoon in the Burmese jungle appears to be about three months, after which they need rest in a rear area. The conditions under which troops operate in the dry weather are so infinitely better and the communications both air and ground so much more reliable that it is in my opinion uneconomical to use more troops than are absolutely necessary under monsoon conditions. It may be vital to fight in the monsoon, but a high wastage rate must then be expected and operations in the dry weather will be reduced or delayed by the need for resting and reinforcing those formations which operated during the monsoon, unless there are available very large reserves to take their places.

(*c*) The increasing accuracy of air bombardment of tactical targets in jungle. This was of the greatest help as divisions which were wholly supplied by air had frequently a very limited supply of artillery ammunition.

(*d*) The increased ability of brigades and larger formations to leave the road and move by tracks through the jungle to attack the enemy's flanks and rear.

Intelligence.

123. *Enemy Strengths and Dispositions.* As mentioned in my first Despatch, the Japanese strength in Burma had increased from four divisions to nine in the twelve months ending June, 1944. One additional division (the 49th) arrived in this Theatre in October.

124. *Enemy Casualties and Morale.* The total number of enemy killed (actually counted) between July and October amounted to 8,859 on the Fourteenth Army front and 3,724 on the Northern Combat Area Command front. No captured documentary evidence is available regarding the number of wounded and sick, but it was undoubtedly high.

These severe losses added to those of the earlier months, coupled with the steady and increasing pressure which we maintained on his retreating divisions, must have weakened his morale. Though the individual officer and man will doubtless continue, in accordance with Japanese tradition, to resist fanatically when occupying defensive positions, I have no doubt that the standard of training and will to battle will deteriorate and that we shall not again meet Japanese forces of their former standard.

PART II. RE-ORGANIZATIONS AND COMMAND ARRANGEMENTS.

Availability of Infantry Formations.

125. (*a*) I mentioned in my first Despatch[9] the acute shortage of infantry, especially British, reinforcements, and I of course discussed the situation with the Supreme Allied Commander on many occasions. On the 24th June, I wrote to him that I had been examining his instructions of the 8th June, to exact the maximum effort during the monsoon season. I pointed out that there were two major difficulties to overcome:-

(i) The need to withdraw certain divisions, which had been engaged for long periods in active operations, for rest, re-organization and training.
(ii) The general shortage of reinforcements.

(*b*) My examination showed that we had two alternatives, each bound to affect operations.

Either we had to-

(i) Accept the necessity for resting formations, and thereby reduce the number available for operations, or

(ii) Decide against any rest, and thereby so reduce the efficiency of formations that, by the end of the Winter, they would be unfit for further fighting.

(*c*) The general reinforcement situation was such that-

(i) It appeared that we could not maintain 2 British Division at war strength.

(ii) Special Force must be substantially reduced.

(iii) We should have the greatest difficulty in finding a formation to replace 36 British Division, about to relieve Special Force, when its replacement became necessary.

(*d*) I, therefore, recommended that-

(i) We must accept the fact that some divisions would have to be rested during the coming Winter.

(ii) The programme of rest should be planned on the basis of using nine divisions; three in the Arakan, with one in reserve, and four in Assam, with one in reserve.

I added that I should leave no stone unturned to discover ways and means for improving the supply of reinforcements.

126. This letter was followed by a discussion with the Supreme Allied Commander and the Commander-in-Chief, India. In consequence, I decided that in future we should try to keep two divisions resting in addition to one division in G.H.Q. (India) reserve. Initially, one of the nine active divisions would be in Army Group reserve.

I also decided that only one division (17 Indian) would leave the Fourteenth Army area for rest and re-organization and that the others would remain in the Shillong – Imphal area. The following formations would move back into India Command: H.Q. 4 Corps, 50 Parachute Brigade, 23 L.R.P. Brigade, 268 Indian Lorried Infantry Brigade, and three Armoured Corps units.

127. By this time our air supremacy, and our improved strategical situation, justified the disbandment of a considerable number of light A.A. batteries. The officers and men thrown up in consequence were available to train as infantry and, added to increased reinforcements from England, enabled me to bring 2 British Division up to strength.

The relief of 36 British Division did not arise during the period covered by this Despatch.

128. As a result of the experience gained from the operations of Special Force, I had decided that the future rôle of such a force be either-

(*a*) To provide mobile infantry brigades specially equipped to make turning movements away from roads and tracks or protect flanks in exceptionally difficult country.

(*b*) Deeper penetration as a Special Force capable of continuous mobile operations for long periods.

I also considered that a change of name, to conform with these rôles, was desirable and the term "Penetration Brigade" was substituted for "Long-Range Penetration Group".

129. Taking into consideration our available manpower and the desirability of providing at least one Penetration Brigade by the end of the year, I asked the Commander-in-Chief, India, early in August-

(*a*) To re-form initially four brigades, of which one would be entirely British.
(*b*) To re-form two more British brigades later, if reinforcements became available.

I estimated that one brigade would thus be ready for operations by mid-December and the other three a month later. The period of re-organization and training of Special Force had to allow for the re-formation of its ancillary services, as these brigades had to be self-contained.

130. A month later, after consultations with the War Office and the Commander-in-Chief, India, it became clear that we should have to reduce Special Force to four brigades, and this I recommended, to the Supreme Allied Commander.

During October the decision to form an Air Landing Brigade and to provide a third brigade for 36 British Division further reduced the possibility of forming Penetration Brigades, because reinforcements for the two former formations could only come from Special Force. I agreed, therefore, that this Force should consist only of three Brigades.

Formation of an Indian Airborne Division.
131. In August, the Supreme Allied Commander asked the Commander-in-Chief, India, to examine the problem of forming an airborne division, the raising of which was supported by the War Office. The main points in the Commander-in-Chief's reply were-

(*a*) The division could be formed and trained by the 15th February, 1945, subject to the conditions given in (*b*) to (*e*) below.
(*b*) A British parachute brigade from outside India must arrive fully trained by the 15th November.
(*c*) 26 Indian Infantry Brigade to be made available as an air landing brigade at the expense of making up 36 British Division to three brigades. (A brigade from Special Force was later substituted for 26 Brigade as an air landing brigade and the latter remained allotted to 36 British Division).
(*d*) 875 glider pilots to be available by the 1st December.
(*e*) Transport aircraft equivalent to twenty squadrons to be made available by the 15th January.

During the prolonged discussions regarding the formation of an Indian airborne division I had provided India Command with my proposals for the re-organization of 50 Indian Parachute Brigade which I assumed would provide the nucleus of such a division.

44 Indian Airborne Division was finally formed by India Command on the 1st November.

Conversions of Divisions to a Standard Divisional Basis.

132. As I wrote in my first Despatch, our earlier operations had shown that divisions organized and equipped for special rôles were uneconomical and wasteful. Later we had had experience of the unsuitability of a division, such as the 2nd British or 25th Indian, equipped solely with mechanical transport, for warfare in mountainous jungle country and of the tactical disadvantages inherent in a Light Division of two brigades such as the 17th Indian.

To overcome this, the organization of a Standard Division – details of which are contained in my first Despatch – was produced, and the Commander-in-Chief, India, had accepted my recommendations.

Army and Corps Commanders were given a free hand to select the most suitable time for the re-organization of their divisions.

When I relinquished command all divisions, except Special Force of which I have already written, had either re-organized or were reorganizing.

17 *Indian Light Division.*

133. 17 Indian Light Division was the only large formation to be rested and re-organized outside the area of Fourteenth Army. I had decided that this Division should be rested in India because it had been in the forward zone for 3½ years and had to be completely reorganized.

Among other changes it had to absorb a third brigade and to change the composition of its brigades from three Gurkha battalions to brigades of one British, one Indian and one Gurkha battalion. The Division was to be ready for service again by February,

Arrangements for Internal Security in re-occupied Burma.

134. As we advanced into Burma, we had to find troops for internal security in re-occupied territory, until such time as the police force could be re-created.

I had of course no intention of detaching battalions from infantry divisions on such duty. The most suitable type of unit was one composed of officers and men who had had experience in the Burma Frontier Force or Burma Military Police. I, therefore, arranged with the Commander-in-Chief, India, for 2 and 4 Burma Regiments to be trained for this duty and earmarked for Fourteenth Army. I said that I should probably need more battalions.

I also asked the Commander-in-Chief, India, to obtain the agreement of the Government of Burma to disband the Northern Kachin Levies and to re-form them into two Kachin battalions for use later for internal security.

Re-organization of the Chain of Command.

135. I had come to the conclusion in August that future operations would make continued control of the Arakan operations by Headquarters, Fourteenth Army,

impossible. I therefore ordered that a re-organization of command should be examined on the following basis:-

(*a*) That the command of 15 Indian Corps should pass from Headquarters, Fourteenth Army, to H.Q., 11 Army Group.

(*b*) That H.Q., Fourteenth Army, should be reconstituted as a mobile Field Army H.Q., for the command of two Corps, and be relieved of the responsibility for the lines of communication.

I was also examining the formation of a new headquarters to be known as H.Q., L. of C. Command, to be located at Comilla. I intended that the Commander of the Lines of Communication should command both the existing Areas (202 and 404) of the L. of C. and thus free the Commander, Fourteenth Army, and Commander, 15 Indian Corps, from the work which the control of the lines of communication involved.

136. As a result of this examination, I gave the following orders:-

(*a*) H.Q., Fourteenth Army, to be reorganized.

(*b*) H.Q., L. of C. Command, to be set up, the commander of which would assume control directly under H.Q., 11 Army Group, of the existing 202 and 404 L. of C. Areas.

(*c*) Establishments of H.Q., Sub-Areas, to be standardised to simplify the future adjustment of boundaries of sub-areas.

(*d*) Two Advanced Echelons, 11 Army Group, one of which already existed, to be formed to assist H.Q., 11 Army Group to control general administration on the L. of C.

The date selected for the transfer of 15 Indian Corps to command of 11 Army Group and the formation of H.Q., L. of C. Command, was the 15th November. H.Q., Fourteenth Army, moved to Imphal at the same time.

137. In re-organizing Command and Administration I was looking ahead. I foresaw that when the re-occupation of Burma was complete, the commander of these Ls. of C. would probably extend his command to include the whole of Burma and that 202 and 404 Areas would then be transferred to the command of the Commander-in-Chief, India. The flexibility of the organization should admit of future adjustments and extensions.

138. This examination of the organization of the L. of C. confirmed my opinion that some re-organization of the establishments of reception camps, reinforcement camps, feeding and welfare arrangements generally on the L. of C. was overdue.

It was not, however, possible to start this re-organization for lack of men, as all British personnel likely to be available were to be absorbed in the formation of H.Q., L. of C. Command, and the re-organization of Headquarters, L. of C. Areas and Sub Areas. I had, therefore, to defer these measures until the manpower situation had improved.

Changes affecting East African Forces.

139. (*a*) It was necessary to re-organize 11(East African) Division to bring it as far as possible into line with an Indian Standard Division.

(*b*) 22 and 28 (East African) Brigades, which formed part of the garrison of Ceylon, were on a different establishment from the brigades of 11 (East African) Division. It was always my intention to re-organize these two Brigades so that they should be inter-changeable with those of 11 Division. It has not, however, been practicable to make this change.

I foresaw, however, that additional brigades would be needed both in Fourteenth Army and 15 Indian Corps. I therefore arranged to withdraw 22 and 28 (East African) Brigades from Ceylon. This left Ceylon with three locally enlisted battalions only.

Re-organization of Armoured Formations.

140. I mentioned in my first Despatch that major changes in the organization of tank brigades were necessary and that-

(*a*) all regiments should be re-equipped with medium tanks,

(*b*) a troop of flame-throwers should be included in each squadron, and

(*c*) an infantry battalion should be included in each brigade.

The Commander-in-Chief, India, has agreed to this re-organization and an infantry battalion has been provided for each brigade, but we are still short of medium and flame-throwing tanks.

Command Changes.

141. There are two other important changes, the policy in regard to which was decided while I was Commander-in-Chief, 11 Army Group, although it was not put into effect until after I had left. Since, however, I was closely associated with this policy, I should, I consider, mention these two changes in this Despatch. The first was the appointment of an Allied Land Commander-in-Chief. The second was the transfer of Headquarters, Allied Land Forces to the vicinity of Calcutta.

142. As long as General Stilwell operated under the command of General Slim no difficulties regarding command arose. When, however, General Stilwell came under the direct command of the Supreme Allied Commander, there was a duplicate chain of command as General Slim operated under my orders and General Stilwell under the Supreme Allied Commander. I pointed out the grave disadvantages of such a system and urged the Supreme Allied Commander to arrange for the appointment of a commander of the Allied Land Forces. He eventually agreed to my recommendation and put forward his proposals to the Chiefs of Staff in September.[10]

143. It had originally been intended that the headquarters of 11 Army Group which, under the new organization was to become H.Q., Allied Land Forces,

should go to Kandy. I pointed out in my first Despatch the grave disadvantages of placing this headquarters at a place so far distant from the area of operations to which both signal and other communications were so bad.[11] I continued therefore, to press during the summer for the move of H.Q. 11 Army Group, to the neighbourhood of Calcutta. The Supreme Allied Commander finally approved this proposal and arrangements were made to move my Headquarters to Barrackpore. The Commander-in-Chief, India, with that readiness to help which always distinguishes him, moved H.Q., Eastern Command, to provide my staff with the necessary accommodation and offices.

144. The need for the closest co-operation between the Army and the Air Forces at all levels of command had led the Supreme Allied Commander to set up a committee to examine and report upon the best method of improving co-operation.

Its principal recommendation was that army and air headquarters should be alongside each other at all levels down to and including composite group level. I strongly supported this proposal, which involved the following, re-organization of air commands:-

(*a*) Eastern Air Command absorbed Third Tactical Air Force and was to work in conjunction with Advance Headquarters, Allied Land Forces.

(*b*) 221 Group became a Composite Group for co-operation with Fourteenth Army.

(*c*) 224 Group was to provide support for 15 Indian Corps in the Arakan.

(*d*) 10 U.S.A.A.F. was to continue to operate with Northern Combat Area Command.

In each case, the army and air headquarters were to be located together. Operations subsequent to those covered by this Despatch have shown the wisdom of these decisions.

PART III. – ADMINISTRATION.

Adjutant-General Questions.

145. *Reinforcements.* I have already mentioned the shortage of infantry reinforcements in discussing the availability of formations, but the demand for all types of reinforcements has continued to exceed the supply. The general position has, except that of certain highly technical trades, however, improved since the situation described in my first Despatch.

Shortages, although a very severe handicap, have not made it necessary to withdraw units but it has been necessary to send some British infantry drafts to reinforcement camps without previous jungle training in order to mainmain battalions at minimum fighting strength. This does not mean that drafts are sent forward wholly untrained since they are given some training by the camp training staffs.

146. *Releases.* As a result of the announcement of the scheme for the "Re-allocation of British Manpower" on the cessation of hostilities in Europe, instructions were

issued to units early in November, together with provisional Class A release rolls. Personnel fell into three categories:-

(*a*) Surplus to manpower requirements.

(*b*) Those called out for vital post-war reconstruction.

(*c*) Compassionate cases.

147. *Repatriation.* The reduction, in September, of the period of overseas service to 3 years and 8 months caused widespread satisfaction. The numbers affected, however, were large and their despatch had to be spread over the following four months, except in the case of the officers and men of the Royal Corps of Signals. The repatriation of Signal personnel had unfortunately to be delayed and spread over the period January to March 1945, whilst officers had to wait longer and were to be sent home between February and April as the replacements had to arrive before repatriates left their units.

148. *Leave.* (*a*) The opening, in August, of the Indian Army leave scheme for officers filled a long felt want. All British officers and British other ranks who had completed 5 years' service abroad were eligible, but the number was so large that leave could only be granted to those with 8 years' overseas service. Even so, it is likely that it will take over 12 months to send these officers home, owing to the limited number of passages.

(*b*) A special war leave programme was arranged between July and October. This enabled Indian other ranks, whose leave was overdue, to go to their homes.

Medical.

149. *Evacuation of Casualties.* While Imphal was still surrounded, all casualties had to be flown to the base hospitals as described in my first Despatch. I had always pressed for the movement of sick and wounded to hospital by air, but until operations in Arakan and Imphal this year there had never been enough aircraft. Their increasing use on this important duty reduced the number of men who had to travel by the old types of transport. As we advanced down the Tiddim and Tamu roads, airstrips were constructed for use by light aircraft in the first place, and, later, by cargo aircraft as the strips were enlarged and their surfaces improved. Casualties were sent to a central air maintenance area in Imphal and thence by returning supply aircraft to the base hospitals. All casualties from the Tiddim road were flown back. From Tamu, sick and wounded travelled both by air and road.

On the Arakan front, the movement of casualties by air was limited almost entirely to those of 81 (West African) Division in the Kaladan Valley, since water transport was available for other formations.

Our casualties from North Burma (36 British Division) were also flown back, at first by light aircraft and later by returning heavy transport planes, to our forward base hospitals in the Ledo area.

150. The organization needed when large numbers of casualties are moved by air was being studied during the past six months. A start was made to reduce the

wasteful "ribbon" distribution of hospitals, which had hitherto had to be maintained along the L. of C. solely for transit purposes, and to concentrate beds in large hospital centres. This policy, as it develops, will allow a much larger number of cases to be retained in the Fourteenth Army area until they are fit to return to their units, and thereby avoid the many drawbacks in their evacuation to base hospitals in India.

151. The following is a summary in round figures of casualties moved between the 25th June and the 12th November:-

	Within Fourteenth Army	Ex-Fourteenth Army	TOTAL
By Road	26,300	—	26,300
By Rail	22,300	—	22,300
By Air	29,800	3,000	32,800
By Sea	9,500	15,100	24,600
By River	3,900	12,800	16,700
	91,800	30,900	122,700

Note. - All casualties are sent by river to the railheads of the India Command.

152. *Incidence of Disease.* The period June to November has witnessed a steady fall in the sick rate. The daily rate per thousand of 4.2 at the peak period in June, compares favourably with the peak figure of 6.0 in 1943. In November, the incidence was only 3.0 compared with 5.0 per thousand in the same month last year. This reduction was mainly due to the fall in the malaria rate, which is due to a steady improvement in malaria discipline.

153. D.D.T. had not been used on a scale adequate to show its capabilities, but experiments were being made.

154. Apart from malaria, there were two other somewhat serious outbreaks of disease; dysentery, which reached its peak in June and July, and scrub typhus, which caused much sickness between August and October. The dysentery died down in October, but emphasised once more the necessity for maintaining a high standard of sanitation. Effective preventive measures against scrub typhus have been discovered by the medical officer who was lent to South-East Asia Command by the Colonial Office and attached to my headquarters.

155. Since my first Despatch, the consulting physician, surgeon, malariologist and psychiatrist have arrived at this Headquarters and their advice has proved most valuable.

156. *Casualties.* The following table gives a summary of our battle casualties from the 1st July to the 1st November and, for comparison, a statement showing the Japanese casualties during the same period. The numbers of enemy killed are those whose bodies were actually counted and they do not include the casualties inflicted by our air action:

CASUALTIES IST JULY, 1944 TO IST NOVEMBER, 1944.

	Killed	Wounded	Missing
Fourteenth Army fronts.			
British	583	2,001	110
Japanese	8,859	—	234
			prisoner
Northern Combat Area Command			
British[12]	513	1,389	47
Japanese[13]	3,724	—	246
			prisoners

The Japanese losses in killed alone exceeded our total losses in killed, wounded and missing.

Welfare and Morale.

157. *British Troops.* The morale of the troops has reached a high level, for they have shown their superiority over the Japanese.

The main interest of the British troops is centred in repatriation. Service in a distant Eastern Theatre is unpopular and the British soldier looks forward to going home. The handling of this important question by the Government appeared in the eyes of the men unsympathetic, but the reduction in the period of service overseas has convinced the men of the sincerity of the Government.

The grant of Japanese Campaign Pay and War Service Increment and the White Paper on Release were generally welcomed.

158. "Mail" and "Rations" improved greatly; the film situation also improved and additional Kinema Sections were allotted to South-East Asia Command. "Live Entertainment" remained inadequate, for there were too few E.N.S.A. shows and Indian Concert Parties. Radio entertainment was increased to thirty hours per week. The newspaper "S.E.A.C." grew in popularity, its circulation by November having reached some 30,000 copies daily. Travelling facilities for men going on leave continued, however, to be bad, in spite of strenuous efforts that were made to improve them. Shortage of railway equipment and rolling stock caused many of the difficulties.

159. I wish to mention three institutions in Imphal which did much to alleviate conditions in the forward area:-

(*a*) An Officers' Club was opened, the popularity of which proved that it filled a long felt want.

(*b*) Toc H Canteen, known as "The Elephant Arms", had an average nightly attendance of 1,000 British soldiers. The attached leave hostel was also popular.

(*c*) The Y.M.C.A., which had remained open throughout the battle, also had an average daily attendance of a thousand. I wish to pay tribute to the Reverend Walter Corbett and his wife for the devoted service they rendered to the troops.

(*d*) I also wish to mention the splendid work of the Women's Auxiliary Service (Burma). This Service operated mobile and static canteens in the forward areas and on many occasions worked right up with the leading formations. The value to morale of a women's service operating canteens in the interests of the troops in forward areas and under monsoon conditions was inestimable.

160. *Indian Troops.* The discipline and fighting spirit of Indian troops has been throughout of the highest quality.

The re-opening of leave on a large scale, and the improvement in economic conditions in the villages, did much to relieve the Indian soldier's mind, but there are still complaints of the irregularities of the postal services, the failings of the family allotment system and graft and exploitation by petty local officials.

The Commander-in-Chief, India, has taken all possible steps to put these matters right.

161. *African Troops.* The morale of both East and West African troops has been satisfactory. They require more training. Owing to the shortage of formations, they had to be committed to action before they were entirely ready for war.

Supplies, Transport and Maintenance.

162. *Movements and Transportation.* A full description of the lines of communication was given in my first Despatch. The main tasks of the Movements and Transportation Directorates during the period of this Despatch were:-

(*a*) The maintenance of Fourteenth Army in Assam and Arakan.

(*b*) The building up of stocks on both the Imphal and Arakan fronts for the post-monsoon offensive.

(*c*) The movement of formations under the relief programme.

163. *Tonnages Handled,* (*a*) *Assam Line of Communication.* The average monthly tonnage of stores for Fourteenth Army, excluding P.O.L., carried between June and November was 31,200, an increase of some 3,000 tons over the monthly average for the previous six months. This increase was creditable in view of the difficulties caused by the monsoon. The completion in August of the American 6-inch pipeline from Calcutta to Dibrugarh has released wagons needed formerly for aviation spirit. I hope that the Assam line of communication will now be able to carry all the traffic, and that the tonnage which can be handled in railheads and depots will be the limiting factor, rather than the capacity of the river, rail and road systems of the lines of communication.

(*b*) *Chittagong Port.*

The average monthly import of stores, excluding bulk P.O.L., was 51,000 tons. This figure is lower by 10,000 tons than the average of the previous three months, and is explained by the smaller number of ships using the port. On the other hand, the average tonnage discharged per ship per day increased.

(*c*) *Arakan Ports.*

The average monthly imports into Cox's Bazaar, Ultaklali and Maungdaw totalled 23,600 tons, which was an increase of 4,500 tons over the average of the previous three months. This increase in tonnage, in spite of the difficulties of working in the monsoon at these small ports, is noteworthy.

164. *Opening of Maungdaw Port.* A new channel into the mouth of the Naf River was discovered, and it was found possible to bring ocean-going ships for the first time to Maungdaw. This saved much overland transport.

165. *Monsoon Reliefs.* The following is a summary of the major moves completed, or in process during the monsoon:-

   (*a*) *Divisions.*
   (i) One division from Assam to India.
   (ii) One division from Ceylon to Assam.
   (iii) One division from India to Assam.
   (iv) One division from India to Arakan.
   (*b*) *Brigades.*
   (i) Six brigades from Assam to India.
   (ii) One brigade from Arakan to India.
   (iii) One brigade from India to Assam.
   (iv) Two brigades from India to Arakan.
   (v) One brigade from Ceylon to Assam.
   (vi) One brigade from Ceylon to Arakan.

The details of these moves are given in Appendix "A", as the times and methods are interesting and instructive.

166. An interesting experiment in transportation was the use made of "jeep trains" by 36 British Division in their advance down the railway.

This new method of haulage was first tried in July on the Myitkyina – Mogaung section of the line, as no locomotives were available. It was found that a jeep, fitted with flanged wheels, could draw some 40 tons of freight and "jeep trains" have since formed part of the transportation organization in that area.

167. *Air Supply.* When discussing "Organization" in my first Despatch, I stated the need for a permanent organization to handle the movement by air of troops and supplies, and I mentioned that my proposals were, at that time, being considered by the Air Commander-in-Chief, South-East Asia Command, and the Commander-in-Chief, India. The last six months has seen the birth of the Army Air Transport Organization, with headquarters at Comilla alongside the recently formed Headquarters, Combat Cargo Task Force. These two Headquarters, the one Military and the other R.A.F. and U.S.A.A.F., worked as a whole, the Army staff being under command of 11 Army Group and the Air staff under Eastern Air Command. The main duties of the Commander of this new organization were:-

   (*a*) To control all the Rear Airfield Maintenance Organizations in South-East Asia Command.

(*b*) To ensure that the requirements of forward formations for air supply or air transport were met in accordance with the policy laid down by Headquarters, 11 Army Group.

(*c*) To advise and assist formations dependent on air supply, and formations training or preparing for air transported operations.

168. Rear Airfield Maintenance Units were formed and the existing Air Supply Companies, renamed Air Despatch Companies, were reorganized to handle daily, 80 tons of stores for air dropping. The duties of these companies included the collection of stores from the nearest depot, packing, loading and the provision of crews for dropping stores. Each Rear Airfield Maintenance Organization also included an Air Despatch and Reception Unit which was a combined passenger and freight section to control the loading of aircraft and to exercise general flying control on the airstrip.

169. I emphasised in my first Despatch the vital part played by air supply in Arakan and at Imphal during the first half of the year. As it was obvious that the success of our future operations would be equally, if not more, dependent on air transport, I was determined that the system of control which I have briefly outlined should be introduced as soon as possible. In spite of the shortage of manpower and other difficulties, it was introduced on the 18th October. As our operations expand changes may become necessary, but the organization is sufficiently flexible to allow this.

170. The extent to which formations were supplied by air is best illustrated by the total monthly tonnages dropped or, when airstrips were available, landed. In June, the figure was 5,854 tons; this fell to 4,019 tons in August, when only two divisions were operating on the Chindwin front and only two brigades of Special Force were in North Burma; it then rose steadily, and by November, when 81 (West African) Division in the Kaladan Valley, certain brigades of 33 and 4 Corps on the Chindwin, and 36 British Division in North Burma were being supplied by air, reached 10,573 tons.

The airfields upon which transport aircraft were based were:-

Airfield.	Formations Served.
Dinjan	Fort Hertz.
Moran	36 British Division.
Sylhet	Special Force, 4 and 33 Corps.
Agartala	Lushai Brigade, 4 and 33 Corps
Comilla	81 (West African) Division.
Chittagong	Corps Troops, 4 Corps.

171. *P.O.L.* In the early part of the year the supply of petrol and lubricants had been difficult, but by decreasing consumption and by increasing our bulk storage and methods of distribution this had improved.

Imperial requirements increased during the last six months from 11 ¼ million gallons to nearly 14½ million per month, but decreased consumption during the monsoon enabled us not only to meet the increase, but to build up our reserve stocks to 30 million gallons by the 1st November. To make this possible we had to:-

(*a*) Increase the storage of P.O.L. in bulk at Chittagong port from 11 million to 20 million gallons.

(*b*) Increase the capacity of tanks at airfields and army depots by 3½ million gallons.

(*c*) Increase the capacity of our rail cars by 485,000 gallons.

(*d*) Greatly extend our pipelines.

172. *Situation as regards Rations.* The supply of fresh meat for Indian troops is still difficult. In October, the supply of sheep and goats only permitted the issue of meat on three days with another half day in Assam and on two days in Arakan during the month. There is little hope of improvement, but I hope to compensate for the loss of protein in the ration by issuing dehydrated fish.

The production of dehydrated goat meat has improved, but is still insufficient. The Commander-in-Chief, India has been asked to increase production and to arrange to import dehydrated meat, if the religious objections of Hindus and Mohammedans can be satisfactorily met.

During October, there were larger stocks of frozen meat in India and frozen meat was flown in to British and African troops of Fourteenth Army. Cold storage plants in forward areas are being built.

173. A new Field Service scale of rations for Indian troops was introduced on the 1st November. The new scale is not only more lavish than the old, but it is designed to give a higher calorific value to meet arduous conditions in this Theatre.

174. Various projects to increase local supplies of fresh food to reduce the tonnage on the lines of communication are being developed. In spite of the shortage of labour and agricultural equipment, much progress has been made and I expect that we shall produce vegetables, livestock and salted fish in sufficient quantities for our needs in 1945.

Maintenance.

175. (*a*) The supply of vehicles, particularly jeeps and load carriers, is unsatisfactory. Fighting units are not yet fully equipped and only by strict economy and careful control of issues is it possible to maintain formations engaged in operations. Administrative units in rear areas inevitably go short, with a consequent loss in efficiency.

(*b*) The design and provision of equipment which can be carried by air has been thoroughly examined. R.E.M.E. are making machine trailers which can be carried by air for their workshops in forward areas. These are improvised from existing equipment until those designed in the U.K. arrive. The Wireless Testing Trailer is reported as being up to the standard of the Home pattern. The selection and preliminary trials of vehicles, other than these, for air transport are made by the staff of G.H.Q., India, to specifications supplied by my staff.

(*c*) I have set up a committee to examine and if possible reduce the number of modifications which are demanded in equipment.

The Engineering Effort. A. *Road Communications.*

176. *The Arakan Road.* At the beginning of July the policy in Arakan was to provide a new single-way brick road alongside the existing one-way road, the latter to be used in its less worn sections for passing places.

By September, the road was nearly finished, but maintenance of the completed section was so abnormally heavy that it was decided to waterproof the surface with bitumen. In view of the probable future operations, this was eventually not done.

Between July and November, therefore, no major road work was done in Arakan other than the widening of the coast road, and the bulk of the engineers were employed in maintenance. 22,000 local labourers, excluding military supervisors, were employed.

177. *Imphal Front.* Before the Japanese offensive in March caused a stoppage of work, the following all weather two-way roads were being built:-

Imphal – Tiddim.
Palel – Tamu.
Tamu – Witok – Mau.

178. *Imphal – Tiddim* (*164 miles*). It was originally intended to improve this road to an all-weather standard and as we advanced much work was done on it.

By September, half the distance had been finished, but the difficulties in maintaining an all-weather standard were out of proportion to the value of the road. I, therefore, decided to concentrate all road building resources in labour and material on the Tamu – Witok – Kalewa route to the Chindwin; though some had to be left to maintain the Tiddim road at a standard adequate to support the force on that line.

179. *Palel – Tamu* (*43 miles*). As soon as operations permitted, the construction of this road to a two-way, all-weather Class 30 standard was restarted and it was hoped to finish it by the end of the year. This was later altered to Class 70 to permit of the passage of loaded tank-transporters, and the date of completion was extended to April 1945. By November 1944, satisfactory progress had been made, 2,500 military and 2,000 local labour being employed.

180. *Tamu – Witok – Kalewa* (*112 miles*). Planned before March as a two-way, all-weather road from Tamu to Witok, this road was subsequently extended to be two-way, fair-weather Class 70 to Kalewa.

The road was virtually finished by November. An all-weather Class 70 road from Tamu to Kalewa on a different alignment was also planned, but by November reconnaissance only had been made.

181. *The "Breach Road" (Bongaigaon-Pandu)*. The Bongaigaon – Amingaon railway has been cut during the monsoon every year except one during the past thirty-two years, and communications in Assam have been interrupted for many months on each occasion.

To provide an alternative route for traffic it was decided to improve to two-way, all-weather standard the road from Bongaigaon to Jogighopa (21 miles) on the north bank of the Brahmaputra River and from Goalpara on the south bank to Pandu (93 miles).

These roads, which were virtually finished by November, should provide a good alternative route if the railway should be breached in future.

182. *Road Construction*. In planning all-weather roads in forward areas the problem has been their construction during the monsoon at a sufficient rate to ensure the adequate support of operations and their subsequent maintenance.

"Bithess", a bitumen-impregnated sheet of heavy jute sacking which was used to cover airfields and prevent penetration of water into the ground, is now being used on roads. It provides an all-weather surface suitable for all but tracked vehicles and can be laid at a rate double that of metalling and tarring road surfaces.

The Engineering Effort. B. Airfields.
183. Few new airfields have been built, but the demands for the expansion of existing airfields, and their conversion for use by heavier types of aircraft, strained my engineer resources to the utmost, in spite of the arrival of new mechanical equipment.

The principal changes have been:-

Cox's Bazaar. Enlarged to accommodate an additional heavy bomber squadron and a fighter squadron.
Chittagong. Enlarged to take two heavy bomber squadrons, a U.S.A.A.F. Lightning squadron, a R.A.F. Wing and an Air Staging Post.
Hathazari. Some twenty miles north of Chittagong. Constructed for one transport squadron.
Fenny. Doubled in size to accept four U.S.A.A.F. Medium Bomber squadrons and one long-range Fighter squadron.
Shamshernagar. Fifty miles south of Syhlhet, previously known as Tilagaon. Completely re-designed from a bomber base to an Air Transport and Air Service Centre. The U.S.A.A.F. lent me an airborne aviation engineer company and a group of engineers to help in building this airfield. Their assistance was valuable and the co-operation between the American, British and Indian engineer units engaged, exemplary. I have mentioned this project in some

detail because, not only is it the largest airfield in India, but it was the model of the new airfields which we subsequently built.

Sylhet, was expanded for the U.S.A.A.F. from a two squadron Heavy Bomber to a four squadron Transport field.

Tulihal, near Imphal, has been enlarged from a fair-weather Fighter to an all-weather four squadron Transport field. Constructed entirely with "Bithess", it is now regarded as the best airfield in the Fourteenth Army area.

I have referred only to major construction in the rear areas. There was, of course, much other less important work, and work on maintenance during the monsoon was heavy.

184. The construction of forward airfields continued in co-operation with Head-quarters, Third Tactical Air Force. An important fact which saved much work was our ascendancy in the air. Dispersal areas were no longer needed and this reduced the mileage of taxi tracks and roads, labour and material.

185. *Airfields in North-East Assam.* Much work was still done on the numerous air-fields built for the U.S.A.A.F. in this area. Although, no new airfields were made, the size of the task can be measured from the following figures which shows the major works finished by mid-November at the eleven main airfields in Assam:-

Runways and taxi tracks, 38 miles.
Number of aircraft standings, 506.
Aircraft parking aprons, 60 acres.
Roads, 111 miles.
Accommodation, for 33,000 officers and men.
Covered storage, 67 acres.

186. It will be remembered that I am writing of the monsoon and of an area where the rainfall is the heaviest in the world. The amount of new construction, involving the clearance of thick jungle, and of maintenance under severe climatic conditions, both in Assam and Arakan, reflects the greatest credit on our airfield engineers.

187. *Airfields in Ceylon.* The improvement and extension of the nine main airfields on the Island continued.

As a matter of convenience, it was decided that, from August, the Engineer-in-Chief, South-East Asia Command, who is at Kandy, should relieve my Chief Engineer of the technical responsibility for the works in Ceylon, the latter's duties being henceforth limited to stores and personnel. The responsibilities of the Chief Engineer, Ceylon Army Command, and of the Air Ministry Works Department, were unaffected by this change.

188. *Airfields in North Burma.* As I have mentioned the operations under General Stilwell, this section of my Despatch would be incomplete without reference to the airfield construction undertaken by the United States Army Air Engineers in North Burma.

As General Stilwell's forces advanced his engineers built three airfields in the Hukawng Valley. On the afternoon of the capture of Myitkyina airfield, 10 U.S.A.A.F., on whom rested the responsibility of building forward airfields, landed by glider the first company of a battalion of airborne aviation engineers. The rest of the battalion followed in transport aircraft within a week. The airfield was in full use two days after its capture and has since been completely reconstructed and greatly expanded.

The concentration of aircraft on Myitkyina airfield was very heavy, nearly 2,000 landings and take-offs being made daily by heavy transport aircraft. More airfields in this area were clearly necessary and three more Engineer Aviation battalions were flown in with their full equipment. By November, three all-weather Transport airfields had been built and two others were nearly finished.

The movement and supply of the engineers at work on these airfields was airborne throughout, as no suitable communications existed overland. To construct five large airfields under monsoon conditions was a noteworthy feat of engineering work. To have done it as an airborne operation was outstanding.

The Engineering Effort. C. Oil Pipelines.
189. The 4-inch pipeline joining Chittagong and Chandranathpur, mentioned in my first Despatch, was finished as far as Comilla by November. Construction of the final link between Comilla and Chandranathpur was in progress. This will give an unbroken line from Chittagong to Manipur Road. The extension of this line to Imphal was begun at the end of September.

190. The American so-called "Infinity Line" from Calcutta to Kunming reached Myitkyina in October. From Ledo there are two 4-inch lines for aviation and motor spirit respectively.

The construction of the second American 6-inch pipeline from Chittagong to Tinsukia, forecast in my first Despatch, was also started. This line will follow the British 4-inch line and the operation of both will be under one control and for the mutual benefit of ourselves and our Allies.

191. The elaborate, pipeline system in the North-East Assam airfields area was handed over to the Americans at the end of July.

Civil Affairs Burma.
192. On the 23rd June, the British Military Administration in Burma had under its control the Fort Hertz and Sumprabum areas, the Hukawng Valley, the western fringe of the Chin Hills District and the northern fringe of the Arakan Division.

On the 12th November, the area included the whole of the Myitkyina District, the northern part of the Bhamo and Katha area of the Upper Chindwin District and all but the southern area of the Chin Hills District. The area under administration in Arakan remained unchanged.

193. The principal centre of activity in Civil Affairs was the Myitkyina District, where the advance of the forces of Northern Combat Area Command brought important new tracts under British control. The main tasks were the restoration of law and order, the care of refugees, the feeding and clothing of destitutes, the organization of medical services, the provision of labour for the Armed Forces and, last but not least, the restoration of confidence among the local inhabitants. Although a great deal was done, the British Military Administration was handicapped by the restriction on the number of Civil Affairs officers allowed to work in the area. The civil population suffered in consequence: had more staff been allowed, action to relieve hardship could have been taken more rapidly and effectively.

194. The chief problem in the Hukawng Valley was the shortage of food, and relief camps had to he organised on a large scale. Seed and agricultural tools were imported, but immediate relief was given by developing the local salt production to the maximum, and thus setting free much air transport for other supplies.

195. During the earlier part of our re-occupation of North Burma, the British Military Administration was handicapped by the movement southwards of large sections of the Shan and Burmese inhabitants. This was due in part to Japanese propaganda and in part to the fear of Chinese troops and the Kachin Levies. They gradually returned as confidence was restored, but in the interval, there was a shortage of potential subordinate officials, police, and agricultural labour. Nevertheless, a police force was organized, order restored, crops sown, and "collaborators" brought to trial.

196. In the Kabaw Valley and the Naga and Chin Hills, the work of the Military Administration was largely confined to the organization of Intelligence, the provision of labour, and general liaison betwen the Army and the local population.

In Arakan, the British Military Administration continued to administer the northern area.

197. The Civil Affairs Service depots for relief supplies and stores were at Chittagong for Arakan, at Manipur Road and Imphal for the Chin and Naga Hills and Upper Chindwin, and at Ledo and Moran (seventy miles southwest of Ledo) for the Northern Combat Area Command area. The difficulty, of course, lay in moving these supplies forward to distribution centres; and Army air and road transport had to be borrowed, until such time as Civil Affairs Service transport companies could be formed.

198. In spite of the shortage of transport, the paucity of communications and bad weather, the whole of the relief supplies for the population of the re-occupied areas were successfully distributed, including some 6,000 tons of rice, 1,500 tons of salt, and large quantities of milk, cloth, etc.

The chiefs, headmen and local inhabitants of the areas released from Japanese occupation were found for the most part to have behaved loyally during our absence and, with a few exceptions, our return was greeted with satisfaction.

Main Administrative Lessons.

199. *Air Supply.* The need of foresight, of standardising drops, of giving the Air Supply Depots ample warning of any change of plan, and of economising resources, were all of paramount importance. As operations went on, formations became more skilful in choosing dropping zones, and pilots more efficient at dropping on them. The necessity for alternative dropping zones was clearly brought out. Finally, the importance of salvaging all parachute material and containers was emphasised.

200. To meet the uncertainties of supply dropping in the monsoon, orders were given that, as soon as there was a failure to drop supplies, all ranks and mules were to be put on half rations until dropping could be resumed. All troops carried three days' reserves and they could therefore carry on for six days: in addition they had their emergency rations.

These precautionary measures turned out to be wise. It so happened that the maximum number of days on which supply-dropping was impossible consecutively was five, but on one occasion the margin was narrow. In a final attempt on the sixth day, the aircraft found only one gap in the cloud over the whole area. Under this gap was the dropping zone.

201. *Vehicles.* The value of the 30 cwt. 6×6 vehicles has been shown. It had the cross-country performance of a jeep, except on narrow tracks, and nearly the capacity of a 3-tonner.

As regards specialist vehicles, experience has shown that they should either all be 4×4 or that their equipment should be capable of being fitted on to a standard chassis. The latter is preferable as, should the specialist vehicle be damaged, its equipment can be quickly transferred.

The highest standards of maintenance and traffic discipline are essential to maintain efficiency under the conditions I have described.

202. *Salvage.* Owing to the length and complexity of the lines of communication, it was found unprofitable to send back many types of salvage. Instead, workshops were set up which manufactured from this salvage a large assortment of articles, and thereby saved transport.

203. *Welfare.* Good administration in units in the provision of food, recreation, etc., was vitally important in the monsoon for the quick restoration of morale after battle. Cinemas are possibly better than E.N.S.A. parties in this Theatre and I hope that before long each brigade will have its own. Corps "Welfare Shops" proved very popular.

Under monsoon conditions, arrangements for the periodical withdrawal of troops from the line in order to have hot baths and a change of clothing are essential and have a high moral value.

204. *Conclusion.* The administrative machine stood up well to the strain of fighting a war and administering a great expanse of territory with inadequate resources and under difficult conditions. Much improvisation has been necessary and all Services have shown great resource and ingenuity in doing their many duties. Their success reflects the greatest credit on all concerned.

PART IV. CONCLUSION.

205. "This Army has by its aggressive operations guarded the base of the American air line to China and protected India against the horrors of Japanese invasion." With these words Mr. Churchill put in clear perspective the vital part that Fourteenth Army has played during the last six months in the struggle against Japan. The crushing of the Japanese offensive against Kohima and Imphal and our pursuit of his retreating columns to the Chindwin were, of course, one battle. We have inflicted upon the enemy a major defeat. It is the first time the Japanese have been driven back so far – and they will go further. The facts speak for themselves and they will give encouragement and assurance to those who fought against a ruthless and cunning enemy, against disease and in rain and heat through the jungles and mountains of Assam and Burma, to inflict the first great land defeat on Japan.

I have quoted the words of the Prime Minister. I also quote a few sentences from an address delivered by His Excellency the Viceroy, Field-Marshal Lord Wavell, when he visited the troops during the course of the campaign: "You will find that, when the history of the war comes to be written, the recent fighting will be put down as one of the turning points of the war, when the Japanese were routed and their downfall really began. Not only have you inflicted a tremendous defeat on the enemy but, even more, you have dealt a damaging blow to their morale – and it is the breaking of the enemy's morale that finishes wars in the end."

206. This Despatch brings to an end the account of my command of 11 Army Group, and I cannot finish it without paying tribute to the magnificent team of officers and men who made up the forces under my command.

Though it is outside the period covered by my two Despatches I must refer briefly to the six months in 1943 in which I commanded Eastern Army out of which Fourteenth Army was born.

In those early days, deficiencies in equipment; shortage of trained reinforcements; lack of welfare arrangements; long service overseas; inadequate leave due to lack of accommodation and transport; indifferent rations; much sickness; slow mails; an apparent lack of interest at home in what was being done and endured on the Burma Front; and an exaggerated opinion of the efficiency of the Japanese had combined to lower the morale and destroy the confidence of the Army.

Without confidence and high morale, equipment and weapons, however good, are useless, and the re-creation of these two qualities was the first task to which we all had to address ourselves during the monsoon of 1943. Confidence could be created by training and improved equipment, morale by confidence and care for the spiritual and physical well being of the troops.

All through that monsoon, the Commander-in-Chief, India, did all that was possible to improve the training and, with his limited resources, the welfare of the troops.

Much was accomplished, and by October, 1943 – when direction of the operations was about to pass to the Supreme Allied Commander; Fourteenth Army was about to be formed, and the weather moderated sufficiently to allow us to move – the work done during the monsoon began to bear fruit. Operations started, slowly at first, but with gathering momentum as their first encounters with the enemy showed the troops that the Japanese soldier, though tough and prepared to die rather than surrender, was not so skilful as themselves nor so well equipped.

The Army must have contained almost more diverse races than any other, even in this war, when so many nations have fought as Allies.

There were battalions from British county regiments distinguished in our history, and officers and men from every county in England, Scotland, Ireland and Wales serving in other arms or with units of the Indian and African forces.

The Indian units of which the bulk of Fourteenth Army was composed, came from many famous regiments, recruited from races whose names have been household words since first we went to India: Rajputs, Dogras, Sikhs, Jats, Mahommedans from the Punjab, Gurkhas, Garhwalis and Madrassis to mention but a few of those who volunteered to fight for the King Emperor.

To the Army were added later divisions from our West and East African Colonies, composed of Hausas, Yorubas and Ibos from Nigeria; Kanjarga, Dagartis and Ashantis from the Gold Coast; Mendis and Timinis from Sierra Leone; Mandingos from Gambia; Nyasas and Yaos from Nyasaland; Manyamwezi and Manyema from Tanganyika; Akamba, Nandi and Kavirondo from Kenya; Baganda and Achole from Uganda; Somalis from Somaliland; Awemba and Angoni from Northern Rhodesia and many others too numerous to mention.

All these men had volunteered to fight for the King.

The success of Fourteenth Army is the best testimonial to its officers and men and I cannot add anything to it. Victory was achieved by fine leading by all commanders from the highest to the most junior section leader; by the skill of the men in the ranks; by high courage in battle; by steady endurance under conditions of climate and health worse than almost anywhere in the world; by a determination to defeat the enemy, and by that spirit, which alone enables an army to exert its maximum strength, of co-operation among all ranks and arms.

It has been an immense source of pride to me to watch the growth of confidence and skill which enabled the officers and men of Fourteenth Army to inflict the first major defeat upon the Japanese and by unrelenting pursuit to drive them with crippling losses in men and material in disorder across the Chindwin.

207. Once again I should like to thank General Sir Claude Auchinleck[14] and the staff at his Headquarters for their generous and unfailing help, without which

11 Army Group could not have driven the Japanese back from the frontiers of India.

I also wish to give a final word of thanks to my own staff for their hard work and fine team spirit, upon which I was able always confidently to rely however acute the crisis or hard the work.

I want especially to mention my two principal Staff Officers, Major-General I.S.O. Playfair, M.G.G.S., and Major-General E.N. Goddard, M.G.A., whose wise advice, good judgment and unfailing loyalty were a great support to me.

Finally, I have no doubt that the defeat of the Japanese forces in Burma is due to the balanced judgment, determination and skill of Lieut-General Sir William Slim, upon whom fell the burden of the fighting.

Notes

1. Operations in Burma and North-East India from 6th November, 1943 to 22nd June, 1944.
2. Now Vice-Admiral The Earl Mountbatten of Burma, K.G., P.C., G.C.S.I., G.C.I.E., G.C.V.O., K.C.B., D.S.O.
3. Now Field-Marshal Sir William J. Slim, G.B.E., K.C.B., D.S.O., M.C.
4. A 4 × 4 lorry is a four-wheeled vehicle, all four wheels of which can be driven by the engine. Similarly, a 6 × 6 lorry is one in which the power can be transmitted to all of its six wheels.
5. Now General Sir A.F. Philip Christison, Bart., G.B.E.. C.B., D.S.O., M.C.
6. Now General Sir Geoffry A.P. Scoones, K.C.B., K.B.E. C.S.I., D.S.O., M.C.
7. Now General Sir Montagu G.N. Stopford, G.C.B., K.B.E., D.S.O., M.C.
8. *War Office footnote:* See also the Supreme Allied Commander's Report, South-East Asia, 1943–1945, Part A., para. 59; Part B., paras. 185–186 and 201–203.
9. Operations in Burma and North-East India from the 16th November, 1943 to the 22nd June, 1944.
10. *War Office footnote:* Additional particulars regarding the re-organization of the command of the Allied Land Forces in South-East Asia are set out in the Supreme Allied Commander's Report, South-East Asia, 1943–5, at Part A., para. 43; Part B., paras. 170–172; 226–227; 231 and 268–269.
11. *War Office footnote:* The views of the Supreme Allied Commander and his reasons for the move to Ceylon are set out in Part A., paragraphs 12–14 of his Report, South-East Asia, 1943–45.
12. Special Force and 36 British Division.
13. Figures include casualties inflicted by American and Chinese forces.
14. Now Field-Marshal Sir Claude J.E. Auchinleck, G.C.B., G.C.I.E., C.S.I., D.S.O., O.B.E.

APPENDIX "A"
MAJOR OPERATIONAL MOVES

Formation	From	To	Started	Finished	Method of Movement
11 (East African Division)	Ceylon	Manipur Road	20th May	24th August	4 flights by sea to Chittagong, then by rail to Manipur Road. 2 flights by sea to Calcutta, thence by rail/river/rail to Manipur Road.
3 (West African) Brigade	Tinsukia	Dhond	22nd August	6th September	Rail/river/rail
23 L.R.P. Brigade	Manipur Road	Bangalore	5th August	21st August	Rail
111 L.R.P. Brigade	Tinsukia	Dehra Dun	8th August	18th August	Rail
268 Indian Lorried Infantry Brigade	Manipur Road	Ranchi	25th August	4th September	Rail/river/rail
23 Indian Division	Manipur Road	Shillong	1st August	31st August	Rail/road
77 L.R.P. Brigade	Tinsukia	Dehra Dun	19th July	6th August	Rail/river/rail
17 Indian Light Division	Manipur Road	Ranchi	29th August	2nd October	Rail/river/rail
14 L.R P. Brigade	Tinsukia	Bangalore	1st September	19th September	Rail/river/rail
255 Indian Tank Brigade	Ranchi	Manipur Road	14th September	13th October	Rail
19 Indian Division	Nasik	Manipur Road	7th October	6th November	Rail/river/road
2 (West African) Infantry Brigade Group (82 (West African) Division).	Ranchi	Dohazari	9th October	20th October	Rail/road/sea
Headquarters 4 Corps	Imphal	Ranchi	10th October	22nd October	Rail/road
3 Special Service Brigade	Colombo	Chittagong	2nd October	24th October	Rail/sea
28 (East African) Brigade	Colombo	Imphal	8th November	29th November	Sea/rail/road
71 Independent Brigade Group	Chittagong	Cocanada	7th November	20th November	Sea/rail
50 Tank Brigade	Poona/Secunderabad	Chittagong	1st November	30th November	Road/rail/sea
82 (West African) Division less 2 (West African) Infantry Brigade Group	Ranchi	Dohazari	31st October	1st December	Road/rail/sea

3

VICE-ADMIRAL SIR ARTHUR J. POWER'S DESPATCH ON NAVAL OPERATIONS IN RAMREE ISLAND AREA, 19 JANUARY TO 22 FEBRUARY 1945

MONDAY, 26 APRIL, 1948

The following Despatch was submitted to the Lords Commissioners of the Admiralty on the 2nd May, 1945, by Vice-Admiral Sir ARTHUR J. POWER, K.C.B., C.V.O., *Commander-in-Chief, East Indies Station.*

East Indies Station.
2nd May, 1945.

The accompanying reports by Flag Officer, Force "W" on naval operations in the Ramree Island area between 19th January and 22nd February, 1945, are forwarded for the information of Their Lordships.

2. I concur in the conclusions of the Senior Officer Advanced Force "W", and in the remarks of Flag Officer, Force "W". Considerable ingenuity and resourcefulness were shown by all the Commanding Officers in this operation, and the endurance and determination of the crews of small craft during Operation "Block" were most creditable. The Royal Indian Navy landing craft crews demonstrated again the zeal and efficiency which have formed a notable contribution to the success of all the combined operations on the Arakan Coast.

(Signed) ARTHUR POWER,
Vice-Admiral.

Enclosure 1.

Office of Flag Officer Force "W"
20th March, 1945.

REPORT ON NAVAL OPERATIONS IN THE RAMREE ISLAND AREA.

The attached report on the Naval Operations at Ramree Island is forwarded.

2. As stated in paragraph 7 of the report I instructed my Chief Staff Officer, Captain E.W. Bush, D.S.O., D.S.C., R.N., to place himself on divisional level with Major-General Lomax at Kyaukpyu and to render all assistance to that officer in his task of clearing the enemy off Ramree Island. Though this step meant that my Chief Staff Officer was divorced from me from 24th January to 24th February, I am of the opinion that the results obtained justified it.

3. As will be seen from the report the naval operations were of a unique kind, calling for resourcefulness, determination and professional experience, and Captain Bush rose to the occasion in the able manner I expected him to, and I consider that the success of the naval operations at Ramree was due to this officer's efforts.

4. I fully concur with paragraph 36 et seq. of the report.

(Signed) B.C.S. MARTIN,
Rear-Admiral.

Enclosure 2.

Office of Senior Officer,
Advanced Force "W",
Kyaukpyu, Ramree Island.
22nd February, 1945.

I have the honour to submit the following Report on Naval Operations in the Ramree Island Area from 19th January to 22nd February, 1945. These operations formed part of the strategic advance of the 15th Indian Corps down the Arakan coast with a view to securing the airfields on Ramree Island from which Fourteenth Army could be supplied on their advance on Rangoon, and operations could be mounted for the capture of that port by sea should it become necessary, and which in fact did prove the case.

Introduction.

2. The initial assault (Operation "Matador") by the 26th Indian Infantry Division, Major-General C.E.N. Lomax, C.B., C.B.E., D.S.O., M.C., and troops under his command, had taken place at 0942 on 21st January, 1945, after preliminary bombardment by the air forces.

3. The Assaulting Brigade, the 71st Indian Infantry Brigade, Brigadier R.C. Cottrell-Hill, O.B.E., M.C., and the "Follow Up" Brigade, the 4th Indian Infantry Brigade, Brigadier J.F.R Forman, had been landed under cover of R.A.F. aircraft and guns of the Fleet without meeting with much opposition On 26th January they were joined by the 36th Indian Infantry Brigade, Brigadier L.C. Thomas, D.S.O., O.B.E., M.C.

4. By 23rd January a firm bridgehead had been established at the north west extremity of Ramree Island. The Naval Officer in Charge, Lieutenant-Commander G.W.S. Goss, R.N.V.R., with Port Party Number 31 had set up his Headquarters on shore, and Kyaukpyu harbour was in the process of being developed as an anchorage. Moored mines had been found in the inner harbour on D day and were being swept by B.Y.M.S.[1] under command of Commander E.J.C Edwards, D.S.C., R.N.V.R., Commander M/S, Bay of Bengal. Sweeping operations were concluded on 24th January and the harbour declared clear of mines.

5. Captain E.T. Cooper, D.S.O., R.N., had, on Brigade level, carried out the duties of Senior Officer Assault Group during the landings and remained in charge of the build up and Ferry Service.

6. The Commander, 26th Indian Division, General Lomax, had disembarked on 21st January, with his staff and taken over control of military operations, which had passed from a Brigade Operation to a Battle on Divisional Scale.

7. In compliance with verbal instructions received from Rear-Admiral B.C.S. Martin, C.B.E., D.S.O., Flag Officer Force "W", I joined General Lomax at Kyaukpyu on the morning of 26th January, with a small Naval Staff, and with the title of Senior Officer, Advanced Force "W". Here in a "tumbledown" house, formerly occupied by the Japanese Military Staff, we were joined by Wing-Commander R. Smith, Royal Air Force, and established a Combined Head-quarters.

Narrative.
8. The Japanese had developed a strong defensive position guarding the beaches near Thames Point. Their main body was established near Ramree Town. A landing at Kyaukpyu was unexpected and tactical surprise was achieved.

9. As soon as our bridgehead was consolidated, the 71st Indian Infantry Brigade was ordered to advance rapidly southward down the west coast road, leaving the 4th Indian Infantry Brigade in defence of the Kyaukpyu Area.

10. The advance of the 71st Indian Infantry Brigade was supported by destroyers and sloops.

11. It was expected that the Japanese would fight a strong delaying action near Mount Peter and Black Hill, to enable their reinforcements to reach the Leiktaung area where a narrow defile, through which our troops must pass, offered a natural defensive position.

12. As events transpired, determined resistance in the Mount Peter – Black Hill area was not as protracted as expected and after some brisk fighting our troops drove the enemy off and passed quickly through the Leiktaung Gap and reached the Yan Bauk Chaung[2] on 26th January, where they were brought to a halt by a strong Japanese force entrenched on the south bank of the Chaung.

13. In the meantime Force WELLINGTON consisting of Royal Marines from the East Indies Fleet, with naval support under command of Rear-Admiral A.D. Read, Flag Officer Force 65, had occupied Cheduba Island on the 26th January (Operation "Sankey") without meeting any opposition.

14. On 30th January, Force WELLINGTON was relieved by the 2 AJMER Battalion Group from the 4th Indian Infantry Brigade (Force CACTUS). On the same day, the 8/13th Frontier Force Rifles Battalion Group of the 36th Indian Infantry Brigade (Force MARTIN), occupied Sagu Kyun (Operation "Pendant")

also without opposition, under cover of naval and air bombardment. The task of this Force was to establish a Naval Landing Craft Base as a springboard for combined landings on South Ramree Island.

15. On 1st February a company of the 8/13th Frontier Force Rifles from Force MARTIN landed without casualties on the south tip of Ramree Island, under cover of naval and air bombardment. The task of this company was to guard the entrance to the Kalemgdaung River.

16. It was the original intention of the Commander 15th Indian Corps, Lieutenant-General Sir A.F. Philip Christison, Bart, K.B.E., C.B., D.S.O., M.C., to capture only as much of Ramree Island as was necessary for the development of airfields to supply the 14th Army during the monsoon, and to launch at an early date a major operation against the mainland in the Taungup area mounted from Kyaukpyu.

17. On the 4th February, however, a directive was received from the Joint Force Commanders to the effect that the maintenance difficulties precluded the major operation against the mainland and the following operations were to be undertaken in lieu:-

(*a*) The whole of Ramree Island to be captured.
(*b*) Raids and such minor landings as could be supported administratively to be carried out on the mainland between Taungup and An Chaung with a view to facilitating the eventual capture of Taungup itself.

18. Further attempts by the 71st Indian Infantry Brigade to cross the Yan Bauk Chaung, paragraph 12, met with no success, in spite of heavy gun support from destroyers and from cruisers of Force 65. It was, therefore, necessary to review the situation in the light of the Joint Force Commanders' directive, and to devise another plan for defeating the enemy.

19. The possibility of an amphibious landing on the beaches on the south of the Yan Bauk Chaung was considered first of all. The idea, however, was rejected on the grounds that the beaches were strongly defended and believed to be mined. Surf conditions on the beaches were an added objection.

20. A solution was found in a decision to order the 71st Indian Infantry Brigade to advance north east towards Sane and outflank the Japanese positions south of the Yan Bauk Chaung, and then to attack Ramree Town from the north west. To implement this decision, part of the 4th Indian Infantry Brigade were ordered south into the Yan Bauk Chaung area.

21. This new move had Naval implications. While the 71st Indian Infantry Brigade had been operating near the coast, it had been possible to give them all the naval gun support they required. But now that the advance had turned inland, the enemy would soon pass out of range of H.M. Ships lying off the west coast of Ramree Island.

22. The Gates at the entrance to the Kalemgdaung River had already been opened by elements from the 36th Indian Infantry Brigade in their occupation of Sagu Kyun and the south tip of Ramree Island (paragraphs 14 and 15). A survey of the river had already been started in anticipation of a requirement to send destroyers into the river to give naval gun support to our troops advancing on Ramree Town.

23. On 4th February, reinforcements of 8/13th Frontier Force Rifles were landed on the southern end of Ramree Island, this time at Kyaukmmaw, (Operation "Mike"), and on the same day two destroyers, preceded by minesweepers, entered the Kaleingdaung River and took up bombarding positions off the Taraung and Ramree Chaungs.

24. By 7th February the outflanking movement of the 71st Indian Infantry Brigade had caused the Japanese to withdraw from their dominating position on the south bank of the Yan Bauk Chaung allowing the 4th Indian Infantry Brigade to cross the Chaung without difficulty, and advance in pursuit.

25. It was not long before Sane fell to the 71st Indian Infantry Brigade, and on the 8th February Ramree Town was captured.

26. A glance at the map in Appendix I [not published] will show that an interesting situation had developed. The bulk of the Japanese who survived the battles were now to the eastward of a line drawn between Sane and Ramree with remnants probably still in the southern part of the Island. To the Japanese there remained only two alternatives, to stand and fight or to escape from the island by water. They chose the latter alternative and in so doing met with disaster.

27. The best method of preventing the Japanese from escaping by boat to the east and the north east had for some time been the subject of close study by the Combined Staffs. The conclusion reached was that with the use of destroyers and all B.Y.M.S., M.Ls. L.C.S.(M) and L.C.A.,[3] the Navy could block effectively the Chaung exits from the Taraung Chaung to the Pakseik Taungmaw River in the east, and exits into the Mingaung Chaung and Pakseik Taungmaw River in the north east. The Army must look after the remainder.

28. The Combined Operation which followed, known as Operation "Block," commenced on 8th February, and was concluded on the 22nd February.

The Army covered the Chaung exits south of the Taraung Chaung by an advance north from Kyaukmmaw with the 36th Indian Infantry Brigade, they also occupied Kalebon to guard the Japanese escape routes north between Sane and the Mingaung Chaung. R.A.F. Fighters straffed boat concentrations and provided cover. Thus the Army and R.A.F. drove the Japanese off the Island into the mangrove swamps where they were successfully dealt with by the Navy.

29. The Navy established their blocks as described in paragraph 27 by placing the Landing Craft (L.C.A. and L.C.S. (M)), camouflaged as far as possible with

foliage, in ambush at the mouth of the Chaungs, while the M.L.s and B.Y.M.S. were used as back stops. Initially there were two Naval blocks known as the North Block (along the course of the Mingaung Chaung and the Pakseik Taung-maw River) and the South Block (from Tan Chaung to the Taraung Chaung).

30. As operations developed and more intelligence of the enemy's intentions was received the South Block was moved to form an East Block (from the lower Zareik Chaung to the upper Didokbank) and later again moved to form the Thanzit Block (from the Wonkpit Chaung to the Awlebyin River). In the later stages the Chaungs were illuminated at night and a greater degree of mobility of craft was introduced.

31. The frontage covered in these operations was considerable. Exits from the mangroves were not confined to those shown on the maps. Hundreds of Chaungs and waterways were found to be in existence, all suitable for native boats. Trees with thick foliage growing down to the water's edge provided ample cover for a small boat. At high water much of the mangrove was flooded, allowing lateral movement from one Chaung to another. The rise and fall of the tide, accentuated by conditions of shallow water and mud near the banks, made concealment of Landing Craft difficult. When the Chaung blocking started the moon was in its first quarter and the tide approaching springs. All these conditions were to the advantage of the enemy.

32. Disadvantages to the Japanese lay in the indescribable horrors of the man-grove swamps. Dark during the day as well as during the night, acres of thick impenetrable forest; miles of deep black mud, mosquitoes, scorpions, flies and weird insects by the billion and – worst of all – crocodiles. No food, no drinking water to be obtained anywhere. It can hardly be possible that in their decision to quit the Island the Japanese could have been fully aware of the appalling con-ditions which prevailed. It proved to be beyond even their endurance to exist for more than a few days. Prisoners taken out of the mangroves during the operations were found to be semi-dehydrated and in a very low physical condition.

33. The Minor Landing Craft crews with Army machine gun units embarked also had a hard time. It was found possible to relieve the Army personnel about every four days but, owing to shortage of spare crews, many of the Royal Marines and Sailors had to remain in their craft for the whole 14 days of this operation.

34. The provision of these widespread units with food, water, cigarettes, etc., and their craft with fuel and repair facilities, presented a formidable administrative problem. Largely by the allocation of a B.Y.M.S. or an L.C.I.(L) as a "Mother Ship" to each block and by the co-operation of the Army "Q" Staff, these diffi-culties were overcome and after the first few days the standard of rations became, on the whole, quite acceptable.

35. Thus concluded the operations for the capture of Ramree Island. Of the 1,200 to 1,500 Japanese in occupation on the day of landing, only a few escaped. The

remainder were either killed in battle or drowned in the mangrove swamps. Only twenty prisoners were taken in spite of all efforts of persuasion towards the close of Operation "Block", when many Japanese troops, without hope of relief or escape, had reached the final stages of exhaustion.

Conclusion.

36. The Naval "set-up" on Ramree Island was very satisfactory. Senior Officer Advanced Force "W" and Staff devoted their attentions to the Planning of Operations, the control of H.M. Ships and Craft, and to co-operation with the Army and the R.A.F. The Senior Officer Assault Group, Captain E.T. Cooper, D.S.O., Royal Navy, and his Staff were fully employed in the execution of the Operations, the maintenance of craft, and the training and supervision of their crews.

37. Co-operation with the 26th Indian Infantry Division, under the able leadership of General Lomax, worked very well indeed. It is no exaggeration to say that throughout the period of our stay on the Island no moves in battle were ordered by General Lomax without the knowledge of the Naval Staff. Similarly, the proper employment of H.M. Ships and Craft was often the subject of joint consideration.

38. This excellent co-operation was made easy by the fact that all three Services worked together under the same roof, used the same mess, and shared the same camp. General Lomax and his staff were always most cooperative and often visited ships and craft employed in support of the Army. The R.A.F. also co-operated fully and effectively.

39. This satisfactory state of affairs is reflected in the following signal received from General Christison, the 15th Corps Commander, on occasion of Ramree Island being declared free of enemy organised resistance:-

> "Congratulations to you all and especially 71st Indian Infantry Brigade and Naval Forces on liquidation of the Garrison of Ramree.
> I have been most impressed by the soundness of your joint planning and the gallant show by all ranks and ratings in execution. Well done."

The following congratulatory message was also received from General Christison:-

> "Hearty congratulations to all officers and ratings on the splendid success of Blocking Operations. You have done good work."

40. The contribution made by destroyers in support of the Army was an important factor in the operations. A total of 64 shoots were carried out, 35 with F.O.B. observation in direct support of the leading Infantry, and seven with Air O.P. observation. Communications with the F.O.Bs. were good throughout, and in addition to the engagement of targets, a great deal of valuable information was passed back in a steady stream from F.O.Bs. via the destroyers, to Combined Headquarters at Kyaukpyu.

41. The standard of gunnery in destroyers was high. Great credit is especially due to H.M.S. PATHFINDER, Lieutenant-Commander J.F. Hallifax, Royal Navy, for their excellent shooting and overall contribution to the success of the Operations.

42. Commander R.W.W. Ashby, D.S.C., R.N.V.R., Senior Officer Arakan Coastal Forces deserves recognition for his share in the very fine performance put up by his M.L.s. Also Commander E.J.C. Edwards, D.S.C., R.N.V.R., Commander M/S, Bay of Bengal, for leadership and devotion to duty in command of the B.Y.M.S.

43. Special mention should be made of Captain E.T. Cooper, D.S.O., Royal Navy, who, as Senior Officer Assault Group, was responsible for the successful execution of all the Combined Operations described in this report.

44. On the Staff side, the work of Lieutenant-Commander R.M.P. Williamson, Royal Navy, in particular, was very valuable.

(Signed) ERIC BUSH,
Captain, Royal Navy.

Notes
1. B.Y.M.S. = British Yacht Minesweeper.
2. Chaung = the local name for the innumerable narrow tidal channels or waterways intersecting the low lying, jungle-covered, Burmese coastal plain.
3. M.L. = Motor Launch.
   L.C.S. (M) = Landing Craft Support, medium size.
   L.C.A. = Landing Craft Assault.

4

LIEUTENANT-GENERAL SIR OLIVER LEESE, DESPATCH ON OPERATIONS IN BURMA, 12 NOVEMBER 1944 TO 15 AUGUST 1945

THURSDAY, 12 APRIL, 1951

The War Office, 1951.

The following Despatch was submitted to the Secretary of State for War on the 4th *February,* 1947, *by LIEUTENANT-GENERAL SIR OLIVER LEESE, Bart., K.C.B., C.B.E., D.S.O., Commander-in-Chief, Allied Land Forces, South-East Asia.*

INTRODUCTION

1. This Despatch covers the period from the12th November, 1944, on which date I assumed the appointment of Commander-in-Chief, Allied Land Forces, South-East Asia, to the 15th August, 1945, when the Japanese surrendered and when I relinquished my appointment. I have included the planning for subsequent operations, as it was initiated and carried on during the period under consideration. But these plans are given in outline only, because their execution is outside the period of my command and because the Japanese capitulation caused many modifications of the basic plan.

I have divided my Despatch into three parts. Part I is concerned with the course of operations and the planning and strategy which determined them. In Part II I have gone into some detail of the administrative aspect, which in this campaign assumed such importance that it justifies this separate treatment. In Part III I have given some appreciations of the contributions made by those who took part in the campaign. It may be that, for the general reader, a perusal of Parts I and III will suffice to produce an adequate overall picture, but for the military student the importance of the administrative side of the campaign needs special emphasis.

Finally, I have attached a table of contents of the Despatch and two other Appendices to which reference is made in the body of the Despatch.

PART I
NARRATIVE OF OPERATIONS
SECTION I (paras. 2–18)
THE SITUATION ON TAKING OVER COMMAND

Location of my H.Q.: Constitution of the command: Note on the topography and climate of Burma: The task: Strategic plans already in existence: The new directive.

---

2. I took over 11 Army Group from General Sir George Giffard on the 12th November, 1944, with the new title of Commander-in-Chief, Allied Land Forces, South-East Asia. This appointment had just been created following the decision to place the American and Chinese troops in South-East Asia under my control. Since the 20th June, 1944, after the capture of Kamaing (in the Mogaung Valley), Northern Combat Area Command had been under the direct operational control of the Supreme Allied Commander (Admiral The Lord Louis Mount-batten, later Earl Mountbatten of Burma). This arrangement had its origin in the refusal of General J.W. Stilwell, who in addition to commanding Northern Combat Area Command was Deputy Supreme Allied Commander, to serve in a subordinate capacity to the Commander-in-Chief, 11 Army Group, although he had agreed to act under the operational control of the Commander, Fourteenth Army, for a limited period, that is, until the capture of Kamaing. When General D.I. Sultan, General Stilwell's successor, came under my command on the 12th November, a difficult arrangement came to an end. An increment of United States staff officers under Brigadier-General T.F. Wessels and Brigadier-General R.T. Maddocks was added to my Headquarters to provide adequate American representation.

On taking over, I received my first Directive from the Supreme Allied Commander.

3. My Advanced Headquarters were in the process of moving from Delhi to Barrackpore, where they opened on the 1st December, 1944. Main Headquarters, Allied Land Forces, South-East Asia, at the insistence of the Supreme Allied Commander, were at Kandy where the Supreme Allied Commander and the Air Commander-in-Chief were located, while the Naval Commander-in-Chief was nearby at Colombo.

It was not, however, possible for me to exercise command from Kandy of an Army Group which was actively engaged on three widely separated fronts, 15 Indian Corps in Arakan, Fourteenth Army in the Chin Hills, west of the Chindwin River, and the British/Chinese/American forces comprising the American "Northern Combat Area Command" in Northern Burma. Even from Barrackpore I was to find that it took me 1,500 miles flying to visit the three fronts. Despite therefore the disadvantages of being separated by so great a dis-tance from the Headquarters of the Supreme Allied Commander and from those of his two other Commanders-in-Chief, it was necessary for me to base myself on my Advanced Headquarters at Barrackpore, which was in fact by far the larger echelon, where all the day-to-day executive business of the Headquarters was carried on. Actually Barrackpore had certain other advantages. First, Head-quarters, Eastern Air Command, were located only a mile or two down the Hooghli. I was thus enabled to maintain that close touch with General G.E. Stratemeyer which was essential to our joint operations while the battle for Burma was in progress. Secondly, I was in a good position to visit Delhi, the Headquarters of the India Base through which all my supplies and personnel had to pass. And, lastly, I was well placed to visit formations training under G.H.Q., India, which had been allocated to my future operations, and in particular those at the Combined Training Centres at Cocanada and near Bombay.

My Main Headquarters at Kandy was in reality a strong liaison section under Major-General I.S.O. Playfair, designed to maintain close contact with Headquarters, Supreme Allied Commander, South-East Asia, and the other Commanders-in-Chief.

4. On the 12th November, when I took over, my command consisted of Four-teenth Army, made up of 4, 15 and 33 Indian Corps, the Northern Combat Area Command and Ceylon Army Command. In addition there were certain forma-tions in India, which although not under my command, were allocated for my future operations.

In Fourteenth Army (Lieutenant-General Sir William Slim), 4 Indian Corps (Lieutenant-General Sir Geoffry A.P. Scoones) consisted of 19 Indian Division and 23 Indian Division, which was in the process of being withdrawn to India. 33 Indian Corps (Lieutenant-General Sir Montagu G.N. Stopford), consisted of 2 British Division, 5 and 20 Indian Divisions, 11 (East African) Division, the Lushai Brigade, 268 Indian (Lorried) Brigade, and 254 Indian Tank Brigade. 7 Indian Division was in the Kohima area and was destined for 4 Corps. 255 Indian Tank Brigade at Imphal and 28 (East African) Brigade were also under Fourteenth Army. Fifteenth Indian Corps (Lieutenant-General Sir A.F. Philip Christison) consisted of 25 and 26 Indian Divisions, 81 and 82 (West African) Divisions, 50 Indian Tank Brigade and 3 Commando Brigade.

Northern Combat Area Command (Lieutenant-General Dan I. Sultan) con-sisted of First and Sixth Chinese Armies, 36 British Division, and 5332 U.S. ("Mars") Brigade. First Chinese Army (General Sun Li Jen) was composed of 30, 38, and 50 Chinese Divisions, while the Sixth (General Liao Yo Hsiang) was composed of 14 and 22 Chinese Divisions. The Mars Brigade (Brigadier-General J.P. Willy) was in fact equivalent to a United States light division and consisted of 475 United States Infantry Regiment, 124 United States Cavalry Regiment, and one Chinese regiment. In addition Northern Combat Area Command possessed one Chinese tank brigade.

Ceylon Army Command (Lieutenant-General H.E. de R. Wetherall) consisted of a few locally enlisted battalions and Base units, and also the small garrisons in the island bases of Addu Atoll and Diego Garcia.

In India, assigned to my operations, but not under my command, were Special Force, made up of 14, 16 and 23 Infantry Brigades, 77 and 111 Indian Infantry Brigades and 3 (West African) Infantry Brigade, which together formed six Long-Range Penetration Groups, 50 Parachute Brigade, two tank regiments (25 Dragoons and 149 R.A.C.), and certain small units. 17 Indian Division was in India in G.H.Q. Reserve and not under my command.

5. In mid-November, a reorganization of the chain of command took place, which had been planned by General Giffard with the object of freeing the Commander, Fourteenth Army, from the control of operations in Arakan, and from the responsibility of administering the long and difficult lines of communication in Assam. In this way he would be enabled to concentrate his full attention on the coming offensive across the Chindwin River into Central Burma. Accordingly on the 15th November, Lines of Communication Command was formed under Major-General G.W. Symes, with its H.Q. at Comilla. It comprised 202 L. of C. Area (H.Q., Gauhati), consisting of four sub-areas and the Fort Hertz Area, and 404 L. of C. Area of four sub-areas; it included a very great number of Base and L. of C. units. The policy was to be that the rear boundaries of Fourteenth Army and 15 Corps would be adjusted as the progress of operations allowed, in order to free them from rearward responsibilities. On the 16th November, 15 Corps was separated from Fourteenth Army and came direct under my command. I thus had under my command three major formations in contact with the enemy, 15 Corps, Fourteenth Army and Northern Combat Area Command, with the L. of C. Command in the rear up to the boundary between South-East Asia Command (S.E.A.C.) and India Command.

6. Before explaining my task and the existing strategical plans, I propose to say a few words on the topography and climate of Burma, which exercised a preponderating influence on all operations there.

The only natural approach to the interior of Burma is through Rangoon, and thence by road, rail or river to Mandalay. We, unfortunately, had to re-enter the country from the north, and for this there are only two routes. The first is from Dimapur (Manipur Road Railhead), then south through the mountains *via* Kohima and Imphal, then southeast through thick jungle hill country to Tamu, thence south down the notoriously unhealthy Kabaw Valley to Kalemyo, across the Chindwin River and then through gradually improving country to Shwebo in the dry belt. The road from Tamu to Shwebo was only a fair-weather track quite unsuited as the main road artery of an army. The other northern road approach was *via* Ledo, and, at the time we are discussing, it was under construction, under American control, as a land route to Myitkyina to link up with the Burma Road.

The only route from the Arakan coast into Central Burma other than a rough foot track through An, was a fair-weather road of small traffic-carrying capacity from Taungup to Prome. Owing to its situation and limitations we were not able to use it until after the capture of Rangoon.

7. Between Eastern Bengal and Central Burma lie the Lushai and Chin Hills, which extend south as the Arakan Yomas and northeast as the barrier between Burma and Assam. They consist of a mass of parallel sharp ridges, running roughly north and south, with many peaks rising to heights of 6,000–9,000 feet. The highest peak of the Arakan Yomas, Mount Victoria, is just over 10,000 feet. These mountains are covered with intensely thick jungle and form a complete military barrier between Central Burma and the Eastern Bengal and Arakan coast, with exception of the two tracks mentioned above.

In the centre of Burma, and containing Mandalay and Meiktila, lies the "Dry Belt," which consists of flat and open country. It has been developed, and an all-weather road system exists, for example, connecting Shwebo, Mandalay, Meiktila, Myingyan and Kyaukpadaung.

It was not until we reached this area that we could expect to fight the Japanese under conditions favourable to our superiority in armour, fire-power and mobility. The Arakan coast is discussed in more detail in the part of the Despatch which deals with the Arakan operations (Sec. IX). It suffices to say that immensely thick jungle runs down to the coast from the hills, the only clearings being the settlements. Suitable beaches for landing operations are very rare and most of the water-ways, especially between Akyab and Taungup, are hemmed in by dense mangrove forests.

8. The climate of Burma, from an operational point of view, is dominated by the arrival of the summer monsoon. The exceptionally severe monsoon rains in Arakan virtually stop all movement by land between May and the middle of December. Elsewhere the rainfall is generally very heavy during the monsoon except in the central dry belt. The monsoon has the effect, too, of raising a swell in the Bay of Bengal from mid-March onwards, until, in early May, days suitable for landing operations are very rare indeed. The monsoon conditions in the mountainous jungle areas make land operations difficult and exceptionally unpleasant, while flying conditions over them become hazardous in the extreme.

The question of health will be discussed in detail with the medical aspect in the Administrative part of this Despatch. It is enough to say here that without modern methods of maintaining health, suppressive drugs, and the discipline required with them, the campaign could not have been fought.

9. Finally, before leaving the subject of topography I make no apology for drawing attention to the huge distances in this theatre. Our road L. of C. from Kohima to Mandalay was 527 miles long, and from Mandalay by road to Rangoon was a further 433 miles.

10. The first task assigned to me in my Directive was to protect the air route to China, to open the Burma Road *via* Myitkyina, Bhamo and Wanting, to Kunming, and to protect the airfields at Myitkyina. I was also to destroy the Japanese Army in Burma, with the proviso that these operations must in no way interfere with my responsibilities for the protection and opening of the Ledo/

Burma Road and the air routes to China. I realised at once, however, that I could do nothing permanently to ensure the safety of the air route or the Ledo/Burma Road until I had defeated decisively in battle the main Japanese forces in Burma.

11. The strategical plans which I took over on arrival were as follows.

Operation "Capital" was aimed at the re-conquest of Central Burma. It envisaged an advance *via* Kalewa with Fourteenth Army into the Mandalay Plain, with the first objective Ye-U and Shwebo, which are both situated in the more open country in the dry belt, and, secondly, Mandalay. Northern Combat Area Command was to conform in this by advancing south to the general line Mongmit – Lashio. The primary object of this operation was to bring the Japanese to battle in country where we could exploit our superiority in firepower, armour and mobility, and to provide an "anvil" for the eventual invasion of Burma from the Rangoon end, since it was considered that the clearing of Burma from the north alone was impracticable.

Operation "Dracula" was the invasion of Rangoon by air and sea. This operation was originally planned for the middle of March, 1945. While I was in the United Kingdom in early October, after leaving Eighth Army, the Chiefs of Staff decided that this operation could not take place, since the resources, principally in formations which it was hoped to send from Europe, could not be released. The original plans envisaged a seven division operation, including one airborne division and three air-transported, the remainder for sea assault and follow-up. The requirements from Europe were two Corps Headquarters, one airborne division, and three other divisions, one of which was to replace the G.H.Q., India, reserve division. Although, however, it was not going to take place in the Spring of 1945, it was still intended that a similar operation would take place after the 1945 monsoon. The airborne and air-transported part of the operation, which was considered essential owing to the difficulties of a purely seaborne assault on Rangoon, was to be mounted in the Chittagong area and a big programme of building of fair-weather airstrips, with all the necessary ancillaries such as fuel installations, had been approved. In order that these could be ready for a post-1945-monsoon assault, I was directed to continue the construction required. These pre-monsoon preparations were naturally at the cost of resources I wanted for my current operations.

The scale and concept of Dracula in its original form should be borne in mind when the way in which Rangoon was captured is described at the end of this part of the Despatch. The difference between the projected operation of early October, 1944, and the actual operation of May, 1945, is the true measure of the development of the operational situation in Burma between those dates.

12. As soon as it was known that the air and sea invasion of Rangoon (Dracula) could not be carried out before the 1945 monsoon, a fresh operation (Romulus) was planned in Arakan. The situation there was unsatisfactory, as we had four divisions locked up by the Japanese threat of an advance up the Kaladan Valley. This threat, which was by a force much inferior in numbers to our own, could

best be liquidated by the capture of Akyab Island, Myebon and Minbya. With this achieved, the Arakan garrison of four divisions could be reduced to one of four brigades during the coming monsoon, and valuable divisions thereby released for further operations, thus partially offsetting the non-arrival of formations from Europe.

13. To recapitulate in brief, the tasks of the formations under my command at the time I took over were as follows.

Northern Combat Area Command to recapture and secure the trace of the Burma Road from its junction with the new road from Ledo and to hold the Myitkyina air bases.

Fourteenth Army to get into the dry belt of Central Burma in order to defeat the main Japanese armies and thus ensure permanent security to the Ledo/Burma Road, to develop airfields there, and to provide an " anvil" for the invasion of Rangoon after the 1945 monsoon.

Fifteenth Corps in Arakan to liquidate the remaining Japanese threat in that sector by a limited offensive to just beyond Akyab, in order that formations could be withdrawn to take part in post-monsoon offensive operations against Rangoon or elsewhere.

14. On the 4th November, eight days before I assumed command, the Supreme Allied Commander had issued an Operational Directive to his three Commanders-in-Chief, regarding an offensive in Arakan, instructing them jointly to initiate the planning, and direct the execution of the following tasks.

An advance by land was to be made down the Mayu Peninsula and the Kalapanzin and Kaladan Valleys with the object of clearing the area north of the general line Foul Point – Kudaung Island – Minbya. This advance was to begin as soon as possible.

An amphibious assault on Akyab Island was to be launched as early as possible in 1945, with the aim of clearing the island by the end of January. The area north of the line Akyab – Minbya was to be consolidated but no exploitation was to take place south of Myebon without the Supreme Allied Commander's authority.

On the 9th November, General Giffard had issued an Operation Instruction to the Commander, 15 Corps, defining his task in Arakan in accordance with the above Directive.

15. A week after I had assumed my new Command, the Supreme Allied Commander issued a Planning Directive (19th November) in which he ordered plans to be made for the execution of "the stages of operation Capital (the plan for the advance into Central Burma) necessary to the security of existing air supply routes and the opening of land communications with China and the exploitation of Capital throughout 1945 as far as may be possible without prejudicing the preparation for the execution of Dracula (the plan for the amphibious assault on Rangoon) at the very earliest date possible after the end of the monsoon in 1945." (I quote the actual words of the directive.)

After stating that the plans for operations to secure the general line Kalewa – Shwebo – Mogok – Lashio (Phase II of operation Capital) had received his approval, the Supreme Allied Commander further directed me in conjunction with the Allied Air Commander-in-Chief, to initiate and co-ordinate plans for the execution of Phase III, with the object of securing the general line Pakokku – Mandalay – Maymyo – Lashio.

I was also directed "to bear in mind the paramount importance of destroying the maximum number of Japanese during this Phase, so as to prevent their withdrawal to South Burma and to facilitate subsequent exploitation." This was fully in accordance with my own views since I had already decided in my own mind that the Mandalay Plain, for the reasons I have already explained, should be the graveyard of the Japanese armies. I may add that I found when I met General Slim that he had long been of the same opinion and that his future strategy was directed to this end.

16. Another Directive which I received about this time (18th November) informed me that the British Chiefs of Staff had ordered that the Cocos Islands, lying midway between Ceylon and Australia and some 1,500 miles from each, were to be developed early in 1945 as an air staging point for heavy aircraft in transit. I was called on to provide for the land defence of these islands, in consultation with the Naval and Air Commanders-in-Chief; the target date given for the completion of the development of the islands being the 1st June, 1945.

I may add here that the Army component of the garrison eventually decided on was one battalion, one Coast and two A.A. batteries, and certain Engineer and Pioneer companies. The disembarkation of troops and stores commenced on the 25th March, 1945, and was completed without enemy interference.

17. There is one other project that arose during the period under consideration. In a Directive issued by the Supreme Allied Commander on the 3rd December, 1944, he instructed his Commanders-in-Chief to plan an operation for the capture of the Hastings Harbour Island Group, which lies off Victoria Point, the southern tip of Burma. The object of the operation was to establish an advanced naval and air base for the exploitation of our naval and air superiority, to assist operations in Burma and to prepare for an early advance on Malaya. I represented to the Supreme Allied Commander that we had insufficient force to do this operation in addition to the Arakan and Fourteenth Army operations, and planning was suspended.

18. I have already mentioned in paragraph 11 that a number of formations were due from Europe, but that this redeployment had been postponed. Two aspects of this deserve mention at once as they were problems which remained during the whole period on which I am reporting.

The first problem was the lack of sufficient formations with which to affect the relief of battle-worn troops. General Giffard, with the help of the Commander-in-Chief, India, had done much to improve the situation, but it was still acute.

It was only possible to spare one division at a time for rehabilitation in India. Moreover, the time and space factor, including the limited number of transport aircraft available in the theatre made this process necessarily slow. To send a division from Burma to India, from the point of view of time and availability, was equivalent to moving such a formation from Italy to rest and refit in Palestine. Further, I could not afford to send more than one division outside the Fourteenth Army area. Reorganizations for specific tasks and reliefs were achieved by resting formations within the Army area. But most of the formations under my command had been in forward areas for six months – some much longer. Lack of trained reinforcements, especially in British personnel, made it difficult to keep some of them up to full establishment.

The second problem concerned the redeployment of formations from Europe. This scheme, known as "Minerva," involved the large-scale transfer of formations, units and cadres initially to the command of General Headquarters, India, for subsequent employment in operations in S.E.A.C. Although it was not implemented to any extent during the period covered by this Despatch, it was a matter under very active consideration the whole time. The principal difficulty was the time lag. In the case of an Indian division in Italy, it would be eight and a half months from the time the order to withdraw from Italy was given to the date of readiness for operations in S.E.A.C.: for a British division from North-West Europe the corresponding delay was eight months. Moreover, the formations could not at this stage be linked up with a particular projected future operation but had to build up a balanced force suitable for any future operations in the theatre. The composition of the force table and the necessary priority of arrival in India were matters of close co-operation between General Headquarters, India, and my Headquarters.

SECTION II (paras. 19–27)

THE OPERATIONAL SITUATION IN NOVEMBER

The failure of the Japanese invasion of Spring, 1944: The importance of the 1944 monsoon operations: The state of the enemy, his strength and dispositions: Relative strengths: Our assets of sea and air power: Air supply.

---

19. In February and March, 1944, Fourteenth Army (15 Corps) had decisively beaten the Japanese in Arakan. This was followed by our outstanding victory in the Kohima – Imphal battle (May–July). Thus the offensive, which the Japanese had launched in the Spring with the object of seizing the gateway to India, had completely failed. They had suffered tremendous casualties, estimated at 100,000 during their offensive and their subsequent retreat during the monsoon, when privation and exposure took a toll to which the thousands of enemy bodies counted by our advancing troops bore witness.

20. During the monsoon, Fourteenth Army and Northern Combat Area Command both exploited success to the full. I wish to emphasise the importance of

these monsoon operations. In the Kohima – Imphal battle we had inflicted a crushing defeat on the enemy and our continuous pressure throughout the rainy season had kept him on the run, allowing him no respite. This was largely due to the tenacity of 5 Indian Division (Major-General D.F.W. Warren) and of 11 (East African) Division (Major-General C.C. Fowkes) which refused to be daunted by appalling conditions of weather and terrain.

21. My problem, which was largely an administrative one owing to the paucity of communications, was how to maintain the impetus of our advance until we could bring the enemy to battle on ground of our own choosing. Moreover, to be fully effective, this impetus had to be maintained over a broad front. It appeared likely that the enemy, having failed to stop us west of the Chindwin, would attempt to hold the Shwebo – Mandalay area; and that his intention would be to reorganize and reinforce his armies behind a covering line, with the view ultimately of passing again to the offensive. His forward covering troops were disposed well north of the general line Lashio – Shwebo – Myingyan – Akyab.

22. The location of Japanese formations at the end of November was as follows:-

In the coastal sector, two divisions (the 54th and 55th), comprising Twenty-eighth Japanese Army, were distributed between Maungdaw and Bassein. The enemy, however, appeared to be withdrawing from the Paletwa area in the Kaladan, leaving only small detachments north of the Khawei – Paletwa line.[1]

Facing Fourteenth Army were three Japanese divisions, the 15th, 31st and 33rd, all much reduced in strength but with fresh drafts arriving. 15 Division was based on the Wuntho – Pinlebu area, and had recently withdrawn its outlying detachments from the area west of the Zibyutaung Range. 33 Division had been forced back east of the Chindwin; it seemed probable that this Division would fight a series of delaying actions along the Kaing – Ye-U road, but there was as yet no indication that they would attempt a firm stand on any particular line. The depleted 31st Division was in Fifteenth Army reserve in the Ye-U area.

53 Division was in the Naba – Katha area. This Division, together with the 15th, 31st and 33rd mentioned above, comprised the Japanese Fifteenth Army. 14 Tank Regiment, which had suffered heavily in the retreat, was believed to be refitting in the Shwebo area.

Facing Northern Combat Area Command and the Chinese Expeditionary Force, there were 56, 2 and 18 Japanese Divisions, disposed between Bhamo and the Salween River. These formed Thirty-third Army, but 2 Division was only on loan and was to return to Burma Area Army reserve.

The Japanese Burma Area Army reserve consisted of 49 Division, in the Pegu Area. The Japanese were known to be particularly sensitive to the threat of sea-borne attack, and our deception schemes were designed to increase their fears. It was therefore unlikely that they would move troops from South to North Burma unless the situation there became critical. This also applied to 72 Independent Mixed Brigade at Moulmein.

In addition to the formations listed above, the Japanese had about 100,000 L. of C. troops. The fighting qualities which these administrative units displayed against General Wingate's brigades earlier in the year proved them to be a factor which could not be ignored. Experience in the Pacific theatre had shown that Japanese base troops were capable of stubborn and suicidal defence. The enemy also had at their disposal two "Indian National Army" divisions, each 6,000 strong, and seven battalions of the "Burma National Army." Both these forces had a considerable potential nuisance value.

To summarise, therefore, the enemy had, in November, ten divisions and two independent mixed brigades in Burma, disposed as follows:- 33 Army (three divisions) facing Northern Combat Area Command in the northeast; 15 Army (four divisions) in the centre extending from the Railway Corridor, through the Zibyutaung Range, to the River Irrawaddy: 28 Army (two divisions) in the coastal sector; and a division in reserve.

23. The situation of our own forces during the latter part of November was briefly as follows.

In 15 Corps, in Arakan, 25 Indian Division (Major-General G.N. Wood) was in contact with the enemy in the general area of Maungdaw and the Maungdaw – Buthidaung road, the eastern portion of which, including Buthidaung, was in enemy hands. Our troops were actively engaged in clearing features of tactical importance prior to the coming main offensive in December.

26 Indian Division (Major-General C.E.N. Lomax) had one brigade forward at the head of the Kalapanzin River, in the area of Bawli, Taung and Goppe Bazaars, and two brigades in reserve. It was in process of being relieved by the newly-arrived 82 (West African) Division (Major-General G. Mc I.S. Bruce) and was about to concentrate for training at Chittagong, in preparation for the sea-borne assault on Akyab in February.

In the upper Kaladan, elements of 81 (West African) Division (Major-General F.J. Loftus-Tottenham) had by-passed the enemy positions in the Paletwa area (Paletwa itself was found deserted on the 17th November) and were advancing south down the Pi Chaung. Their patrols, on the 30th November, were within two miles of Kaladan village, which lies some eight miles south-south-east of Paletwa.

3 Commando Brigade was concentrated at Teknaf and was responsible for the security of the Naf Peninsula.

50 Indian Tank Brigade had not concentrated by tine 30th (November, and 22 (East African) Brigade did not arrive till the end of December.

33 Corps was leading the advance of Fourteenth Army, with 5 Indian Division on the right, and 11 (East African) Division on the left. 5 Indian Division, which had advanced *via* Tiddim, was concentrating in the Kalemyo area prior to being relieved. (Kalemyo itself had been entered by the leading elements of 11 (East African) Division on the 15th November.) Between the 1st July and the 30th November, 5 Indian Division had killed fifteen of the enemy for every one of

its own men killed. The actual casualty figures, excluding the Lushai Brigade area, and only including fresh bodies and wounded which the enemy were actually seen to remove, were:-

	Killed.	Wounded.	Missing.	P.O.W.
Japanese	1316	533	—	53
5 Indian Division	88	293	22	—

11 (East African) Division was advancing on Kalewa from the west and north. Two brigades moving along the Myitha Gorge, supported by tanks, were meeting strong opposition some six miles west of Kalewa. The third brigade was advancing south down both banks of the Chindwin and had reached a point seven miles north of the town by the 30th November.

2 British Division and 20 Indian Division, which had been in rest areas further north, had begun to concentrate forward, the former in the Yazagyo area and the latter about Htinzin. (Yazagyo and Htinzin lie in the Kabaw Valley, about 26 and 35 miles north of Kalemyo respectively.)

The Lushai Brigade formed an Intelligence screen on the right flank of 33 Corps. By the end of November, the Brigade had cleared the area to the south of 5 Indian Division and was successfully harassing the enemy as far east as the Myittha River, with patrols penetrating as far south as Tilin.

Headquarters, 4 Corps, had reopened at Imphal on the 1st November, after a period of rest in India. On the 6th November, the Corps had been ordered to detail a brigade of 19 Indian Division (Major-General T.W. Rees) to capture Pinlebu and reconnoitre routes from the Chindwin eastwards to the railway, with a view to the move of larger forces on the general axis Sittaung – Indaw. Early reports received from both ground and air forces indicated that such a move would be feasible, and, on the 18th November, 4 Corps were allowed to direct the whole of 19 Indian Division, which had moved forward from Imphal to the Tamu – Sittaung area, on to Pinlebu. In addition to reconnoitring routes east of this place, 19 Indian Division was given the task of discovering whether the roads from Pinlebu southwards could be opened for a further overland advance. By this means, coupled with the operations of 33 Corps, the possibility of completing Phase II of Capital without airborne operations was to be investigated. The two leading brigades of 19 Indian Division began to cross the Chindwin at Sittaung and Thaungdut in the third week of November and, by the end of the month, had occupied Nanbon and Paungbyin against minor opposition.

Meanwhile, in the middle of November, 4 Corps took over 268 Indian Brigade – an independent formation composed of five battalions – from 33 Corps. The leading elements of this Brigade were, at this time, disposed on the east bank of the Chindwin, opposite Sittaung. 7 Indian Division (Major-General F.W. Messervy) which was also to form part of 4 Corps, was still resting in the Kohima area. It was not to be committed across the Chindwin, as, at this period, it was expected it might be required later to be flown into the Shwebo area as a reinforcement.

In Northern Combat Area Command, 36 British Division (Major-General F.W. Festing) on the 30th November captured Pinwe, six miles north of the important railway junction of Naba, after the village had been fiercely defended by the enemy for over two weeks. The Japanese left behind many dead and much equipment. 38 Chinese Division had occupied Myothit, 16 miles north-east of Bhamo, and pushing on had encircled Bhamo itself and the air-strip east of the town, despite strong enemy counter-attacks. Other Chinese troops were advancing down the Bhamo – Namhkam and Bhamo – Mongmit roads.

24. Bearing in mind the undoubted fighting qualities of the Japanese soldier, and the fact that the enemy was operating on interior lines, his strength of ten and two-third divisions (with auxiliary troops) appeared formidable. The question was how much of this force could be concentrated against Fourteenth Army, or, in other words, how many divisions we could force the enemy to employ against Northern Combat Area Command and in Arakan, in order to weaken this concentration.

Northern Combat Area Command comprised 5332 ("Mars") Brigade, which was the equivalent of an American light division, and five Chinese divisions. The latter had little administrative tail, as the Americans provided much of the administration, and were smaller than Indian divisions. They also varied a good deal in their state of training. While it was unlikely that the Japanese could be induced to send more troops to this front, provided that the pressure by Northern Combat Area Command did not weaken, they might at least be expected not to withdraw any substantial force from it. There were two enemy divisions in the coastal sector, including Bassein. It was hoped that, in spite of the advantages of terrain and communications which the Japanese defence enjoyed, they would not be able to reduce this force by more than a regiment or two. In the south of Burma, our deception schemes were framed with the object of tying down the garrison there, which amounted to rather less than two divisions.

Thus I hoped that Fourteenth Army might not be opposed by a force greater than five Japanese divisions, one independent mixed brigade, a tank regiment and approximately 50,000 L. of C. and auxiliary troops.

25. The Commander, Fourteenth Army, had at his disposal six and two-third divisions (2 British Division, 5, 7, 17, 19 and 20 Indian Divisions), 268 Indian Brigade, 28 (East African) Brigade, and two Indian tank brigades (254th and 255th). But our transportation resources, air and road, were limited and it appeared impossible to maintain more than four and two-third divisions and two tank brigades beyond the Chindwin.

To launch an offensive, across a great river (the Chindwin) and with precarious communications, with only four and two-third divisions against five and one-third, even though some of the latter had been badly mauled, was to take a risk. But it was a calculated risk. Our troops had already shown themselves to be superior to the enemy and, once we reached open country, our superiority in armour, firepower and mobility would tell.

26. I relied also upon two other great assets in particular – our complete sea and air supremacy. As will be seen from the narrative of operations, it was thanks to

sea power that we were able to capture and then to stock and operate the great air bases on Akyab and Ramree Islands, upon which the air supply of Fourteenth Army so much depended. Sea and air power enabled us to deliver the final assault on Rangoon.

27. The factor of air supremacy was of the highest importance. In jungle fighting, tactical mobility is afforded by air transport. Air supply allows the carrying out of the outflanking manoeuvres necessary to pin enemy resistance, by-pass it, and isolate or destroy it. By the use of air lines of communication, as with sea lines of communication, not only are the tenuous and limited overland routes supplemented, but one checkmates the Japanese technique of establishing road blocks in one's rear; the advance can continue unchecked and the enemy detachments are left to starve or are mopped up in due course.

Supply by air formed a large and vital part of the whole gigantic transportation effort which the prosecution of this campaign entailed. The full details appear in the Administrative part of this Despatch. It is enough here to say that during the peak month of April, 1945, when Fourteenth Army was racing for Rangoon, over 68,100 tons were delivered by air, over 11,000 men were brought forward and nearly 10,000 casualties evacuated. The stores carried by air included engines and other essential material for the building of the Inland Water Transport fleet at Kalewa, which was to operate the inland water transport supply link to Myingyan, and the light locomotives which were to operate on stretches of railway east of the Irrawaddy.

Throughout the campaign, the availability of aircraft for supply and transport was a major influence on the course of operations.

But in addition to air supply, our air superiority gave our land forces many other advantages. Our bases, rear areas and land communications were secure from air action, while these vital parts of the Japanese army were under constant attack by the Allied Air Forces. The close support of bomber, fighter/bomber and fighter squadrons was denied the enemy, while our own army reaped the benefit of tactical air support. Air transport gave mobility and flexibility to Allied troops while this was not available to the Japanese owing to their inferiority in the air. The use of an air L. of C. released the large number of troops necessary to defend a long land L. of C. Finally, the Allied Air Forces provided regular air reconnaissance, which was denied to the enemy by our command of the air.

SECTION III (paras. 28–49)
OPERATIONS IN DECEMBER

The abandonment of the airborne operation: The decision to advance on a two Corps front: 33 Corps operations to the capture of Shwebo: 4 Corps operations: Operations by Northern Combat Area Command: The capture of Bhamo: Note on operations in Arakan.

---

28. An account of the operational situation of our troops at the end of November has been given in paragraph 23. In this section I propose to give an account

of operations up to the virtual completion of Capital, Phase II, that is, the securing of the Ye-U and Shwebo areas in the dry belt area of Central Burma. In the original plan for Capital, the advance of 33 Corps to Ye-U and Shwebo was to have been assisted by an airborne operation. It soon became obvious, however, that the specially trained and equipped troops, essential for such an operation, were not going to be available. It is worth, therefore, at this point reviewing the situation as regards airborne troops in the Command, or available for it, generally.

29. On the 1st November, 1944, just before I assumed command, H.Q., 44 Indian Airborne Division had been formed from elements of the recently disbanded H.Q., 44 Indian Armoured Division. The organization and training of this Airborne Division was to be the responsibility of the Commander-in-Chief, India, who, however, kept in close touch with me, through the Supreme Allied Commander, in regard to matters of policy. It was agreed that the Divisional H.Q. and Divisional troops were to be concentrated for training by the 1st January, while the remainder of the Division was to be concentrated in the Bilaspur – Raipur area by the end of March. The Division as a whole was to be ready for war by the 15th October, 1945, that is, in time for immediate post-monsoon operations. The existing 50 Indian Parachute Brigade formed the nucleus of this new Division, and this formation was the one which had been originally earmarked to take part in operations in Burma to assist 33 Corps. It had, however, been used in an infantry rôle in the Imphal battle and had suffered severely. It had not been fully reconstituted and so was not now available. A second parachute brigade was to have been formed from Special Force, but as sufficient volunteers were not forthcoming, recruiting was extended to other units in India, and to A.L.F.S.E.A. units which were not involved in operations. By mid-1945 the Division was more or less complete except for the Signals element, which could only be made up when forces were redeployed from Europe after the German defeat. The provision of aircraft for the training of this Division was a perpetual worry, since they could only be supplied at the expense of the more immediately pressing needs of air supply for the Burma battle.

30. Failing any part of the Airborne Division proper, the only other troops I could hope to be able to call on for an airborne operation were Special Force. This Force had suffered seriously from disease, especially malaria, during its 1944 campaign. When I inspected it in December, 1944, I formed the opinion that, despite its splendid achievements and fine *esprit-de-corps*, it was no longer battle-worthy and that it could not be used for the Capital airborne operation. Moreover I considered that there was no longer a justifiable rôle for a force such as this, which, like all forces of this nature, was particularly expensive in over-heads such as Headquarters and Signals. I therefore recommended its disbandment, and later, on the 23rd February, was informed by India Command that the War Office had approved my recommendation.

31. I was thus compelled to abandon the plan of an airborne landing as part of Capital, Phase II. I was also forced, reluctantly, to give up the idea of reinforcing the Northern Combat Area Command front by flying-in another division. I had hoped to move 7 Indian Division, which was resting at Kohima, into the Pinwe – Wuntho "railway corridor" by air, but examination showed that our air transport resources would be inadequate without prejudicing the maintenance lift required for the advance of Fourteenth Army. Instead, therefore, I instructed the Commander, Fourteenth Army, to direct 19 Indian Division on to Indaw (less the brigade already advancing on Pinlebu). General Sultan for some time had been worried about his right flank. I was therefore glad to close the gap between him and Fourteenth Army.

32. General Slim now recast his plan and decided to advance with two Corps up. This decision fully accorded with my own views, as, to maintain the strongest pressure on the retreating enemy, it was necessary to do soon on as broad a front as possible.

33 Corps remained directed on Ye-U and Shwebo, but he moved up 4 Corps on their left, directed initially on Pinlebu. The orders issued to Commander, 4 Corps, on the 7th December were:-

(*a*) Advance as rapidly as possible to make contact with 36 British Division in the area Indaw – Wuntho.

(*b*) Capture Pinlebu as quickly as possible and exploit towards Wuntho with a view to cutting the railway behind, and destroying any Japanese forces to the north.

(*c*) Take over part of the sector of 36 British Division, thus enabling General Sultan to employ this Division in operations further to the east.

(*d*) Concentrate 4 Corps in the Ye-U – Shwebo area as rapidly as possible, and by the 15th February at the latest.

Further, General Slim pointed out that the Japanese forces opposing 4 Corps were neither in great strength nor in good shape. It was therefore legitimate to take certain risks to achieve a rapid advance.

33. By the end of November, it will be remembered, the leading division of 33 Corps, 11 (East African) Division, was approaching Kalewa. It entered that village on the 2nd December, after stiff close-quarter fighting in the Chaunggyin area, six miles to the west. A battalion then crossed the Chindwin on the night of the 4th–5th December in the face of only slight opposition, but was held up two miles to the east. North of Kalewa, the brigade advancing southwards astride the river encountered stubborn resistance on the east bank, seven miles north-east of the village; but an outflanking movement caused the enemy to abandon his position and a link-up with the rest of the Division was effected. It is of interest to note that by the 10th December, Indian sappers had in 36 hours achieved the feat of erecting across the Chindwin a thousand foot Bailey pontoon bridge. The enemy unsuccessfully attempted to destroy it by air attack two days later. Two

brigades of 11 (East African) Division crossed the river, but met determined opposition in their efforts to extend their bridgehead. By the 14th December, however, a semi-circular area, extending from a point six miles north-east of Kalewa to Shwegyin, five miles to the south-east, had been cleared. The withdrawal of the Division for rehabilitation then began, on relief by 2 British Division, and was completed by the end of the month.

34. On the day before 11 (East African) Division's crossing, 32 Brigade of 20 Indian Division had crossed the Chindwin about thirty miles to the north, at a point seven miles, southeast of Mawlaik. The passage of the river was made mainly by rafting, and 5,065 men, 1,456 mules and 30 tons of equipment were put across this formidable obstacle in 100 hours, for the loss of one mule. The Division then advanced rapidly eastwards in difficult flooded country until it reached the Indaw – Pyingaing road. It there turned south, reaching the Pyingaing area in time to attack in the rear the enemy rearguard which was blocking the advance of 2 British Division who had come through the Kalewa bridgehead. The enemy were routed, suffering heavy casualties. 32 Brigade then continued its advance southwards, reaching a point 19 miles south of Pyingaing by the 31st December. In the meantime, the rest of 20 Indian Division (Major-General D.D. Gracey) had moved south from their concentration area at Htinzin and relieved 5 Indian Division at Kalemyo and Khampat. Divisional Headquarters and 100 Brigade then pushed on across difficult country and occupied Maukkadaw on the Chindwin, 17 miles south-west of Pyingaing, on the 25th December. Thence, following 32 Brigade, their advance was directed on Budalin, the important Japanese communication centre 54 miles south-east of Maukkadaw, flank protection being afforded by 80 Brigade advancing west of the Chindwin.

35. 2 British Division (Major-General C.G.G. Nicholson) remained concentrated in the Yazagyo area until the 12th December, when it began its forward move to the Kalewa bridgehead. The leading Brigade, the 6th, passed through 11 (East African) Division on the 21st and advanced rapidly along the road from Kalewa towards Pyingaing. West of Pyingaing the advance was checked by a strong rearguard position. With the assistance of 32 Brigade of 20 Indian Division as stated above, the enemy was cleared, and Pyingaing was captured on the 24th. Determined resistance was again encountered in the Wainggyo Gorge, nine miles south-west of Pyingaing, but was overcome with tank support. The advance of 2 British Division continued with great speed. Dominating features astride the road 12 miles east of Pyingaing were cleared, and a large enemy detachment was successfully ambushed on the 28th December. On the 31st, the Kabo Weir, 11 miles north of Ye-U was captured intact. This was an important economic gain, since the Kabo Weir controls the irrigation of an extensive area of rice-growing country. It was a propitious entry into the Shwebo plain – the enemy's demolition party, sent to blow up the weir, arrived to find us in occupation. On the 2nd January, 5 Brigade had established itself at Ye-U and the Division was driving the enemy back on to Shwebo, the northern outskirts of

which were reached by the 8th January. 64 Brigade of 19 Indian Division had already reached the eastern outskirts on the 7th, having come *via* Kanbalu. Shwebo town was finally occupied on the 10th January, after the Japanese rearguard had fought to the last man. 6 Brigade of 2 British Division was then concentrated at Shwebo after relief by 268 Indian Brigade in the Kabo Weir area. This advance of 150 miles in 20 days was a fine performance by an all-British Division.

36. On the extreme western flank of 33 Corps, a general redistribution of forces of Lushai Brigade took place early in December, Brigade Headquarters being located 18 miles north of Gangaw. Deep patrolling was maintained east to the Chindwin, while two battalions continued to close in on Gangaw *via* the Myittha Valley. They reached the area three miles north of Gangaw by the 14th December, but here they bumped strong positions which the enemy continued to hold stubbornly despite strong air attacks. Meanwhile, Irregulars had occupied Mingin, on the river 24 miles S.S.E. of Kalewa. Other Irregulars had penetrated 30 miles south of Gangaw and were engaging the enemy in the Tilin area. Lushai Brigade came under command of 4 Corps on the 23rd December.

  I may add here that this formation and its Commander, Brigadier P.C. Marindin, after the fall of Kalewa and the clearing of the west side of the Chindwin (in which operations they had played an important rôle), received the congratulations of the Supreme Allied Commander on the outstanding results they had achieved under exceptionally severe conditions during the past 12 months.

37. 4 Corps (Lieutenant-General F.W. (later Sir Frank) Messervy, who had succeeded Lieutenant-General Sir Geoffry A.P. Scoones on the 8th December) was in the area of the Upper Chindwin.

  268 Indian Brigade (Brigadier G.M. Dyer) now consisted of six battalions. The two leading battalions, advancing from the Chindwin, *via* Pantha, reached Indaw and an area 15 miles to the east-north-east by the 15th December. They then pushed on a further 20 miles, through the Japanese advanced elements, and occupied two villages east of the escarpment, thereby blocking the road south-west from Pinlebu. The remainder of the Brigade crossed the Chindwin and followed up this advance, operating in the gap between 2 British and 19 Indian Divisions. It was transferred back to 33 Corps on the 26th December.

38. 19 Indian Division (Major-General T.W. Rees) advanced from the Sittaung bridgehead, through Wuntho. 62 Brigade, advancing rapidly from the bridgehead, occupied Pinlebu on the 17th December after overcoming some opposition along the escarpment nine miles west-south-west of Pinlebu. Wuntho, on the Myitkyina – Mandalay railway, was reached on the 19th, and Kawlin on the 20th December. Further north, 64 Brigade, passing through Pinbon on the 15th December, made a rapid advance of over 60 miles in seven days and occupied Banmauk on the 17th, making contact with 36 British Division and thus establishing a continuous front with Northern Combat Area Command. After concentrating about Wuntho,

62 and 64 Brigades conformed with the main southerly axis of advance, and, by the 23rd, they reached Kokkogon, 25 miles south-east of Wuntho.

39. This advance of 192 miles in 20 days was a wonderful achievement for troops who were in action for the first time. Not only did they overcome the scattered but desperate opposition of enemy rear parties, but they surmounted tremendous physical difficulties, cutting a road through steep, jungle-covered hills, and man-handling their guns and vehicles over long distances. On one occasion, they even had to cantilever the track out on timber supports round a cliff face. Two of the three columns were accompanied by their motor vehicles, though it was often necessary to winch them up the hills. In spite of all these difficulties it is much to the credit of the R.E.M.E. mobile workshops that these two columns only lost 29 vehicles between them. This loss was compensated by the addition to the divisional motor transport of 47 broken down and abandoned Japanese vehicles which we successfully repaired.

40. On the 26th December, the Division passed under command of 33 Corps, with 62 and 64 Brigades in contact with the retiring enemy on a 20 mile front. 64 Brigade pushed on, smashing an enemy rearguard at Kanbalu on the 2nd January, and, with 2 British Division, assisted in the capture of Shwebo on the 10th January.

41. 7 Indian Division (Major-General G.C. Evans, who had succeeded Major-General Messervy on the 12th December) which had been rehabilitating at Kohima, was now entering the forward zone. Its leading brigade relieved 98 Brigade of 19 Indian Division, which had been employed on road construction along the Thanan – Tonhe track, in the middle of December. By the end of the month, 7 Indian Division was concentrating six miles south-west of Tamu, ready either to be flown in to the Schwebo area or to follow 19 Indian Division.

42. 28 (East African) Brigade concentrated in December near Sunle on the Tamu – Kalewa road. When the change of plan described in the next section took place in the second half of December, this Brigade was ordered south up the Gangaw Valley, in rear of Lushai Brigade. By the end of December, it had reached Myintha, 29 miles north of Gangaw.

43. On the Northern Combat Area Command front in Northern Burma, 36 British Division had been advancing down the Railway Corridor. Following on the capture of Pinwe on the 30th November (already mentioned in para. 23), Naba, Indaw and Katha were occupied in quick succession by the 10th December, and consolidation of the area proceeded without enemy interference. The situation at the end of the month was that 29 Brigade was concentrating at Tigyaing on the Irrawaddy, while 72 Brigade had crossed the river south of Katha and reached a point 25 miles south-west of Shwegu, on the south bank of the Shweli River. At this time 26 Indian Brigade joined 36 British Division and

moved up to Indaw. Up till now, the Division had comprised only the two British Brigades mentioned above.

44. Two regiments from 50 Chinese Division proceeded from behind 36 British Division and crossed the Irrawaddy to concentrate at Kontha, 24 miles south-east of Mawlu. By the 30th December, one regiment had reached Shwegu and the other a point 30 miles southeast of it. 5332 (United States) Brigade ("Mars" Brigade) was operating over a widely separated area from Bhamo to the southeast of Shwegu. 38 Chinese Division captured Bhamo on the 15th December after a siege of four weeks. The remnants of the Japanese garrison, some 300 strong, succeeded in breaking out south of the town, but suffered severe casualties in doing so. After mopping up in the Bhamo area, 38 Chinese Division supported 30 Chinese Division in the advance on Namhkam. On the 28th December, one regiment crossed the Sino-Burmese frontier and occupied Loiwing (five miles north-north-east of Namhkam), together with its two all-weather airfields.

45. 30 Chinese Division met vigorous opposition 20 miles north-west of Namhkam in its initial advance down the Bhamo – Namhkam road, but, with the assistance of 38 Chinese Division and elements of Mars Brigade, it fought its way to within seven miles of Namhkam by the 31st December. The Japanese had recently reinforced this front and it was evident that a determined effort was being made to check our advance in this area, to permit of the withdrawal of their 56 Division from Wanting towards Hsenwi and Lashio.

46. 22 Chinese Division, advancing south from the Bhamo area, occupied Siu, 48 miles to the south, on the 10th December, and captured Tonkwa, seven miles to the south-west, on the 12th against determined resistance. After this, 22 Chinese Division was concentrated in the general area of Sikaw, and began its fly-out to Kunming on the 22nd December. The removal of this Division, and of 14 Chinese Division which had preceded it, will be referred to in more detail in the next section of the Despatch. This depletion of our strength occurred at a critical juncture. The magnitude of the air effort involved in the move can be judged by the fact that between the 22nd and 28th December alone the numbers transported were 8,423 Chinese troops, 95 United States personnel, four jeeps, 12 75-mm. guns and 701 animals. This of course represented a very serious loss in lift by transport aircraft, which would have been invaluable elsewhere on the front.

47. Nevertheless, when the original Phases of Operation "Capital" are consider, it will be seen that the advance of Northern Combat Area Command was lagging behind that of Fourteenth Army, which had completed Phase Two with great speed.

48. Further east, elements of the Chinese Expeditionary Force made progress in December down the Lungling – Namhkam road, reaching a point eight miles north-west of Wanting.

The Chinese Expeditionary Force was not, of course, under my command but their movements at this time affected my operations.

49. Finally, although the planning and details of the operations in Arakan are dealt with in a later section of this part of the Despatch, the main events should be noted. On the 9th December, 81 (West African) Division crossed the Kaladan River. On the 15th December, Buthidaung fell to 82 (West African) Division. In the coastal sector, the advance of 25 Indian Division had been very rapid. On the 23rd December they reached Donbaik and on the 26th they were at Foul Point looking across the water at Akyab Island. Akyab itself was occupied on the 3rd January.

SECTION IV (paras. 50–69)
THE READJUSTMENT OF PLANS IN DECEMBER

The diversion of resources to China and its adverse effects: The enemy's dispositions: The poor quality of Intelligence about the enemy: Fourteenth Army's plan for the battle of the Mandalay Plain: Comments on the plan.

---

50. While operations for the completion of Phase II of Capital were thus, in December, going extremely well, other events had necessitated a considerable readjustment of plans for the achievement of Phase III – the capture of the Mandalay area; and as these were the plans which resulted in the final destruction of the enemy forces in Burma, their development deserves a full account.

51. The first event which affected all our plans, imposed considerable delay on our subsequent advance, and had other serious effects, had its origin in another theatre of war. Owing to the deterioration of the military situation in China, General Wedemeyer, Chief of Staff to Generalissimo Chiang Kai Shek, had asked for the transfer of troops from Burma to China. As a result of orders received from the Chiefs of Staff at the beginning of December, the Supreme Allied Commander ordered me to transfer 14 and 22 Chinese Divisions to China, and instructed the Allied Air C.-in-C. to lend the necessary transport aircraft for their support. One Chinese Division was flown out from the Myitkyina area to China between the 4th and 15th December and the second followed about a week later. This transfer involved some 1,300 Dakota sorties. This was serious enough, but on the 10th and 11th December some 120 transport aircraft, 75 of which had already been allotted to Fourteenth Army maintenance, were also removed to China. These were in addition to the temporary diversion of aircraft for the fly-out of the two Divisions mentioned above.

52. Now it had been obvious that the rapidity of Fourteenth Army's advance must become increasingly dependent on adequate air supply, as our troops reached out into Central Burma and outran their land lines of communication. This sudden and unexpected reduction in transport aircraft therefore seriously complicated our already difficult administrative problem, thus inevitably hampering our

operations. The loss of air-lift involved curtailed our freedom of action, and severely limited the degree of exploitation which our forces were able to carry out. General Slim calculated that Fourteenth Army's operations were retarded by at least two weeks. The Japanese thus gained valuable time in which to react to our moves. This, by itself, would have been bad enough, but the weakening of Northern Combat Area Command by the loss of two Chinese divisions had another adverse effect on our strategy. I was now forced to accept a slower advance by Northern Combat Area Command. 36 British Division was directed on Mongmit, one brigade to cross the Irrawaddy at Tigyaing and the other at Kantha. 50 Chinese Division was directed to relieve 22 Chinese Division in the Siu area and advance towards Lashio, their initial objective being Namtu. 30 and 38 Chinese Divisions were ordered to advance on the axis Namhkam – Lashio, the latter to support the former by outflanking operations. The Mars Brigade, directed initially on Mongwi, was to form the link between 36 British Division and 50 Chinese Division, operating in the gap between them. General Sultan, with whom I discussed the above plan, was convinced that the Japanese would fight hard for the Burma Road and anticipated a long and severe battle for Lashio and Namhkam. He considered that the enemy's resistance on this front would be unaffected even by the capture of Mandalay, since the Japanese troops could still be maintained by the direct route from Indo-China.

53. On the other hand, my principal problem was to ensure that Northern Combat Area Command continued to contain all the Japanese forces opposing it. This could only be done by maintaining the strongest pressure, but I was now being forced to accept a weakening of this pressure. Northern Combat Area Command never fully recovered from this depletion of its strength. The advance lost its momentum, thereby releasing further enemy troops for operations against Fourteenth Army. Principally owing to the loss of aircraft, Fourteenth Army's lower crossing of the Irrawaddy actually took place about 14 days later than the planned date. This meant that 19 Indian Division, which had crossed the Irrawaddy north of Mandalay, had to hold on in their bridgehead against a greater concentration of enemy for 14 days longer than was originally expected. The result was that the Division became involved in very bitter fighting and suffered severe casualties. I have given some space to the very adverse effects of the transfer of troops and aircraft from the theatre at such an inopportune moment, despite the representations made by the Supreme Allied Commander and myself, as at that time it appeared that the consequences of the reduction of Northern Combat Area Command's effort might seriously prejudice the whole success of the operations of Fourteenth Army. It was, however, agreed by the Chiefs of Staff that two United States Combat Cargo squadrons would be returned to South-East Asia Command by the 1st February, 1945.

54. General Slim's plan of concentrating the whole Fourteenth Army in the loop of the Chindwin and Irrawaddy, as given in paragraph 32, was based on the belief that the Japanese would fight to cover Mandalay and the Shwebo airfields; that is,

that they would stand west and north of the river. About mid-December, however, it became apparent that the enemy was not going to do so and was withdrawing his main forces southwards. It is therefore worth while reviewing the enemy's situation at this stage.

55. At the end of November, the enemy's alignment was as I have described in paragraph 22. By the 3rd December, however, we had cross the Chindwin at three points and held bridgeheads at Sittaung, Mawlaik and Kalewa. The Japanese, of necessity, had conformed to the advance of Fourteenth Army and Northern Combat Area Command by withdrawing southwards. The enemy situation on the 7th December was that 33 Japanese Division held from Gangaw to the north of Kalewa, with 15 Japanese Division on its right extended up to the railway above Wuntho. 31 Japanese Division remained in the Ye-U area, while 53 Japanese Division filled the gap between Wuntho and the Irrawaddy, with 18 Japanese Division on its right up to the Bhamo – Namhkam road. 56 Japanese Division held between Namhkam and the Salween River. 2 Japanese Division had been withdrawn from this front and was believed to be in reserve in Central Burma in the vicinity of Pyinmana. Further south, 49 Japanese Division remained in the Pegu area.

56. By mid-December, the results of our policy of applying continuous pressure over a broad front began to be apparent. The enemy appeared to be readjusting his dispositions as follows. In 15 Army's sector, in the north, 53 Japanese Division was crossing the river and taking up positions east of the river; 15 Japanese Division was also withdrawing across the river into the Mandalay area. 31 Japanese Division was withdrawing from the Ye-U area into the strong natural bridgehead, west of the Irrawaddy, formed by the Sagaing Hills, while 33 Japanese Division was apparently pulling back to a line running west-south-west from Myinmu to Pauk, in prolongation of the line to be held by 31 Division. Pauk was the junction of 15 Army with 28 Army, which controlled the Irrawaddy Valley. It was known that 28 Army was building up a strong force in the Yenangyaung oilfields area comprising one Independent Mixed Brigade, a part of 49 Japanese Division, and a considerable force of I.N.A. troops.

57. The following points will be noted about this new positioning of the Japanese forces. Once the enemy had decided not to fight on the line of the escarpment running through Pinlebu and Pyingaing he had virtually lost the battle for the "dry belt" of Central Burma. The line of the escarpment represented the last opportunity he had of compelling us to fight him on a narrow front and on something approaching level terms. From this line onwards the country opened out and our superiority in mobility, firepower and armour, would increasingly assert itself. There would be two divisions (the 53rd and 15th) disposed in depth east of the Irrawaddy, protecting Mandalay from the north, with their left flank protected by the river. The Sagaing Hills position (31 Division), which the Japanese had been preparing for some time, would deny us observation across the river and

provide an outlet for counter-attack. Also, in conjunction with 33 Japanese Division further west, it would cover any reserve formations which the enemy might bring up south and east of the Irrawaddy.

58. The main reasons which compelled the enemy to make this alteration in his plans were probably three in number.

First, helped by our air superiority we had sprung a strategical surprise upon him by the speed with which we had got strong forces across the Chindwin.

Secondly, the troops (15 and 33 Divisions), with which he had intended to hold a covering line, had been given no respite during the monsoon and were thus no longer in a condition seriously to impede our offensive. Resistance to our entry into the Shwebo plain was crumbling before our rapid advance. We were now learning gradually just how badly damaged some of the enemy formations were from their earlier defeat.

Thirdly, the time and space factor would not allow the enemy to bring his reserve troops up from the south. Not only was he short of transport, but, lacking air supremacy, his movements by day were restricted, and his lines of communication damaged by bombing.

59. At this point I would like to draw attention to a factor which will re-appear from time to time in this Despatch, and that is the poorness both in quantity and quality of Intelligence about the enemy in the Burma theatre. I found that, compared with the African and European theatres, the information which we received about the enemy from all sources was very bad, and we were often virtually fighting in the dark. Although there was a large number of special and guerrilla organizations, full benefit was not obtained from these sources owing to overlapping and the differing channels by which they reported. Very often little more operational Intelligence was available than was obtained from forward troops. I was very keen to improve this state of affairs as it made planning extremely difficult, and it did grow better somewhat later on.

60. General Slim had at once appreciated that the Japanese had now no intention of seriously defending the Shwebo Plain, and that the enemy's covering forces were virtually evacuating the river loop, while the main forces would be grouped in depth, protected by the great river obstacle. It appeared that the Japanese intended to fight for Mandalay and on the line of the Irrawaddy, but it must be remembered that, at this stage, reports only showed them to be retiring on to their new positions. There was still doubt as to whether they meant to make a main stand on these positions, or merely to delay us on this line. One report received on the 16th December definitely stated that the enemy would not hold Mandalay, but would continue withdrawal southwards. This was a contingency which had to be borne in mind. If the enemy had stood to fight north and west of the Irrawaddy, it was General Slim's plan to destroy him there. But he had always had in his mind an alternative plan which he could employ if the enemy decided –

as he did in fact – to fight east of the river. The time had now come to put this alternative into action.

61. The essence of the new plan was a regrouping and redirection of the two Corps. 33 Corps, consisting of 2 British Division, 19 and 20 Indian Divisions, 268 Indian Infantry Brigade and 254 Indian Tank Brigade, was directed to capture the area Monywa – Mandalay, thus holding the Japanese forces by frontal attack. 4 Corps, consisting of 7 and 17 Indian Divisions, 28 (East African) Brigade and 255 Indian Tank Brigade, was to be switched from the left of the Army to the right flank, and, thrusting down the Gangaw valley, was to seize a bridgehead at Pakokku and capture the communications centre of Meiktila. It was this blow at his most vital point that was to be the basis of the enemy's destruction, and it was hoped he would not realise its significance until too late.

By cutting the enemy's L. of C. at Meiktila, a main frontal attack across the Irrawaddy would be avoided, the escape route cut, and, by isolating the northern flank of the Japanese Army, the enemy would be forced to give battle in the Mandalay Plain. 19 Indian Division, transferred to 33 Corps under the regrouping plan, would play an important part. Crossing the Irrawaddy, it would threaten Mandalay from the north prior to 4 Corps thrust at Meiktila. This, it was hoped, would concentrate the enemy's attention on Mandalay and maintain his main forces in the northern sector. Subsequent exploitation was to be by 33 Corps down the Mandalay – Rangoon railway axis and by 4 Corps down the Irrawaddy Valley.

62. On the 19th December, the above plan was embodied in an Operation Instruction issued to the Commanders of 4 and 33 Corps. In it the Army Commander stated that it was his intention to exploit the rapidity of the enemy's withdrawal to the utmost, and, in conjunction with Northern Combat Area Command, to destroy the Japanese forces in Burma, to advance rapidly to the general line Henzada – Nyaunglebin, and to seize any possibility that might offer of capturing a South Burma port.

63. To achieve this object, formations were to regroup not later than 0001 hours on the 26th December as follows:-

```
              { 2 British Division
              { 19 Indian Division (ex 4 Corps)
   33 Corps   { 20 Indian Division
              { 268 Indian Infantry Brigade (ex 4 Corps)
              { 254 Indian Tank Brigade

              { 7 Indian Division
              { 17 Indian Division (when available, expected the 1st February)
              { Lushai Brigade (ex 33 Corps)
    4 Corps   { 255 Indian Tank Brigade (ex Army reserve)
              { 11 Cavalry
              { 28 (East African) Brigade (ex Army reserve)
```

...roops of the 19th Indian Division, more commonly referred to as the Dagger Division, firing 3-inch ...ortars in support of the advance along the Mawchi Road, east of Toungoo in Burma. The mortar ...roved a most effective weapon in jungle warfare. (*James Luto Collection*)

...ransport and a towed 25-pounder, part of the British 36th Division, pictured moving past a ...urmese temple on way to Tigyiang. (*James Luto Collection*)

Men of the South Wales Borderers, part of the British 36th Division, move forward along a swampy jungle road under sniper fire. (*James Luto Collection*)

A battery of 25-pounders firing on Japanese positions in Pinew in support of operations by the British 36th Division, 30 November 1944. (*James Luto Collection*)

A picture of Major Scott of the 8th Frontier Force Rifles, 19th Indian Division. (*James Luto Collection*)

A notice board warns the occupants of a Jeep of the dangers ahead on a stretch of the Mawchi Road during the advance by elements of XIVth Army in June 1945. (*James Luto Collection*)

Landing craft on the beach at Akyab Island, 4 January 1945. (*James Luto Collection*)

British troops of the first wave are pictured going ashore from their landing craft during the amphibious landings against the Japanese-held island of Ramree on 21 January 1945. (*James Luto Collection*)

Men of the RAF's Advance Assault Party pictured on Ramree Island examining a dummy Japanese tank, the gun being nothing more than a length of bamboo. (*James Luto Collection*)

An aerial view of a Bailey Bridge being constructed across the Chindwin River at Kalewa. At the time that this was completed, for use by the men of the 11th East African Division, it was the longest such bridge in the world. (*Historic Military Press*)

The drive on Mawchi. A Japanese 150mm gun, knocked out by Sherman tanks, is examined by two Indian soldiers of the XIVth Army on the Mawchi Road, June 1945. (*James Luto Collection*)

Royal Artillery Gunners firing on Japanese positions on the Imphal Plain whilst supporting the operations of the 17th Indian Division, also known as the 'Black Cats'. (*James Luto Collection*)

Men of the 6th Gurkha Rifles go into action at Singu on the Irrawaddy bridgehead, with Sherman and Grant tanks in support, February 1945. (*James Luto Collection*)

A battery of 3.7-inch howitzers, commanded by one Major Hackett, fire at enemy positions on Burma Hill whilst supporting the 36th Division. The battery was also under fire at the time. (*James Luto Collection*)

Troops of the 98th Indian Infantry Brigade, part of the 19th Indian Division, advance past burning buildings in a village near Mandalay. *(James Luto Collection)*

The Japanese 33rd Army surrendered to the 17th Indian Division at Thaton, north of Moulmein, in the last week of October. This image was taken shortly before the handover ceremony in which Japanese commanders handed their swords to Major General W.A. Crowther DSO. *(James Luto Collection)*

NOTE. – The above redistribution left 5 Indian Division, which had been withdrawn to rest in the Kohima area, in Army reserve. 17 Indian Division, allotted to 4 Corps, was still in India, but would be available for exploitation. The organization of these two Divisions was being changed; in each of them two brigade groups were being motorised, and one brigade group made air-transportable.

A.L.F.S.E.A. reserve (in India) consisted of 23 Indian Division, but it would be joined by 11 (East African) Division (already withdrawn) and Lushai Brigade (about to be withdrawn).

64. The tasks allotted to 33 Corps were:-

(*a*) To capture or construct airfields in the Ye-U – Shwebo areas.
(*b*) To capture Monywa.
(*c*) To capture Mandalay.
(*d*) To be prepared to advance on the general axis Mandalay – Nyaunglebin.

NOTE. – Up to this date, 33 Corps had been acting on an Instruction issued on the 1st October which directed them to advance eastwards and capture the Ye-U area, with the object of establishing airstrips.

65. The tasks allotted to 4 Corps were:-

(*a*) To capture Pakokku.
(*b*) To seize a bridgehead across the Irrawaddy.
(*c*) To capture Meiktila and the Meiktila group of airfields.
(*d*) To be prepared to advance southwards on the general axis Myingyan – Henzada.

NOTE. – The previous Instruction to 4 Corps, dated the 7th December, directed its concentration in the Ye-U – Shwebo area by the 15th February at the latest (see paragraph 32).

66. This Instruction also laid down that the Kalemyo – Gangaw – Pakokku road would be constructed to a standard sufficient only to pass 4 Corps through, and that it would not be maintained thereafter. The Kalewa – Ye-U – Shwebo road was to be constructed to a fair-weather standard only, since time and the available engineer and transport resources would allow no more.

With regard to administration, the allocation of air supply lift was laid down (I shall refer later in this Despatch to the actual tonnage allotments), and the following important instructions were given:-

(*a*) Temporary airstrips were to be constructed every 50 miles, capable of taking C-46 aircraft.
(*b*) Formations, when beyond maintenance distance from Indianggyi, were to move by march route, owing to the shortage of available air-lift and the consequent need for the maximum economy in motor fuel.
(*c*) The potentialities of the Chindwin River as a supply-carrying L. of C. were to be exploited to the utmost, since we were not able to construct an all-weather road route from Kalewa to Shwebo.

67. The following points in regard to the above plan deserve emphasis. First, a wide, but converging, advance was being made against a retreating enemy – a strategy which is bound to discover weak points in his dispositions. Secondly, the significance of the switch of 4 Corps from the left to the right flank; this switch, with its object the creation of a surprise thrust over the Irrawaddy in the neighbourhood of Pakokku, and then the seizure of the Meiktila airfields by a sudden armoured assault, reinforced by air-transported troops, was the key of the whole battle plan. Secrecy was therefore of paramount importance. The advance of 4 Corps was to be led by 28 (East African) Brigade to give the impression that 11 (East African) Division was again in the line under command of 33 Corps, and that 4 Corps was still operating north of Mandalay. Whereas, in point of fact, 11 (East African) Division and 5 Indian Division had both been withdrawn for rest and refitting after the capture of Kalewa. We calculated that, by bringing the enemy to battle in the Mandalay plain, we should be able to defeat his northern wing in detail and thus have an open corridor for a rapid advance towards Rangoon, since at last we would be operating in country suitable for the employment of armoured and mechanised forces. Thirdly, the boldness of the plan should be noted. Not only were we taking considerable (but calculated) administrative risks, but the whole essence of the operation lay in deception and speed. Two divisions and a tank brigade had to move down the Gangaw Valley for 320 miles making their own roads, establish a bridgehead, and then make a mechanised dash on Meiktila. It would not, of course, be possible to conceal our movements from the enemy; however many ingenious devices were operated by Fourteenth Army, to persuade the enemy that 4 Corps was still concentrating on the left of 33 Corps and that any movement in the Gangaw Valley was merely a demonstration by a small force to distract his attention from our main thrust toward Mandalay. Further deception measures were also designed to tie down enemy forces which might otherwise be moved up from South Burma. Finally, I draw attention to the selection of Meiktila as an objective. It was the focal point of all Japanese communications to their 15 Army, and their chief airfield centre. The manner in which the enemy reacted to its seizure affords sufficient proof of the value they attached to it.

68. There is one other point I would like to mention at this stage. Ever since its formation in 1942, Fourteenth Army had been operating in jungle-clad mountains. It was now entering flat, open country, where mechanisation would have full scope, and speed, mobility and dash would have to replace the slow and cautious tactics imposed by enclosed terrain. As much training as circumstances allowed was carried out to meet these changed conditions. The results achieved bear witness to the skill, energy and versatility of both Commanders and men.

69. For the accomplishment of these plans, and particularly for the exploitation which their success would make possible, one thing especially was required and that one thing we had not got – a sufficiency of transport aircraft. I continued to press the point, and finally, early in January, the Supreme Allied Commander sent

his Chief of Staff, Lieutenant-General F.A.M. (later Sir Frederick) Browning back to the United Kingdom to put the case personally before the Chiefs of Staff, and point out how great was the prize at stake. This had the desired effect, as on the 26th January, the Supreme Allied Commander received a signal saying that the transport aircraft would not only be made up but increased. Besides the two Combat Cargo squadrons which it had already been agreed would be returned from China by the 1st February, two R.A.F. Dakota squadrons would be made available, one being on loan, from 1st March. In addition, it was proposed to raise the aircraft establishment of all R.A.F. transport squadrons in the theatre. Thus, by March, our estimated essential requirements in air-lift were going to be met in full.

SECTION V (paras. 70–91)
THE IRRAWADDY CROSSINGS.

The establishment of 19 Indian Division's bridgeheads: The advance of 33 Corps up to the river: The bringing forward of 17 Indian Division: The plans for the crossings: Operations in 19 Indian Division's bridgehead: The four main crossings described: Progress by Northern Combat Area Command.

------

70. I will now resume the narrative of operations from the point reached at the end of Section III. While 64 Brigade of 19 Indian Division was engaged at Shwebo, the other two brigades were switched eastwards, *via* Myemun and Kinu, to the Irrawaddy. Destroying all resistance in their path and relying on speed to achieve surprise, they rushed the river and effected two crossings. 98 Brigade established a bridgehead at Thabeikkyin, 28 miles northeast of Shwebo, on the 9th January, after overcoming enemy defence in the village; 62 Brigade followed suit at Kyaukmyaung, due east of Shwebo, on the 16th. The river at Thabeikkyin runs between steep rock banks, jungle-covered almost to the water's edge. It is only about 500 yards wide, but is swift and deep. Concentrated artillery harassing fire rendered raft assembly difficult by night and impossible by day, but our crossing at this point was evidently unexpected and the enemy infantry build-up was slow. At Kyaukmyaung, the river is some 800 yards wide; the current is not strong, but shifting sandbanks caused difficulties. The terrain on both banks is flat and covered by scrub, except for open cultivation round the village itself. The leading troops of 62 Brigade actually reached the river on the 12th January, but enemy rear parties between Onbauk and Kyaukmyaung had to be cleared, and engineer equipment brought forward. The first crossing was made on the night 16th–17th January. As at Thabeikkyin, the enemy kept up a steady harassing fire with guns and mortars, but again we were allowed time to strengthen our bridgehead before any infantry or tank counter-attacks developed.

71. During the period of the above crossings, 64 Brigade concentrated at Onbauk, ready to reinforce 62 Brigade. Meanwhile 2 British Division continued its sweep south into the loop of the river against steadily mounting resistance. On

the right flank, 20 Indian Division, advancing from Maukkadaw across difficult country, captured Budalin on the 10th January, after four days of the most bitter fighting. A week later, they were within five miles of Monywa, which, despite our bombing, still functioned as the chief Japanese river port on the Chindwin.

72. In the new 4 Corps sector, Lushai Brigade crowned its splendid fighting career by capturing Gangaw on the 12th January after a month's serious fighting. The village itself was entered unopposed after the enemy positions covering it had been stormed with the aid of heavy air support. 28 (East African) Brigade (Brigadier T.H.S. Galletly) then relieved Lushai Brigade, which was flown out later to India for rest and refit. While the above operations were in progress, 7 Indian Division had begun its advance south. By the 7th January, it had reached Natchaung, some 12 miles south of Kalemyo and a hundred miles from its concentration area at Tamu. It was being followed by 255 Indian Tank Brigade, which on this date (7th January) was concentrated 72 miles south of Tamu. The steady advance southwards on this front was maintained. Enemy resistance in the Tilin area was quickly overcome and Tilin itself occupied by 28 (East African) Brigade on the 22nd January, by which date Headquarters, 4 Corps, had opened at Kan.

73. The passage of 4 Corps south to Pakokku presented considerable engineer problems. There was an unmetalled track of sorts from Kalemyo to Pakokku, but it required widening throughout its length and much bridging. The only difficult sections were some rocky hill stretches amounting in all to about 40 miles. The main problems were, first, to work on a narrow road without impeding the continuous stream of traffic which flowed throughout the 24 hours and, secondly, the movement of engineer units and equipment forward in the limited amount of transport that was available, and their maintenance. In general the plan adopted was that the divisional engineers worked forward bringing the track up to a standard to carry three-tonners and Corps engineers followed making it passable for heavy lorries and transporters, including construction of the water crossings. Although the policy was that this road would be abandoned after the passage of 4 Corps it was in fact kept open as a subsidiary L. of C. until the Inland Water Transport link from Kalewa to Myingyan was in operation. Nevertheless it was a rough passage to travel by this route and drivers who had experienced the Kabaw Valley during the monsoon were unanimously of the opinion that they would rather drive through two feet of mud than three feet of dust. The latter, between Tilin and Pauk, on occasions proved to be a barrier even to the usually ubiquitous jeep. It is worth remarking, none the less, that the original plan of moving 4 Corps up over the route taken by 19 Indian Division would have been far more difficult and, with the engineer resources at our disposal, would have probably been impracticable.

74. 7 Indian Division was not to be thwarted by any of the difficulties described above. While work on the road was in progress, 89 Brigade, operating in two

columns, executed a skilful flanking movement through the hills, which forced the enemy to vacate their strong positions covering Pauk on the 27th January. By the 31st January, 7 Indian Division was seven miles east of Pyinchaung, after forcing the double crossing of the Yaw Chaung against unexpectedly light opposition. 28 (East African) Brigade was operating to the south, covering the right flank of the Corps.

75. On the 8th February, the joint Fourteenth Army/221 Group R.A.F. Headquarters opened at Monywa. This now included the Rear Headquarters, 221 Group, which had been left behind at Imphal when Army Headquarters moved forward, only a small operations staff then accompanying the Army Headquarters. 221 Group Headquarters, under Air Vice-Marshal S.F. Vincent, and Headquarters Fourteenth Army maintained a joint Headquarters for the remainder of the campaign.

76. It was now becoming operationally essential to bring up more formations. To do so involved administrative risk, but we could now look forward to some improvement in the transport aircraft situation after the 1st February and a further large improvement on the 1st March. By the end of January, therefore, 17 Indian Division was concentrated forward in the Gangaw Valley, together with 255 Indian Tank Brigade, as already mentioned. I also told General Slim that he could bring forward 5 Indian Division, which had been reorganized like 17 Indian Division, when he required it.

77. The distance between 19 Indian Division's bridgehead at Thabeikkyin, to the projected 4 Corps' crossing in the vicinity of Pakokku is some 160 miles. Between Thabeikkyin and the other 19 Indian Divisional bridgehead at Kyaukmyaung – about 24 miles – the river flows through jungle-clad hills and is comparatively narrow, being some 500 yards wide. From Kyaukmyaung downstream, the country opens out and the width of the river varies from 2,000 yards to 4,500 yards at its junction with the Chindwin (between Myingyan and Pakokku). The current in the dry season is about two knots in the wider stretches, but navigation is obstructed by islands and sandbanks. Generally speaking, the south bank dominates the northern approaches, but this does not apply to the loop, where the Sagaing Hills (which the Japanese were careful to hold) on the north bank dominate not only the river to the east and south, but all approaches to it from the north. I would sum up my impressions of this wide and treacherous river by saying that I cannot imagine a more formidable military water obstacle.

78. Our primary object in the north was to divert attention from the projected 4 Corps' crossing near Pakokku. To achieve this, the first crossings, as already stated, had been made by 19 Indian Division on the extreme left flank of Fourteenth Army. This, it was hoped, together with the deception measures we were employing, would lead the enemy to appreciate that the rest of 4 Corps would follow 19 Indian Division, and that our main effort from there would be directed on Mandalay. This illusion would be strengthened by the steady advance of

36 British Division from the north. The question now arose as to the priority of our further crossings. If the next crossing were again to be effected by 33 Corps, it would further indicate that our main objective was Mandalay. On the other hand, it was essential that 4 Corps should secure their bridgehead early, in order to allow sufficient time for the mechanised force designed for the thrust on Meiktila to pass through it – an operation which, once he realised its significance, the enemy would strain every nerve to delay. General Slim, therefore, decided that one division from each Corps should cross simultaneously: 20 Indian Division from 33 Corps and 7 Indian Division, from 4 Corps. He considered that even if the enemy regarded 4 Corps' crossing as the greater menace, he would not be able to react in time to upset our plans in this sector, in view of the existing threat to Mandalay and the pressure exerted by 33 Corps elsewhere.

79. The Japanese were completely deceived by 19 Indian Division's crossing. They believed, as we had intended they should, that this Division was the advanced guard of 4 Corps and they decided to exterminate it before its two bridgeheads could be consolidated. I had hoped, when I had originally directed 19 Indian Division on to Indaw in the "railway corridor," that Northern Combat Area Command would be able to exert sufficient pressure from the north that the Japanese would be unable to concentrate in strength against the left flank of Fourteenth Army. Unfortunately, as I have already indicated, the sudden transfer of the two Chinese divisions to China had disrupted General Sultan's plans, and temporarily halted Northern Combat Area Command's advance. This enabled the enemy to concentrate the bulk of his 15 and 53 Divisions against the Kyaukmyaung bridgehead, thereby pinning 19 Indian Division to this restricted area for a much longer period than would otherwise have been the case.

Moreover, the Commander, 15 Japanese Army, was able to support these two Divisions, not only with the bulk of his Army artillery, but also with batteries drawn from 31 and 33 Divisions, and with tanks. Covered by what General Slim described as "the heaviest artillery concentration our troops had yet endured," the Japanese infantry hurled themselves against our defence night after night, keeping up their attacks for nearly a month. Not only did 19 Indian Division hold its ground, but, despite heavy casualties, it actually expanded its bridgehead. Gradually, as their losses mounted, the enemy attacks lost their sting until it became apparent, even to the Japanese, that we could not be dislodged.

I wish to pay tribute to the gallantry and determination displayed by 19 Indian Division in this their first major encounter with the enemy. Although, like all troops new to battle, when opposed by veteran formations, they had to buy their experience, their firm stand at this stage against serious odds contributed materially to the success of our operations elsewhere. It is perhaps worthy of note that this Division, except for a few small units, was composed entirely of pre-war regular troops.

80. It may serve to clarify the picture of this vital phase of operations if, before describing what occurred at each crossing-place, I summarize the crossings which

were made. Four crossings of the Irrawaddy were undertaken. Briefly they were as follows:-

(*a*) 19 Indian Division crossed north of Mandalay at Thabeikkyin (9th January) and Kyaukmyaung (16th January), as already described. They then, as will be shown later, advanced south on Mandalay, shifting their bridgehead south to Singu.

(*b*) 20 Indian Division crossed near Allagappa, west of Mandalay, in the Myinmu area, on the 12th February, with the object of advancing east along the south bank of the river towards Mandalay.

(*c*) Twelve days later (24th February), 2 British Division crossed at Ngazun, a village between Mandalay and 20 Indian Division's bridgehead.

(*d*) Meanwhile 4 Corps (7 and 17 Indian Divisions with 255 Indian Tank Brigade), with Meiktila as its ultimate objective, had advanced down the Gangaw Valley crossed the Irrawaddy at Nyaungu, to the west of Pakokku, between the 13th and 19th February.

It will be noted that the Army Commander's decision that simultaneous crossings should be made on both 33 and 4 Corps' fronts was successfully implemented; 20 and 7 Indian Divisions crossed within 24 hours of each other.

The crossings will be described in the order in which they took place.

81. First I will deal with 20 Indian Division's advance to, and crossing of, the river. After the capture of Budalin, 20 Indian Division continued its advance with all three brigades up. On the right, 32 Brigade, directed on Monywa, there met with fanatical resistance. This important river port was captured on the 22nd January after three days fierce fighting. In the centre, 80 Brigade occupied Wadan, on the Ayadaw – Monywa road, and pushed southward. On the left, 100 Brigade, advancing from Ayadaw, made a lightning thrust at Myinmu, on the Irrawaddy, which fell on the 22nd January after bitter hand-to-hand fighting. An incident occurred here which illustrates the Japanese mentality: a detachment pinned against the river, formed up and marched straight into it, deliberately committing mass suicide by drowning. For the capture of both Monywa and Myinmu we received magnificent air support. The next three weeks were spent by 20 Indian Division in closing up to the north bank of the Irrawaddy between the Mu and Chindwin Rivers. The Japanese rear parties remaining on the north bank put up a stubborn resistance. While this area was being cleared, we pushed patrols out across the river. These operated with the greatest daring, not only reporting on possible crossing places, but in the words of the Army Commander, maintaining "a reign of terror among the Japanese posts on the southern bank." The enemy responded by sending a small detachment round the left flank of 20 Indian Division; this detachment crossed the Mu River from the east bank, under an artillery concentration, and recaptured Nyaungyin, a village two miles east of Myinmu. They then split up into small harassing parties, which had to be hunted down and eliminated.

82. The area finally selected for the crossing of 20 Indian Division was at the bend, south of the village of Allagappa. The river here is about 1,500 yards wide and the current is strong (three knots). High ground to the south-east gave the enemy observation over the area initially. Not being an ideal crossing-place, it was only lightly defended. Moreover it was the junction of 31 and 33 Japanese Divisions, which, as was hoped, led to confusion when we struck. The crossing was made by 100 Brigade on the night 12th–13th February, and, by the following night, a bridgehead six miles wide by two miles deep had been developed. The success of this operation was in great measure due to the diversionary attacks made elsewhere by 32 Brigade which attracted troops away from the real crossing. This crossing by 20 Indian Division is also notable for the fact that it was supported by the only Corps artillery concentration attempted during the whole campaign. Generally, the artillery's rôle was unspectacular but it should not be thought for that reason that it was unimportant. The often few guns in action, brought forward sometimes by tremendous effort, played a vital rôle and Commanders repeatedly commented on the effectiveness of the fire support that was provided.

Early on the 15th, hostile air action, caused considerable damage to our already scant river crossing equipment, but the damaged boats were replaced by the evening of the 17th. By the 16th February, our bridgehead had been sufficiently extended to allow crossings to be made in daylight.

83. 4 Corps' crossing, which I shall next describe, was a model of its kind. For some weeks before the actual crossing, widespread deception measures were instituted indicating that a minor operation was in progress down the Gangaw Valley with the Yenangyaung oilfields as its objective. Shortly before the crossing, obvious preparations were made further east, towards Pakokku. The real crossing was timed for the night 13th–14th February. At dawn on the 13th, 28 (East African) Brigade, which had been fighting its way down the Yaw Chaung, suddenly appeared on the west bank of the Irrawaddy opposite Chauk, after capturing Seikpyu. These feints were entirely successful. The Japanese moved more troops to both Pakokku and Chauk, while, as will appear, we crossed practically unopposed at Nyaungu roughly half-way between these two places.

84. Nyaungu was selected as the crossing site for two reasons. First, it was on the boundary between 15 and 28 Japanese Armies and experience had shown that the enemy were notoriously weak at tying-in at such points. Secondly, it was, for topographical reasons, the most unsuitable place for a crossing, and, consequently, its defence had been largely entrusted to an "Indian National Army" division.

85. Three crossing-places were selected. The longest, a diagonal crossing of two and a half miles, was to be made by the assault brigade (33 Brigade of 7 Indian Division). The other two were about 1,800 yards and 1,300 yards wide respectively. The current was about one and a half knots. This, combined with a steady

east wind (i.e. with the current), rendered navigation between the islands and sandbanks difficult. The approaches on the west bank were open and completely overlooked from the steep 100-foot cliffs on the opposite side. No power craft were used for the first assault wave. Paddling silently in the darkness for over two miles, they landed at the foot of the cliffs and gained the crest without a shot being fired. The second flight attempted the shorter crossing, using outboard motors, but were heavily fired on. The drivers were killed or wounded and the attempt failed. By this time, however, troops of the first wave had established a small bridgehead and they were immediately reinforced by the rest of 33 Brigade and a detachment of tanks, which crossed in broad daylight practically un-opposed. The Divisional Commander's selection of the crossing site had been justified.

86. 33 Brigade captured Pagan on the 15th February. The build-up in the bridge-head continued. On the west bank 114 Brigade entered Pakokku on the 18th after overcoming strong opposition to the west of it. It then started to clear the large island which lies off Pakokku. By this time (20th February), the Japanese were attacking the bridgehead from the south, but prisoners stated that our crossing was regarded merely as a diversion. 28 (East African) Brigade were also heavily counter-attacked in Seikpyu area on the 16th. They regrouped at Gwebin, but were again severely attacked on the 20th and withdrew to Letse. Here the threat to our right flank was held. It was evident that the enemy still continued to regard the feints which had been made on both sides of Nyaungu as a greater menace than the real crossing, despite our build-up in the bridgehead.

87. While 7 Indian Division was operating on and across the river, the other divi-sion of 4 Corps, 17 Indian Division (Major-General D.T. Cowan), was closing up ready to cross, leaving its air-transportable brigade (99 Brigade) at Palel ready to fly in. By the 22nd February, two brigades of 17 Indian Division and 255 Indian Tank Brigade had actually crossed into the bridgehead. 5 Indian Division (Major-General E.C. Mansergh) who had taken over the Division after the death of Major-General D.F.W. Warren in an aeroplane crash less its air-transportable brigade (99 Brigade), was, during this period, also being brought forward. It was directed on Nyaungu, *via* the Kabaw Valley, Ye-U and Monywa. The intention was that this formation should assist 17 Indian Division in the Meiktila area and, also, exploit southwards.

88. Back in 33 Corps' sector, the last crossing of the Irrawaddy was made by 2 British Division at Ngazun, some 10 miles to the east of 20 Indian Division's bridgehead, on the night 24th–25th February. The river here contains many large sandbanks and shifting shoals and varies in width between 1,000 and 1,500 yards. The current is considerable (two and a half knots). It was originally hoped to cross further to the east, but reconnaissance showed that beach obstacles had been erected, and defences manned, in all suitable areas. It was planned to land on three beaches simultaneously: Beaches A and B lay some two miles and one mile

respectively west of Ngazun Village, and C Beach on the large island north of the village, which it was necessary to secure since it enfiladed the other two crossings and was patrolled by the enemy. The crossings had to be made diagonally to avoid sandbanks, thus lengthening the time the boats were exposed to view and, unfortunately, the moon was nearly full. The first assault wave on to Ngazun Island (C Beach) was fired on, but about one company touched town and charged through the enemy positions. The supporting wave, however, failed to land and the enemy held their ground, pinning the first wave's boats to the beach by their fire and preventing their return. The assault on A Beach met heavy fire from artillery, mortars and infantry. Many boats were sunk and the assault had to be abandoned. The situation was serious and it looked as if the crossing might fail, but there remained B Beach. Here the 1st Battalion, The Queens' Own Cameron Highlanders, who had the longest crossing to make, also encountered heavy fire but they effected a gallant landing, storming up the steep 30-foot bank and establishing a bridgehead. Again, however, no boats got back.

89. What followed was an outstanding feat of control, staff work and discipline. It was, obviously, essential to reinforce with infantry the bridgehead on B Beach at once, but this entailed a complete change of plan. The possibility of partial failure had been foreseen and an alternative plan had been prepared, but the fact that it was rapidly and successfully executed in darkness – the moon had set – despite the inevitable confusion of the initial failures, and despite the shortage of equipment, many craft not having returned, reflects great credit on all concerned, from the Divisional Commander (Major-General C.G.G. Nicholson) downwards.

By first light on the 25th February, two battalions of 5 Brigade were established complete on the south bank and one battalion of 6 Brigade complete on Ngazun Island. By the 26th the whole of both 5 and 6 Brigades were over, together with a squadron of tanks, and on this date Ngazun Village was captured. On the 27th February, the bridgehead had been extended to a depth of five miles and 4 Brigade had begun to cross, after being relieved in the Ondaw area by 268 Indian Infantry Brigade. 268 Indian Infantry Brigade had taken over the Sagaing area to enable 2 British Division to concentrate on their crossing, and were responsible for the open flank between 19 Indian Division and 2 British Division. Our troops received strong air support throughout these operations: Ngazun was only captured after it had been set on fire by the Royal Air Force.

90. I would like to emphasise here the magnitude of Fourteenth Army's achievement in crossing this great river obstacle, in the face of a brave and determined enemy and with a minimum of modern equipment. It is worth considering that the Irrawaddy is four times as wide as the Rhine, while the Japanese soldier in well prepared positions is no less formidable than the German. It is the greatest tribute to the Commander, officers and men of Fourteenth Army that such a hazardous and exacting operation was crowned with success. By the end of February, four divisions and a tank brigade were firmly established on the left bank of the river.

91. Before going on to the next phase of operations and the Japanese reactions to our crossings, which are described in the next section, I will draw attention to the progress made in Northern Burma on the Northern Combat Area Command front since my last mention of it (paragraphs 43–47). Namhkam fell to 30 Chinese Division on the 15th January. 38 Chinese Division entered the village of Muse on the 22nd, linking up with the Chinese Expeditionary Force which had just captured Wanting, thus reopening a through route from Burma to China. The American "Mars" Brigade were operating in the area 30 miles north-west of Hsenwi, into which 56 Japanese Division from the Wanting area was withdrawing. The main body of 36 British Division (26 and 72 Brigades) was advancing south on Mongmit and, at the end of January, it had reached a point on the Shweli River 18 miles to the north of that place. One detached brigade (29 Brigade) of this Division had made considerable progress down the east bank of the Irrawaddy, capturing Twinnge, 15 miles north of 19 Indian Division's bridgehead at Thabeikkyin on the 24th January. It then turned due east along the main road to Mongmit.

SECTION VI (paras. 92–101)

THE SITUATION IN FEBRUARY

A.L.F.S.E.A. Operation Instruction of the 27th February, 1945: The change in scope of the Burma operations: The Japanese plans for a counter-offensive: Operations to enlarge our bridgeheads: The Northern Combat Area Command front.

---

92. Directly it became apparent that our crossings of the Irrawaddy had succeeded over a wide front, I issued, on the 27th February, an Operation Instruction to General Slim, General Sultan and General Christison in order to co-ordinate operations in the immediate future. It will be remembered that on the 26th January, the Chiefs of Staff had promised to increase our transport aircraft to meet our essential requirements by the 1st March. With this in mind, I instructed Fourteenth Army to destroy the Japanese forces in the Mandalay area and to capture Rangoon before the monsoon. Northern Combat Area Command were directed to seize the general area Kyaukme – Lashio and then to turn south-west and co-operate in the Mandalay area battle. After this they were to exploit out towards Loilem. 15 Indian Corps, whose tasks I had already a month before extended to include developing the air bases on Akyab and Ramree Islands for the supply of Fourteenth Army, and to operations as far south as Taungup, were now directed, in general, to contain the maximum number of enemy forces, particularly by operating up the An and Taungup – Prome routes. (These operations by 15 Indian Corps will be discussed in detail in a later part of this Despatch.) Since this Operation Instruction contains my brief appreciation of the situation at the time, I have attached a copy at Appendix A.

93. It will be seen at once that the outline of operations given above represents a great development from the situation in November, 1944. Then we were direct-

ing our efforts to enable us to launch a major expedition against Rangoon after the 1945 monsoon. Now we were aiming at capturing Rangoon by land advance from the north, an operation which for long had been regarded as impracticable. There were additional reasons for this change. After the Yalta Conference, the Chiefs of Staff had sent the Supreme Allied Commander a new directive. This was not only influenced by the speed and success of our advance in Burma, and the opening of the Ledo/Burma Road, but also by the general quickening of the tempo of the American operations against Japan in the Pacific and in the Philippines. The new directive ordered South-East Asia Command to defeat the Japanese Army in Burma and capture Rangoon; thereafter to open the Straits of Malacca and to capture Singapore. After the Chiefs of Staffs' promise to give us the necessary transport aircraft, on the 5th February I received a directive from the Supreme Allied Commander ordering me to "secure the Ledo/Burma Road, capture Rangoon by 1st June, 1945, and destroy the main Japanese forces in Burma excluding the Tenasserim." In furtherance of the second half of his directive from the Chiefs of Staff, Admiral Mountbatten decided to capture the island of Phuket, as an air base and a station for the assembly of naval landing craft, with a target date in June 1945. This proposal was put up to the Chiefs of Staff on the 26th February, and received their general approval on the 2nd March.

94. 34 Indian Corps was formed for this operation. It had been obvious for some time that if operations were to be extended beyond the Burma theatre, additional formations would be required, and in particular another Corps Headquarters. There was only one immediate source of man-power, namely Special Force, until the redeployment of forces from Europe began. I therefore recommended the immediate formation of a Corps Headquarters and Corps Signals to plan and train for future operations and, in February, the Supreme Allied Commander asked the Commander-in-Chief, India, to implement the formation of such a Headquarters from the assets becoming available from the disbandment of Special Force. By the end of February, H.Q., 34 Indian Corps, had been established at Poona, becoming an assigned formation. Placed under its command were 23 Indian Division, which was the General Headquarters, India, reserve division, but which was released for my operations by General Auchinleck; 81 (West African) Division, which had just come out of the Kaladan, and 3 Commando Brigade, which had carried out highly successful operations at Akyab, Myebon and Kangaw with 15 Indian Corps. Planning by 34 Indian Corps for the Phuket operation began in Delhi on the 1st March, under Lieutenant-General O.L. Roberts, who was appointed to the command of the Corps early in March. (See also Sec. XVIII.)

95. Returning to the operations in Central Burma, if the Japanese reactions to our successful crossings of the Irrawaddy are to be understood, it is necessary to look at their plans and the situation as it must have presented itself to them at the time. It had been the intention of the Commander of the Japanese Burma Army that

the main battle should be fought on the banks of the Irrawaddy. By the second half of February it must have been clear that this battle was not going very well, but the position did not yet seem irretrievable. At that time 19 Indian Division had broken out of their bridgehead at Kyaukmyaung and begun their advance on Mandalay (I refer later to these operations), but they had not yet crossed the formidable Chaungmagyi Chaung, which most effectively bars the approach to Mandalay from the north. 2 British Division had only penetrated five miles inland from Ngazun. 20 Indian Division were being bitterly attacked and were still confined to a narrow semi-circle of ground. They had not yet linked up with 2 British Division. 7 Indian Division had already captured Pagan, but believing, as they did, that 4 Corps was still operating on the left of 33 Corps, the enemy regarded this crossing merely as a diversion which could be dealt with by the troops on the spot. General Kimura therefore decided to restore the generally adverse situation by a counter-offensive. The main effort was to be by 15 Army, which, reinforced by most of 18 Japanese Division, was to launch an offensive with 18 and 31 Divisions from Madaya and Sagaing towards Wetlet (on the Shwebo railway line from Sagaing). On the right flank of this counter-offensive 33 Army, with 56 Division and a regiment of 18 Division, was to hold the areas round Lashio and Namtu, whilst on the left 28 Army was to defend the Irrawaddy valley about the Yenangyaung and Mount Popa areas and launch an offensive in the Pakokku area. The scale of the latter – it was to be made by a composite force of less than divisional strength – showed that the real threat in that area was not yet appreciated. The general offensive was to begin on the 10th March.

96. This plan involved considerable movements of formations, which, in view of the state of the Japanese communications and our air superiority, were executed with remarkable speed. Besides the move of 18 Japanese Division (less a regiment) from opposite Northern Combat Area Command to the Mandalay area, the remainder of 49 Japanese Division (less the two regiments already committed on the Northern Combat Area Command front and in the Yenangyaung area respectively) together with a regiment of 55 Japanese Division (from the Henzada – Bassein area) were ordered up south of Mandalay. In addition, a regiment of 2 Japanese Division, destined for Siam, was stopped at Pegu and counter-marched north. From the Arakan front, 54 Japanese Division was ordered to concentrate north of Yenangyaung and to block the An and Taungup – Prome roads with detachments. This attempt at reinforcement from Arakan by the Japanese must have been in the nature of a forlorn hope and reflects their lack of knowledge of the situation there. Thanks to the energetic operations carried out by 15 Indian Corps, very few troops reached the Irrawaddy from Arakan. In short, General Kimura decided to abandon Arakan, weaken South Burma and reduce the forces holding the Northern Combat Area Command front to a minimum in order to concentrate his troops in the Mandalay sector which he regarded as the vital one. As will be seen later, he was too late.

97. The bringing forward of 17 and 5 Indian Divisions, which had been made possible by the increase in transport aircraft promised by the 1st March (*vide* paragraphs 69 and 93), had raised the number of divisions in Fourteenth Army to six. Had the Japanese redistribution of their forces, mentioned above, been effected in full, it would have meant that their total strength opposed to Fourteenth Army would have been increased by the equivalent of three divisions, i.e., up to a total of eight divisions (less one regiment), excluding the two I.N.A. divisions. In view of this disparity in formations, General Slim asked that 36 British Division should be placed under his command. I was, however, unable to accede to this request at this juncture (though I was in a position to do so later), both because it would have upset the Northern Combat Area Command plan and also because of administrative difficulties connected with air supply. It will be remembered that I had already instructed General Sultan to accelerate his advance and co-operate in the coming Mandalay battle (*vide* paragraph 92). But while, on paper, I had apparently ordered six divisions to destroy a force of nearly eight, there were several factors, which have been mentioned before, operating in our favour. We were now beginning to realise how far the state of the enemy was deteriorating. We had overwhelming air superiority and all the great advantages of security from air attack, close air support, regular air reconnaissance, air supply and air movement of troops – advantages which were denied to the Japanese, owing to their marked inferiority in the air. We possessed great advantages in mobility and in armoured strength, and were in terrain where we could exploit them. And, last but not least, there was the proved fighting value of our own troops and their now most marked moral ascendency over the enemy.

98. In 33 Corps' sector, 19 Indian Division made substantial gains in the third week in February, capturing Singu after stiff fighting and inflicting heavy casualties. On 98 Brigade's front, there were indications that the enemy was pulling out from the Thabeikkyin area, after ten days of continuous attacks. 98 Brigade was, therefore, ordered to clear the area between Thaibeikkyin and the southern bridgehead and rejoin the remainder of the Division. This operation was successfully completed by the 20th February, on which date 19 Indian Division commenced its drive south on a two brigade front against continued resistance. 2 British Division encountered only light opposition to their build-up, as the enemy in this sector had concentrated his strength in an all-out effort to destroy 20 Indian Division. In 20 Indian Division's bridgehead, a prolonged and bitter struggle was raging, but the Japanese, following their usual custom, flung their reinforcements in piecemeal and their casualties continued to mount. By the 16th February, we had passed to the offensive, capturing Alethaung Village after savage hand-to-hand fighting. Fierce counter-attacks followed against the extreme west of our position; but, by the 26th we had taken Tabingon and extended our bridgehead to a width of eight miles and a depth of two and a half.

99. In 4 Corps' sector, after the capture of Pagan on the 15th February already recorded, 7 Indian Division's bridgehead at Nyaungu was considerably enlarged.

By the end of February, 33 Brigade was thrusting east, along the south bank of the Irrawaddy, with Myingyan as its ultimate objective. Meanwhile, 89 Brigade was striking south towards Singu. On the north bank, 114 Brigade continued operations about Pakokku. On the right flank of 4 Corps, west of the river, 28 (East African) Brigade had repulsed enemy attacks south of Letse. Further west, a detachment composed of the Chin Hills Battalion and the Lushai Scouts was pushing back the Japanese rear parties in the area of Point 468, west-north-west of Letse. As already stated (paragraph 87) 17 Indian Division (less its air-transportable brigade) and 255 Indian Tank Brigade, had concentrated in 7 Indian Division's bridgehead at Nyaungu by the 22nd February. The success or failure of the whole Fourteenth Army plan depended on its subsequent operations and they will be described separately.

100. On the Northern Combat Area Command front 36 British Division (less 29 Brigade), advancing on Mongmit from the north, effected a strongly opposed crossing of the Shweli River during the first week of February. The first attempt failed, but the second one, made with increased air support, was successful near the bend of the river north of Myitson. Myitson fell on the 9th February and the advance continued against stiff resistance. On the 17th, the enemy counter-attacked in strength, using flame-throwers and much artillery. They succeeded in penetrating our forward positions, but were ejected by a spirited attack by an Indian battalion after bitter hand-to-hand fighting. Our further progress towards Mongmit continued to meet with determined resistance. 29 Brigade, advancing on Mongmit from the west, captured Nabu on the 18th February and, by the end of the month, had reached a point approximately half way between Nabu and Mongmit. Further east, 50 Chinese Division entered Namtu on the 23rd February, capturing eleven locomotives and a quantity of rolling stock. Further east again, 30 Chinese Division captured Hsenwi on the night 18th – 19th February against light opposition. This village lies on the Burma Road about 30 miles north-east of Lashio. The enemy in this sector appeared to be falling back to positions immediately north of Lashio, with a view to defending that town.

101. Although the Japanese were withdrawing along the whole of Northern Combat Area Command's front, they were doing so at their leisure. Since the weakening of Northern Combat Area Command's front by the loss of two divisions and the securing of the road trace through Namhkam and Muse by the capture of Hsenwi, the pressure had slackened and this front was not fulfilling the task I wanted done, namely the containing of the Japanese forces there and the prevention of enemy concentration against Fourteenth Army. It was for this reason that, in my Operation Instruction of the 27th February (see Appendix A), I directed the Commanding General, Northern Combat Area Command, to secure the general area Kyaukme – Lashio with all speed.

SECTION VII (paras. 102–117)
THE BATTLE FOR MANDALAY
The importance of Meiktila: The capture of Meiktila and its effect on the Japanese plans: The capture of Mandalay: Japanese counter-offensive to retake Meiktila.

---

102. While the Japanese were concentrating their forces against 33 Corps (*vide* paragraphs 95 and 96) the thrust at their vitals by 4 Corps was developing. I use this term advisedly for all the Japanese communications radiated from Meiktila and Thazi; north to Mandalay and Lashio, south to Rangoon, north-west to Myingyan, west to Kyaukpadaung and thence to the oilfields at Chauk and Yenangyaung, and east, *via* Kalaw, to Siam. Meiktila was the advanced supply base for all the Japanese forces in Burma, with the exception of those in Arakan. At Meiktila, too, were located the principal Japanese airfields, the capture of which would be of inestimable value to us. If we could seize Meiktila, and hold it, the whole structure of the Japanese defence in Central Burma was bound to collapse.

103. The great dash on Meiktila started on the 21st February, when a mechanised and armoured column composed of 48 Brigade (17 Indian Division), with tanks, broke out of the Nyaungu bridgehead, captured Hnawdwin 15 miles to the east, and were then temporarily held up by deep ravines beyond the village. Here they were joined by the rest of the Division and 255 Indian Tank Brigade (less one regiment left with 7 Indian Division). The advance continued the same day, but to avoid the difficult country between Pyinsin and Welaung, the Division fanned out, 48 Brigade and a proportion of armour moving on Taungtha, *via* Kainye, and 63 Brigade with the main body of the Tank Brigade directed south-east on Seiktin and then north-east, *via* Welaung. Both columns reached Taungtha on the 24th February after overcoming desperate resistance and clearing many minefields. By the evening of the 24th, our leading troops had progressed five miles south-east of Taungtha, towards Mahlaing. By 0900 hours on the 26th we had captured the important Thabutkon airfield intact, smashing through a deter-mined Japanese effort to protect it. The fly-in from Palel of the air-transportable brigade (99 Brigade) of 17 Indian Division began next morning, by which time our tanks were engaged within five miles of Meiktila.

104. This rapid drive merits attention. It was the first opportunity we had had of utilising our mechanised and armoured superiority on a large scale and the Japanese were completely bewildered and overwhelmed. The enemy positions, manned by such scratch forces as could be hastily collected, were subjected to heavy air attack, encircled by tanks and lorried infantry, and rendered untenable. Forced into the open, the enemy suffered enormous casualties. The "Cab Rank" method of air support was here employed most successfully for the first time in Burma, squadrons remaining over the operations area and being directed on to fleeting targets from ground control centres. These were known as Visual

Control Posts (V.C.Ps.) which comprised an Army and a R.A.F. officer and which were usually located at brigade headquarters. It proved a most efficient method, though uneconomical from an Air Force point of view, of providing instantaneous air strikes during rapidly moving operations. The finding of the necessary officers for these V.C.Ps., and their training had in the past been matters of some difficulty. The efforts which had been made to overcome these were now rewarded in full.

105. The Japanese garrison at Meiktila totalled 3,500, according to a document captured later. Unfortunately, our arrival in the area coincided with that of one regiment of 49 Japanese Division, which was being rushed from Pegu to Mandalay. The enemy was also strong in artillery. The commander of the garrison, General Kasuya, had acted with vigour in the short time at his disposal. The defences were strong and ingeniously sited, and all available men, including hospital patients, were put in to man them. The large lakes to the west of the town narrowed the areas of approach and, in all sectors, the lines of advance suitable for tanks were well covered by artillery, which included many anti-aircraft batteries used in their anti-tank rôle. All this in an area where the deployment of armour was already hampered by broken, country and deep irrigation cuts.

106. As dawn broke on the 28th February, the attack on Meiktila went in from four directions. On the north-west, 48 Brigade drove down the axis of the main road, while 63 Brigade attacked from the west. Simultaneously, 255 Indian Tank Brigade, with two infantry battalions, attacked from the east and north-east. The tanks experienced difficulty in deploying and the infantry were at first pinned down by heavy fire, but later succeeded in capturing Point 859, which dominates the town from the south-east. 48 Brigade were temporarily held up by a blown bridge, but by nightfall Point 859 had been consolidated and Meiktila had been entirely surrounded. There followed three days and nights of hand-to-hand fighting as savage as any yet experienced in the campaign. The enemy put up the most fanatical resistance and houses and dug-outs were only cleared after the last defender had been bayonetted. By the morning of the 4th March, all Meiktila north of the railway had been cleared, but on both sides of the lake suicide parties still held out, which it took some days to eliminate. In this bitter fighting, the Japanese garrison had been practically annihilated – over 2,000 bodies being counted in the town alone. The booty captured included 48 guns.

107. In the meantime, the fly-in of 99 Brigade of 17 Indian Division, which had begun on the 27th February (paragraph 103), was completed early on the 2nd March, three days ahead of schedule, and the Brigade moved forward into battle. In all, 353 sorties were flown without the loss of a single man, a very fine achievement by the R.A.F. and U.S.A.A.F.

108. On the 4th March, leaving the complete clearance of the town to 63 Brigade, columns of all arms were despatched along all the roads radiating from Meiktila. The important road and railway junction of Thazi was reported clear, but, in

other sectors, columns of reinforcements, guns and lorries heading for Meiktila were encountered. The fighting in the actions which resulted amounted to pure slaughter. The enemy, caught completely on the wrong foot, was engaged by aircraft, tanks and infantry and thrown into utter confusion. Here again, the "Cab Rank" method proved most efficacious.

109. To say that our capture of Meiktila came as a surprise to the enemy Command would be an understatement. Not only was the blow utterly unexpected, but their Intelligence was for some time completely baffled as to what troops had inflicted it. The general counter-offensive plans for early March had to to put aside, as, until Meiktila was recaptured and our forces south of Mandalay destroyed, no major attacks could be launched north and west of the Irrawaddy. On the other hand, failure to recapture Meiktila could result in disaster for practically the whole of the Burma Area Army. Although captured orders show that Kimura realised this, yet, curiously enough, other documents show that he still intended to prosecute what he called "The decisive battle of the Irrawaddy Shore." The result was that he adopted half-measures. He countermanded the moves directed against 33 Corps (*vide* paragraph 95) and diverted these formations on to Meiktila, stressing, in his orders, the vital necessity for speed. He also directed General Yamamoto in the west (Yenangyaung area) to sever 4 Corps' communications by capturing their Pakokku bridgehead by an advance up both banks of the Irrawaddy. But he gave no orders to his forces who were about Mandalay or south of the river to withdraw, evidently considering he could restore the situation about Meiktila while continuing the battle in the north. Here, as so often before, the Japanese under-estimation of their enemy was to prove fatal to them.

110. The forces which Kimura concentrated to recover Meiktila were as follows: 18 Japanese Division (less 114 Regiment), brought south from the Northern Combat Area Command's front: 119 Regiment (53 Japanese Division), from south of Mandalay; 214 Regiment (33 Japanese Division) from the Irrawaddy front, opposite Pakokku; and 49 Japanese Division (less 153 Regiment) which had been hurried north from Pegu. These forces were reinforced by Army Troops, including medium artillery and some tanks. It was a formidable concentration and it was being rapidly effected. Our forces in Meiktila comprised 17 Indian Division and one tank brigade. The only reinforcement available was 5 Indian Division, which moved forward from Jorhat (700 miles distant) on the 5th March. Its forward concentration was carried out with great speed and the whole Division (less its air-transportable brigade) had reached 7 Indian Division's bridgehead at Nyaungu 10 days later. The fly-in of the remaining brigade from Palel to Meiktila was completed on the 17th March, but I will refer to this again. It will be seen, therefore, that the enemy was concentrating the equivalent of six brigades, plus Army units, against our four infantry brigades and one tank brigade. There was nothing perturbing about this, but it must be remembered that our communications were vulnerable; our forward airfields were exposed to attack, as, also, was the road back *via* Taungtha, while the road west, *via* Kyaukpadaung,

was of course still under enemy control. Our object, therefore, was to hold Meiktila, acting as offensively as possible, while 7 Indian Division kept open the bridgehead area and enabled 5 Indian Division to pass through.

111. As already stated (paragraph 109), the enemy commander at Yenangyaung had been ordered to seize our bridgehead at Nyaungu, thus cutting our L. of C. to Meiktila. Yamamoto's plan was to make a converging attack from the west, on the right bank, and from the south and east on the left bank. This offensive, however, was uncoordinated. The I.N.A. Division attempted an assault from the east against 114 Brigade in the bridgehead, but its attacks were half-hearted and were driven back with heavy casualties. To the south, a Japanese force, assembling for an attack near Singu four miles north-east of Chauk, was caught and routed by 89 Brigade. The attack on the bridgehead from the west was prevented from developing by 28 (East African) Brigade, which successfully repulsed a series of attacks. Thus ended the threat to our communications at Nyaungu.

112. 28 (East African) Brigade deserves some remarks. Besides 11 (East African) Division, the original East African contingent included two independent brigades, the 22nd and the 28th, which were originally allotted for defence duties in Ceylon. Shortage of formations, however, had resulted in both brigades being sent to Burma, primarily to undertake duties on the L. of C. The Commander, Fourteenth Army, soon found himself forced, through lack of sufficient troops, to employ 28 (East African) Brigade in the line, although the formation had not really reached a sufficiently advanced state of training to be pitted against the enemy. It will be remembered that a reverse was suffered resulting in a withdrawal to the Letse area. Reinforced, however, by an Indian battalion and some artillery, the Brigade fought well, as shown above. In accordance with the decisions reached at a Conference with the G.O.C.-in-C, East Africa, held in February, 28 (East African) Brigade was flown out of Burma to Dohazari in March and April, and broken up, as the first step in the reduction of the East African forces, which, owing to the man-power situation, were to be reduced to the one division by early 1946.

113. On the east flank of the Irrawaddy battlefront, over a 100 miles up river, another great battle was raging. 19 Indian Division, which had broken out of its bridgehead on the 20th February, had begun its drive down the east bank of the river, advancing with great speed and determination. The two Japanese divisions (the 15th and 53rd) opposing 19 Indian Division completely failed to stop it. Strong positions were either assaulted, with tank and air support, or were bypassed. In a "leap-frogging" advance, 98 Brigade were the first troops to reach the Chaungmagyi, establishing a bridgehead on the 5th March; while, further north, 64 Brigade was still mopping up in the Pinlein area and 62 Brigade was fighting at Yenatha, which they captured on the 6th. The result of this method of advance was that we reached and passed through Madaya before the enemy had time to retire to the strongly prepared positions covering the two water barriers

north of the town. This spectacular advance ended on the 9th March, on which date 98 Brigade was attacking Mandalay Hill and 64 Brigade the village of Patheingyi, two miles to the east. Meanwhile, 62 Brigade had turned off southeast from Madaya on the 8th March and struck through the forest-clad hills towards Maymyo, which was occupied on the 11th; the astonished Japanese only offering slight resistance. The following day a large enemy convoy of lorries and staff cars in this area was surprised and wiped out. The capture of Maymyo cut the enemy's communications between Mandalay and their forces facing Northern Combat Area Command on the Kyaukme – Lashio front.

114. Mandalay contains two areas of tactical importance: Mandalay Hill and Fort Dufferin. The former is a great rock feature, covered with pagodas and Buddhist monasteries, which rises some 750 feet above the surrounding paddy fields, completely dominating the city from the north-east. Fort Dufferin lies southwest of Mandalay Hill and about two miles from the river. It is encircled by a moat about 80 yards wide, while its 20-foot walls are backed with an earth embankment some 72 feet thick at the base. The manner in which these ancient types of defences withstood many of the most modern and scientific forms of attack, including skip-bombing and rocket attacks by aircraft, is not without interest. It is worth recording, however, that low-level bombing attacks by Thunderbolts caused a gap in the walls large enough to enable a tank to get through.

115. The attack on Mandalay Hill was launched by 98 Brigade early on the 9th March, and the hill was captured after 24 hours of the most bitter hand-to-hand fighting. The enemy fought to the end, the last defenders being killed by means of petrol drums, set on fire, which were rolled down into the tunnel they were holding. There followed three days of street fighting. By the 14th the city had been cleared and Fort Dufferin invested. A gallant attempt by 98 Brigade to storm the fort failed, the attackers being held up by the thick weed in the moat. Old fashioned siege warfare methods were then adopted, in order to avoid the casualties which a direct assault would have entailed: but even medium artillery, firing from 500 yards, and aerial rocket projectiles failed to break the massive walls, with their earth embankment. By the 19th March, however, the Japanese had had enough, and that night the remnants of the garrison attempted to escape through the ruins. The majority were intercepted and only a few got away. An immense quantity of equipment, chiefly ordnance stores, fell into our hands and 160 civilian internees were rescued. The capture of Mandalay was a fitting climax to a great advance. Between the date it crossed the Irrawaddy on the 9th January and the fall of Mandalay, 19 Indian Division had accounted for 6,000 Japanese killed, actually counted on the ground.

116. General Kimura's plan (paragraphs 109 and 110) to recapture Meiktila, both by cutting our communications thereto and by direct assault was energetically pursued. Early in March, a strong enemy force re-occupied Taungtha and the dominating hills to the northeast. This meant that nearly 5,000 unarmoured

vehicles, comprising the administrative "tail" of the formations in Meiktila, could not get through. As already stated (paragraph 110) 5 Indian Division had reached Nyaungu on the 15th March and to it was then allotted the difficult task of reopening the road to Meiktila.

117. In the Meiktila area, there was continuous fighting. While mobile columns of infantry and tanks were successfully operating against the enemy who were attempting to close in on the town, inflicting heavy casualties and capturing many guns, the Japanese were concentrating on capturing the airstrip, two miles north of Meiktila, on which our supplies depended. On the night 15th–16th March, their attacks reached the north-west corner of the airstrip where they dug in. They were successfully counter-attacked but their guns still dominated the strip, and the air-transportable brigade of 5 Indian Division, which was then being flown in landed under artillery fire. Several aircraft were destroyed, but the American Air Commandos were undeterred and no sortie turned back. The enemy then attacked in strength and succeeded in capturing the airstrip. This resulted in an immediate severe curtailment of supplies, including ammunition, since we had to fall back on "dropping" as opposed to "landing." There followed a week's fierce fighting to regain the strip. The enemy dug in in the broken country to the north, which was almost impassable for tanks, and strengthened the position with numerous anti-tank guns and minefields. This meant that the clearance of the strip was a job for the infantry, together with elements of the R.A.F. Regiment and R.A.F. Servicing Commandos, and it was achieved against the most determined opposition with the magnificent support of R.A.F. fighter-bombers. The Japanese artillery, however, still covered the airfield at almost point-blank range and further bitter close-quarter fighting was necessary before the enemy was routed. The whole area was cleared by the 29th March. The enemy's suicidal resistance cost him nearly all his guns and we inflicted tremendous casualties.

SECTON VIII (paras. 118–130)
THE CLEARING OF THE MANDALAY PLAIN

The end of operations by Northern Combat Area Command: The opening of the road to Meiktila: The capture of Kyaukse: The clearing of Ava and Sagaing: The Japanese decision to withdraw: Shortage of transport aircraft: The achievements of 33 Corps.

---

118. In early March decisions were taken which resulted in Northern Combat Area Command's operations ceasing altogether by the end of the month. Generalissimo Chiang Kai Shek was preparing his forces for an offensive in the Autumn of 1945, and for this he proposed to form an army of some thirty-six divisions, whose spearhead would be the five Chinese divisions from Burma, which had been trained at Ramgarh in India. He also required the American Mars Brigade from Burma to train fresh divisions in China on the lines of the

Ramgarh-trained divisions. On the 8th March, the Supreme Allied Commander visited Chungking to confer with the Generalissimo on these matters. General Wedemeyer was not present as he had gone to Washington to consult the Combined Chiefs of Staff on the same issue. Admiral Mountbatten pointed out to the Generalissimo how vital the continued operations of the Chinese forces in Burma were, since the issue of the main battle was not yet decided, upon which our chance of capturing Rangoon before the monsoon depended. While he insisted on their eventual withdrawal, the Generalissimo appeared to agree to the Chinese divisions continuing the present operations, but in actual fact the Chinese forces never came beyond Lashio and Hsipaw. Moreover, the Combined Chiefs of Staff confirmed the Generalissimo's request for the Mars Brigade, whose retention I had particularly pressed, by an order for their move to China at once. As will be seen from the account of operations below, this put a virtual end to the offensive operations of Northern Combat Area Command, though, of course, I realised that it would be considered that the American forces in Burma had achieved their primary object once the Burma Road was opened to connect with the road they had built from Ledo. I had hoped that Northern Combat Area Command, beside co-operating in the Mandalay battle, could assist our further advance by sending weak forces southwards towards Loilem, but this was not to be.

119. On the 9th March, 36 British Division, captured Mongmit, and, advancing south-west reached Mogok on the 20th. They were then directed on to Kyaukme, which lies some 45 miles due south of Mogok. 50 Chinese Division, advancing southwards from Namru, entered Hsipaw on the 16th March, and then turned west down the road towards Kyaukme. 38 Chinese Division captured Lashio on the 7th March, and by the end of the month had pushed south-south-east 38 miles along the Lashio – Mongyai road. Other troops from this Division turned south-west down the Lashio – Hsipaw road and, by the 26th March, had linked up with 50 Chinese Division in the Hsipaw area.

120. This limited advance was the end of Northern Combat Area Command's operations. Unfortunately, the relaxing of the pressure had, as already shown, allowed the Japanese to reinforce the Mandalay sector from this front. The bulk of 18 Japanese Division had been brought into the Meiktila battle, while later 56 Japanese Division with the remaining regiment of the 18th were ordered to withdraw their main forces for the main battle and hold the right flank with minimum strength. On the 30th March, I issued orders for 36 British Division to come under command of Fourteenth Army on reaching Kyaukme. I also directed, that one brigade should be flown into Mandalay as quickly as possible. The whole of 36 British Division was then to relieve 19 Indian Division and assume control of operations in the Maymyo – Mandalay – Ava area. This would relieve the strain on Fourteenth Army until the Japanese had been pushed further south, but it could only be regarded as a temporary expedient since the American aircraft, on which 36 British Division was dependent for maintenance, were to be withdrawn

in May, before which the Division would have to be flown out to India. 36 British Division, less 26 Indian Infantry Brigade which remained in Burma, was actually flown out between the 1st and 21st May.

121. Returning now to the main battle on the Fourteenth Army front: while our forces in Meiktila were engaged in frustrating and destroying the Japanese built-up against them, the remainder of 4 Corps was engaged in pushing back the enemy west of the Irrawaddy, and in expanding the Nyaungu bridgehead south-wards towards Chauk and eastwards towards Myingyan. On the 18th March, 33 Brigade (7 Indian Division) attacked prepared positions south of Myingyan, securing the road and railway crossing. On the 21st with tank support, they forced an entry into the town, and by the 23rd the whole of Myingyan had been cleared. Meanwhile, a detachment of the same Brigade had cleared the Chindwin – Irrawaddy confluence area to the north-west. The capture of Myingyan was a very important gain since it opened the way for our Inland Water Transport (I.W.T.) on the Chindwin. The administrative plan was to transport supplies by water from Kalewa to Myingyan, and thence by rail to Meiktila. It will be remembered that we had no all-weather road from Kalewa to Shwebo; the alternative route by water was therefore very important. A very great deal of transport and constructional effort was being expended on this I.W.T. L. of C. as can be seen in more detail in the part of this Despatch which deals with administration, and it paid good dividends.

122. At the same time as 7 Indian Division (33 Brigade) was attacking Myingyan, 5 Indian Division (161 Brigade) was advancing on Taungtha. The hill *massif* north of the town dominates the whole of this area and, after an assault launched on the 28th March, this feature was captured the following day. On the 30th, Taungtha was occupied. 161 Brigade was at once relieved by 33 Brigade from Myingyan and continued the advance, passing through Mahlaing on the 31st March and making contact with 17 Indian Division in the vicinity of Thabutkon. The road to Meiktila was open, and the rear echelon of 17 Indian Division, followed by the whole of 5 Indian Division (less the air-transportable brigade already in Meiktila), moved forward immediately.

123. As already described (paragraph 111), Yamamoto's offensive against 4 Corps' bridgehead had completely failed. His forces on both banks of the river were pushed back and, by the end of March, 89 Brigade (7 Indian Division) had entered Lanywa on the west bank and were successfully probing south from Singu, and west towards Kyaukpadaung, east of the river. 7 Indian Division (less 33 Brigade) was placed under command of 33 Corps on the 29th March, when that Corps entered the area in which the Division was operating. 33 Brigade reverted to under the command of 7 Indian Division on the 31st March.

124. 20 Indian Division linked up their bridgehead with that of 2 British Division to the east on the 2nd March. The prolonged period of severe defensive fighting had ended and all three brigades broke out of the bridgehead. By the 10th March,

80 Brigade had taken Gyo to the south-east, capturing eleven guns. On this date, also, 32 Brigade began its break-through against stiff opposition and advanced three miles. By the 12th March, 100 Brigade (from the west flank of the Myinmu bridgehead) had captured the important road junction of Myotha, inflicting heavy casualties. The advance continued eastwards against steadily increasing resistance. By the 23rd March, 80 Brigade were two miles west of the important enemy base of Kyaukse, where they were held up. With a view to outflanking the Japanese positions, 32 Brigade began an encircling movement south-west of the town. A week's hard fighting ensued before Kyaukse was entered on the 30th March, the booty captured including rolling stock, motor transport, and a quantity of valuable stores. The fall of Kyaukse was a severe blow to the enemy, strategically as well as administratively, since it formed the bastion behind which their disorganized forces, streaming back from north and west, were attempting to rally. Since crossing the Irrawaddy on the 12th February, 20 Indian Division had killed over 3,000 Japanese (counted), and captured 50 guns.

125. While the other two brigades of 20 Indian Division were advancing on Kyaukse, 100 Brigade (less one battalion) and two armoured car regiments made a spectacular raid against the enemy's communications to the south. Moving with great speed, this mechanised column captured Pyinzi on the 20th March and Pindale the following day. Turning eastwards, it then captured Wundwin on the 22nd, destroying large enemy dumps. It then turned north, surprising and killing a considerable force of Japanese encountered at Kume, 18 miles due south of Kyaukse.

The effects of this daring raid can well be imagined; it inflicted severe casualties, captured guns, and created havoc in the enemy's rear. But it did much more than this: it completely disrupted the Japanese system of command over a wide area, just at a time when its smooth working was essential to restore their crumbling battle fronts.

126. 2 British Division began its break-out from the Ngazun bridgehead on the 7th March. 4 Brigade captured Myintha on the 8th, and cleared the area to the west to the common boundary with 20 Division during the following week. 5 Brigade captured Kyauktalon on the 11th March and pushed rapidly eastwards. By the 15th, they were within two miles of the Myitnge River. On this date also, 6 Brigade operating to the south of 5 Brigade against strong opposition, inflicted heavy casualties on the enemy and reached a point two miles south of Tada-U. On the 17th March, 5 Brigade captured Ava Fort, liquidating a stubborn defence and, by the 21st, Japanese pockets of resistance had been mopped up, the Ava – Mandalay road opened, and junction effected with 19 Indian Division. 6 Brigade in the meantime had reached the Myitnge River and proceeded to inflict severe casualties on the enemy retreating before 19 Indian Division. 4 Brigade, transferred from the west, passed through 6 Brigade on the 18th and continued the advance towards Sado. While 19 Indian Division continued to advance southwards, 2 British Division were deflected south-west clearing the triangle Myitnge

– Myingyan – Meiktila. On the 27th March, 4 Brigade cleared Pyinzi and on the 31st reached Mahlaing. 5 and 6 Brigades cleared the area between Myitnge and Myingyan, linking up with 268 Indian Infantry Brigade at Natogyi, 17 miles east of Myingyan, on the 30th March. 268 Brigade had cleared Sagaing at the north end of the Ava bridge on the 18th March, and then advanced south-west *via* Myotha.

127. By the end of March, Kimura evidently realised that "The decisive battle of the Irrawaddy Shore" had ended for him in decisive defeat, for he ordered a general withdrawal. His plan now was for 33 Japanese Army, comprising 18, 49 and 53 Japanese Divisions, to stem our advance in the east down the railway axis, and for 28 Japanese Army, comprising Yamamoto's force and other detachments, to hold us in the west in the Irrawaddy Valley. Not for the first time, the Japanese Commander had left it until too late. From now on his losses in artillery and transport were to hamper his defence and restrict his mobility.

128. Another event occurred about this time to add to the Japanese difficulties. On the night of the 24th March the Headquarters staffs of the Burmese forces, which they had raised during their occupation, deserted. Three days later there was open revolt. The Burma Defence Army had turned against its masters. The revolt was widespread and considerable numbers of Japanese were killed. This rising, although in no way decisive, proved of great value to our operations, and forced the enemy to divert forces to deal with it. On joining the Allies the force was re-named the "Burma National Army".

129. But we ourselves were now faced again with the ever recurrent crisis of transport aircraft. General Sultan had agreed to hand over 36 British Division to Fourteenth Army, for General Slim to use for mopping-up work in the Mandalay area, with a view to the release of 19 Indian Division into Army reserve. 36 British Division would in any case have to be flown out to India as soon as possible as it could not be maintained for long, and it also needed a rest after a year's continuous fighting. An examination of the position on the 19th March had shown that we had insufficient transport aircraft to meet our present needs. This was likely to have the serious result that another division – probably a British one – would have to be flown out in April to relieve the supply situation. Further, I felt that the time had come when we should start to insure against the probable removal of the United States aircraft in the fairly near future. Admiral Mountbatten accordingly held a conference at my Tactical Headquarters at Monywa on the 22nd March, to discuss air supply. The following attended: Lieutenant-General Sultan, Air-Marshal Park, Major-General Stratemeyer, Lieutenant-General Slim, Major-General Fuller and Air Vice-Marshal Vincent. All the resources in transport aircraft which could be made available were to be used to help Fourteenth Army in their battle of annihilation and their subsequent dash for Rangoon. I asked for sufficient aircraft to enable me to keep 2 British Division in Fourteenth Army, and for a few over to enable General Christison to continue

mobile operations in Arakan to contain the enemy there. Owing to the nature of the country, operations up the An track or inland from Taungup were impracticable on an effective scale without air supply. I also suggested that as many now unwanted American and Chinese troops as possible should be flown out, so as to release transport aircraft for Fourteenth Army. But I insisted that no transport aircraft could be spared for this task from those supplying my forces at this critical stage.

130. Before leaving this phase of operations, it is interesting at this point to review the achievements of 33 Corps. By this means it is possible to see the magnitude of the cumulative defeat of the Japanese forces. On the 3rd April, 1944, Headquarters, 33 Corps, had opened at Jorhat and had proceeded at once to organize the operations which led to the relief of Kohima. Exactly one year later, the troops comprising this Corps were able to claim the following successes: Japanese killed (and actually counted) 19,547, prisoners taken 720, guns captured or destroyed 252. The following advances had taken place: on the right 597 miles, in the centre 549 miles, on the left 645 miles. The Japanese had been cleared from an area of 35,000 square miles. At least 11,000 inhabited localities had been liberated, including the city of Mandalay.

SECTION IX (paras. 131–158)
OPERATIONS IN ARAKAN

General remarks: Topography: The 15 Indian Corps plan: The Divisional plans: Opening stages of the offensive: The advance to Foul Point: Operations inland and in the Kaladan Valley.

---

131. I think that this is the appropriate place to turn from Fourteenth Army to the operations of 15 Indian Corps in Arakan. The object of these operations has already been given (paragraph 12), as has the outline of the plan (paragraph 14). Some reference has been made also to the progress there in November and December (paragraph 49). In this and the two ensuing sections, I propose to describe in more detail these plans and operations, showing how, from first being directed at the release of formations for post-monsoon operations against Rangoon, they developed so that their new object became the assistance of Fourteenth Army to capture Rangoon before the monsoon, by containing enemy forces, establishing air supply bases and, finally, by mounting an ancillary sea-borne operation against Rangoon itself.

132. In the Arakan sector, we were faced with peculiar difficulties. The first was topographical. The country entirely favoured the Japanese. The tangled, jungle-clad mountains run down to a narrow coastal strip of paddy or mangrove swamp, which is intersected by unfordable tidal creeks. These creeks or "chaungs" present problems which few who have not experienced them can imagine. They are mostly bordered by mangrove forest to a considerable depth on each side, which makes landing altogether impossible except at the extremely rare landing places,

of whose importance the enemy was obviously aware. These landing places, however, are only short stretches of muddy bank. The chaungs vary a very great deal in size, some being arms of the sea, while others are narrow and winding streams, hedged in both sides by the mangrove forest. In the latter case visibility is only to the next bend in the chaung. Near the sea, tidal conditions add to the difficulties. North of Akyab a few beaches can be found, but south to beyond Taungup, the mangrove swamp conditions are at their worst.

133. The other great difficulty is the weather, which is a major strategic factor. The exceptional severity of the monsoon in Arakan is apparent when one realises that the rainfall is over fifty inches during the months of July and August. During June and September the rainfall varies betwen fifteen and twenty inches for the former and between twenty and thirty inches for the latter month. This has two main effects. Movement on land is more or less impossible except between mid-December, when the ground dries out, and the breaking of the monsoon about mid-May, or a little earlier. Not only do the waterways rise and flood, but the paddy fields, which form most of the open country are under water and impassable. The impracticability of the employment of armour is obvious, and the absence of all-weather roads makes a land of L. of C. impossible during the rains. The second effect of the monsoon is that sea conditions prevent the use of landing craft except in virtually inland waterways. The number of days on which landing is impossible becomes progressively greater during April, and it will be seen later how the Japanese in fact anticipated no landings from the open sea after mid-April, until the monsoon was over.

134. Fortunately we had two advantages which enabled us decisively to overcome both the natural difficulties and the Japanese. We had secured complete command of the sea and the air and were thus able to utilise to the full the mobility conferred by this supremacy. Thus although the country favoured the land defence, we were in a position to force the enemy to fight on ground of our own choosing and to make ourselves independent, to a great extent, of overland Ls. of C. The campaign therefore hinged upon a series of combined operations, rapidly and efficiently mounted by a combined headquarters. Excellent teamwork was established between Lieutenant-General Sir Philip Christison, commanding 15 Indian Corps, Rear-Admiral Martin, commanding a naval force consisting, in part, of his own landing craft of Force "W", which was arriving from England, and a scratch force of landing craft from India, and Air Commodore (later Air Vice-Marshal) the Earl of Bandon, commanding 224 Group, R.A.F. The planning and execution by these Commanders and their staffs was excellent. In conjunction with these amphibious operations, the operations further inland by 81 and 82 (West African) Divisions fulfilled a very important rôle. Fighting under very arduous conditions, they kept the enemy spread over a wide front, containing the equivalent of about three Japanese regiments, and, by preventing the enemy from concentrating more troops in the coastal sector, materially assisted the speed of operations there.

135. To recapitulate what has been said in the early paragraphs of this Despatch, the primary object of the Arakan campaign was to liquidate the very unsatisfactory position which then existed. We had four divisions contained there by a very much inferior enemy force, which was able to threaten to outflank our positions by an advance up the Kaladan Valley. By a limited offensive to capture Akyab, Myebon and Minbya, we would eliminate this threat, and, by the coming monsoon, be enabled to reduce our garrison to about four brigades. The remaining formations could be withdrawn for post-monsoon operations, which at that time (November, 1944) were visualised as including an amphibious and airborne assault on Rangoon.

136. The Supreme Allied Commander had, on the 4th November, directed that plans were to be prepared and executed to accomplish the above object as follows:-

(*a*) A land advance, to start as soon as the drying of the ground allowed it, down the Mayu Peninsula and the Kalapanzin and Kaladan Valleys, with the object of clearing the area north of a general line Foul Point – Kudaung Island – Minbya.

(*b*) An amphibious assault on Akyab Island to take place as early as possible, with the aim of clearing the island by the end of January.

(*c*) Consolidation of the area north of the line Akyab – Minbya, but no exploitation to take place south of Myebon without the Supreme Allied Commander's authority.

These instructions had been passed on to the Commander, 15th Indian Corps, by General Giffard in an Operation Instruction dated the 9th November.

137. General Christison's plan to fulfil these directions for the clearing of Northern Arakan was as follows: 25 Indian Division (Major-General G.N. Wood) was to clear the Mayu Peninsula, and seize Foul Point and Kudaung Island. 82 (West African) Division (Major-General G. McI. S. Bruce) was to operate inland, as left flank guard to 25 Indian Division's advance, along the general axis of the Mayu River as far as Htizwe. This entailed the capture of Buthidaung and the crossing of the Kalapanzin River. On arrival at Htizwe, the Division was to turn east, over the Kanzauk Pass, and relieve 81 (West African) Division in the Kaladan Valley, and thence continue south towards Myebon. About 30 miles further inland, separated from 82 (West African) Division by a considerable range of hills, 81 (West African) Division (Major-General F.J. Loftus-Tottenham) consisting of only two brigades, was allotted the task of clearing the Kaladan Valley as far as Myohaung, by an advance down the axis of the Pi Chaung and the Kaladan River. After Myohaung, it was to hand over to 82 (West African) Division, and withdraw into Corps reserve at Chiringa as the first step towards the reduction of formations in Arakan. 26 Indian Division (Major-General C.E.N. Lomax) with 3 Commando Brigade under command, was to capture Akyab by a seaborne assault mounted from Chittagong and then to

exploit eastwards through the chaung country to the line Minbya – Myebon, while 82 (West African) Division came down the road from Myohaung. It will be seen from this plan that the main thrust was down the coast where our mobility could be exploited, while the two African divisions inland kept the enemy spread on a broad front, preventing him from concentrating in the coastal sector and safeguarding the land communications, first of 25 Indian Division and later of the rear of 15 Indian Corps. We thus would eliminate the threat of Japanese out-flanking operations, hitherto a worry.

138. As far as the timings of these operations were concerned, the advance of 81 (West African) Division was to begin first, and it was to secure the general line from Kaladan Village westwards to the Pi Chaung by the 1st December. The advance in the Mayu sector was not due to start until the 12th December, by which date the country would dry up sufficiently to allow the movement of armour and guns, and for air support to be given from fair-weather strips. Never-theless, 15 Indian Corps carried out what amounted to a preliminary offensive prior to this date. All ground which we had voluntarily vacated west of the Kalapanzin River prior to the monsoon was re-occupied, while, in the coastal sector, 25 Indian Division reached Udaung 13 miles south-east of Maungdaw. The first objective allotted to 25 Indian Division and 82 (West African) Division when the main offensive opened was the general line Indin – Htizwe, which was to be secured by the 31st December.

139. In the matter of ground communications, the advantage lay with the Japanese in that they controlled the mouths of the Mayu, Kywede and Kaladan Rivers, the Htizwe – Kanzauk jeep track, and the road south from Kyauktaw, on the Kaladan, to Myohaung. These advantages were, however, counteracted by the fact that our advance down the coast could be based on the sea, while, further east, the Kalapanzin waterway from Buthidaung could be used to supply any parallel advance in that area. In the Kaladan Valley, the enemy's river and road communications were offset by the fact that 81 (West African) Division was on air supply, with the consequent freedom of manoeuvre which it allowed.

140. The plan of 25 Indian Division was, briefly, for 74 Brigade to advance down the coastal plain, "cutting its tail" as it went and being supplied from the sea, while 53 Brigade advanced down the Kalapanzin Valley, being supplied by air until the Kalapanzin River could be opened for Inland Water Transport from Buthidaung. 51 Brigade was to follow, and clear enemy pockets which had been bypassed in the Mayu hills. The essence of this plan was our refusal to present General Sakurai with his favourite target – a vital maintenance road in our rear. The Divisional Artillery was supplemented by the support of two destroyers which, as events proved, filled a most useful rôle in shelling enemy hill positions defiladed from our own guns. The chief task during the planning period was to procure sufficient boats to maintain the advance of 53 Brigade and to arrange for their overland transportation through the narrow tunnels on the Maungdaw –

Buthidaung hill road across the Mayu Range to the Kalapanzin River. Some 650 craft were required for this project.

141. In 82 (West African) Division, 4 Brigade had already relieved a brigade of 26 Indian Division in Taung Bazaar. The remainder of 82 (West African) Division was to concentrate just prior to D-Day (12th December) astride the Buthidaung road, immediately east of the Mayu spine, whence a simultaneous advance was to be made by 2 Brigade, with tank support, on Buthidaung and by 1 Brigade further south on Baguna. 1 Brigade was then to cross the Kalapanzin River and capture the high ground on the east bank. This feature dominated the river and the 53 Brigade "regatta," mentioned at the end of the preceding paragraph, could not start until it was cleared. When 1 Brigade was firmly established, 4 Brigade was to drive down towards it from Taung Bazaar. Subsequently, when the whole Buthidaung area had been cleared, 82 (West African) Division, less one brigade left for rear protection, was to advance through Kindaung on Htizwe. The rate of advance was to be co-ordinated with 53 Brigade to ensure that the Divisional task of protecting the Corps' eastern flank was effectively carried out. From Htizwe, 82 (West African) Division was to cross the Kanzauk Pass into the Kaladan Valley, relieve 81 (West African) Division north of Myohaung, and then to continue the advance south.

142. The 11th December saw 74 Brigade of 25 Indian Division beginning its advance in the coastal sector – a flying start in order to attract the enemy's attention away from the Buthidaung area. On the 12th December, 51 Brigade extended its hold east towards Buthidaung against slight opposition. By the 14th December, 53 Brigade had concentrated in the eastern foothills of the Mayu Range, four miles south of Letwedet. Forward elements of 82 (West African) Division had debouched from the Tunnels, passed through 51 Brigade, and had reached Buthidaung and Baguna. By the 15th December, 2 (West African) Brigade had secured Buthidaung and cleared it of the enemy, and 82 (West African) Division had secured its first objectives. The advance of 15 Indian Corps was thus successfully launched on both the 25th and 82nd Divisional fronts.

143. Further east, in the Kaladan Valley, the main body of 81 (West African) Division had crossed the Kaladan River by the 12th December, while on the west side of the river a detachment attacked and drove the enemy from positions south of Kinthe (14 miles south of Kaladan Village). The crossing of the Kaladan is described in more detail in paragraph 154 below. The West Africans had carried out a highly successful advance against opposition, covering 50 miles in 42 days. This rate of advance may not sound very rapid, but it was achieved through extremely dense and difficult country. There is no doubt that its speed took the Japanese by surprise and forced them to withdraw southward, abandoning areas which they had intended to hold, but which were now outflanked.

144. A significant report was received about this time (mid-December) stating that the Japanese had started to improve the track over the An Pass, leading west-

wards from Minbu on the Irrawaddy, to Dalet, on the west coast. This route was obviously intended to provide interior lines of supply from the middle Irrawaddy to the Arakan coast, or else a means of withdrawal in the reverse direction. The only other practicable route lay much further south, a fair-weather road from Taungup inland to Prome.

145. In the early stages of the advance of 25 Indian Division, the enemy were amply in evidence in the hills, but they were so rapidly outflanked that only on one occasion did they succeed in launching an attack on the advancing column. This was repulsed with heavy loss to the attackers. What did happen however, was that the Japanese on more than one occasion attacked areas in our rear which were devoid of troops. The enemy shelling did nothing to impede our advance; moreover it proved somewhat profitable, since ruthless counter-battery action was invariably forthcoming from the watchful destroyers NAPIER and NEPAL lying off the coast, which also, on occasions, even dispersed enemy detachments attempting to destroy bridges on the line of our advance. By the 20th December, 74 Brigade of 25 Indian Division had already covered half the distance from Maungdaw to Foul Point.

146. On the 19th December, the Navy turned their attention to a strategical target and the NAPIER shelled the town of Rathedaung, east of the Mayu Range and on the far bank of the Mayu River, which was the Headquarters of the Japanese "Sakura Detached Force." Their fire was controlled by an Army Air Observation Post and the incident constituted an innovation in inter-Service liaison in this theatre. The results were most satisfactory. Indin Village was occupied on the 21st and its airstrip was soon in commission. In country where operational airfields were not easy to construct, this acquisition proved of great value in subsequent operations. 74 Brigade's next bound was to Donbaik, the scene of the battle of early 1943. The enemy had recently improved this strong position, and it might have provided us with a problem. But the Japanese had been left far in the rear and the defile was occupied on the 23rd December before the enemy could get any garrison back to man their defences. They did, however, cut in behind our troops, but our advance continued unchecked. The incident merely served to illustrate once again the importance of sea power; had we been dependent on supplies by road, this severance of land communications could not have been thus ignored. As it was, the Brigade was effectively maintained by Naval landing craft and the I.W.T.

147. 74 Brigade reached Foul Point, at the tip of the Mayu Peninsula, on the 26th December, after an advance of 30 miles in 14 days, and by the 27th December, the dominating hill features in the neighbourhood were in our possession. This opened the mouths of the Mayu and Kywede Rivers for the operations of light Naval craft and for sea-borne maintenance. The whole of the south of the peninsula was reported clear of the enemy and the Brigade began to concentrate for future operations.

148. While 74 Brigade had been making rapid progress in the coastal sector, 53 Brigade had been advancing east of the spine with 82 (West African) Division, moving down the axis of the Mayu River. Some determined resistance from enemy covering positions had been encountered and, in addition, 82 (West African) Division had been impeded by adverse tidal conditions at major river crossings. After the occupation of Buthidaung and Baguna (paragraph 142) 82 (West African) Division began an opposed crossing of the Kalapanzin River. The following day, a second surprise crossing was effected a few miles further south, but the enemy held grimly to the foothills overlooking the road and the advance was checked.

149. While these operations were in progress, the immense task of assembling and launching the large fleet of boats on the Kalapanzin River was begun. This feat was completed in five days, on the 21st December. On the fleet of over 600 craft the maintenance and transport of 53 Brigade depended. It will be remembered (paragraph 140) that they had been collected at Maungdaw and then transported across the Mayu Range, by the hill road and its tunnels, to Buthidaung.

150. Meanwhile, by the 18th December, 53 Brigade had occupied Seinnyinbya, seven miles south of Buthidaung. Leaving a detachment heavily engaged in this area, the Brigade effected a double river crossing and occupied the large village of Kwazon on the 21st December; while another detachment advanced, against opposition, down the east bank of the river. On the 19th December, 1 Brigade of 82 (West African) Division to the north made a great stride forward and occupied Kindaung, forcing the crossing of the Saingdin Chaung. 4 Brigade, released from its protective rôle at Taung Bazaar, was at this time rounding up scattered enemy parties north of Buthidaung, preparatory to rejoining the Division in its advance on Htizwe. After securing Kindaung, 82 (West African) Division encountered stubborn resistance. A number of attacks failed to dislodge the enemy rearguards from their strong hill positions, despite concentrated air support. On the 22nd December, however, the enemy was outflanked by a strong force which moved down the river in boats and seized the high ground north of Zedidaung against stiff opposition. From this area, we were able to overlook the enemy's line of retreat and his resistance collapsed. The Kalapanzin Plain, north of the Saingdin Chaung, had been cleared of the enemy.

151. On the 27th December, when 74 Brigade had already reached Foul Point, 53 Brigade began their last bound. It entailed the crossing of the Mayu River (two miles wide), the capture of Rathedaung, and finally of Kudaung Island, which was the objective. This island lies due north of Akyab, in the junction of the estuaries of the Mayu and Kywede Rivers. One battalion ferried from Kwazon to the west bank of the Mayu, drove on to Pyinshe (seven miles south of Kwazon), sweeping prisoners into their net. On the 29th December, they crossed the river to Htizwe, forestalling the West Africans in the occupation of this objective. Two days later they occupied Rathedaung unopposed, after it had been bombarded from the sea

by the destroyer NEPAL. On the same day (31st December) another battalion occupied Kudaung Island, thus fulfilling the Brigade's task.

152. The success of all the foregoing operations of 53 Brigade had been made possible by the fleet of boats already mentioned. Not only were they vital for the supply of the Brigade but they conferred the tactical mobility which was so essential. The great effort which they had involved was fully justified. The task of maintenance of the Brigade still remained. Navigational difficulties were not at an end, for the lower Mayu is an arm of the sea rather than a river. Great assistance was, at this stage, rendered by Naval motor launches, which by the end of the month were able to round Foul Point.

153. On the 17th December, 22 (East African) Brigade began to take over the defence of the Tunnels area, thereby releasing 51 Brigade to mop up a number of bewildered Japanese detachments, who were garrisoning strongholds on the Mayu Ridge, by-passed by the advance of the other two brigades of 25 Indian Division. By the 22nd December, 51 Brigade began to spread southwards down the coastal plain and concentrate at Indin, where it remained until it later rejoined 25 Indian Division in Akyab. It had taken 25 Indian Division less than three weeks to secure their final objectives on either side of the Mayu Range, a fortnight ahead of schedule. The enemy had withdrawn east to Kanzauk and a large column was known to have moved from there to Myohaung. It thus appeared unlikely that 82 (West African) Division would encounter much determined resistance on its way into the Kaladan Valley.

154. Earlier, during their advance down the Kaladan Valley in the Spring of 1944, 81 (West African) Division had suffered a check at Kyauktaw. They were unaccustomed to open country and Kyauktaw lies in a cultivated valley four miles south of the confluence of the Kaladan River and the Pi Chaung. This time it bad been planned to cross the river north of the confluence and to outflank Kyauktaw to the east, while leaving a holding force on the west bank. This would act as a protective detachment against any counter-thrust and mislead the enemy as to our intentions. Accordingly, on the 4th December, 6 (West African) Brigade advanced east from Kyingri on the Pi Chaung, with the intention of crossing the Kaladan at a point some ten miles north of the confluence of the two rivers. The first troops of the Brigade made the crossing on the 6th December; by the 9th the whole of 6 Brigade and Divisional Headquarters were across, and three days later only a detachment of battalion strength remained west of the river. Beyond shelling the bridgehead, the Japanese were slow to react to this crossing and subsequent concentration, and it was not until the 15th December that they launched a night attack against 6 Brigade, which was covering the bridgehead. This attack was repulsed after bloody fighting.

155. It should be noted here that the Japanese had a heavy preponderance in guns; 81 (West African) Division only possessed pack artillery, whereas the enemy possessed not only field but a considerable number of medium guns. In this close

country, air support could not always redress the balance. In order to maintain the momentum of our advance, despite the fact that we were out-gunned, it was desirable to avoid open fighting. It was therefore decided to execute a wide hook through the hills to the east, by-passing Thayettabin (through which the road runs from Kyauktaw) and emerging only to cut the enemy's communications about Myohaung.

156. The advance from the bridgehead started on the 19th December and the leading troops of 6 Brigade, with 5 (West African) Brigade following, were already eight miles south-east of Tinma on the following day, with a major left hook developing. A small deception detachment was left in the Tinma area for several days, which successfully diverted the enemy's attention from the main outflanking movement. The Division moved swiftly, reaching Thandada, six miles south-east of Thayettabin, by the 22nd December. The enemy had been out-witted and the majority of his force, including all his guns, were still north of Thayettabin, expecting to fight in the area which they had selected.

157. The next few days were spent by 81 (West African) Division in establishing a firm base in the hills south-east of Thayettabin. The Japanese pulled back and concentrated west of Point 317 – an isolated feature which runs parallel to, and just east of, the road Thayettabin – Myohaung. Despite three days of saturation bombing, from the 29th to 31st December, and vigorous ground attacks supported by further air strikes, the new enemy positions in this area were not carried till the 9th January, and then only in the face of a determined defence.

158. At this stage, 4 Brigade of 82 (West African) Division came into the picture. This Brigade, moving *via* Kanzauk, reached Apaukwa on the 9th January and came under command of 81 (West African) Division, on the 10th, for the operation to capture Myohaung. Myohaung and Minbya were now the enemy's concentration areas and there were good reasons for anticipating that he would defend this zone strongly. It included the only road fit for vehicles; it covered the flank of their activities 180 miles to the east; and finally, the Dalet – An – Minbu track was not yet ready for traffic, and further time was required to complete its construction. The somewhat abnormal amount of artillery known to be in the area also indicated the probability of determined resistance. Before, however, describing what actually happened on this front, it is necessary to revert to the operations which took place in the coastal sector.

SECTION X (paras. 159–185)
CAPTURE OF AKYAB AND SUBSEQUENT EXPLOITATION

Modified plans for the capture of Akyab: The enemy's withdrawal: The Myebon and Kangaw operations: The battle for Myohaung: Operations of the West African divisions.

---

159. For the past two years planning teams had been studying how best to re-capture the island of Akyab by amphibious assault. On the 10th December, I had

issued an Operation Instruction, based on plans made and instructions received before I took over command, for the mounting of an amphibious operation from Chittagong. 26 Indian Division (Major-General C.E.N. Lomax) was earmarked for this assault, which was scheduled to take place about the 15th February but it looked as if it might have to be made later, since the landing craft of Naval Assault Force "W" were only partially assembled. In this original plan the choice of a landing beach caused a good deal of anxiety. The tests recommended by the Scientific Advisers to the Supreme Allied Commander had not yielded any conclusive results on the consistency of the beaches, and inland swamps and waterways limited the landing places from which deployment was practicable. It was, however, decided that a beach on the south coast of the island, between Fakir Point and Akyab Town, showed most promise. It was, however, narrow – about 900 yards – and looked like restricting the assault to a one brigade front. The garrison of the island had been some 2,000 infantry, supported by artillery. As usual our Intelligence of the enemy garrison was very poor and we later found out that the Japanese had started to thin out in the autumn, and by December only about a battalion remained.

160. As described in the last section, our offensive in Arakan had opened well, and unexpectedly fast progress had been made. It was essential to maintain this momentum and take full advantage of the enemy weakness. Thus the situation demanded that quicker, and therefore simpler, ways of capturing the island be devised than the original fairly large-scale amphibious operation in mid-February or later. Accordingly Lieutenant-General Christison, with Rear-Admiral Martin and Air Commodore the Earl of Bandon, prepared new plans. These were considered by the Supreme Allied Commander, with the Naval and Air Commanders-in-Chief and myself, at a conference at my Advanced Headquarters at Barrackpore on the 21st December. From the outset it was realised that, in the event of the enemy weakening further, even these new plans would be too slow and elaborate, and it was agreed that if circumstances allowed it, emergency plans for the quickest possible occupation of the island – known as Operation "Lightning" – should be carried out. The plans for a fully opposed landing were, nevertheless, very carefully examined. It should be remembered that this operation was the first combined operation to be undertaken in the theatre, and the importance of its complete success, as affecting the subsequent larger ones we were going to undertake, was very much in the minds of all concerned.

161. This revised operation took the form of a river crossing operation using combined operations technique, by 25 Indian Division, on to the north-west corner of the island, followed by the capture of Akyab town from the landward side. The method to be adopted, and the concept of subsequent operations, may be summarised as follows. The initial landing was to be made by 3 Commando Brigade, half of which was composed of Royal Marines, mounted in the Naf River, to be followed by 74 Brigade of 25 Indian Division from Foul Point. Full

air and naval support would be available. Meanwhile 53 Brigade of 25 Indian Division was to clear Kudaung Island, which lies to the north of Akyab, and exploit to Akyab Island and also eastwards through Ale Chaung to Ponnagyun on the Kaladan River, about 14 miles from its mouth. 25 Indian Division was then to exploit success, seizing all commanding ground on the Boronga Islands, and on the Pauktaw Peninsula to their north. It was then to advance by way of the rivers and establish a base south-east of Minbya, prior to attacking Myebon. 82 (West African) Division, after relieving 81 (West African) Division, was to clear the area south of Kyauktaw and join 25 Indian Division at Minbya.

162. It must be remembered that, when the above revised plan was decided on, our offensive, though going well, was still in its early stages. On the 21st December, when the plans were being discussed, 25 Indian Division had entered Indin Village on the coast, about 22 miles from Foul Point, and Kwazon on the Kalapanzin River, nearly 30 miles further to the north. It was therefore quite possible that a fair proportion of the Japanese forces in the Mayu Peninsula might withdraw on Akyab, and that we might have to land against a reinforced garrison totalling some 4,000 men. There was every reason for supposing that the enemy would not surrender the island without a struggle – not because it was vital to them, but because of its strategical value to us. Apart from its political importance as an administrative centre for liberated areas, its possession would enable us to assist our forces driving south down the Kaladan. It would provide us with a forward base, which was becoming increasingly necessary now that Cox's Bazaar was 100 miles in rear of our forward troops. Our nearest railhead, Chittagong, was about 70 miles further back still. Finally, transcending even the importance of the port and harbour, there were the airfield potentialities of the island. An air base was essential both for the support of further operations in Arakan and, above all, for the maintenance of Fourteenth Army in Central Burma.

163. The situation on the 1st January necessitated further modification of the plan, which had already been anticipated. The Akyab garrison was known to have been further weakened, although to what extent was still uncertain. 25 Indian Division had reached Foul Point, Rathedaung and Kudaung Island well ahead of schedule. 81 (West African) Division was successfully containing the enemy by its pressure in the Kaladan. It was, therefore, imperative to block the Japanese Minbya – Myebon escape route as early as possible. The immediate possession of Akyab thus became essential to our further progress, and the quickest emergency plan for its capture was put into action. 3 Commando Brigade, mounted in the Naf River as previously planned, was to carry out an assault landing on the north-western beaches of the island, supported by such naval and air bombardment as could be prepared at short notice. Brigade was to cross the two mile wide mouth of the Kywede River in country craft, from Kudaung Island. 74 Brigade would be ferried across the four mile wide Mayu estuary from Foul Point and follow up 3 Commando Brigade. D-Day was fixed for the 3rd January.

164. On the 2nd January, an artillery officer in an air O.P. over Akyab, seeing no signs of the enemy, landed on the airstrip in the centre of the island. He was informed by the local inhabitants that the enemy had left. The question, of course, immediately arose as to whether the assault landing should go in as planned. I insisted that it should, except that there would be no sea and air bombardment unless such support was called for. To have changed the plan at this juncture would have involved delay, and, also, it was not certain that the Japanese had evacuated the whole island – the possibility of some opposition in the coastal areas remained. My experience in the past had always been that, in cases when opposition has suddenly given way, one should still go in on the original battle front, though without the planned supporting fire. If, instead, the advance is changed to something resembling an advanced guard, time is bound to be wasted when the necessity for redeploying occurs, and momentum is consequently lost.

165. The operation, therefore, proceeded as planned in its final form (para. 161). Neither landing was opposed and Akyab Town was occupied on the 4th, our troops receiving a rousing reception.

   Patrols found the Boronga Islands and the Pauktaw Peninsula clear of the enemy. Work on the airfields began immediately and, as a result, a squadron of Spitfires was able to fly in just in time to punish the first enemy air attack on shipping in the harbour on 9th January, by shooting down five out of six of the Japanese aircraft.

166. It was learnt that the Japanese had evacuated Akyab Island 48 hours prior to our arrival. The last elements – a battalion and some anti-aircraft troops – had proceeded to Ponnagyun on the west bank of the Kaladan River. Two battalions of 53 Brigade, following in rapid pursuit, had a sharp engagement with these troops, forcing the main body to fall back across the river. Despite their heavy casualties, however, this force made a spirited attempt on the night of the 9th January to rescue their compatriots still marooned on the west bank. They effected a landing from armoured landing craft but most of these were sunk, and the attempt ended in disaster.

167. In order to maintain contact, and to oblige the enemy to keep troops facing west, the detachment (two battalions) of 53 Brigade, mentioned above, was then directed towards Minbya. After a series of chaung crossings, it reached the Thinganet River at a point four miles south-west of Minbya. A number of sharp actions disclosed that the Japanese were holding the area between the Thinganet and Yede Rivers, just west of Minbya and covering their road L. of C. to Mychaung. It had always been the intention that we should exploit to Minbya and Myebon directly Akyab had been secured. Now that Akyab was in our hands and probing towards Minbya already begun, the opportunity had been created to block the Japanese L. of C. Before dealing with this phase of operations, however, I wish to say a final word about Akyab.

168. The final capture of the island may at first appear as something of an anti-climax after all the preparations and planning that it had at various times involved. A project which had originally been planned as a fairly considerable combined operation became an unopposed river crossing. Nevertheless I would like to dispel this impression, and to stress the significance of this operation apart from the strategic gain of Akyab itself (which I have already mentioned in para. 162). The original date for the full-scale assault was the 15th February and, at one time, it looked as if a three weeks' postponement might be necessary owing to lack of the resources required. It was the tireless efforts and moral ascendency of our men in the early stages of the offensive, as well as the bold and efficient handling of the campaign by Lieutenant-General Christison and his Naval and Air colleagues, which made it possible and necessary continually to ante-date D-Day, until the landings were finally made some six weeks before 15th February.

The Japanese evacuated Akyab not because they wished to but because they had to. The battle that might have been fought on Akyab beaches, and which we should rejoice was not, had already been won in the jungles to the north. The Japanese were fully alive to the value of Akyab to us: it can in fact be said that their evacuation of the island reflected their reactions to battles fought elsewhere in Burma during the previous six months. Finally, here again I had it forcibly brought home to me how poor our Intelligence was in this theatre. It was not until a very short time before Akyab fell that we realised, for the first time, the weakness of the Japanese in Arakan. The real state of the Akyab garrison we never knew.

169. On the 12th January, one week after the occupation of Akyab, 3 Commando Brigade (consisting of Nos. 1 and 5 Army Commandos and Nos. 42 and 44 Royal Marine Commandos), and 74 Brigade (25 Indian Division), carried in craft of the Royal Indian Navy, and supported by naval and air bombardment, mounted an operation from Akyab and made a successful, but opposed, landing on the Myebon Peninsula, 35 miles east-south-east of Akyab. Complete surprise was effected and a bridgehead quickly established. The Naval Forces were commanded by Captain D.C. Hill, R.N. Naval bombardments were carried out by H.M.I.S. NARBADA and JUMNA. This move rendered the position of all the Japanese forces in Arakan, north of Myebon, precarious. They had either to withdraw through the bottleneck east of Myebon, *via* Kangaw, or face destruction. The original intention was that 74 Brigade should advance up the various chaungs and capture Minbya from the south, after the Myebon Peninsula had been cleared. It was now essential to cut off the enemy troops still in the Kaladan and to relieve the pressure on 81 (West African) Division.

170. By the 13th January Myebon itself and the high ground to the west had been occupied by 74 Brigade with tank support against increasing enemy resistance, and exploitation north through Kantha and east towards Kangaw began. At this stage, Naval launches successfully co-operated by patrolling the chaungs, sinking twenty of the enemy's supply craft besides a number of sampans. The Japanese

reacted sharply to this disruption of their communications, sending four relatively heavily armed assault craft into action against the naval motor launches. The enemy ships were promptly sunk. At a later stage, too, the small Naval craft materially assisted in bringing about the eventual destruction of the enemy force north of Myebon.

171. There followed a week of severe fighting against the strongest enemy concentration that the troops of 25 Indian Division had yet encountered. Kantha was occupied on the 17th January, and the enemy driven from an important hill feature to the north of it. By the 21st, 74 Brigade had reached a line running east and west two miles north of Kantha. This effectively sealed off the Myebon Peninsula and the mouth of the Myebon River. It remained to cut the enemy's other avenues of escape in this area. These were the water route down the Daingbon Chaung, and the vital road to the east of it, which runs north and south through Kangaw. Recent air reconnaissance and captured documents had shown, that a series of strong enemy defences existed from Kangaw Village (which lies nearly eight miles north-east of Myebon on the main and only road), across to the hills on the opposite side of the river to the Myebon Peninsula. This defence system faced north and north-east, effectively blocking the approach to Kangaw from that direction. It was, therefore, decided to cancel the projected advance of 74 Brigade by chaung route to Minbya, leaving it to deal with the enemy on its immediate front, and to move a force by water from Myebon south down the Myebon River and then up the Daingbon Chaung, thus out-flanking the main Japanese positions, though the whole area contained defences. The landing was to be effected as close to Kangaw as possible and, relying on a brief period of tactical surprise, a swift advance made to cut the road. The troops most readily available for this operation were 51 Brigade of 25 Indian Division, which had been brought forward to Akyab from Indin, with 3 Commando Brigade under command. 74 Brigade was to continue its exploitation towards Minbya under the direct command of 15 Indian Corps, and 53 Brigade was brought forward to Myebon.

172. The objective – the main road where it skirts the foothills just north of Kangaw – was, as indicated above, too strongly defended to invite approach by any overland route. The direct water approach, *via* the Myebon and Kyaukngamaw Rivers, was completely dominated by enemy hill positions near Zinyawmaw. The only alternative was to put out into Hunter's Bay, turn east through the Thegyan River, and then north up the Daingbon Chaung to a selected landing place two miles south-west of Kangaw Village. This route lay through 20 miles of tortuous waterways and mangrove swamps in the heart of enemy occupied country. It had one supreme advantage however; any approach from this direction was likely to be unexpected. It was only due to naval surveys that this route could be used at all.

173. On the 22nd January a naval force commanded by Captain D.C. Hill, R.N., landed 3 Commando Brigade as planned, on the east bank of the Daingbon

Chaung, two miles from Kankaw. This landing achieved complete tactical surprise, but was hampered by very difficult conditions of thick mud and mangrove swamps which prevented the early putting ashore of guns and tanks. Moreover, the position was made worse by the fact that we occupied a narrow strip of flat, open country, largely flooded, while the enemy overlooked our area from positions on jungle-clad features on which accurate artillery fire could not easily be brought to bear. Naval bombardments in support of the Army were carried out by the NARBADA and JUMNA, and close support was given by motor launches and support craft.

174. The ensuing week was to see some of the heaviest fighting of the whole Burma campaign. The Japanese quickly reacted to the threat which we had produced. By their preparations for the defence of Kangaw, they had already shown that they appreciated the importance of the area. Our unexpected landing, if successful, would cut the only escape route for the wheels and guns of all their forces in the north. The Commandos were heavily shelled and continuously counterattacked throughout the next 48 hours. They suffered considerable casualties, yet yielded no ground. On the night of 23rd–24th January, 51 Brigade of 25 Indian Division landed, and one battalion pushed through the beachhead. The enemy resisted fiercely from extremely strong bunker position, and continued to build up against us.

175. Starting on the 25th January, a three days' air offensive was arranged to soften up the main hill features commanding the road. The bombing was well concentrated and accurate, and 51 Brigade attacked on the 28th. One battalion reached and captured an under-feature near Kangaw Village, but was later called off by the Brigade Commander as the feature proved to be completely dominated from the east. Another battalion secured a precarious footing on a small feature further east, and held on despite strong counter-attacks. On the 28th January alone, the enemy fired about 1,000 shells into our restricted positions, using guns of all calibres, including 150-millimetre and 25-pounders, the latter presumably captured in Malaya. Considerable casualties were inevitable, including some divisional troops.

176. It had become evident that the enemy defences protecting the road were stronger than originally anticipated. It was, therefore, decided to abandon further attacks on the hill features north of the road and concentrate our forces on the right flank, where, by securing Kangaw Village and the hills to the east of it, the object of effectively blocking the road could be achieved. A strong enemy counter-attack on the night 28th–29th January was repulsed with loss. On the 29th, we drove the enemy from Kangaw Village and captured the small hill which dominated it, and from which any movement on the road could be prevented by fire. On the early morning of the 31st January, the Japanese launched the most desperate attack of the whole Arakan campaign, but gained no ground and received severe punishment. It was now eleven days since the initial assault on

Kangaw had been made, a period in which our field, medium and Naval artillery, together with the Thunderbolts and Spitfires of the R.A.F. had hammered the enemy without intermission. The capture of Kangaw and of an important hill to the east of it which had followed on the 1st February, marked the turning point of the battle; the enemy's escape road from Myohaung and Minbya had been finally cut. 51 Brigade then secured a dominating position north of the road, which effectively prevented any possibility of a break-through from the north. As will be seen later, 82 (West African) Division had already begun their task of driving the Japanese up against this block. This result could not have been achieved without the work of Naval craft and beach parties, which continued to land supplies under heavy fire.

177. I have dealt with this action in some detail both in justice to the gallantry and endurance displayed by our troops and in view of its strategical importance. It provides a striking illustration of the principle, that, if you wish to bring a retreating enemy to battle, you must hit him where he is most sensitive. This we did, by cutting the only road escape route for all the Japanese forces to the north. In their struggle to regain this vital area the Japanese threw in three regiments, as well as Divisional and Army troops. They suffered at least 2,000 killed and lost 16 guns, 15 large motor craft, and quantities of other equipment. Against this, our casualties were under 600 and the morale of 3 Commando Brigade and 51 Indian Infantry Brigade, after six days of the most gruelling hand-to-hand fighting, was very high.

178. On the 1st February, part of 74 Brigade crossed the Min Chaung from the neck of the Myebon Peninsula, and, after establishing themselves on the east bank, launched operations against the Japanese positions two miles north-west of Kangaw. Faced with encirclement by the rapid advance south of 82 (West African) Division (which I will shortly describe), the enemy began to withdraw into the mountains to the east. By the 8th February, the leading brigade (the 2nd) of 82 (West African) Division was in contact with the enemy nine miles north of Kangaw, but the Japanese continued to resist as the jaws of the trap closed. On the 9th, 2 (West African) Brigade passed under command of 25 Indian Division and a series of co-ordinated attacks were made on successive enemy positions. It took another nine days before the whole area was cleared. The toll of captured guns rose to 26, but the enemy threw all their remaining artillery into the chaungs, and gun muzzles protruding from the water bore silent witness to the magnitude of the Japanese disaster.

179. 51 Brigade of 25 Indian Division and 3 Commando Brigade were now withdrawn from operations, as part of the phasing-out programme of 15 Indian Corps, which was to take place before the monsoon. 53 Brigade, after completing its task of clearing the chaung country between Akyab and Minbya, had already been concentrated in Myebon. Thus 25 Indian Division was left with two brigades in the area, the 53rd and the 74th.

180. While operations to close the Japanese escape road at Kangaw were in progress, the West Africans were engaged in driving the enemy in the Kaladan Valley south on to the Kangaw block. It will be recalled (*vide* paragraphs 157 and 158) that by the 10th January, 81 (West African) Division was fighting in the hills about 15 miles north-north-west of Myohaung, with 4 Brigade of 82 (West African) Division under command, at Apaukwa, which lies on the Kaladan River 16 miles north-west of Myohaung. Care had to be taken at this stage to avoid forcing the enemy into making a too early withdrawal before the trap was closed by 25 Indian Division in his rear. The Kangaw landing was timed for the 22nd January, and it was therefore decided to clear Myohaung by a determined drive on the 25th.

181. Operations southwards towards Myohaung began on the 15th January. By the 19th, Teinnyo had been occupied, and our forward troops were established six miles north of Myohaung. Opposition continued stubborn for the next four days, particularly east of the road, and there were no signs of the enemy resistance weakening, though we continued to press forward. Early on the 23rd January, however, a disquieting report was received indicating that the enemy had grasped the implication of the Kangaw landing the previous day and was about to evacuate at least part of his forces *via* the Lemro River. It had always been intended that, as soon as Myohaung had fallen, 82 (West African) Division should relieve 81 (West African) Division and effect a crossing of the Lemro River. It was not possible immediately to cut the enemy's projected escape route east of Myohaung from the north, since he held strong positions protecting it, but it was feasible to attack him from the north and the west.

182. Urgent orders were issued to 1 Brigade of 82 (West African) Division, which was now near Kanzauk (on the Yo River), to move south it Yotarok (12 miles south of Apaukwa) and then to advance on Myohaung and the road Myohaung – Minbya, from the west. Simultaneously, 2 (West African) Brigade, engaged in protecting the Forward Maintenance Area at Buthidaung, was directed to hand over this responsibility to 22 (East African) Brigade and to rejoin 82 (West African) Division in the Myohaung area. Both these Brigades moved with great speed, 1 Brigade arriving to take part in the final phase of the Myohaung operations on the 24th January, on which date 81 (West African) Division completed the occupation of all the commanding features north of the town and east of the Lemro River, while 82 (West African) Division (1 Brigade) seized a dominating feature five miles south of the town, after an air attack. What remained of the garrison disintegrated during the night, and the ancient capital of Arakan was entered on the 25th.

183. Major-General F.J. Loftus-Tottenham and 81 (West African) Division had thus completed their task. The Division was now withdrawn to Chiringa, north of Cox's Bazaar, where it was concentrated until its final withdrawal. For more than four months the Division had advanced through most difficult country,

against continuous opposition. The enemy had been obliged to weaken his Mayu and Akyab garrisons in an attempt to stem this threat to his Minbya L. of C., which served all his forces in Arakan. With no land lines of communication, and little physical contact with the outside world, 81 (West African) Division (which it must be remembered only consisted of two brigades), had out-manoeuvred and out-fought parts of the Japanese 54th and 55th Divisions and cleared the greater part of the Kaladan Valley.

184. 82 (West African) Division (Major-General H.C. Stockwell, who had succeeded Major-General Bruce on the 12th January) took up the advance south of Minbya encountering only slight opposition. The situation on the 30th January was that one battalion of 53 Brigade (25 Indian Division) was operating west of the town, the remainder of 53 Brigade having been transferred to Myebon. 82 (West African) Division had its Divisional Reconnaissance Regiment and its Anti-Tank Regiment west of the Lemro River, and these were investing the town from the north. The rest of the Division, east of the river, was advancing on Hpontha. But the garrison at Minbya did not wait to be assaulted. The major portion withdrew south on the night of the 30th, the remainder stayed till the 2nd February by this date the road south had been cut, but they managed to escape to the south-west.

185. Minbya was occupied on the 2nd February. Forward elements of 82 (West African) Division were now in contact with the enemy from Zibingyi to Hpontha, 20 miles north of Kangaw. Here the Divisional Commander divided his forces, pushing south from Hpontha on the 3rd February. 1 and 4 Brigades were directed on Kyweguseik in order to intercept the Japanese forces withdrawing from Kangaw. I will deal later with this phase of the operations. 2 (West African) Brigade pushed south on to the Kangaw block, overcoming considerable opposition. As already recorded, they passed under command of 25 Indian Division on the 9th February, when within nine miles of Kangaw. By the 14th February, they were driving the enemy from the high ground north of the road; and the junction of the two geographical divisions of the Arakan campaign had been effected.

SECTION XI (paras. 186–211)
THE EXTENSION OF THE ARAKAN CAMPAIGN
Reasons for the extension of the campaign: The capture of Ramree and Cheduba: New instructions to the Commander, 15 Indian Corps: The new plan and its subsequent modification: The withdrawal of 25 Indian Division: The Letpan landing: Occupation of Taungup.

186. After the capture of Akyab and Myebon, we had reached our original objectives. The clearing of the Minbya area was only a matter of time. As was described in the last section, we were exploiting these gains to the maximum, but, nevertheless, the campaign as originally planned was virtually completed. A new situation, however, had been created by the speedy and successful advance of Fourteenth

Army in Central Burma. A decisive victory in the Mandalay Plain would make the prize of Rangoon a possibility. Everything had to be concentrated on helping on Fourteenth Army. Other operations in Burma became subsidiary. The first and major way in which Fourteenth Army could be helped was by directing all possible means towards increasing the supply tonnage which they received, and since all other supply lines were working to fullest capacity, this meant increasing their supply by air. By their advance, Fourteenth Army had left their main air supply bases, which were in the Imphal and Chittagong areas, far behind. By the establishment of new and closer supply bases, giving a shorter journey, the tonnage could be materially increased for the same number of available aircraft. Akyab, and Ramree Island to the south were the best available places for these new air supply bases, as, in addition to giving a shorter flying distance, they were reasonably easy of access by sea. There were, however, a number of difficulties, which will be discussed later. The first task of 15 Indian Corps was therefore to develop to the maximum these air supply bases. The second way in which 15 Indian Corps could assist Fourteenth Army was by containing the maximum number of troops in the coastal sector, including those further south in the Taungup, Sandoway and Bassein areas. This meant continued offensive action. At the same time the original object – the withdrawal of formations was not lost sight of. Not only did I need the troops for post-monsoon operations, but it was also essential to cut down the administrative commitment in Arakan itself, so that the maximum tonnage could be built up in Akyab and Kyaukpyu for Fourteenth Army. Our resources, particularly in harbour-craft, severely limited the rate at which these stocks could be built-up, and we were working to a very small margin of time before the monsoon broke.

187. The next step in the extension of the campaign was, then, the capture of Ramree Island, which lies some 70 miles to the south-east of Akyab. The acquisition of Ramree would deprive the enemy of a vital link in his inland water communications, on which he was so dependent, and furnish us with a valuable forward sea and air base. The harbour of Kyaukpyu, at the north end of the island, provided sheltered anchorage for large ships, and an all-weather airstrip to operate transport squadrons for the maintenance of Fourteenth Army could be constructed. The particular importance of the establishment of an air supply base on Ramree Island lay in the following facts. It shortened the air-lift journey as already stated, thus allowing more sorties by the available aircraft. The mountain barrier between Ramree and Fourteenth Army's lines of advance was lower than that which had to be crossed in the flight from Akyab, a matter of great importance with the approach of the monsoon. The airfield capacity of Akyab alone was not great enough, as the fair-weather fields had to be put into action as soon as possible to relieve the present air supply situation, while with the approach of the monsoon, all-weather airfields had to be built so that air supply could continue as far as possible during the rains.

188. The plan was to launch a seaborne assault against Ramree, using 26 Indian Division, which had been trained, but not used, to carry out a similar operation against Akyab, and then to effect a landing on Cheduba Island, 12 miles to the south-west, with a force of Royal Marines. The timing of this operation in relation to the rest of the operations in Arakan is worth noting. On the 21st January we assaulted Ramree, on the 22nd we landed at Kangaw, while the Myebon operation was still in progress. Three days later the West Africans (81 Division) captured Myohaung in the Kaladan Valley. Under such pressure the Japanese command must have been in no small difficulty.

189. Strong Naval Forces under the command of Rear-Admiral B.C.S. Martin transported 71 and 4 Brigades (26 Indian Division) from Chittagong, and landed the troops at Kyaukpyu on the 21st January under cover of a heavy Naval and Air bombardment. The Naval bombardment force consisted of the QUEEN ELIZABETH, flying the flag of Vice-Admiral H.T.C. Walker, PHOEBE, RAPID, NAPIER, FLAMINGO and KISTNA. For the first time an Aircraft carrier, the AMEER, took part in Burmese operations, her aircraft spotting for the QUEEN ELIZABETH. The whole of Kyaukpyu village was in our hands by nightfall. On the next day, the Brigades started to move south, and, by the 24th, they had advanced 30 miles down the west coast, to within three miles of the formidable Yanbauk Chaung. Although the Japanese fought tenaciously, we recaptured a number of British 25-pounder guns. It was apparent, however, that the northern part of the island was not being held in strength. Incidentally, the local inhabitants gave our advancing troops the greatest welcome they had had since the commencement of the campaign.

190. On the 26th January a force of 500 Royal Marines, supported by a Naval Squadron consisting of the NEWCASTLE, wearing the flag of Rear-Admiral A.D. Read, KENYA, NIGERIA, PHOEBE, AMEER and four destroyers, landed on Cheduba Island. The Marines met with no resistance. It had not been expected that the Marines would be able to clear the whole island and they were to be relieved after landing by 36 Brigade (26 Indian Division); but this actually proved to be unnecessary. The other tasks allotted to 36 Brigade were to capture the small island of Sagu Kyun, south of Ramree, which it accomplished on 30th January under cover of the fire of NORMAN and RAIDER, who silenced enemy guns, and then to assault the southern end of Ramree itself, and exploit northwards.

191. On the night of the 26th, and again on the 28th, 71 Brigade made two unsuccessful attempts to cross the Yanbauk Chaung. The enemy were obviously determined to hold this excellent natural obstacle. It was, therefore, decided to leave a holding detachment on the northern bank and to switch the axis of advance north-eastwards, towards Sane on the east coast. On the 1st February, 36 Brigade landed on the southern tip of Ramree against only slight opposition. The same day, the Japanese in the Sane area were subjected to heavy bombardment by the Royal Indian Navy. On the 2nd February, leading elements of 71 Brigade drove the enemy out of Sane.

192. In the meantime 22 (East African) Brigade were transferred from Akyab to Kyaukpyu, thus releasing 4 Brigade of 26 Indian Division for more active operations further south. 4 Brigade forced a crossing of the Yanbauk Chaung on the 6th February. The enemy were now trapped by the three-pronged advance of 71 Brigade due south from Sane, 4 Brigade south and east from the Yanbauk Chaung, and 36 Brigade north and north-west, after its landing in the south. They were being driven towards Ramree town, in the south-east corner of the island, whence their escape was cut off by the Naval blockade under the orders of Captain E.W. Bush, R.N. On the 8th February, 71 Brigade had reached the hills north of Ramree. There they were heavily engaged, though a patrol which entered the town itself that afternoon was informed that it had been evacuated. The enemy were, however, unable to stop our tanks and, by the 9th, they were driven from their positions overlooking the town – the Japanese defence, determined as it had been, had failed, but they made a final effort to break the sea blockade and extricate their garrison. On the evening of the 11th February, they launched an air attack on our two destroyers, which were guarding the sea approaches. Under cover of this diversion, forty powered craft left Taungup to rescue their troops in Ramree. The attempt ended in complete disaster. Thirty-six vessels were intercepted and sunk by our light naval forces. Four actually got through, but were sunk on the return trip with all hands. By the 15th February, all organised resistance on Ramree Island had ceased, but mopping up continued for some time.

193. Earlier, on the 25th January, I had issued orders to the Commander, 15 Indian Corps, extending his tasks in accordance with what has been discussed earlier in paragraph 186.

I directed him now to:-

(*a*) Clear the Japanese out of Northern and Central Arakan.
(*b*) Establish a bridgehead at Taungup.
(*c*) Open the road from Taungup to Prome if possible.
(*d*) Develop the air bases at Akyab and Kyaukpyu.

The last task had precedence over the others and I laid down that their accomplishment was not to interfere with this commitment.

As already pointed out, the construction had to include both fair-weather airfields to meet our present needs, and all-weather fields to allow air supply to continue during the monsoon. These requirements not unnaturally conflicted. The target for all-weather construction was accommodation for three transport squadrons at Akyab by the end of April and three at Kyaukpyu by mid-May. In fact we managed to get three squadrons working from all-weather bases in each place in early May. The fair-weather bases were wanted as early as possible and by the 20th March there were two transport squadrons working from Akyab, with two more eleven days later. During April, half a squadron operated from Kyaukpyu for the supply of troops in Arakan only. I make no apology for going into this matter of airfields in some detail, as the responsibility for their construction, as of the great majority of the others in the theatre, rested with the Army, as did their stocking and subsequent supply.

194. It will be noticed that in the instructions given in the preceding paragraph, the Commander, 15 Indian Corps, was ordered to open the Taungup – Prome road if possible. This looked an attractive-enough project on the map, as it appears to give direct access from the sea to the Irrawaddy Valley. In practice, however, it was a very doubtful proposition. It was only a fair-weather road, the greater part passing through the thickest bamboo jungle. Taungup, the sea terminal, was no port, merely a village up a narrow winding creek, with a landing place on a bend in the creek. Ships bringing supplies would have to anchor a long way off and the passage up the creeks would be made by lighters and other harbour craft. The latter were not available in the quantity required, after the needs of Akyab and Ramree had been met. The road itself required very extensive engineer work and the time factor alone precluded the road paying any dividend before the monsoon; moreover unless the road was made all-weather before the rains, it would be closed for the whole period of the monsoon. In actual fact, our troops did not pass over this road until after the 1945 monsoon. Finally, if the road was to be opened, the operations necessary to do this in a reasonable time had to be given some air supply; this we could not do.

195. By early February, the Japanese main forces had been split up into two groups. The Northern Group was in the Dalet Chaung–An area, covering the An Pass. The Southern Group was in the Taungup area, covering the Taungup Pass. The enemy also had troops in the Sandoway area, in the Bassein delta, and in the Prome – Henzada area, which were within reach of the Arakan front. Our own troops at this time (early February) were located as follows. 25 Indian Division was engaged on the general line Kangaw – Myebon, with 82 (West African) Division driving the enemy south on to this line. 3 Commando Brigade was concentrated in Myebon, after five weeks hard fighting. 26 Indian Division, with 22 (East African) Brigade under command, was clearing up Ramree Island, and, in addition, raiding the Japanese road communications between the An Chaung and Taungup, with a view to ascertaining the intentions of the Japanese garrison in that area.

196. As indicated above, the operations of 15 Indian Corps were directed, not merely to clearing Arakan, but to containing the enemy and to preventing them from crossing the Yomas and interfering with the advance of Fourteenth Army. It was, by this time, almost certain that the Japanese were using the An Pass road and that they intended to withdraw their Northern Group (54 Division) by that route. General Christison's task was, therefore, to frustrate this plan, and, also, to threaten the Taungup Pass to prevent the enemy's Southern Group (55 Division) being diverted to fight Fourteenth Army. In this task, the R.A.F. were to assist by intensive bombing of the Taungup – Prome road with the object of producing

landslides in certain vulnerable mountain sections of it. I may add here that this was successfully achieved, the road being rendered impassable for long periods.

197. My intention was that 15 Indian Corps should destroy 54 Japanese Division in the An area and contain 55 Japanese Division by thrusting inland from Taungup on the axis of the Taungup – Prome road. Unfortunately, as will appear later, the plan to destroy 54 Japanese Division had in the end to be abandoned owing to shortage of transport aircraft. Encircling operations – the only type which could sucessfully destroy the enemy in the thick Arakan jungle country – were only possible if supplied, by air, which would enable our forces to be independent of a land L. of C.

198. General Christison decided first to destroy the Northern Group, in the Dalet Chaung–An area, by a pincer movement of 25 and 82 Divisions, then to eliminate the Southern Group, in the Taungup area, by a similar pincer movement of 82 (West African) Division from the north and 26 Indian Division from the coast. The exploitation up the Prome road could then follow. To ease the maintenance problem and assist the vital build-up of air bases, 81 (West African) Division and 50 Tank Brigade (less two squadrons) were to leave Arakan at once, and a provisional programme for the evacuation of other formations was prepared.

199. It will be recalled (*vide* paragraph 185) that, by the 9th February, 2 Brigade of 82 (West African) Division had nearly reached Kangaw, while 1 and 4 Brigades were *en route* from Hpontha to Kyweguseik to intercept the Japanese forces withdrawing from Kangaw. 82 (West African) Division (less 2 Brigade) was now directed to advance on An with all possible speed, leaving a detachment to mask Kyweguseik, which was found to be strongly held. Maintenance would be by air, since they would be going through some of the thickest and most mountainous country in the whole of Arakan. While 82 (West African) Division was continuing its difficult approach march towards An, 53 Brigade (25 Indian Division) was to make yet another landing, this time at Ru-Ywa, a village some 14 miles due west of An. 2 (West African) Brigade, from Kangaw, was then to pass through this bridgehead and advance on An from the south-west, thus forming the southern arm of the pincer movement against this village, the northern arm being formed by the other two brigades of 82 (West African) Division. After 2 (West African) Brigade had passed through the bridgehead, 74 Brigade of 25 Indian Division was to land and, advancing north up the coast, capture Tamandu, a village three miles east of the enemy's inland water transport base of Kantaunggyi, and the western terminus of the road to An. 25 Indian Division was also directed to find a small pursuit force to follow up its success at Kangaw, which was to press rapidly south, through Kyweguseik, on to Tamandu from the north. This secondary pincer movement was designed to destroy the large body of enemy troops known to have been virtually trapped in that area.

200. It was also decided to carry out a combined naval and artillery bombardment of Tamandu while the Ru-Ywa operation was being mounted. This had the

double object of riveting the Japanese commander's attention to this area (since it was known that the enemy there expected attack), and of destroying important installations. This bombardment, which was carried out by the NARBADA, KISTNA, JUMNA and FLAMINGO, began on the 5th February and lasted for ten days and nights. The area was utterly wrecked and, later, when the Ru-Ywa landing was made, it became apparent that, as a deception measure, this operation had achieved its object.

201. On the 16th February, naval forces, commanded by Captain D.C. Hill, R.N., landed 53 Brigade at Ru-Ywa against slight opposition. Enemy gunfire from the Tamandu area was dealt with by the NARBADA and JUMNA. This initial success, and the subsequent build-up, were largely due to audacious minor operations carried out during the three nights preceding the landing. Detailed reconnaissance by 3 Commando Brigade of the mangrove swamps west of Ru-Ywa revealed an unoccupied island four miles from the proposed bridgehead. A battery of medium artillery was unobtrusively transported to it by naval landing craft, a light airstrip was constructed, and supplies dumped. The enemy never succeeded in locating this battery and its support proved invaluable. The Japanese made a determined attack on the bridgehead on the 19th February, which was only beaten off after severe hand-to-hand fighting. On the 20th, while the enemy were still attempting to dislodge our troops, the first flight of 2 (West African) Brigade arrived from Kangaw. By the 25th, this Brigade was four miles east of Ru-Ywa, having passed through 53 Brigade. On the 25th February also, 74 Brigade started to land. In spite of most difficult conditions the supply of the troops ashore was maintained by naval landing craft, and the sloops, motor launches and support craft continued to afford fire support to the Army, especially in the Dalet – Tamandu area.

202. In the north of the sector, 82 (West African) Division, which had occupied Kyweguseik on the 24th February, was making surprisingly good progress despite physical difficulties; every step of the path had to be cut and impassable cliffs imposed wide diversions. They were, however, doing useful work as they were continually cutting off and destroying enemy parties, of the order of 50 strong who had formed part of the Kangaw garrison.

203. Meanwhile, 74 Brigade, supported by tanks, had begun its advance north. By the end of February, it had pushed the enemy back over the Me Chaung and this obstacle was crossed on the 3rd March. 53 Brigade was carrying out extensive patrolling east and south of Ru-Ywa and several small clashes occurred. 2 (West African) Brigade continued its advance on An from the south-west, meeting only slight opposition, but experiencing great topographical difficulties. 74 Brigade after crossing the Me Chaung, pushed ahead towards Tamandu against considerable opposition. On the 4th March, with the aid of tanks, they overran several enemy positions, the enemy's anti-tank artillery making no impression on our Shermans. After a sharp but successful engagement in the vicinity of the road

junction south of Tamandu they exploited northwards to the village, which they found derelict and deserted and which was proudly handed over to them by a naval party which had landed a few hours earlier. Severe fighting, however, continued east and north of Tamandu for some days until the enemy's fierce resistance was broken by the combined efforts of 74 Brigade and the West Africans advancing from the north. On the 7th March 1 Brigade crossed the Dalet Chaung and occupied Dalet Village. Simultaneously, 4 (West African) Brigade crossed the Chaung further south and established itself in the hills five miles north-north-east of Tamandu. 2 (West African) Brigade had reached the Tamandu – An road and established a block at the Me Chaung crossing.

204. It was at this stage that the overall shortage of transport aircraft forced me to intervene and upset the Corps plan. When I issued General Christison with his orders as given in paragraph 193, he had been allotted 130 tons per day of the air supply capacity. But in early March Fourteenth Army was heavily engaged in the Mandalay and Meiktila areas and the continued success of its operations, with Rangoon as the goal, depended largely on increasing its air supply. At the same time, the build-up of supplies at Akyab and Ramree had to be speeded up, if sufficient stocks were to be accumulated on these islands, prior to the monsoon, for the possible continued maintenance of Fourteenth Army. This was absolutely essential, since the land communications would prove quite inadequate during the rains, and I could not gamble, at this stage, on capturing a South Burma port and establishing maintenance from it. The interests of 15 Indian Corps had to be subordinated to those of Fourteenth Army, who were playing for high stakes. I was reluctantly obliged to reduce the air supply lift allotted to 15 Indian Corps from 130 to 30 tons per day, though I realised that this meant the abandonment of General Christison's plan – which was going well – for the encirclement of 54 Japanese Division. Orders had, therefore, to be issued to all three brigades of 82 (West African) Division to break contact and make for the An – Tamandu road; but, as will appear later, this did not mean that the Japanese in the An area would be left unmolested.

205. In accordance with the policy for easing the maintenance situation, 25 Indian Division was now directed to withdraw to Akyab by the end of the month (March). 22 (East African) Brigade, from Ramree, was to relieve 53 Brigade at Ru-Ywa, at once, but, until the Forward Maintenance Area at Tamandu was firmly established, 74 Brigade was to remain in the area under command of 82 (West African) Division.

206. The achievements of 25 Indian Division are well summarized in the farewell order issued to this formation by the Commander, 15 Indian Corps, on their departure:-

"You have to your credit the clearance from the Mayu Peninsula of the famous 55 Japanese Division and the capture of Akyab and clearance of the surrounding districts, the Myebon operations and the surprise landing and resultant decisive battle of the whole campaign – Kangaw. You finished off your campaign to clear the Northern and Central Arakan of the Japanese 54 Division by the brilliantly executed landing at Ru-Ywa – leading to your final capture of the enemy's base at Tamandu.

Throughout these operations you have shown magnificent fighting qualities and the highest morale. You have to your credit the successful accomplishment of probably the most difficult combined operations any British force has ever attempted.

You have inflicted 8,300 casualties on the Japanese and taken 37 guns."

207. On the 13th March, naval forces under the command of Captain E.T. Cooper, R.N., transported 4 Brigade of 26 Indian Division from Kyaukpyu and landed it unopposed due east of the village of Letpan, 36 miles south of Ru-Ywa. The landing was supported by naval gunfire from the ROEBUCK, ESKIMO, CAUVERY and JUMNA. This final landing on the Arakan coast was effected in order to cut the main road behind the enemy's forward troops. It brought us nearer Taungup and the western entrance to the last pass across the Yomas into the Irrawaddy Valley. The advance of 4 Brigade down the road axis towards Taungup was rapid, despite considerable opposition, until it was held up, on the 25th March, by hill positions three miles south of the Tanlwe Chaung, about five miles from Taungup.

208. In the meantime, the enemy had succeeded in establishing a strong block on the Tamandu – An road, to the west of 2 (West African) Brigade, and the supply situation of this Brigade was, for some days, critical. The road was, however, reopened on the 26th March. 2 Brigade was ordered to withdraw west to the Tamandu area, while 1 (West African) Brigade, now the most easterly troops on the An road, readjusted their dispositions east of Letmauk (seven miles east of Tamandu). On the 17th March, 22 (East African) Brigade was concentrated at Ru-Ywa and assumed charge of that area. It was then ordered to move south in support of 4 Brigade of 26 Indian Division, which was advancing towards Taungup. By the 23rd March, forward troops had reached the north bank of the An Chaung at Kywegu, meeting only slight opposition and, by the end of the month, they had reached Letpan.

209. The time had now arrived, in the beginning of April, to relieve 26 Indian Division, as the continuation of the phasing out of 15 Indian Corps. 36 and 71 Brigades had remained on Ramree Island and thus it remained only to relieve 4 Brigade in the Taungup area. 25 Indian Division had already been withdrawn, and so there remained on the mainland, in addition to 4 Indian Brigade, only 82 (West African) Division, disposed between Tamandu and Letmauk (where 1 (West African) Brigade was in contact with the enemy), and 22 (East African) Brigade, which was advancing south from Letpan. In the Irrawaddy sector, the rapid advance of Fourteenth Army was bringing it appreciably closer to Minbu, at the eastern end of the An – Minbu road. It was, therefore, clearly the respon-

sibility of 15 Indian Corps to prevent the Japanese forces about An withdrawing east to oppose Fourteenth Army. Since, without air supply, it would not be possible to despatch a column to block the enemy's escape route east of An, the best alternative was to maintain an offensive force before An, whose rôle would be to keep the enemy facing west, without actually driving him from his present positions. This task was allotted to 1 (West African) Brigade. The Japanese appeared remarkably sensitive to the activities of this force and the ruse was entirely successful. This new operation up the An road released 2 and 4 (West African) Brigades. 2 Brigade was immediately ordered south to relieve 4 Indian Brigade, thus freeing this formation to rejoin 26 Indian Division on Ramree prior to its departure for India. 4 (West African) Brigade was used to secure the base at Tamandu, and, when this became no longer necessary, it too was transferred to Taungup.

210. During the second week in April, it seemed evident that the Japanese were thinning out north and north-east of Taungup. Reported withdrawals of their troops between Taungup and Sandoway into the hills east of Taungup also indicated that the enemy were now more concerned with preventing our advance across the Yomas, than in maintaining their defence of the coast further south. Patrols of 4 Indian Brigade found Taungup deserted on the 15th April. This Brigade was relieved by 2 (West African) Brigade on the 17th and sailed for Ramree. On the 19th April, 22 (East African) Brigade captured the village of Dalet on the Tanlwe Chaung nine miles north-east of Taungup. On the 28th April, 4 (West African) Brigade actually occupied Taungup, and with this fitting conclusion 82 (West African) Division and 22 (East African) Brigade passed under my direct command. The formations of 15 Indian Corps had completed their task and were withdrawn to India, less Headquarters, 15 Indian Corps and 26 Indian Division in Ramree.

211. The campaign had fulfilled its objects. The Japanese had been driven out of Arakan. The air bases, which enabled Fourteenth Army to continue its rapid advance, had been secured, 54 Japanese Division and the Sakura detached force of 55 Japanese Division had been largely destroyed. The balance of 55 Division, already seriously depleted by our 1944 offensive, was kept deployed on the coast until too late to offer any serious resistance to Fourteenth Army.

SECTION XII (paras. 212–227)
PLANS FOR THE CAPTURE OF RANGOON

The situation in Central Burma at the end of March: General Slim's plan for the drive south: The decision to go for Rangoon by sea: Reasons for this decision: Directive issued by the Supreme Allied Commander on the 17th April.

---

212. It will be remembered (paragraph 92) that on the 27th February I had directed General Slim to destroy the Japanese forces in the Mandalay Plain and to seize Rangoon before the monsoon. During the second half of March the clearing

of the Mandalay Plain proceeded with very great loss to the enemy (paragraphs 102 to 127). The remnants of 15 Japanese Army were being driven by 33 Corps east of the road Mandalay – Thazi and were endeavouring to retreat south along the tracks in the foothills. Their 33rd and 28th Armies had suffered severe casualties and lost many guns, but, although their fighting value had decreased, it was by no means negligible. It was important that they should not be given time to recover from the battering they had received. Our own losses, considering the nature of the fighting, had not been excessive and, with one important exception, they had been replaced. (This exception was in the British battalions. While we had the reinforcements at Comilla, we lacked the transport aircraft to fly them in.) The morale of our troops was magnificent and had to be seen to be fully realised.

213. General Slim's task now was to get to Rangoon before the monsoon broke, which might be in early May. Time was thus very short. Our biggest problem, as always, was administrative. It was not possible to maintain more than five divisions south of the line Meiktila – Yenangyaung, and our supply difficulties were, of course, going to increase in direct proportion to the length and speed of our advance. Thus the enemy might be able to concentrate superior forces against one, or even more than one of our possible lines of advance if he were given time to recover his balance.

214. Since a simultaneous advance in strength down both the road and rail axis, on the east, and the river axis, on the west, was ruled out for maintenance reasons, the question arose on which axis our main thrust should be concentrated. Speed being essential, the striking force would have to be on a fully mechanised basis. The eastern axis was selected for two reasons. First, the river (western) line of advance contained many more water crossings. Since we must expect all bridges to be blown, these obstacles would seriously delay our progress. Secondly, an advance down the eastern axis would cut off many more of the enemy. Those escaping east from the Irrawaddy would have to cross a range of difficult jungle-clad hills, possibly at a time when the monsoon would be at its height, and then have to attempt to break out, through flooded country, across the Mandalay – Rangoon road, along which we should have established a cordon.

215. General Slim decided that the advance down the eastern axis should be made by 4 Corps, because 5 and 17 Indian Divisions were already organized each with two mechanised brigades and one air-transportable brigade, and because this Corps was already concentrated in the Meiktila area, well south of 33 Corps. This plan entailed moving 2 British and 20 Indian Divisions from the north-east to the south-west into the Irrawaddy Valley, where they would join 7 Indian Division, which had already been placed under 33 Corps. 19 Indian and 36 British Divisions would constitute the army reserve. The general method of advance to be adopted by 4 Corps was to be the seizure of an airstrip, or a site for one, by a rapid bound forward, followed by the fly-in of an air-transportable brigade. While this

brigade held the airstrip area, the rest of the division would make its next bound. Airstrips would be required every fifty miles. Divisions were to advance by leap-frogging, each division halting on reaching its objective while the other passed through. South of Toungoo, all the formations of 4 Corps would be on air supply, while those to the north would be maintained by road, suppemented by rail as far as the number of locomotives, the amount of rolling stock, and the state of the line permitted. 33 Corps was allotted enough supply air-lift for one division, the rest of the Corps thus being dependent on supply by road and inland water transport.

216. On the 18th March, the Commander, Fourteenth Army, had issued an Operation Instruction to his Corps Commanders dividing the forthcoming operations into three phases:-the present battle, the re-grouping stage, and the advance south. The intention was stated thus:-
"On completion of the task of destroying the Japanese forces in Central Burma, Fourteenth Army will:-

(*a*) Capture Rangoon at all costs and as soon as possible before the monsoon.
(*b*) Capture Yenangyaung, Magwe and Prome.
(*c*) Secure the area Myingyan – Mandalay – Maymyo – Chauk, and the road and railway axis Meiktila to Rangoon."

217. The instructions given to the two Corps for the regrouping stage were that 4 Corps, consisting of 5 and 17 Indian Divisions, with 255 Indian Tank Brigade and one armoured car regiment, was to secure Pyawbwe, strike at Japanese forces and concentrate for a thrust south. 33 Corps was to clear Mandalay – Maymyo – Kyaukse, to operate 20 Indian Division to the south and the south-west, to operate 2 British Division south-west, and move 19 Indian Division south to follow up and take over from 4 Corps up to Meiktila.

The instructions for the advance south stated that Fourteenth Army with 19 Indian Division would hold secure the area Mandalay – Thazi – Meiktila. 4 Corps was to capture Rangoon at all costs before the monsoon. 33 Corps was to capture Seikpyu and Chauk first, containing Yenangyaung, then capture in succession Magwe, Yenangyaung, Prome and finally Rangoon, if possible before 4 Corps.

218. The magnitude of the undertaking should be noted. About five weeks were available before the monsoon broke. Its arrival would cut the land line of communication from Kalewa to Shwebo and vastly increase the difficulties of air supply. The serious consequences of the delay imposed on our advance by the transfer of airlift and forces to China (see paragraphs 51 and 52) were now fully apparent. To reach Rangoon in time meant that Fourteenth Army's advance had to average at least ten miles a day against opposition and despite demolitions – a formidable proposition. There was also the very disturbing possibility that the Japanese, instead of withdrawing their defeated forces southwards, would retire into the mountains that lay to the east of the road and railway between Mandalay

and Rangoon. Maintenance would be possible by the road from the Lampang railhead in Siam, *via* Kengtung, Takaw and Loilem. The presence of such a force on our flank would inevitably have weakened the drive south, while we certainly could not afford to operate eastwards against it in any strength.

Fortunately, this threat did not materialize.

219. I had, for some time, been considering the necessity of a subsidiary operation to assist Fourteenth Army. At the end of March, I decided that I must recommend to the Supreme Allied Commander that a sea-borne attack on Rangoon, in addition to Fourteenth Army's thrust, was essential.

220. Both General Slim and I were full of hope that Fourteenth Army would reach Rangoon before the monsoon, despite the difficulties which faced them. But at the same time I had to take into account the possibility of failure to do so. It is not too much to say that the results of such failure would have been disastrous. The long land L. of C. – it is over 600 miles from Manipur Road railhead to Meiktila – was not designed to withstand monsoon conditions, as an important length of the road, running from Kalewa to Shwebo, about 108 miles, was constructed to fair-weather standard only. Air supply on a considerable scale was in any case essential to supplement what came by land and river. But during the monsoon, flying conditions were often hazardous, and would certainly interrupt air supply altogether for periods, at a time when our land L. of C. was interrupted and possibly the I.W.T. traffic on the Chindwin was reduced too. Moreover, I knew, and the Americans had been quite candid and warned me, that if we did not get into Rangoon by June, their American transport aircraft which formed a large proportion of the theatre resources, would be taken off to China. Thus we might well have the position where our troops, halted only a comparatively short distance from Rangoon by the monsoon rains, would have to be withdrawn back to Mandalay or even to the Chindwin, with all the attendant losses in vehicles and morale, for reasons of supply. How real this danger was, was afterwards proved by the fact that, even after Rangoon was captured and opened in May, the R.A.F. were unable, at times, during the June monsoon rains, adequately to supply even the small forces which we still had to maintain in Central Burma. General Slim had repeatedly asked me to put in an amphibious operation to assist his army to capture Rangoon, because he felt he could not guarantee reaching it before the rains.

221. In the early part of this Despatch (paragraph 11) I mentioned that a combined operation for the capture of Rangoon, known as Dracula, had had to be postponed. This operation was, however, never actually cancelled. As far back as the 5th February, the Supreme Allied Commander had issued a Directive in which my tasks were defined as follows: "To secure the Ledo – Burma road, capture Rangoon by 1st June, 1945, open the port of Rangoon and destroy the main Japanese forces in Burma, excluding the Tenasserim coast." In this Directive the Commander-in-Chief, East Indies Fleet, was instructed "To furnish such Naval

support and amphibious resources as may be required for combined operations," and, mention was also made of the Indian Airborne Division, which was to be held under the Supreme Commander's operational control. This amounted, in effect, to "Operation Dracula," though in a modified form, and I considered the time had now come to put it into effect, that is, to carry out a combined sea, land and air operation against Rangoon, though on a much smaller scale than was originally planned.

222. Everything indicated that the enemy was going to make determined efforts to halt us in the Yenangyaung area on the Irrawaddy axis, and that we should meet defence, in depth on the road-railway axis to the east. From captured documents and the evidence of Staff officers obtained later it is clear that the enemy intended to halt us successively at Pyawbwe, Pyinmana and Toungoo. It was only his inability to carry out the necessary moves in time that prevented these plans from fully materialising.

223. Moreover, there was the problem of Rangoon itself. The garrison was at this time known to be some 10,000 strong. Although these were largely Base troops, experience in Manila and elsewhere in the Pacific theatre had shown that these troops were capable of stubborn and suicidal defence, and I had had no indication from my Intelligence that the enemy might abandon Rangoon. Nor with the clearing of Rangoon town itself was the problem by any means solved. Before supplies could be brought in by sea, the twenty-four odd miles of the Rangoon River approach had to be cleared of mines, and naturally the minesweepers could not start until the banks were cleared of enemy. It was not difficult to foresee a position where the remnants of the Rangoon garrison, turned out of the town itself, might have fallen back across the Rangoon and Pegu Rivers and have put up a protracted defence of the areas on each side of the Rangoon River as far as its mouth. These areas are intersected with creeks, and with the monsoon rains it would be nearly impossible to deploy forces effectively against the enemy who remained. Thus with Rangoon actually in our hands, we could find ourselves in a worse position than ever, until we opened the Rangoon River. With a seaborne attack the Rangoon River had to be opened first, and the capture of Rangoon town could be closely followed by the opening of the port to traffic. The strength with which Rangoon might be held had made me, earlier on, consider the possibility of going for the less defended ports of Bassein or Moulmein, but it was soon clear that, since these had no all-weather road communications with the main body of Fourteenth Army, Rangoon was the only useful objective.

224. I therefore recommended to the Supreme Allied Commander that a force of two divisions – one for the assault and one for the follow-up – under the command of 15 Indian Corps, should be used to capture Rangoon from the sea. I realised that if my recommendation was accepted, it meant postponing or even cancelling the Phuket operation for which planning was well advanced, and which I had previously agreed to try to carry out.

225. The Supreme Allied Commander approved my recommendation after discussion at a meeting with the Naval and Air Commanders-in-Chief and myself at Kandy on the 2nd April, a few days after I had sent my signal making the recommendation. He made the proviso that the decision as to whether the second (follow-up) division should actually be committed would be taken later. On the 17th April he confirmed his approval in an Operational Directive addressed to his Commanders-in-Chief, in which we were instructed "To carry out an amphibious/airborne operation with the object of the early capture of Rangoon should this not have been previously achieved by Fourteenth Army from the north." D-Day for the initial amphibious assault was to be the 2nd May, and this date should be borne in mind when the progress of Fourteenth Army's advance southwards is followed in the next section of the Despatch.

226. I should like to stress here the hazardous nature of the Rangoon operation. Heavy storms are a common occurrence just before the breaking of the monsoon and, in any case, at this time of year there was a heavy swell outside the Rangoon River. This, combined with the exceptionally long run-in for minor landing craft from the lowering position, made the task extremely difficulty and its success somewhat uncertain.

227. Planning started on the 8th April under the experienced team who had been responsible for our combined successes in Arakan. On the 18th April I issued the necessary detailed instructions to the Commander, 15 Indian Corps. The details of the plan itself and its execution are dealt with in a later section of this Despatch.

SECTION XIII (paras. 228–256)
FOURTEENTH ARMY'S DRIVE SOUTH
The regrouping phase: Fighting in the Irrawaddy Valley: The capture of Prome: 4 Corps' axis: Successive captures of Pyawbwe, Pyinmana and Toungoo: Japanese plans to defend Pegu: The advance to Pegu: Capture of Pegu.

---

228. Early in April, 5 Brigade of 2 British Division and 268 Indian Brigade, advancing south-west from Myingyan – Natogyi area and destroying many isolated enemy detachments *en route*, encountered stubborn resistance at Mount Popa. This is an extinct volcano, 5,000 feet in height, whose steep slopes afforded excellent defensive facilities. Here a force of about 600 Japanese, supported by field and medium artillery, held out until the 20th April, when they were finally eliminated, losing much equipment including vehicles and guns. While this action was in progress, the remainder of 2 British Division was being flown out to India. The fly-out began on the 11th April from Myingyan and was completed by the 25th. For administrative reasons, it had become necessary to reduce the forces in Central Burma by one division, and 2 British Division was required as the follow-up division of the force for operation "Dracula," the capture of Rangoon

by a combined airborne and seaborne landing, which was discussed in the last section.

229. 7 Indian Division (less 33 Brigade) was, in the meantime, operating down both sides of the Irrawaddy, while 33 Brigade was directed on the important communications centre of Kyaukpadaung. This town fell on the 12th April, after a strong enemy counter-attack had been repulsed just to the west of it. 33 Brigade then turned west and captured Chauk on the 18th April, the booty taken included five guns (including two medium), and much transport. On the 19th, 89 Brigade cleared Singu, four miles to the north-east. 33 Brigade, advancing south from Chauk, met fierce resistance at Yenangyaung. This extensive oilfield area was completely cleared by the 23rd April after three days' stiff fighting. On this date, 89 Brigade were concentrating seven miles north of Yenangyaung preparatory to crossing the river. West of the Irrawaddy, 114 Brigade had reached a point 17 miles south-west of Seikpyu without meeting any organized resistance. During its advance, 7 Indian Division had inflicted heavy casualties, captured more guns and much booty.

230. After clearing the Myittha – Wundwin area on the railway axis, 20 Indian Division changed two of its brigades from an animal transport to a motor transport basis, and began its rapid move south-west across to the Irrawaddy. This quick re-organization was rendered possible by the fly-out of 2 British Division, whose vehicles thus became available for re-allotment. The advance of 20 Indian Division was directed on Taungdwingyi, which lies some 43 miles east-south-east of Magwe and roughly half-way between the Mandalay – Rangoon railway and the Irrawaddy. This place was the vital rail and road junction of the Japanese communications linking their east and west fronts. Completely under-estimating our mobility, the Commander of 28 Japanese Army had only garrisoned this important point with I.N.A. troops. Covering the 65 miles from Meiktila in three days, 32 Brigade reached Taungdwingyi on the 18th April. The booty taken included a useful haul of 1,500 gallons of petrol and 3,500 gallons of oil. Surprise was complete; for some days afterwards, enemy convoys, routed *via* Taungdwingyi, continued to be welcomed by 20 Indian Division. 32 Brigade was followed by 80 Brigade, which entered Natmauk, 28 miles north-north-west of Taungdwingyi, on the 15th April. Both Brigades then continued their rapid advance westwards to the Irrawaddy. 32 Brigade reached the river at Myingun, nine miles south-east of Magwe, on the 19th without opposition. On the same day, 80 Brigade occupied Magwe after slight opposition from astonished Japanese administrative units. We thus controlled the Irrawaddy at two points 22 and 33 miles south of Yenangyaung respectively. Considerable equipment was captured in Magwe and, once more, unsuspecting convoys entering the town were captured.

231. With their retreat cut off at Magwe, the Japanese troops to the north of it, on the east bank, were compelled to cross the river. They joined the main body of

Yamamoto's force, which was pulling out down the west bank after the fall of Yenangyaung. Their retreat was harried by two brigades of 7 Indian Division, 89 Brigade crossing the river and linking up with 114 Brigade, which was already operating on that side. The Japanese in their effort to move south were pushed off the main roads and their retreat became increasingly difficult.

232. The situation in 20 Indian Division's area on the 26th April was as follows. 80 Brigade in the Magwe area had pushed patrols across the river, which reported enemy motor transport moving west out of Minbu. Magwe itself was being heavily shelled from the west side of the Irrawaddy. 100 Brigade was passing through 32 Brigade on the road leading from Satthwa to Allanmyo. After clearing opposition 26 miles north of Allanmyo on the 27th, 100 Brigade again made contact just north of the town. Allanmyo fell the following day, after 36 hours fighting, and we captured five guns. Meanwhile, 80 Brigade, advancing south from Magwe, was destroying many parties of the enemy who were trying to cross the river from the right bank and escape eastwards. At Allanmyo, 100 Brigade were 252 miles from Rangoon on the 28th April. By the 2nd May, breaking through all enemy attempts to stop it, it had advanced a further 40 miles and captured the great river port (now in ruins) of Prome, the eastern terminus of the road from Taungup. The last escape route of the remnants of the Japanese forces in South Arakan was now blocked.

233. I will now turn to the main axis of the drive south, the road and railway between Mandalay and Rangoon. After the failure of his counter-offensive in the Meiktila area, the Commander, 33 Japanese Army, decided to halt our advance north and west of Pyawbwe, 24 miles south-east of Meiktila, where good natural defensive positions exist. He withdrew 18 Japanese Division, through Thazi, to take up positions covering Pyawbwe from the north and he ordered 53 Japanese Division to withdraw from west of Meiktila and occupy positions west of Pyawbwe. 49 Japanese Division, which had already suffered severely at our hands, was to act as a rearguard, delaying our advance down the Meiktila – Pyawbwe road. Further to the east, 15 Japanese Division was being withdrawn through Taunggyi and Loikaw so that it could reinforce the railway lower down.

234. Pushing south from Meiktila, on the 5th April, 48 Brigade of 17 Indian Division met heavy opposition eight miles down the Pyawbwe road. Leaving a detachment to deal with this, the Brigade by-passed the enemy position and advanced another five miles, overcoming further opposition north of Yindaw. They were eventually held up by minefields and heavy mortar fire at the village itself. 99 Brigade, operating east of the road, cleared village after village, eventually being held up nine miles south-south-east of Meiktila. 63 Brigade on the right flank made an advance of five miles. It was evident even at this early stage of the advance that 49 Japanese Division was putting up a determined stand. On the 6th April, the enemy again re-occupied the positions eight miles south-east of Meiktila from which they had been cleared by a detachment of 48 Brigade the

previous evening. We attacked again, this time annihilating the defenders. Yindaw still held out, but was bypassed by a battalion and 255 Indian Tank Brigade, less a squadron, which was operating with 99 Brigade. On the 7th, this battalion and a detachment of tanks overcame enemy opposition near Ywadin, seven miles due west of Pyawbwe, and were then held up by a blown bridge. Meanwhile 63 Brigade reached Ywadin.

235. On the 8th April, on the main Meiktila – Pyawbwe road, Yindaw still held out, but its reduction was left to 161 Brigade of 5 Indian Division, which was following 17 Indian Division according to plan. 48 Brigade by-passed it and fought their way forward to within eight miles of Pyawbwe, shelling the enemy with some of their own guns, which had been captured on the 6th. Meanwhile 99 Brigade was still fighting north of Yindaw, inflicting heavy casualties. On the 9th April, 5 Indian Division captured Yindaw, killing almost the entire garrison and capturing three guns. On this date, 99 Brigade with tank support captured part of the high ground three miles north of Pyawbwe and reached the landing ground just north-west of the town. 48 Brigade, attacking astride the road, broke through stubborn resistance, inflicting heavy losses and capturing, two guns. 63 Brigade occupied a village two miles west-south-west of Pyawbwe, taking three guns and then probed forward to the outskirts of the town. Meanwhile our armoured columns were operating south-west and south of Pyawbwe, capturing artillery and slaughtering the gun crews. Altogether a total of fifteen guns (some medium) were taken by 17 Indian Division during the fighting on the 9th April.

Pyawbwe fell on the 10th to co-ordinated attacks by infantry from the north and west and armoured troops from the south-west, the latter assault proving decisive.

236. Our victory at Pyawbwe was one of the most costly defeats the enemy had suffered during the whole campaign. During our advance, 49 Japanese Division, already greatly depleted in strength, was practically exterminated. Their 53 Division attempting to occupy its allotted defence zone west of Pyawbwe was struck in the flank and severely mauled before it ever got there. During the fighting in and around the town itself, 18 Japanese Division lost 2,200 killed, and we captured 31 guns, eight tanks and much transport. The tactical handling of 17 Indian Division by Major-General D.T. Cowan in this fighting was excellent. The enemy were expecting an attack from the north and they were attacked by infantry from this direction, but what surprised and disrupted their defence were the armoured columns operating from the south. The whole battle was a massacre by tanks, guns, infantry and aircraft. 33 Japanese Army was shattered.

237. The advance from Pyawbwe was taken up by 5 Indian Division, which passed through 17 Indian Division on the 11th April. 123 Brigade Group reached Yamethin on that date and our armour contacted the enemy seven miles to the south. During the night, an enemy detachment some 400 strong, with an anti-

tank battery, entered the town from the east and occupied buildings and trenches commanding the road. This detachment fought to the last man and it took two days to eliminate them, the process being considerably hastened by accurate air strikes. In the meantime, a by-pass road was constructed west of the town to allow our unarmoured vehicles to get forward. On the 12th the Japanese achieved a minor success in one of their rare air attacks, 16 vehicles of a petrol and ammunition convoy being destroyed by them.

238. While Yamethin was being finally cleared, an armoured column and 161 Brigade Group had advanced and contacted the enemy on the 15th, astride the road and railway on the general line of the Sinthe Chaung, 27 miles from Yamethin and three miles north of Shwemyo. While this portion of the enemy was being subjected to successful air strikes which caused them heavy casualties, an armoured column operating west of the road and railway crossed the Sinthe Chaung and broke into Shwemyo itself, which it completely cleared the same day (16th April). Meanwhile the engineers, though harassed by enemy artillery fire from the Shwemyo Bluff, bridged the Sinthe north of Shwemyo and bulldozed a by-pass over difficult ground. This enabled 161 Brigade Group to outflank the Japanese positions north of the town, and harbour south of it for the night 16th–17th. In their efforts to establish a bridgehead across the Sinthe Chaung the next day, however, this Brigade was held up.

239. 123 Brigade Group, ten miles north of Shwemyo, were preparing for an attack on the Shwemyo Bluff, while 9 Brigade Group concentrated in the Tatkon area, four miles north-west of the entrance to the Shwemyo Bluff defiles. This Bluff is a steep feature rising to 700 feet, dominating the road and railway on the east side. It was expected that the Japanese would hold this strong position, and they did, but they did not anticipate an attack from the jungle-covered hills east of the Bluff, which was the line of advance selected by 123 Brigade. This assault on the 18th caught the enemy in flank and rear and was completely successful. 123 Brigade were then relieved in this area by 99 Brigade of 17 Indian Division, to free them for a further advance.

240. Early on the 18th April, 161 Brigade succeeded in forcing a crossing of the Sinthe Chaung and repaired the bridge. They then, in conjunction with 255 Indian Tank Brigade, inflicted heavy casualties on the enemy over a wide area well south of Shwemyo, destroying three guns. By the evening of the 18th, the armoured column was only twelve miles north of Pyinmana, despite mined road blocks and demolitions, which were covered by enemy detachments concealed in the thick country on either side of the road. The airstrip near Shwemyo was taken over on the 18th April by the air-transportable brigade which had moved up by road, leaving the rest, of 5 Indian Division free for their next bound forward.

241. Our tanks reached Pyinmana on the 19th April. Finding it held, they bypassed it and captured the valuable Lewe airfield, just to the south of the town,

on the 20th. By nightfall, they had reached Yeni, 43 miles from Toungoo and 218 miles from Rangoon. 161 Brigade took over the defence of Lewe airfield after its capture by the armoured column, preparing it for the glider fly-in of aviation engineers. They also cleared the northern part of Pyinmana, the Japanese garrison still resisting stubbornly in the southern sector. Meanwhile 123 Brigade passed rapidly through 161 Brigade and reached Thawatti, almost catching up with our armour three miles further south. Continuing their rush south, both our tanks and our infantry reached a village 15 miles north of Toungoo on the 21st April. On this date, the enemy in Pyinmana were finally liquidated.

242. The last lap of the race for Toungoo was now being run. There were three competitors. 5 Indian Division were driving hard down the axis of the main road. The enemy columns, which had been driven off the main road were attempting by forced marches, along jungle tracks on both sides of the main road, to reach Toungoo ahead of us. These columns were being looked after by our aircraft, but, we too, had our difficulties in the shape of mines, demolitions, and heavy rainstorms – the first two delayed our tanks on the road, while the third hindered their movement off it. The third competitor was 15 Japanese Division, which was moving by motor transport parallel to 5 Indian Division, and some 60 miles to the east of it, down the Taunggyi – Loikaw road, which turns west at Kemapyo, *via* Mawchi, to Toungoo. We owe it to the Karen guerillas, under their British officers, and to the airstrikes by the R.A.F. directed by these same British officers, that this enemy division lost the race. Ambush after ambush, demolition after demolition, airstrike after airstrike, delayed its advance and, although a forward element got within artillery range of its objective, it was too late.

243. After a sharp action on the 22nd April by our tanks in a village eight miles to the north, our troops swept into Toungoo itself. The leading light tanks of 123 Brigade column ignored the traffic signals of an indignant Japanese policeman in the centre of the town, and ran him down. Subsequent enemy resistance in the western half of the town was swiftly overcome and the whole area cleared. Surprise had been complete. By the evening of the 22nd, our leading tanks and infantry were in Oktwin, eight miles to the south, where they captured a loaded train (complete with two engines) which was on the point of departure. The importance of Toungoo to us lay in its airfields from which fighters could operate over Rangoon, distant 166 miles. Since our captures in Toungoo fortunately included an I.N.A. division (some 3,000 strong), there was no shortage of labour to get the airstrips into running order. In the 21 days of continuous fighting since 4 Corps broke out from Meiktila, it had advanced 170 miles and killed 4,800 Japanese, of which 1,677 had been accounted for by 5 Indian Division between the 12th and 22nd April. These were casualties actually counted on the ground; the total enemy killed considerably exceeded this figure, which does not include the many losses inflicted by our armour in quick-moving tank actions, and by our aircraft.

244. Continuing their dash south, 5 Indian Division's armoured column on the 24th April found the Pyu Chaung, 30 miles south of Toungoo, held and the bridge destroyed. Nevertheless, by the 25th, a crossing had been effected and Pyu succumbed to an artillery concentration. The progress of 161 Brigade was delayed by the bridge two miles south of Toungoo being washed away, necessitating the construction of a 180-foot Bailey, which was completed early on the 25th. The Brigade then pushed forward through Pyu in hot pursuit of our armour which, on the night 25th–26th, had reached Milestone 128 from Rangoon, 29 miles north of Nyaunglebin. Incidentally, 17 Indian Division had been scheduled to pass through 5 Indian Division on the 24th April, and indignation swept the former when it was learnt that the latter had invaded what should have been 17 Indian Division's area of operations. I mention this small point as it illustrates the fine aggressive spirit which permeated not only 4 Corps, but the whole of Fourteenth Army in this campaign.

245. The Japanese Air Force was so overwhelmed by the Allied Air Forces at this time, and indeed throughout the whole Burma campaign, that its existence is apt to be overlooked. Nevertheless, the enemy did on occasions attempt to delay the onward rush of 4 Corps. On the 24th April, for example, twelve Oscar fighter-bombers twice bombed and strafed the Tennant and Kalaywa airfields north of Toungoo, and then attacked the armoured column to the south. Our casualties in these attacks were light, whereas the hostile aircraft were intercepted by Spitfires and lost half their number.

246. The loss of Toungoo must have convinced General Kimura that the situation was critical. There is no doubt, evidence later showed, that the Japanese Commander intended as a last resort to hold a line through Toungoo and Prome until the coming of the monsoon forced us to ease the pressure of our offensive. Our break-through at Toungoo destroyed this last hope. Whether he intended to hold Rangoon, or whether he meant to withdraw the remnants of his forces across the Sittang, it was essential that the road and railway through Pegu – the only land communications link between Rangoon and Moulmein – should be kept open. Thus the defence of Pegu now became absolutely vital. Kimura had apparently no hope of retaking Toungoo itself, but he directed 15 Japanese Division to accelerate its move west from Mawchi and block the Toungoo – Mawchi road at the point where it enters the hills. The object was twofold. First, this threat to 4 Corps might delay its advance and cause it to divert troops; secondly, this position would protect the flank of those elements of 33 Japanese Army still north of Mawchi, who were retreating south. The Japanese Commander's next step was to concentrate every available man for the defence of Pegu. 24 Independent Mixed Brigade was rushed north from Moulmein to the Pegu – Mokpalin area. He also formed two new Mixed Brigades from the Rangoon garrison, which were largely composed of administrative and naval personnel. The Rangoon Anti-Aircraft Command, the largest in Burma, provided the guns for this scratch force,

all its batteries being utilised for this purpose. These two brigades were moved up to Pegu on 27th April with orders "To destroy the enemy north of Payagyi and Waw", which lie 10 and 15 miles north and north-west of Pegu respectively. While this was going on, the major portion of the small detachments guarding the mouth of the Rangoon River were moved back into Rangoon "To cover demolitions". With effect from the 28th April, therefore, Rangoon was practically denuded of troops, except for 5,000 I.N.A.

247. I must make it clear however that it was not until the 1st May that I received any indication that Rangoon was going to be evacuated, and it was only after 15 Indian Corps landed that it became certain. This was another example of how poor our Intelligence was in comparison with the European theatre and how, so often, we were virtually fighting in the dark. It was known that Pegu was being reinforced at the expense of Rangoon, but it was always considered that Rangoon itself would be the centre of a desperate resistance. I need not emphasise how serious the delay caused by such resistance would have been.

248. On the 24th April, General Kimura and his Headquarters retired to Moulmein. They were accompanied by Ba Maw and several ministers of his puppet Government. With them went Subhas Chandra Bose – the Commander-in-Chief of the "Indian National Army" – leaving behind him several thousand of his troops, with orders to fight to the last. They surrendered directly we reached Rangoon, thereby easing our labour problem.

249. 19 Indian Division, following up 5 and 17 Indian Divisions, took over the Toungoo area on the 26th April, the actual locations of its brigades on this date being 98 Brigade in Toungoo itself, 62 Brigade at Lewe airfield, and 64 Brigade back in Meiktila. 98 Brigade immediately began operations to clear the leading elements of 15 Japanese Division east of Toungoo, and our artillery engaged the enemy guns shelling Toungoo. The next week was spent in mopping up scattered parties of the enemy in the vicinity; on the 29th April, for example, 200 Japanese were surrounded and killed just south-west of the Lewe airfield, and a further 150 ten miles south-west of Toungoo. Although it falls outside the period covered by this section of the Despatch, it may be recorded here that 19 Indian Division, who were responsible for a large area, held 15 Japanese Division with one brigade, the 98th. At this stage (early May), troops were not available to evict the enemy from the strong positions which they had prepared in the hills some five miles east of Toungoo, and this enemy force, which continued to be reinforced by scattered detachments escaping from the north, continued to be some menace to our communications.

250. The armoured column, which on the night 25th–26th April was 29 miles north of Nyaunglebin, made a further rapid advance on the 26th, capturing Nyaunglebin and driving forward a further 19 miles; that is, to within 80 miles of Rangoon. The resistance encountered was reported as "increasingly disorga-

nized" and many casualties were inflicted; also three locomotives were captured, together with rolling stock loaded with rations. On the 27th April, the armoured column met determined opposition at a village near Milestone 68 and fighting continued throughout the day, Japanese suicide parties, who attempted to destroy our tanks with pole-charges, having to be eliminated. 17 Indian Division had passed through 5 Indian Division on the 26th and was busy mopping up and repairing crossings behind the armoured column. Five bridges south of Nyaung-lebin had been destroyed by the enemy and another washed away by a flooded chaung. Valentine bridge-layer tanks had enabled our armour to cross, but our lorried infantry was temporarily held up pending the arrival of Bailey bridging.

251. By the morning of the 28th, the armoured column had pushed forward another six miles, but again met strong resistance at Milestone 62, twelve miles north of Pegu. This was cleared by nightfall, the Japanese losing 300 killed. Difficult country now lay ahead with reservoirs and marshy ground. Both the main road and the side-tracks were mined and booby trapped, and these obstacles were strongly covered by fire. Nevertheless, by the 29th April, 63 Brigade, supported by tanks, had fought its way through Payagyi and reached the outskirts of Pegu, despite stiff opposition, both ground and air. To the north of Pegu, an armoured detachment moved east, just south of the Moyingyi Reservoir, and cut the Pegu – Mokpalin road at Waw, 15 miles north-east of Pegu.

252. 4 Corps was now straining every nerve to get to Rangoon before 15 Indian Corps could reach the city through the sea-gate. In the present campaign they had captured or destroyed 299 guns and killed over 16,000 Japanese, over 6,500 of whom had been accounted for between the 1st and 28th April. They had cheerfully advanced and fought on reduced rations to make room for more ammunition and petrol. 17 Indian Division was now only some 50 miles from its goal, and, it must be remembered, it was this Division which had carried out such a gallant withdrawal from Burma three years earlier, and, only the previous year, had fought so magnificently in the defence of Imphal. 17 Indian Division had an old score to settle, and, if it was humanly possible, it was going to be settled. But the obstacles to be overcome were serious. Between 4 Corps and Rangoon lay the wide Pegu River, forming a very strong defensive position. In this position was concentrated every available man that General Kimura could raise, including, as we afterwards found out, the whole of the Rangoon garrison. They had orders "To hold to the last", and the fanatical courage of the Japanese soldier has never been questioned.

253. The Pegu River, astride our line of advance, was bridged in three places; the main road bridge west of Pegu, the railway bridge (branch line) about a mile to the north, and the main railway bridge about three miles further north. The enemy had prepared strong positions on both banks of the river, including Pegu itself, through which the river flows. I do not believe, however, that these defences, strong as they were, would have delayed 4 Corps – animated as it was by

a fierce determination to reach its objective – for very long, had not a catastrophe intervened. A violent tropical storm broke on the afternoon of the 29th April and continued throughout the night. All movement of tanks or wheeled vehicles off the road became impossible; no aircraft could land or take off; the Pegu River rose in full flood. It was a foretaste of the coming monsoon, and I was indeed thankful that the early capture of Rangoon was not dependent on our land advance alone.

254. Despite the deep mud, 48 Brigade advanced on the 30th, stormed the Japanese position at Milestone 51 at the point of the bayonet and, by nightfall that part of Pegu which lies north of the river was in our hands. North of Pegu, we had an even more important success. On the 30th, as our attack progressed, the enemy blew all the three bridges, but at both the railway bridges, our infantry, crawling under heavy fire over the wrecked girders, seized and held a small bridgehead. This most gallant feat was the turning point of the battle; an attack on Pegu from the north-west had been planned, but the ford eight miles up river was found to be impracticable. The crossings at the railway bridges, however, gave us what we wanted – a bridgehead on the west bank. Meanwhile, another infantry column drove the enemy from a village six miles east of Pegu.

255. On this date also (the 30th April), we rescued 350 British, American and Indian prisoners of war. Their escort, on finding the road to Moulmein cut at Waw, abandoned their charges, but only to be destroyed by our advancing troops. It was fitting that this rescue should have been made by 17 Indian Division, to which some of these prisoners had belonged when they were captured in 1942.

256. The attack on Pegu progressed throughout the 1st May, in a deluge of rain. 99 Brigade attacked from the north, west of the river, supported by 255 Indian Tank Brigade firing from among the ruins of the northern part of the town on the opposite bank. The Japanese A.A. artillery had its hands full, both in its normal and anti-tank rôles, and we captured twelve guns. By nightfall, the town had been practically cleared and the same night the indomitable 17 Indian Division resumed its advance south. It was a gallant effort. Since our airstrips had been put out of action, the troops had had to be further reduced to half rations. They were hungry and soaked to the skin, but their magnificent spirit was undimmed, and Rangoon lay ahead. But they were not to gain this coveted prize. Their progress was barred by mines averaging 130 to every mile of road, demolitions and, last but not least, mud. By the afternoon of the 3rd May, when 17 Indian Division was still 32 miles from the city and held up by a flooded chaung, Rangoon was being entered by 15 Indian Corps. 4 Corps had been frustrated, not by the Japanese, but by the elements. In their advance from Pyawbwe they had covered 260 miles in 20 days. Although they did not actually liberate its capital, the reconquest of Burma was in the main effected by Fourteenth Army, and to them largely belongs the honour and glory.

SECTION XIV (paras. 257–265)
THE CAPTURE OF RANGOON
The plan for the seaborne operation against Rangoon: The airborne operation: Rangoon discovered virtually abandoned: The link-up with Fourteenth Army.

---

257. While Fourteenth Army were thrusting south, the planning of the seaborne invasion of Rangoon was proceeding. It will be remembered that, as stated at the beginning of this Despatch, when the various projects were discussed, how considerable an operation this invasion in its original form was to have been. It was now proposed to carry it out on a very much smaller scale, but the inherent difficulties of the operation remained the same, with the exception that the weather conditions would be a great deal worse than at the time of year originally contemplated for this operation.

258. In preparing the plan for a seaborne assault on Rangoon, the first consideration was the clearance of the Rangoon River and its channel, to permit the approach of major landing craft. Throughout its whole length of 24 miles it had been mined both by the Japanese and by our own minelaying aircraft. Since minesweepers could only work with the flow of the tide, it was estimated that they would require four days to complete their task. Before minesweepers or major landing craft could enter the river, the coastal defences on the west bank, especially those at Elephant Point, would have to be eliminated. Owing to the difficulties of approach to the mouth of the river, it was not practicable to neutralise these by fire nor was a sea landing on the Point itself possible at this time of year. The only solution was to seize Elephant Point by an airborne operation, so as to allow the sweeping of the entrance to the river and the approach of major landing craft. In any case a very long run-in for minor landing craft was involved, about 24 miles. On the east bank, the village of Kyauktan and the town of Syriam on the Pegu River were both believed to be garrisoned, the latter being held in strength. Thus it was apparent that preliminary operations, probably extending over several days, would be necessary before Rangoon itself could be attacked.

259. The plan in broad outline was as follows. 15 Indian Corps was to consist of 26 Indian Division, now at Ramree, as assault division, with 2 British Division, which had been withdrawn into the Calcutta area, as follow up. The airborne operation was to consist of a parachute battalion dropped on the 1st May, west of Elephant Point, with the task of destroying the defences in that area. This would permit the entrance of minesweepers which would sweep a channel up the river as far as its junction with the Bassein Creek at Thakutpin, some twelve miles from Elephant Point. The way being thus opened for the first flight of assault troops, 36 Brigade of 26 Indian Division was to land half-way between Elephant Point and the Bassein Creek on the 2nd May (D-Day). Simultaneously with the landing of 36 Brigade, one battalion of 71 Brigade was to land on the east bank, near the mouth of the Hmawwun Chaung, and exploit towards Kyauktan. The remainder

of 71 Brigade was to build up this bridgehead as landing craft became available, followed by 4 Brigade. These two Brigades, after capturing Kyauktan, were to drive northwards to the outskirts of Syriam. On D plus 9, 6 Brigade of 2 British Division would take over the area from 71 Brigade, thus releasing 71 and 4 Brigades for the capture of Syriam and the clearance of the southern bank of the Pegu River. The remaining two brigades of 2 British Division were to follow up and assault Rangoon.

260. One of the main difficulties was the shortness of time available for preparing for this operation. The greater part of the Parachute Brigade was on leave and so an improvised Gurkha battalion had to be got together for the operation. It was very much to the credit of the Indian Airborne Division that this was efficiently organized and the operation carried out up to time. The consideration which limited the size of the airborne operation was the available air-lift. To find enough aircraft to lift the battalion, the two American Air Commandos had to be taken from 4 Corps. At the same time we could afford no reduction in air supply lift and so pilots had to be called on to fly at very high rates during this period, a call to which they, needless to say, responded magnificently. Finally, it will be remembered that 2 British Division had been flown out of Burma into India. To take part in this operation it had to be re-equipped. This was done by G.H.Q. India, in what must have been record time, brigades being re-equipped in turn within seven to ten days of their arrival, and although the whole Division was not in the end used, the first brigade embarked to schedule.

261. On the 1st May, heavy air attacks were made on all known defences on both banks of the Rangoon River and the Parachute Battalion was dropped success-fully at 0630 hours. They captured Elephant Point practically unopposed. It was only now that we received the first indication that the Japanese had virtually abandoned Rangoon. Aircraft reported the message "Japs gone" painted on the roof of the Rangoon jail, which was known to be a prisoner of war camp.

262. By the 2nd May, the invasion fleet had been successfully and correctly assembled – no mean task – and lay off the river estuary on the agreed lowering position, which as I have said before was a considerable distance from the beaches. The weather, however, before dawn on D-Day was extremely bad with high seas, low cloud and drenching rain, and the Naval Commander (Rear-Admiral Martin) predicted odds of three to one against it being possible to land the assault battalions on the east and west banks of the river. Despite this, it was decided that the operation should not be postponed and the magnificent work of the landing craft crews entirely justified this decision. Admiral Martin's signal to the fleet of "Guts and good seamanship" was an apt slogan for the occasion. The landings were successful, the only opposition coming from the elements. By 2000 hours the same night, 36 Brigade had reached and crossed the Bassein Creek. It was on this day that it might be said that the first element of the Imperial forces re-entered Rangoon. An R.A.F. pilot, after seeing signals from

the ground and a Union Jack flying over the jail, landed at the airfield seven miles north of the town. He was greeted by the local inhabitants, and made his way into the city and, after contacting our prisoners in the jail, went down river in a country boat and gave 26 Indian Division the news. By 2200 hours on the 3rd May, 36 Brigade had occupied Dala Village, opposite the Rangoon docks, against minor opposition. They had also crossed the river and entered the dock area. This was found to have been wrecked by our bombers, but the only serious damage to the residential part of the town was to the water and lighting installations. Meanwhile, 71 Brigade had occupied Syriam, the only resistance coming from snipers, and were preparing to cross the Pegu River.

263. The liberation of Rangoon had cost us just under one hundred casualties. Only one landing craft, unfortunately containing key engineer and medical personnel, was lost on a mine. By the successful re-entry into Rangoon through the sea-gate, the port was re-opened at least 14 days earlier than if it had been left to Fourteenth Army to take from the north, even as events turned out. The value of these 14 days at this critical period needs no emphasis.

264. By the 5th May, the occupation of the city was complete and exploitation north in progress. On the following day 26 Indian Division linked up with Fourteenth Army at Milestone 29 on the Rangoon – Pegu road, and the north-south bisection of Burma was complete, with 18,000 Japanese troops being cut off to the west. On this date, also, 26 Indian Division passed temporarily under command of Fourteenth Army and 15 Indian Corps thus completed its campaign in Burma.

265. With the capture of Rangoon a major phase of the war against Japan had been completed, a phase important in itself and decisive as far as Burma was concerned. It will be to the eternal credit of the sea, land and air forces of South-East Asia that this phase was completed before the 1945 monsoon.

SECTION XV (paras. 266–274)
THE NEW SITUATION
Opening of a new phase: Internal Security situation: Tactical situation after capture of Rangoon: The administrative situation and the effect on future plans.

---

266. The capture of Rangoon marked the completion of operation Capital and the end of a definite phase in the operations in Burma. From this time onwards I was concerned with the dual task of finishing off the liberation of Burma, and at the same time completing preparations for the campaign in Malaya. For the sake of clarity, I propose to deal first with our operations in Burma, leaving the plans for Malaya to a later section of my Despatch. But it must be remembered that the planning was in fact being carried out concurrently with the operations.

267. Before describing the continuance of operations, one other matter requires mention. This was the internal security aspect, which could not now be ignored.

Both during the retreat in 1942 and during the recent advance large quantities of British and Japanese arms and ammunition had fallen into the hands of the civil population. Furthermore, British and American Long-Range Penetration Brigades, and guerilla organizations, had armed the northern hill tribes on a substantial scale. And finally the Japanese had issued arms to locally raised forces.

The civil population was therefore in possession of a large number of weapons, and there was every chance of a serious outbreak of both dacoity and communal strife. Indeed, dacoity had already been met in the Akyab area, necessitating the detaching of troops to suppress it.

In January the Burma Government had raised the question of the reconstitution of the Burma Army, and I had recommended the raising of seven infantry battalions in addition to those already under my command. The raising of the first of these was begun in June but until the end of the period under review the question of internal security was, as can be understood, constantly in the minds of myself and my subordinate Commanders.

268. My main object at this time, early May, was to complete the liberation of Burma by the destruction of the remaining enemy forces in the country. Apart from direct operations against the Japanese cut off to the west of the Mandalay – Rangoon corridor, it was necessary to exert pressure to the east and south, along the Taunggyi and Mawchi roads, in order that the maximum advantages could be obtained for post-monsoon operations.

269. Our estimate of the Japanese effective fighting strength in Burma at this time was 77,000, of which 18,200 were west of the Irrawaddy. Enemy formations were much intermingled and disorganized as a result of their defeats, and it was therefore difficult to determine accurately their exact groupings. Their locations, however, were generally known, and the Japanese Burma Area Army fell into five main groups. (See Appendix B.)

First, west of the Irrawaddy in the Thayetmyo area, were 54 Division, 72 Independent Mixed Brigade, 153 Regiment from 49 Division and remnants of 112 Regiment of 55 Division.

Second, concentrating in the Pegu Yomas between the Rivers Irrawaddy and Sittang, was a considerable but ill-organized force, consisting of H.Q. 28th Japanese Army and Army troops, 55 Division less 112 Regiment, remnants of 18, 49 and 53 Japanese Divisions, two Brigades formed from the original Rangoon garrison and a number of Lines of Communication and Base troops.

Third, 113 Regiment was east of Sittang, around Taunggyi.

Fourth, in the area of Mawchi and to the north were H.Q. 15th Japanese Army, 56 Division (less 113 Regiment), 15 Division, 144 Regiment of 55 Division and various other units.

Fifth, to the east of the Sittang from Shwegyin down to Moulmein, were H.Q. Burma Area Army, H.Q. 33rd Japanese Army, 31 and 33 Divisions, 24 Independent Mixed Brigade and L. of C. and Base units.

270. This force was not in fact as formidable as it first appears. 56 Division and 24 Independent Mixed Brigade were the only major formations which had not been severely handled, with the loss of a large proportion of their artillery and transport. Moreover these two formations alone had managed to retain their inter-communication systems reasonably intact. There was therefore, I appreciated, no immediate possibility of a major counter-offensive, and the only possible intention of the Japanese would be to extricate those troops west of the Sittang from their almost hopeless situation.

271. I also appreciated that, in broad terms, the Japanese would endeavour to hold the east bank of the Sittang as a rear-guard position under cover of which the bulk of their forces now west of the river could be withdrawn east into Siam or south to Moulmein. While this was in progress the Japanese were likely to oppose any advances by our forces on the Taunggyi and Mawchi roads as likely to turn their position, and cut off or disrupt an organized withdrawal south or east of his forces west of the Sittang. Elements of 56 and 15 Japanese Divisions did in fact oppose our advance on the Taunggyi and Mawchi roads respectively until the surrender.

It was obvious that the extrication of the Japanese formations west of the river was an operation involving tremendous difficulties. There were the truly formidable natural obstacles of the Irrawaddy, the Pegu Yomas mountains and the Sittang to be crossed, during the monsoon, by jungle tracks and without wheeled transport or river crossing equipment. They were also already cut off from all normal supply and while they might live by foraging they could not be maintained in ammunition and other expendable military stores. Our air superiority forbad the use of air supply.

272. Against this situation, Fourteenth Army was in general extended over several hundreds of miles on the Yenangyaung – Rangoon and Mandalay – Rangoon axes. It was only possible under such conditions to hold key points and patrol the intervening gaps, while the movement eastwards of the considerable body of enemy might well disrupt our tenuous lines of communication.

Although we had gained a valuable fortnight by the capture of Rangoon from the sea, the administrative situation now limited our capabilities for further action, coupled as it was with the necessity to begin immediately the preparations for the attack on Malaya. Although it is dealt with in Part H of this Despatch, I think it desirable to draw attention here to the two routes by which our supplies arrived, and to point out that I was responsible not only for the maintenance of the Army, but also for that of all Naval and Air Force bases in Burma and for the carriage to distribution centres in Burma of civil supplies.

The Northern supply route ran by rail to Manipur Road in Assam thence by road through Imphal to Kalewa then by Inland Water Transport to Myingan, and finally by rail to Thazi for distribution. It could be supplemented by air transport from Imphal to Myingan, but this method was as liable to monsoon interruption as was the worn-out road route. In fact, the rapid deterioration of this route had already caused 4 Corps to be put on half rations as a precautionary measure.

The Southern supply route was by sea to Chittagong, Akyab or Kyaukpyu and thence by air to Central Burma or Inland Water Transport to troops in Arakan.

273. It was therefore essential to open, develop and stock Rangoon as the main base for Southern Burma, and improve its communications northwards as rapidly as possible. This was underlined by the administrative problems with which we would be faced when operating in the Moulmein area, for here roads were few, and monsoon conditions precluded the maintenance by sea of an advance down the Tenasserim coast. Finally, no further resources of aircraft or shipping were available, and I was forced to the conclusion that no major operation could be undertaken at any distance from the main Mandalay – Rangoon road or railway.

274. I accordingly directed General Slim to complete the destruction of the enemy west of the Sittang and to maintain constant pressure against Moulmein, Mawchi and Taunggyi.

SECTION XVI (paras. 275–281)

OPERATIONS IN MAY

New orders issued fey General Slim: Arakan operations: 4 Corps operations: 33 Corps operations: Note on guerilla organizations.

---

275. To carry out the tasks I had now given him (see para. 274) General Slim issued fresh orders to his subordinate commanders. Besides 4 and 33 Corps, General Slim had 26 Indian and 36 British Divisions, and 64 Indian Brigade (19 Indian Division), under his direct control.

He instructed 4 Corps (General Messervy) to capture Mokpalin and Bilin, east of the Sittang and reconnoitre towards Moulmein: to destroy any enemy forces attempting to escape from the Pegu Yomas across the Mandalay – Rangoon road and railway; and to capture Thandaung on the road from Toungoo to Mawchi.

33 Corps (General Stopford) at the same time was ordered to destroy the enemy in the Irrawaddy Valley, open the Prome – Rangoon road and railway, and capture Bassein. 26 Indian Division was ordered to advance on Prome from Rangoon to meet 33 Corps, and on the 15th May a battalion group from 2 British Division (then in the Rangoon area) was sent to carry out the capture of Bassein.

Finally General Slim ordered 64 Indian Infantry Brigade to relieve 36 British Division on the Taunggyi – Thazi road and capture Kalaw, the Brigade coming under command of 4 Corps on the 18th May.

276. In Arakan there remained 82 (West African) Division directly under my control, and to them I allotted both operational and administrative responsibility between the Dalet Chaung and Gwa. I also instructed General Stockwell to patrol east of the Taungup – Prome road to establish contact with 33 Corps as the monsoon conditions made it impossible to move the whole Division on this route.

277. *4 Corps operations during May*, 1945: 5 Indian Division was ordered to open the road from Payagyi to Mokpalin and also clear the area between Pegu and the

southern end of the Pegu Yomas of enemy. 9 Indian Infantry Brigade opened the road as far as Waw against determined Japanese resistance, and then continued towards the Sittang River. The heavy rainfall, however, rendered the deployment of tanks and artillery difficult if not impossible, as the west bank of the Sittang is flat and, during May, flooded. With the enemy overlooking them from jungle-clad hills on the east bank and without adequate river-crossing equipment it was not possible to launch an attack to capture Mokpalin, or do more than patrol across the Sittang River on a wide front, until after the monsoon.

Meanwhile 123 and 161 Brigades were engaged in widespread patrols under appalling climatic conditions, seeking out the numerous Japanese in the area to the south of the Pegu Yomas. Throughout the month their toll of Japanese dead mounted; the enemy became desperate in their attempts to escape, and on occasions would deliver fierce attacks upon our patrols.

Meanwhile 17 Indian Division was disposed between Penwegon and Nyaunglebin, and spent the whole month in most active patrolling, designed to kill the enemy wherever found and to prevent a concentrated attempt at a break out. In this they were highly successful, and proved conclusively their superiority to the Japanese in this type of operation. As an example, at Konin on the 21st May a patrol of 99 Brigade in one encounter killed 148 Japanese at a cost to themselves of 4 wounded.

19 Indian Division from Toungoo had by the 10th May advanced 5 miles along the road to Thandaung, but 98 Brigade, the leaders, were being strenuously opposed. On this date 62 Brigade, with tank support, took over the lead and fought its way forward in the face of extensive mining of the road and determined resistance from prepared positions on the high ground dominating the area. On the 25th May 98 Brigade took over again, and three days later captured the road junction at Thandaung, though pockets of the enemy continued to hold out in the surrounding hills.

278. It is convenient at this juncture to deal with 64 Indian Infantry Brigade and the operations on the Thazi – Taunggyi road. On the 10th May it relieved 36 British Division, which was due for withdrawal from operations after a year's hard fighting from Myitkyina in the north to Thazi. The Brigade met most determined resistance in the locality known aptly as "The Staircase", 12 miles north of Kalaw. Here 56 Japanese Division, probably the least battered formation left in the Burma Area Army had a well prepared defensive position supported by artillery. However, after prolonged and bitter fighting "The Staircase" fell to our troops on the 31st May and Kalaw was entered a week later.

279. 33 *Corps operations in May:* The operations of 33 Corps in May consisted initially of an advance south by 20 Indian Division on the east of the Irrawaddy to meet 26 Indian Division marching from Rangoon north to Prome, and thereby to seal off the enemy forces, which consisted of elements of 54 and 55 Japanese Divisions, and 72 Independent Mixed Brigade, to the west of the Irrawaddy. At the same time 7 Indian Division, 268 Indian (Independent) Infantry Brigade and

the Lushai Brigade, were driving the enemy south before them down the west bank of the Irrawaddy, and so closing the net. The linkup between 20 and 26 Indian Divisions was made on the 15th May at Taikkyi, 60 miles north of Rangoon, and 26 Indian Division then came under command of 33 Corps.

As had been anticipated, the enemy now attempted to concentrate on the west bank of the Irrawaddy in the general area Thayetmyo – Kama, and to force his way across into the Pegu Yomas. General Stopford accordingly directed 7 Indian Division to operate agains this crossings on the west bank of the river between Allanmyo and Kama, while 20 Indian Division consolidated the Prome – Rangoon road and railway axis and prevented the enemy establishing escape gaps across the river into the Pegu Yomas. 20 Indian Division was also ordered to push west on the Prome – Taungup road to make contact with patrols of 82 (West African) Division and so cut off stragglers from 55 Japanese Division.

In early May under the increasing pressure of 7 Indian Division, the Japanese began their attempts to break-out east over the river. 54 Japanese Division succeeding in establishing a bridgehead at Zalon, 10 miles north of Prome while one regiment of 49 Japanese Division and 2 Japanese Brigade actually succeeded in crossing just north of Prome and making good their escape.

General Stopford, faced with the problem of trying to prevent all escape crossings over some 50 miles of river with the limited number of troops available, decided to concentrate against the Zalon bridgehead. First 80 Brigade of 20 Indian Division and later 33 Brigade of 7 Indian Division were directed against the bridgehead and throughout the remainder of May both 7 and 20 Indian Divisions were involved in much bitter fighting against the enemy concentrations on the west bank and against the crossings.

Most of these crossings were destroyed or beaten back, but some small parties were able to slip across the river.

Very heavy casualties were inflicted on the enemy during this period and by the end of May the fighting in the Zalon area had reached its conclusion. The west bank was virtually clear of the enemy and those who had succeeded in crossing were being hunted into the foothills of the Pegu Yomas. 268 Indian Infantry Brigade was left on the west bank to mop up the stragglers.

280. Bassein was occupied by a battalion group of 6 Brigade without opposition on the 25th May, our troops receiving a joyous welcome from the local inhabitants.

281. It was during this period that the Burma National Army, now renamed the Patriot Burma Forces, began to take an active part in the operations. The Japanese had raised the Burma Defence Army of some 3,000 men, and this force had come over to our side in March. From this date they fought the Japanese in co-operation with our troops, particularly our Force 136, and the degree of co-operation improved steadily as time went on, reaching its climax in the battle of the break-out in July. During May these organizations operated courageously

and successfully in a guerilla rôle east of the Sittang. They were particularly successful when they worked in co-operation with 221 Group, R.A.F., attacking enemy headquarters, dumps and stores, and damaging communications. Their efforts were by no means to be ignored, and the results attained were a fit reward for the arduous conditions under which they lived and in which the R.A.F. pilots flew. Their presence compelled the Japanese to abandon their attempts to escape in small parties, and forced them to adopt the alternative of a concentrated breakout, which ended so disastrously for them.

SECTION XVII (paras. 282–291)

THE FINAL BATTLES

Reorganization of the Allied Land Forces: Formation and tasks of Twelfth Army: Operations in the Irrawaddy Valley: The Lower Sittang Battle: The Battle of the Break-out: Conclusion of operations.

---

282. Continuing the narrative of events, it was towards the end of May that it became necessary to reorganize my forces in order to carry out the operations planned to take place against Malaya. These plans I will describe in a later section, so here it is but necessary to state that they involved the removal to India of Headquarters, Fourteenth Army, and certain formations and units. In India General Slim was to be responsible for the planning and preparations for the new venture, while Burma became the responsibility of a new Army – Twelfth Army, under the command of General Stopford.

283. On the formation of Twelfth Army (28th May, 1945), 33 Corps ceased to exist. The formations allotted to Twelfth Army were (by the 2nd June, 1945) 4 Corps (consisting of 5, 17 and 19 Indian Divisions), 7 and 20 Indian Divisions, 82 (West African) Division, 255 Indian Tank Brigade, 6 British and 268 Indian Infantry Brigades. 26 Indian Division and 254 Indian Tank Brigade were in the process of moving back to India, but the gucrilla forces mentioned in paragraph 281 remained to operate under Twelfth Army. To deal with internal security, 505 District and No. 1 Area were formed, with their Headquarters at Meiktila and Rangoon respectively. Besides administrative units, they had at their disposal a total of eighteen infantry battalions.

284. My directions to General Stopford were to complete the destruction of the Japanese forces remaining west of the Sittang, and to liberate that part of Burma (including the Tenasserim Civil Division) which Japanese forces still occupied. He was also charged with the introduction of the Civil Affairs Service (Burma) into the country, the maintenance of law and order, and the re-formation of the Burma Army.

285. In order to carry out my orders, General Stopford instructed 4 Corps (disposed between the Sittang and the Pegu Yomas) to block any attempts the Japanese might make to break out of the Yomas, to advance along the Taunggyi

road and the Mawchi road, and to maintain a brigade opposite the Sittang crossing near Mokpalin. Meanwhile 7 Indian Division (with 268 Indian Infantry Brigade under command) were to clear the Allanmyo – Kama – Prome area of Japanese stragglers, and operate with offensive patrols into the Pegu Yomas from the west. 20 Indian Division were to act likewise in the area to the south of the Yomas, and 6 Infantry Brigade and 255 Indian Tank Brigade were held in reserve in Rangoon, with the task of forming a mobile column in the event of an enemy thrust towards Rangoon, and in addition to operate water patrols in conjunction with the Navy in the Irrawaddy Delta.

286. The operations under control of 7 Indian Division in the Irrawaddy Valley around Allanmyo proceeded as planned, and many Japanese raiding and foraging parties were destroyed. Patrols probed the Pegu Yomas and met increasing resistance, until by mid-June it was apparent that the valley was clear and that the Japanese in the Pegu Yomas were preparing an attempt to break out eastwards through 4 Corps' area. Of this Corps, 5 Indian Division was about to leave to join Fourteenth Army in India, and therefore 7 Indian Division was switched to 4 Corps, leaving 268 Indian Brigade, now joined by 22 (East African) Brigade, in the Irrawaddy Valley.

287. The relief of 5 Indian Division in the area between Pegu and the Sittang by 7 Indian Division coincided with a counter-attack by elements of 18 and 53 Japanese Divisions across the Sittang from Mokpalin. This was a determined drive towards Pegu, designed to assist the Japanese in the Southern Pegu Yomas to break out eastwards by pinning down 7 Indian Division. The country in which the battle was fought was one large lake, overlooked by the Japanese artillery position in the hills east of the Sittang. Conditions were such that at times it was impossible to use the Gurkha battalions owing to the depth of water on the "land" over which they were to operate. Our lack of artillery was made good by the magnificent efforts of the R.A.F., and 7 Indian Division was able to stem the attack. A battalion (4/8 Gurkha Rifles) was at one time surrounded at the end of a peninsula, but fought its way out through the Japanese lines, and by the end of July the situation was restored to what it had been before the Japanese attack. Owing to lack of co-ordination the Japanese efforts did not assist their comrades in the Pegu Yomas, and resulted in their sustaining casualties much larger than those of 7 Indian Division.

288. Operations on the Mawchi road continued throughout June and July. 19 Indian Division made slow but steady progress despite Japanese resistance, and dreadful climatic and topographical difficulties. On the Taunggyi road the Japanese resistance was less, and by the 25th July Taunggyi itself was in our hands.

289. During June, 4 Corps' formations not engaged in the operations described in the two preceding paragraphs were engaged with patrols and sporadic engagements with the Japanese concentrating in the Yomas. V Force provided most valuable information, and enabled us to locate the Japanese and forecast their

plans. 4 Corps estimated their numbers at just under 10,000, but this figure was in fact only half the total. The discrepancy was due to the unexpectedly large number of non-divisional Japanese troops caught in the trap, who took part in the break-out. Finally, on the 4th July, an operation order was captured giving the entire Japanese break-out plan; the only detail lacking was the date selected for D-Day, but other Intelligence placed D-Day as approximately the 20th July.

290. With this information at his disposal General F.I.S. Tuker, acting for General Messervy who was on leave, was able to dispose 4 Corps to block all intended lines of escape. The Japanese held to their plan to the last detail, and the resulting slaughter was tremendous. Between the 21st July and the 4th August over 10,000 casualties were inflicted on the Japanese, not counting wounded. Of these only 740 were taken prisoner.

291. The Battle of the Break-out, it transpired, was the last battle of the war. For the 10 days which intervened between the conclusion of the battle and the end of the period covered by this Despatch, a lull ensued during which little of note occurred. Patrols and small advances were the order of the day, and the Royal Air Force continued to add to the destruction they had caused throughout the campaign.

SECTION XVIII (paras. 292–301)
PLANS FOR MALAYA

Joint Planning Staff Paper of the 23rd February, 1945: Operations Roger, Zipper and Mailfist: Cancellation of Roger: D-Day for Zipper: Zipper appreciation and plan.

---

292. It is now necessary to revert to February, 1945, to consider the evolution of the plans for the recapture of Malaya. Throughout the post-Rangoon operations to which the last three sections have been devoted, planning and preliminary action for subsequent operations had been continuing, and their effects on current operations, particularly command and organization, have been recorded. The assaults on Malaya and Singapore (operations Zipper and Mailfist) had absolute priority, and every unit required for these operations was either moved to India or concentrated in Rangoon (which was to be the forward base for the assault forces) for rest and reorganization.

293. On the 23rd February the Supreme Commander had held a conference at Fort William, and at it approval was given to the outline plan produced by the Joint Planning Staff in their Paper No. 88 of the 6th February. It was appreciated that the Japanese would endeavour to hold Malaya and in particular, Singapore, as a barrier to prevent our entry into the area of the South China Sea. Similarly, without Singapore we would be unable to extend materially our operations eastwards. The object of the paper was to examine the best outline method of reaching Singapore.

294. It was anticipated that the Japanese would build up their strength in Malaya, and therefore it was desirable to mount the operation as speedily as possible and by the quickest route. This rendered undesirable an approach *via* the Sunda Straits, Sumatra, or the Andaman Islands, as the establishment of a forward base in these areas would still leave that base at a distance too great for a direct assault on Singapore. By various means we attempted to give the impression that we would move on Singapore by one or more of these routes. It was therefore agreed that the forward base should be on the Malay Peninsula, and an examination was made of the geographical features of the area.

295. The Tenasserim coast was ruled out as a suitable area for a landing owing to the monsoon conditions. The further south the better would these conditions become, until, in the Straits of Malacca, sea conditions were suitable throughout the year.

The Phuket operation was feasible, but the very narrow waterway dividing Phuket Island from the mainland made it necessary to provide a force capable of withstanding any build-up against it. The size of this force depended naturally on the anticipated size of the build-up, and this in turn depended on the length of time during which the British force was to be the only one ashore in Malaya. Another landing would, of course, divert some of the build-up, but the scarcity of landing craft meant a considerable time lag before the next amphibious operation could take place, and for that reason therefore the Army commitment at Phuket had to be considerable if the proposed airstrips were to be protected from artillery fire. While relatively near Rangoon, the seizure of Phuket did not, of course, obviate the need to make another landing on the Malay Peninsula nearer to Singapore.

296. A study of the beaches and anchorages revealed that the Port Dickson/Port Swettenham area also was suitable, though by no means perfect, and the distance on to Singapore was reduced to about 200 miles. This plan would make the maximum use of the capture of Rangoon, and it was considered that with the seizure of a bridgehead in this area it would be possible to disrupt Japanese communications along the Malay Peninsula by the joint use of air power and guerilla forces. It was therefore agreed at this meeting on the 23rd February to examine this project in detail, target dates being decided as the 1st June for Phuket (Roger), early October for the Port Swettenham/Port Dickson landing (Zipper) and December for Singapore (Mailfist).

297. Planning accordingly was begun in detail, while the operations in Burma proceeded.

As has been recorded (para. 224), the Roger operation was postponed by the decision to capture Rangoon from the sea, as the only landing craft available were used for this operation. On the capture of Rangoon in May, the rapid deterioration of the Japanese air and naval forces and the availability of sufficient aircraft carriers, was such that the Supreme Commander decided that he could accept the risk of not seizing Phuket Island at all, and planning thereafter was concentrated on Zipper and Mailfist. Furthermore the situation had now developed to an extent which made it feasible to undertake Zipper in August and we anticipated the capture of Singapore by the end of 1945.

The shipping resources available were, as ever, strictly limited, and it was decided that the assault should be carried out by a Corps. 34 Corps, formed *in embryo* in India for the Phuket operation under Lieut-General O.L. Roberts (see para. 94) was therefore allotted to the new task of undertaking operation Zipper. General Roberts and the Naval and Air Force Commanders examined the problem, and produced by the 23rd June an appreciation and outline plan. They divided the operation into three phases; the securing of the bridgehead, the advance to the Johore Causeway and the assault on Singapore. The last phase was Mailfist, and the two projects were combined into one.

298. At a meeting with the Supreme Commander at Delhi on the 30th May I was reluctantly compelled to tell Admiral Mountbatten that the effects of repatriation on my units was such that I must request a postponement of Zipper from August to early September.

It had been decided by the War Cabinet that the period of overseas service necessary to qualify for repatriation was to be reduced by four months, and this decision resulted in British units being decimated by wholesale departures of battle experienced men to the United Kingdom. Training and reorganization was essential, and the Supreme Commander, considering this and certain other factors, accepted my recommendation. General Slim (who had by now taken charge of Zipper planning – see para. 282) and his colleagues were so informed, and detailed examination led to the 9th September being selected as D-Day.

299. The appreciation of the Japanese resistance to be expected, led us to antici-pate that the landing would be lightly opposed, and that the subsequent build-up against it would be at the worst three divisions, and at the best not more than two, in addition to the garrison of Singapore itself. Against this we were able to deploy two divisions and one brigade on D-Day, rising to three divisions and a Parachute brigade by D plus 8 and a fourth division by D plus 25. This force, plus non-divisional troops, comprised 34 Corps. My plan after the seizure of the bridge-head was based on making a rapid advance on Singapore in order to avoid if possible a serious battle for the Island. If opposition proved light, 34 Corps was to begin the advance south as soon as possible, and we estimated this might be possible by D plus 13. It would even then be necessary to leave two divisions to secure the Port Dickson/Port Swettenham area, but the build-up from India and Rangoon was to come in any case. My plan was to bring in 15 Indian Corps to take over rearward commitments, and thereby allow the Commander, 34 Corps, to devote his entire energies to the advance south. I planned also a series of amphibian hooks down the coast, in order to cut off the Japanese facing 34 Corps and to prevent them retiring on to the Singapore garrison. To control these

diverse operations and to conduct the battle on the ground, General Slim and his Fourteenth Army Headquarters was scheduled to arrive with the second Corps.

300. The landing itself was to be covered by carrier-borne aircraft for the first 8 to 10 days, by which time a strip had to be operating ashore. It was essential also to capture a port through which stores could be landed to supplement the small amount which could be taken over the beaches. The conclusion reached therefore was that the main assault by three brigades should go in over the Morib beaches on D-Day, with the object of securing the airstrips in the area and also Port Swettenham. Also on D-Day, another brigade was to land at Sepang to seize the road bridges there; this subsidiary landing would be a support to the main one. In addition, on D plus 3, three more brigades were to land on the somewhat obvious beaches by Port Dickson, with the object of enlarging the bridgehead and seizing another usable port.

301. The plan described in outline above, was in fact carried out subsequent to the Japanese capitulation, but its execution did not take place during the period covered by my Despatch. Furthermore the Japanese surrender caused certain alterations to it, and I have therefore decided that it would be undesirable to go into fuller detail myself. At this point therefore I shall conclude the Operational portion of my Despatch, and follow with Part II which examines the very vital Administrative aspect of the campaign in considerable detail.

PART II
ADMINISTRATION SECTION XIX (paras. 302–310)
THE MAINTENANCE PROBLEM
The Northern, Southern and Air Lines of Communication generally: The size of the problem.

---

302. The Japanese failure to solve their administrative difficulties in their attempt to invade India led them to disaster at Kohima and Imphal. The fact that we overcame the difficulties of administration resulted in the re-conquest of Burma. The problem that faced us was immense, and the effort that was put into its solution was as great. In the final analysis of military history this may be the outstanding feature of the campaign, and it is with this in mind, that I intend to go into this aspect more fully than is usual in a Despatch.

303. The outstanding administrative problem of an army is usually its maintenance; that is, the unfailing supply of all the commodities which keep that army fighting in the field. The base for our operations was India. The railheads were at Chittagong (with short extensions to Dohazari and to the north for the Arakan coast); Dimapur (Manipur Road), railhead for Fourteenth Army; and Ledo and Chabua for Northern Combat Area Command and the United States air ferry route to China. These railheads thus joined the only three road entries to Burma from the north. A certain degree of flexibility was provided between the Assam

lines to Dimapur, Ledo and Chabua and the Eastern Bengal lines to Chittagong by the rail link between Lumding and Badarpur, though this link was of limited capacity owing to gradients. The whole system of communications between India and Burma has already been fully described by my predecessor, General Giffard, in his Despatch.[2] I will therefore only deal with the more forward communications which immediately affected the campaign. These were three in number: the Northern line of Communication, the Southern Line of Communication and the Air Line of Communication.

304. The Northern L. of C. was made up, at its fullest and longest development, of three main sections from the Manipur Road railhead. The first was 320 miles of road from the railhead, *via* Imphal and Tamu, to Kalewa. It was in part a mountainous route, and the stretch from Tamu onwards could at first only be called a road by courtesy, though subsequently brought up to all-weather standard. The second section was by river from Kalewa to Myingyan, about 240 miles downstream, in Inland Water Transport craft. During the dry weather there was also the fair-weather road from Kalewa *via* Pyingaing to Shwebo and thence on by the Central Burma all-weather road system, but our engineer resources never allowed the conversion of this stretch to higher standard. The third section was by a combination of railway and road from Myingyan southeast to Thazi and thence south to Rangoon, about 430 miles. In addition, a secondary I.W.T. L. of C. ran down the axis of the Irrawaddy. Demolitions and bombing had cut the railway into sections, which were operated to a limited extent with motor transport bridging the gaps. The Northern L. of C. is thus seen to total nearly a thousand miles, using road, rail, and water transport. The resources to operate this immense and complicated L. of C. had either to be brought in by road form the Manipur Road railhead or be flown in. The limitations and development of this L. of C. will be described later.

305. On the Southern L. of C. maintenance was initially by sea from the main base ports in India to Chittagong and to small river ports such as Cox's Bazaar and Maungdaw. After the capture of Akyab and Ramree Islands the bulk of this maintenance was sent direct to Akyab and Kyaukpyu. The latter were however capable of only limited development, with the harbour-craft which we had available.

The Southern L. of C. could, by land and by coastal craft, only serve the Arakan operations. There were only two overland routes from the coast inland to Central Burma, one a rough track *via* An, incapable of development as a road L. of C. without thorough and expensive construction, for which we had neither the time nor the resources. The other was the fair-weather road from Taungup to Prome. The reasons why this route was never opened up have been discussed fully in Part I of this Despatch. It is sufficient here to say that it could not have been developed to a sufficient capacity in time to be any use, even if we had had the engineer resources available. Thus the only way the Southern L. of C. could feed Central Burma and Fourteenth Army was by air transport, and this is what it did. The development of this L. of C. will be described later.

306. At the start of the offensive, the air supply organization was based on groups of airfields near Imphal in the north, Comilla, Agartala and Chittagong in Eastern Bengal. With the limited land lines of communication and no access to Central Burma by sea, air supply was the only way of getting in sufficient maintenance for Fourteenth Army's operations. That is, when all other means were being worked to absolute maximum capacity, there remained a large essential tonnage which could only be brought in by air. Were this essential tonnage reduced, I would be forced to cut down my forces. The total tonnage which could be lifted by air, however, depended not only on the number of available transport aircraft squadrons but on the location of the transport airfields at economic ranges from the delivery airfields. In the case of the C 46 and C 47 aircraft which were being used, this was about 250 miles. It was not long therefore before the advance of the Army took it beyond the economic range of the air bases mentioned above. To move these bases forward on the Army's L. of C. was impracticable owing to the undeveloped nature of the country and the limitations of the L. of C. itself. The air bases near Imphal were already uneconomical since everything for them had to be moved by road from the Manipur Road railhead to Imphal. The desired result could, however, be achieved by opening new and improved air supply bases on the coast, where the material of war could be delivered by sea. This showed at once the vital importance to the maintenance of Fourteenth Army of Akyab and Ramree Islands, where airfields could be constructed, and where there were ports capable of development, even if limited. From these bases, aircraft could operate at economic range to Central Burma and the Irrawaddy and road/railway axes south to Rangoon. It was a question of capturing the areas in time to allow their development and stocking before the monsoon.

307. There was one other route into Burma, the road from Ledo, *via* Myitkyina to join with the Burma Road to China. This was under construction under American control (as has been said already). Northern Combat Area Command in their operations down this road axis towards Lashio were almost entirely supplied by American air transport, operating from the Chabua group of airfields north-west of Ledo.

308. Two factors should be considered when the Ls. of C. are under examination. First, land Ls. of C. in an undeveloped country like Burma and with a determined enemy like the Japanese are liable to be cut by hostile action. On the other hand, our complete air and sea supremacy made transport by these elements secure.

Secondly, I must again draw attention to the factor of the weather. During the monsoon, say 15th May to 15th November very roughly, we had to expect all fair-weather routes to be out of action; even all-weather roads were subject to wash-outs and damage. Although flying was certain to be intermittent and hazardous, air supply became often the only practicable means, but it was entirely dependent on all-weather airfields. All administrative planning had to include provision for the continuance of adequate maintenance under monsoon conditions. The absolute importance of completing the construction of all-weather airfields for supply aircraft before the monsoon was therefore obvious.

309. From the brief description of the Ls. of C. it is plain that the main problem throughout the period of this Despatch was the maintenance of Fourteenth Army. The difficulty of this problem was not only qualitative but quantitative. Requirements of course varied with the number of formations and nature of operations; but, as an example, during April,1945, the daily maintenance tonnage required by Fourteenth Army, including R.A.F. and Civil Affairs (Burma) requirements, averaged 2,090 tons (long) per day, while the equivalent requirement by 15 Indian Corps was 84 tons per day. (The size of 15 Indian Corps at this period had been reduced to allow the maximum tonnage for Fourteenth Army.) Of these amounts, the quantities delivered by air averaged, for Fourteenth Army 1,845 tons, and for 15 Indian Corps 16 tons.

310. To sum up, we were entering Burma by the back door, with wholly inadequate land communications. We were fighting an enemy who had a first rate port behind him and good rail and road communications, since he was operating with his supply system on the same lines that Burma's internal supplies were carried in normal times. We were enabled to conquer him as a result of the tremendous effort that was put into overcoming the administrative difficulties and in particular by supplementing the inadequate land Ls. of C. with an air L. of C., developed to an unprecedented extent. The details of this conquest of the administrative problem set by the natural and geographical peculiarities of the Theatre are the main burden of this part of this Despatch.

SECTION XX (paras. 311–334)
THE DEVELOPMENT OF THE NORTHERN
LINE OF COMMUNICATION

Formation of L. of C, Command: Supply routes to the Advanced bases: The Assam Railways: The problem of replacement vehicles: The development of the Chindwin I.W.T. link: Changes in the organization of the L. of C.: Changes in the organization of Supply and Transport: Further changes in the organization of the L. of C.: The development of the Burma Railways: Petrol distribution: Some statistics.

---

311. I propose to deal with the development of the land Ls. of C. first, as a proper understanding of the difficulties and limitations of these Ls. of C. is essential to any real comprehension of the administrative aspect of the campaign as a whole, including the air supply aspect. I regard it as absolutely essential, too, that it should be realised what a prodigious effort had to be put into the land Ls. of C., as the spectacular results of air supply and the successful capture of Rangoon, with the consequent restoration of a more normal L. of C. tend to obscure the extent and duration of this effort.

312. The organization and development of the Northern line will be described first. When I took over command in November 1944, orders had already been issued for the formation of L. of C. Command, which actually took place on the 15th November. The two L. of C Areas 202 and 404, were transferred from the command of Fourteenth Army to the new L. of C. Command, the Commander of which, Major-General G.W. Symes, was directly responsible to me. Hitherto H.Q., Allied Land Forces, South-East Asia (or H.Q., 11 Army Group as it had been called before it became an Allied Command) had been represented by Advanced Echelon North at Manipur Road and Advanced Echelon South at Comilla. These Advanced Echelons were almost entirely concerned with movements and with the processing of stores, etc., along the complicated L. of C. To ensure continuity and relieve Commander, L. of C. Command of purely movement problems these Advanced Echelons were retained under the new organization. Fourteenth Army was thus relieved of L. of C. responsibilities and could concentrate on the main offensive. The boundary between Fourteenth Army and 15 Indian Corps and L. of C. Command very nearly coincided with the political boundary between India and Burma with a deviation south-east of Chittagong. The whole of L. of C. Command lay in India, 202 Area consisting of most of Assam, including Manipur State, while 404 Area consisted of that part of Bengal lying east of the Meghna River, and a part of Assam lying to the south of Shillong.

313. The system of maintenance at this time on this L. of C. was that supplies were sent forward from the India Base by rail and Inland Water Transport to the Advanced Bases at Gauhati on the Brahmaputra, and at Manipur Road (Dimapur) in Assam. It can be seen that this was not a simple, straight run through. In India Command there was the transhipment at the Ganges Ferry at Mokameh Ghat and, for stores coming by rail from Calcutta, the change from broad to metre gauge railway at Parbatipur. Further tran-shipments were necessary at the Brahmaputra ferries at Dhubri Ghat, Amingaon or Tezpur or at the I.W.T. transhipment points at Pandu or Neamati. The distribution from the Advanced Bases was affected by motor transport (L. of C. Transport Column) to Tiddim, and thence *via* Tamu to the Corps Maintenance Areas.

314. The Assam Railway system worked well on the whole, any occasional short fall on stores tonnage being quickly rectified by increased despatches later. Where target figures were not reached, it was usually due to a temporary shortage of wagons or to the lack of stores ready to load. Only one serious accident occurred during the period of this Despatch, when a buckled rail caused a derailment and the loss of 18 wagons by fire. Throughout the period there were extensions and improvements made to the transhipment, marshalling, reception and departure yards. Engine shed accommodation and yard layouts were improved and the ferry and personnel ghat lines developed.

315. When control of the L. of C. was taken over from Fourteenth Army by H.Q., Allied Land Forces, South-East Asia in November through L. of C.

Command, the responsibility for and control of the movement of replacement vehicles forward of Calcutta also passed from H.Q., Fourteenth Army to my H.Q. This not only freed Fourteenth Army from all responsibility in rear of the Army boundary, but, through the closer control which my H.Q. could exercise, being on the spot, it resulted in a larger number of vehicles being got forward. Delivery was, in theory, to be made to the nearest depot in Fourteenth Army's area, at this time at Imphal, but as the advance into Burma progressed, it was unfortunately often found necessary for Fourteenth Army to send back part of the way, owing to shortage of drivers.

316. In December 1944, India Command came to our rescue and accepted the responsibility for moving up replacement vehicles to Manipur Road by the rail/road route, but, unfortunately, the supply of civilian drivers proved inadequate to meet increasing demands. Recourse had to be made to pulling back drivers from the L. of C. Transport Column, to using spare drivers of units going forward, and of combing our reinforcement camps for drivers. By these expedients, the forward flow of replacement vehicles was maintained at a sufficiently high level to meet essential requirements. Thus, for example, in March 1945, over 7,000 vehicles, including trailers were sent forward, whereas, before December 1944, it had never been found possible to exceed 2,000 replacement vehicles per month.

317. It was during December 1944 that an important development of the Northern L. of C. started, namely the building of the Inland Water Transport base on the Chindwin near Kalewa. As part of the policy of developing the Northern L. of C. to its fullest extent, it was obvious that we should have to make the maximum use of the river waterways. At this time it was not possible to estimate exactly to what extent this I.W.T. link could be developed, but as will be seen later it subsequently became of the utmost importance.

318. In January 1945, the success of operation Capital – Fourteenth Army's offensive into Central Burma – necessitated the extension of administrative planning for the maintenance of the army south of Mandalay. It now became clear that we could not spare the resources for the reconstruction of the road from the Chindwin crossing at Kalewa, *via* Pyingaing to Shwebo up to all-weather standard. At the same time, the development of the River Chindwin L. of C. showed great promise. It was therefore decided to put the maximum effort into the I.W.T. project and to abandon any idea of using the road between Kalewa and Shwebo during the monsoon. In any case, it would not be possible to maintain the Bailey pontoon bridge across the Chindwin when it started to rise with the advent of the rains. The Chindwin River had thus to be developed as fast as possible to bridge the gap between Kalewa and the all-weather road system of Central Burma: this link in the chain and the extent to which its capacity could be raised governed the overall capacity of the Northern L. of C. once the monsoon had started. As the lower terminal of the I.W.T. link, and as the Advanced Base for supplying the forces in Central Burma, Myingyan was chosen, and plans for

its development were prepared. Myingyan was on the existing all-weather road system of Central Burma and there was also the possibility of being able to use stretches of the railway. It was well placed with regard to Meiktila, the road/railway axis to Rangoon and the Irrawaddy River axis to Prome and beyond.

319. The development of the I.W.T. project deserves to be discussed in detail, since in many ways it is unique in the annals of warfare. There were three main ways in which we could build up the fleet; from craft transported in sections from India, from craft built on the spot out of timber felled in the jungle, and by salving and capturing boats already on the river. All these methods were used to the fullest extent. During January, I.W.T. Operating Companies, Craft Erection and Workshop Companies, Salvage Companies, a Higgins Barge Erection Section and – somewhat to their surprise – a Railway Workshop Company were moved to Kalewa. It should be remembered that the whole project started right from nothing. The boat-building yards, jetties, piers and accommodation had first to be built on an open sand bank. Timber was felled in the jungle, hauled by elephants and shaped in improvised sawmills, the work being carried out by an Artisan Works Company and a Forestry Company R.E. Craft were despatched in sections from Calcutta by rail to Manipur Road and thence carried by road 304 miles to Kalewa, where they were reassembled. The cutting of a large boat into section for re-erection elsewhere was no easy task technically, as anyone who saw the experiments carried out near Calcutta will agree. The transport of these awkward loads over the already congested road L. of C. also presented many problems. About 50 craft of all types were normally under construction at the same time. Between January and April 1945 (inclusive), no less than 415 rivercraft were built, comprising 11 different types, including barges, tugs, ramped cargo lighters, launches, etc., all of which were prefabricated types. The vessels constructed even included two gun boats for the Royal Navy, armed with Bofors and Oerlikon guns, which were commissioned for operations on the Chindwin. This must represent a high watermark of inter-Service co-operation. Engines and other vital stores were at times brought in by air transport. Much improvisation was necessary to maintain the rate of constructions, as, for example when fencing wire was used for welding electrodes.

320. Local construction was concentrated on the building of blunt-ended pontoons, which, lashed in threes and decked over, made a raft of 30 tons capacity. These rafts were towed by the power pre-fabricated craft. By the end of April, 541 pontoons had been built and put into service. In addition to these, 174 ex-enemy and other crafts of various types were salvaged and powered with engines, largely flown in from India. When Mandalay was captured in March, the Government Dockyard was found to contain a large quantity of dismantled machinery. The power plant, smithy and foundry were soon put into working order and assisted the Kalewa boat-building operations. A measure of the size of the whole Kalewa project is perhaps indicated by the fact that over five million rivets were used.

321. The target for the capacity of the I.W.T. link between Kalewa and Myingyan was 700 tons a day by the arrival of the monsoon. Operation started on a small scale between Kalewa and Alon (120 miles downstream) on the 1st February and by the end of February the capacity of this link rose to 255 tons per day. The full link to Myingyan started operation on the 26th March, with an initial lift of 200 tons per day, rising to 380 tons per day by the 1st April. During April the capacity rose until by the end of the month 575 tons per day was reached. In four months 25,688 tons of stores had been lifted from Kalewa to Alon and Myingyan, with a record day's lift of 1,147 tons.

322. In January, Railway Operating Construction and Maintenance Companies were concentrated at Manipur Road, awaiting call forward by Fourteenth Army, to start traffic on such stretches of the Burma Railways as proved possible. At the same time plans for getting in locomotives were made – a matter of some difficulty, as the only methods available were road and air transport. The problem was solved with the aid of our American allies, as will be described later. During this month, too, the Movements and Transportation staff attached to Fourteenth Army became part of the new provisional Movements and Transportation, Burma, organization, while its composition remained much the same.

323. At the end of January I sent a signal to the War Office, H.Q., Supreme Allied Commander, South-East Asia and the Commander-in-Chief, India, giving my views on the future organization of my lines of communication. These proposals were, of course, modified as the situation developed. The basis of my proposals was the progressive establishment of districts, each coming direct under my command, as L. of C. Command would not be able to exercise effective control as the lines of communication extended. Coincident with the formation of the districts would be the handing back of territory to G.H.Q., India. I saw the development in seven main phases. Phase I was the establishment of 505 District for the administration of North Burma, and part of Central Burma. Phase II would consist of the handing back to G.H.Q., India, of the whole of 202 Area, except for some territory round Imphal which would pass to 505 District, and part of 404 Area including Silchar. Geographically this roughly amounted to handing back the Province of Assam with Shillong. Phase III, which was to be simultaneous with Phase II, consisted of the raising of 404 Area to District status. The importance of the Southern L. of C. had greatly increased, as will be seen later, with the development of the Akyab and Kyaukpyu air supply bases. Phase IV would consist of the abolition of L. of C. Command as such and Phase V of the abolition of Advanced Echelons North and South, with consequent saving in staff. Phase VI consisted of the establishment of 606 District in South Burma in due course, and Phase VII of the eventual handing over of 505 and 606 Districts to the H.Q. appointed for Burma when operations there concluded.

324. During January certain changes in organization of the Supply and Transport system took place, whereby a basic allotment of Supply and Transport units to

formations was fixed. By this time we were suffering from a severe manpower shortage in R.A.S.C. and R.I.A.S.C. personnel. I obtained War Office approval, however, for the disbanding of two Anti-Aircraft regiments and so was able to transfer some 400 gunners to the R.A.S.C., converting them to form supply and petrol platoons.

A serious shortage nevertheless still remained, and in February India Command agreed to the dilution of static supply units in rear areas with civilians, thereby releasing soldiers to reinforce forward supply units. This scheme was extended later to include all supply units, and a considerable number of educated Burmese civilians in the liberated areas volunteered, for such employment. In addition, several entirely Burmese small supply units were formed, which proved particularly useful as Local Purchase sections. The men in these units were enrolled in the Burma Army Service Corps.

325. A change took place during February in the system of working the L. of C. Transport Column. This organization has already been referred to on more than one occasion. Some indication of its size is given by the fact that during the previous month (January) it operated some thirty General Transport companies on the 320 mile stretch of road between Dimapur and Kalewa. Up till February, the L. of C. Transport Column had worked on the "Round the Clock" system. In order to provide sufficient drivers for day and night running, it was necessary to reduce the number of load vehicles operated by the companies. This, together with certain other disadvantages, resulted in the tonnage lifted being less than the maximum which could be achieved. The rapid advance of Fourteenth Army, the lengthening of the road L. of C., the increased allotment of vehicles, and the desirability of having a more flexible organization, rendered it necessary to introduce a new system of working.

326. Under this new system, all General Transport companies operated their full scale of vehicles, that is 120 instead of 99 under the "Round the Clock" system, and they were not divorced from their own workshop sections. A Commander, R.A.S.C./R.I.A.S.C. Transport Column was provided at a scale of one for every six companies, thereby relieving the H.Q., L. of C. Transport Column of duties which had hitherto made it top-heavy. Finally, the companies, as far as possible, worked through the daylight hours only, the loading and unloading at depots being done at night. This system proved a success: the average time of "turn-rounds" remained unaffected, but the tonnage lifted increased and vehicle maintenance improved. The "turn-rounds" for the vehicles of the L. of C. Transport Column for the various sections of the road were as follows:-

Manipur Road – Imphal/Palel, two days.
Imphal/Palel – Moreh, two days.
Moreh – Indainggyi, two days.
Indainggyi – Kalewa, one day.
Kalewa – Shwebo, three days.
Shwebo – Monywa, two days.

327. While on the subject of road transport, I would like to add a few remarks on the work of the R.E.M.E. and I.E.M.E. Services. Most of the road from Imphal to Kalewa especially the mountain stretches, was very bad and vehicles, especially the larger 5 and 10 tonners inevitably sustained considerable damage. This was in spite of the careful driving of their Indian drivers, to which General Symes, G.O.C., L. of C. Command, has paid special tribute, as did United States officers who visited this L. of C. Considerable economy in recovery facilities was achieved in January, 1945, by locating a single recovery organization with the H.Q., L. of C. Transport Column, and making it responsible for the whole stretch of road. Other special measures included the equipping of each Recovery Company with twelve extra jeeps, which formed "Spanner Patrols." These "Spanner Patrols," which had by this time become a standard E.M.E. service with Fourteenth Army, had their origin in the earlier advances by 5 Indian and 11 (East African) Divisions. The condition of the roads would not permit the sending out of recovery vehicles as rearwards movement was only possible at certain times. In addition divisional and corps workshops had to be left behind. Fitters in the "Spanner Patrols" went up and down the roads in jeeps, doing what repairs they could, while vehicles needing workshop attention were put into parks for later repair. A lesson that was learnt was that such parks required careful guarding, if the vehicles in them were not to become unserviceable by the theft of vital parts and equipment.

328. Mandalay was captured in March and the implementation of my plans for the reorganization of the L. of C. became necessary. The raising of the new District to take over in rear of Fourteenth Army was comparatively simple and was brought about by the end of the month. The return of 202 Area to India, which was also part of my plan, was a much more complicated business, especially as it involved consideration of the question whether 404 Area should not also be handed over. It was not until May, 1945, after prolonged discussion with G.H.Q., India, at which the Supreme Allied Commander, the A.O.C.-in-C, South-East Asia, and the G.O.C.-in-C, Eastern Command, India, were represented, that it was decided that 202 Area would be transferred to control of India Command, while I retained 404 Area, but raised to District status. I may add here that the actual handover did not take place until the 1st June, 1945, on which date also H.Q. L. of C. Command was disbanded, and 404 Area came under my direct control. The overall administrative organization of Burma was considered at the same time and my proposal to form 606 District for South Burma out of the H.Q. L. of C. Command, which became redundant, was agreed. Thus after the fall of Rangoon, I should have three Districts, 404 controlling Chittagong and Arakan, 505 controlling Northern and Central Burma including Mandalay, and 606 controlling Southern Burma, including eventually Tenasserim.

329. Certain changes in organization had taken place on the Movements and Transportation side of the Northern L. of C. A new L. of C. Movement Control Group, No. 8, which had moved up in February, on the 15th March took over

from the Movements and Transportation staff of L. of C. Command, which was moved to Arakan. This Group came under the direct control of my H.Q., which had also taken over the Movement Control Area (L. of C.), Manipur Road from L. of C. Command at the beginning of the month.

330. The final development of the Northern L. of C. was the rehabilitation of stretches of the Burma Railways. The line from Shwebo to Sagaing was found to have been damaged beyond repair, except as a long-term project.

The line from Myingyan to Meiktila was, however, capable of development. I have already said that it was thanks to our American allies that the locomotives were brought in. How this was done deserves description in greater detail. Six five-ton petrol-driven locomotives were flown in sections to Myingyan and there reassembled. General Stratemeyer provided a Liberator from his own H.Q. for this special task. For use on the line north and south through Meiktila, three giant MacArthur locomotives, each weighing over 70 tons, were loaded on special trailers (converted Macks) and brought in by road to Kalewa, and on to Myingyan, which involved ferrying over both the Chindwin and the Irrawaddy. A senior technical officer of the U.S. Army supervised this often hazardous journey, where these monstrous vehicles at times had to negotiate hairpin bends overlooking deep precipices. Six steam locomotives and tenders, each locomotive weighing some 21 tons, were carried complete on transporters to Kalewa and thence loaded on to ramped cargo lighters and carried down river to Myingyan. In addition, 2,540 tons of heavy railway stores and material were brought in by road, I.W.T. and air.

The above, together with a few recaptured and reconditioned locomotives and rolling stock of the Burma Railways enabled us to reopen rail communication from Mandalay and Myingyan with a very limited though valuable capacity, and to begin the work of railway rehabilitation from Central Burma southwards against the day when we could also work northwards from Rangoon. On the 23rd April, the line from Myingyan to Meiktila was opened with jeep trains giving a lift of 150 tons a day, of which 70 tons a day could be taken forward as far as Pyawbwe.

331. When we captured Mandalay, a complete Japanese Base Workshop was found in the town almost intact. This was a great asset, as it saved bringing forward heavy equipment. It is interesting to note that – contrary to the generally held belief – the Japanese machinery in this Base Workshop included good quality high precision machine tools. The same applied to the mobile workshop that we captured, and their machinery lorries were equal to ours.

332. One further aspect of the Northern L. of C. deserves consideration, namely, petrol distribution. In a country with poor and, owing to the monsoon season, precarious communications, the advantages of distributing petrol by pipeline are especially obvious. It was agreed in December, 1944, that the control of both the six-inch American pipeline from Chittagong to Tinsukia in North-East Assam,

and the British four-inch pipeline to Manipur Road, which ran parallel to it, should be vested in the American Chief Engineer, who controlled all the American pipelines in Bengal and Assam. The allocation of products to British and U.S. consumers was to be made by H.Q. Supreme Allied Command, South-East Asia. About the same time a joint Allied Land Forces, South-East Asia, and India Command Committee decided that in future the grades of petrol should be reduced to three, namely, 100 octane aviation spirit, 80 octane motor transport spirit and petroleum spirit (unleaded). This reduction in the number of grades reduced our storage problems and those in India.

On the 9th February, the hitherto uncompleted section of the British four-inch pipeline between Chittagong and Chandranathpur began pumping, thus giving a continuous flow to Manipur Road. This pipeline was by the 2nd March extended to Imphal, and storage tanks to deal with a flow of three and a half million gallons per month had been constructed there. The opening of this pipeline eased the strain on the road transport a great deal, as hitherto all the petrol for Imphal, including very large Air Force requirements, had had to be brought from Manipur Road by motor transport. Later this pipeline was extended beyond Imphal to Moreh, thus bridging an exceptionally bad sector of hill road from Palel. The supply onward was by road tanker to Kalewa, by I.W.T. from Kalewa to Myingyan and from Myingyan forward by road and rail.

333. Finally, a few more general observations on this exceptional road L. of C. are called for. With a single road of limited capacity, there comes a time when, if its length is extended sufficiently, no matter how much is put in the rear end, practically nothing comes out at the forward end. On the Northern L. of C. we had nearly reached this stage, despite the tremendous effort that had been put into its development and operation. The magnitude of the road transport can be gauged by the following figures. Between November, 1944, and April, 1945, the quantity of stores sent forward, excluding petrol, oil and lubricants, varied between 31,000 and 45,000 tons per month, while petrol, etc., came to between 16,000 and 27,000 tons per month. The personnel lift forward varied from 25,000 to 50,000 men per month.

The L. of C. Transport Column had a daily average of 8,830 tons on wheels in March, and 9,932 tons in April; during the latter month a total lift forward of 91,378½ tons was achieved between Manipur Road and Shwebo.

334. For comparison with these figures, it is interesting to analyse the actual requirements of Fourteenth Army and how they reached it. I have already said that in April Fourteenth Army's average daily requirements were 2,090 tons. These were made up as follows:-

	Tons
Supplies	445
Petrol, oil, lubricants	406
Ammunition	175

Ordnance stores	110
Canteens	20
Engineer requirements	143
Construction and Transportation projects	225
R.A.F. requirements	196
Civil Affairs (Burma)	5
Stocking, maintenance of Sub-areas, Reserve Divisions, etc.	365
	2,090

During April, a daily average of 1,845 tons was delivered by air, while the balance came by road and I.W.T. to Myingyan. This, more than anything else, shows the total inadequacy of the Northern L. of C. Owing to the inability of the Chiefs of Staff to meet our constantly increasing demands for additional transport aircraft, we were compelled to develop this wasteful route to the utmost, despite the gross disproportion between the effort expended and the results which it was possible to achieve. It should dispel any idea that the fullest attempts to send up supplies by ground L. of C. were not made before we made our urgent appeals for more transport aircraft to be sent to the theatre.

SECTION XXI (paras. 335–350)
THE DEVELOPMENT OF THE SOUTHERN
LINE OF COMMUNICATION
Development of Chittagong and the smaller Arakan ports: I.W.T. projects: Development of Akyab and Kyaukpyu: The final stages in Arakan.

335. The development of the Southern L. of C. was on different lines. I have touched on the main characteristics of this L. of. C. in paragraph 305. Initial maintenance was by sea from the main base ports in India to the Advanced Base at Chittagong, and by rail to Chittagong from the Advanced Base at Mymensingh (north-east of Calcutta). As in the case of the Northern L. of C., rail tranship-ments were necessary, at Santahar owing to change of gauge, at the ferry at Tistamukh and into Inland Water Transport at Goalundo and Sirajganj. Distri-bution from the Advanced Bases was by sea to Cox's Bazaar and Maungdaw, by motor transport to Bawli Bazaar, by I.W.T. and animal transport to Taung Bazaar, and by air from various airfields, as will be described in the next section. Shipments were also made direct from India to Cox's Bazaar and Maungdaw, but it must be borne in mind that these were only small river ports, used in normal times for local coastal traffic.

336. Chittagong itself is a port of very limited facilities. Some construction was undertaken, notably a 700 foot timber jetty and a screw pile petrol and oil jetty. The port lighting was greatly improved and the water supply scheme completed in December, 1944. Chittagong and the area round about was important, how-ever, for an additional reason. It will be remembered from Part I of this Despatch

that the original operation Dracula – the large-scale combined airborne and sea-borne invasion of Rangoon – was in November, 1944 postponed by the Chiefs of Staff but not actually cancelled. The area round Chittagong was the mounting base for the airborne part of this operation and I was ordered to proceed on the assumption that the postponed operation would be launched immediately after the 1945 monsoon. This meant that construction had to be virtually complete before the 1945 monsoon, that is by about May, 1945. The planning and con-struction of this mounting base, involving, as it did, fair-weather airfields, petrol pipelines, bulk tankage, camps, hospitals and water supply, required considerable administrative planning and co-ordination by my Headquarters. Not only were nearly all the branches of the Army administrative services affected but also the R.A.F. to a very large extent. Unfortunately the work done on this base was of little or no use for my current operations or their development; on the contrary, it involved a diversion of constructional effort that I could very ill afford to spare.

337. I have mentioned above the employment of the smaller Arakan ports such as Cox's Bazaar and Maungdaw. As might be expected, these came into their maxi-mum use in December when 15 Indian Corps' offensive was launched. Two jetties had been completed at Cox's Bazaar during the previous month and the remain-ing two at this period. During December, imports at Cox's Bazaar, including Ultakhali, amounted to 30,000 tons and at Maungdaw to 20,000 tons. After the capture and development of Akyab and Kyaukpyu in January, the traffic at these ports declined. Maungdaw was closed on the 31st March while Cox's Bazaar continued to operate on a reduced scale; the jetties at Ultakhali were destroyed by fire in April.

338. The early stages of 15 Indian Corps' offensive saw two interesting and important developments in maintenance by I.W.T., which have already been mentioned in Part I. The most spectacular feat was the transportation over the Maungdaw – Buthidaung hill road of the 650 craft required for the maintenance of 53 Brigade (25 Indian Division) in its advance down the Kalapanzin Valley. The most careful calculation and loading were required to enable the vehicles carrying these boats, which were of varied types, to negotiate not only the diffi-cult mountain road but particularly the tunnels which were low, narrow and winding. The reassembling and launching of this fleet, at Buthidaung, was com-pleted in the remarkably short space of five days; but this did not end the dif-ficulties. The intricacies of navigation down the Kalapanzin, which in its lower reaches is really an arm of the sea, remained. The manner in which these navi-gational difficulties were overcome by the Inland Water Transport service and infantry, with the aid of the Royal Navy, deserves the highest praise.

Meanwhile, further east on the Kaladan River, 81 (West African) Division, which was on air supply, had developed flotillas of local craft for the local move-ment of supplies. These they operated themselves.

339. It will be remembered from Part I that the original operation planned for the capture of Akyab was to have been mounted from Chittagong. Owing, however,

to the limited capacity of the port, maintenance had to be arranged direct from depots in India, and despatched from Calcutta. This resulted in loss of flexibility, so that when Akyab was captured by a river-crossing operation on the 3rd January, it was found that the shipping from Calcutta could not be made to arrive before the 20th January; even then it was loaded with stores, etc., planned for the original February assault. The landing on the Myebon Peninsula, which took place only nine days after the capture of Akyab, was mounted and maintained from that port. The export commitment inevitably delayed the stores build-up in the island, and, for a time, our resources there were slender. Energetic action, however, overcame the emergency and the development of Akyab as an Advanced Base began; the build-up and maintenance being effected by sea from India.

The next major operation was the landing at Kyaukpyu on Ramree Island, which was mounted from Chittagong. The reasons for the air supply bases here and on Akyab Island have been dealt with in Part I. The development of the air-fields and the air supply aspect will be dealt with in the next section. The port and Advanced Base development, however, was an essential part of the development of the Southern L. of C. This development began directly Akyab and Kyaukpyu were captured. To achieve the results required as quickly as possible, a Sub-Area was established early in February in each place to develop the advanced base, and over 20,000 construction and administrative troops were allotted to each Sub-Area.

340. Despite the fact that shipments were made direct from India to both Akyab and Kyaukpyu, their intensive development placed a very much heavier load on Chittagong. Imports of stores rose from 23,000 tons in January, 1945, to 60,000 in April, while bulk petrol imports increased from 38,000 tons during November, 1944, to 82,000 in April, 1945. Exports were contingent on forward requirements and were not limited by port capacity. Port working was satisfactory throughout the period. Further development of the Eastern Bengal Railway system was proceeding; important improvements being made to the railhead facilities and to the water supply scheme for railway operation, as well as extension of marshalling yards and loops, and the development of stations and sidings. In mid-March, my Headquarters assumed direct responsibility for the Chittagong area and ports, which had hitherto been under Headquarters L. of C. Command.

341. The only aspect which gave a certain amount of anxiety was in connection with railway traffic. Serious congestion began to arise at Chittagong in mid-February due to unbalanced arrivals by both sea and rail. This condition was made worse later in the month by the arrival of large quantities of Bailey bridging. In March an embargo had to be placed on all traffic *ex* India to Chittagong, until the position could be restored by relating and phasing despatches more closely to the releasing capacities of the depots. This was done during the latter half of March by improving railway working in the Chittagong district, and by the provision of more load-carrying motor transport in the depot area. Unfor-

tunately congestion again occurred early in April, and forwardings, except in the case of priority items, had again to be restricted. A strong contributory factor which led to this state of affairs was the necessity, owing to the break-up of the airfield, for moving 42,000 tons of airfield construction stores from Chittagong to Pathangar, halfway between Chittagong and Comilla, in addition to the large normal supply traffic.

342. An interesting side-light on the Ramree operation deserves mention. It will be remembered that 26 Indian Division was originally earmarked for the assault on Akyab, but that the operation was in fact carried out by 25 Indian Division, which had advanced down the Arakan coast. 71 Brigade of 26 Indian Division was doing Combined Operation training in India at Cocanada with 41 Beach Group. The speed of 15 Indian Corps' campaign necessitated their early return to Burma. Ships fitted out at Calcutta were rushed to Vizagapatam where the Brigade and Beach Group were embarked, and then sailed to Chittagong where they arrived on the 4th January. In spite of bad weather, vehicles were discharged, waterproofed and re-embarked, and the force mounted by the 8th January, when the convoy, sailed on to stage at Akyab. This convoy was followed shortly afterwards by the remaining Ramree assault convoys, which sailed on the 17th, 18th and 19th January.

343. Due to the combined results of our own bombing, the Japanese denial measures and general neglect during the occupation, the port and accommodation facilities at Akyab and Kyaukpyu were found to be almost negligible. At Akyab the main stone jetties and approaches required extensive repairs, and the removal of two ships sunk alongside was necessary. In addition considerable new construction was required. Development began on the 15th January. By the 12th February, seven pontoon jetties had been built, and a fortnight later the stone jetty had been sufficiently repaired to be used for personnel. A new solid timber piled wharf 600 feet long and twelve feet wide was built in a space of six weeks, and by the end of April, not only had a wreck at the main jetty been removed but the jetty itself had been completely repaired, all the stone for which had had to be imported. For all this work, only one Port Construction Company was employed, which carried out its task more efficiently, despite shortages of material. The target set for the development was 1,200 tons daily before the monsoon and 800 tons daily during it. By the beginning of April, the target had been exceeded and on the 3rd April a record discharge of 2,406 tons was achieved. The initial working of the port in the early stages was by 41 Beach Group but the responsibility was handed over early in February to a Port Commandant.

344. At Kyaukpyu there were no existing facilities at all. Development as a beach port began on the 21st February. Despite the fact that only one Port Construction Company was available, and that it had to do most of the sorting of stores besides its proper work, by the end of April five pontoon jetties with Bailey Bridge approaches had been built, a timber pier 130 feet long with a 122 foot

pontoon head had been completed, and a start made on a trestle jetty. As in the case of Akyab, the initial working of the port had been by 41 Beach Group who soon handed over to the Port Commandant. The target port capacity was the same as for Akyab, but with very incomplete facilities. This target was early exceeded, a record discharge of 1,767 tons being achieved on the 17th March.

345. The development of Kyaukpyu port and the Ramree Advanced Base was complicated by the fact that in March it became necessary to switch the main-tenance of 15 Indian Corps' mainland operations to them. As the development of the Base was then in its early stages, the requirements of 15 Indian Corps could not be met in full without prejudicing its completion. Priority was given to the development of the Base, as this was now essential to ensure the readiness of the airfields for the supply of Fourteenth Army as it advanced southwards towards Rangoon, and the 15 Indian Corps Commander's plan for destroying the enemy had to be modified considerably. I have already referred to the necessity for taking 15 Indian Corps off air supply at this tune, since all transport aircraft were required for the maintenance of Fourteenth Army.

346. Bulk petrol tankage projects were planned for both Akyab and Kyaukpyu, with a target completion date of the 1st May. In the case of Akyab, however, this was accelerated to the 15th April; and the first tanker discharged on the 21st, just in time for the intensive air supply effort to support Fourteenth Army in the last critical stage of their advance. Nevertheless, the situation gave cause for anxiety. Squadrons were greatly exceeding the rates of maximum effort, which resulted in abnormal consumption of petrol, oil and lubricants. Although the actual con-sumption was far in excess of estimate, our petrol stocks just held out. Aero engine lubricants were flown in from Chittagong and even from Western Bengal, and the emergency was met.

347. In the meantime the various landing operations on the Arakan coast had taken place. The operations at Kangaw, the success of which will be remembered from Part I, were maintained by Naval landing craft and I.W.T. from the Base Maintenance Area which had been established at Myebon. The operations against Ru-Ywa were mounted and maintained from Myebon and Kangaw. The Tamandu operations were maintained from Akyab, and the Letpan landing by Naval landing craft and I.W.T. from Ramree.

348. The last important event on the Southern L. of C. was the mounting of the modified Dracula operation from Ramree in April. This was done under super-vision of 453 Sub-Area. With the very limited port facilities available, this task caused considerable interference with the build-up of the Advanced Base, but as progress was well advanced by this date, the repercussions were not serious. To start with, the only available facilities at Kyaukpyu were a small beach and a ricketty jetty. I.W.T. creek steamers were used for the embarkation of personnel while "Z" craft and ramped cargo lighters were employed for loading vehicles and stores. The weather fortunately remained calm and the mounting was carried

out in accordance with the programme in spite of a number of last minute changes due to the rapidity with which the whole plan had been prepared.

349. In spite of the meagre facilities available, and the additional strain put on the port by the mounting of Dracula, the discharge of maintenance cargo ships was maintained at a most satisfactory rate. The work done in Kyaukpyu during April was a fine performance, the extent of which can be gauged by the following figures for the transit traffic for the month:-

Personnel	51,320
Vehicles	2,172
Stores	34,090 tons

350. Finally, to put the scale of the developments described above into their proper proportion, I will quote yet a few more figures. It will be remembered that in April the average daily tonnage requirements of Fourteenth Army was 2,090 tons of which an average of 1,845 was delivered by air transport. The requirements of 15 Indian Corps were only 84 tons per day, made up as follows:-

Supplies	16 tons
Petrol, oil and lubricants	16 tons
Ammunition	8 tons
Ordnance	4 tons
Engineers	16 tons
R.A.F.	8 tons
Stocking, etc.	16 tons
	84 tons

Until I was finally compelled to take away all air supply from 15 Indian Corps, 16 tons daily was delivered by air and the rest by sea to Akyab and Kyaukpyu.

From these figures it can clearly be seen that the tremendous development of the Southern L. of C. was almost entirely for Fourteenth Army. The reason for and value of 15 Indian Corps' operations, which made this development possible, and thus their contribution to the reconquest of Burma is clear to see.

SECTION XXII (paras. 351–365)
THE DEVELOPMENT OF THE AIR LINES OF COMMUNICATION
The air supply situation in November, 1944: The organization of F.A.M.Os. and R.A.M.Os.: Opening of Chittagong air base: Formation and organization of C.A.A.T.O.: The switch to Akyab and Ramree Advanced Bases: The air supply situation in April, 1945: Airfield construction: Casualty evacuation: Situation after the capture of Rangoon.

351. The total inadequacy of the overland Northern L. of C., in spite of the enormous effort which was put into its improvement, resulted in the development to an unprecedented extent of the only practicable alternative, supply by air, which became the main channel for the supply and maintenance of the fighting forces in

the field. The results achieved in the final stages of the campaign, during the rapid advance to Rangoon exceeded in scale anything done in any other theatre of operations or indeed in the history of warfare. While recognising that this system of the supply of an army in the field, and the organization required for it, are still in their infancy, and that much has still to be learned, it is clearly of the greatest value to give the closest examination to this, its first really large-scale and continuous practical employment.

352. It will be remembered from Part I that the original plans for Capital – the invasion of Central Burma by Fourteenth Army – were based on using air supply on a very large scale. In November, 1944, when I took over command, the average daily supply lift by air was 247 tons. The way in which this was handled is best shown in tabular form, giving the locations of the air supply bases and the proportion of the lift handled at each base.

Location	Squadrons	Rear Airfield Maintenance Organizations (R.A.M.Os)	Average tons a day	Remarks
Imphal	194 R.A.F. 2 U.S.A.A.F. (C.C.) 3 U.S.A.A.F. (C.C.)	No. 1	31	2 Combat Cargo Sqn. U.S.A.A.F. moved from Sylhet to Imphal on the 21st November, 1944.
Kangla	436 R.C.A.F.	No. 2	–	Arrived November, but did not operate until December.
Tulihal	4 U.S.A.A.F.	No. 6	19	
Agartala	31 R.A.F. 62 R.A.F. (less det.)	No. 3	129	
Comilla	Det. 62 R.A.F.	No. 4	24	
Hathazari	Det. 1 U.S.A.A.F. (C.C.)	No. 5	44	
Total	Seven (plus) Squadrons	Six R.A.M.Os.	247 tons	

From the table it will be seen that three main airfield areas were involved; the Imphal area, which includes Kangla and Tulihal, the Comilla area with Agartala, and the Chittagong area with Hathazari.

353. A word on the R.A.M.Os. is perhaps necessary. These were Rear Airfield Maintenance Organizations which operated on the despatching airfields. With each R.A.M.O. there was one or more Air Despatch Companies. The duties of these units were the packing, loading and, in the case of air-dropped supplies, the ejection of these supplies. I would like to emphasise the necessity for having trained units such as these for dealing with stores when air supply is operated on a large scale. The proper packing, etc., of supplies and stores, always against time, is a job for experts.

Normal supplies for the force dependent, including petrol, supplies and ammunition, were held at each R.A.M.O. Specialised items, engineer stores, ordnance and medical stores had to be held where accessibility to the main depots was best.

This had a limiting effect on complete flexibility, but was the only practicable compromise between splitting stocks and the complete use of air flexibility.

354. The corresponding organization at the receiving airfield was the Forward Airfield Maintenance Organization (F.A.M.O.). In this connection I may remark that air landing was always established as soon as possible, as dropping results in a wastage of about 25% of the lift, and in addition many heavy stores, such as Bailey bridging, cannot be dropped at all. The organization at the forward landing grounds is most important. Speed is always essential first in completion of the forward airstrip itself and then in the quick unloading of aircraft. In the case of the C. 46 and C. 47 aircraft in use in Burma, fifteen minutes was the target unloading time for each aircraft. Considerable endurance and efficiency was required to achieve this target, as many loads were both awkward and heavy. As the commodities were unloaded, they were taken by lorry to the nearby depots, from which bulk issue was made to formations, except in the case of troops in the vicinity, who received their supplies from a Detail Issue Depot. Both F.A.M.Os. and R.A.M.Os. made heavy demands on labour, and Pioneer companies formed a vital part of the whole air supply system.

355. The use of air supply had the subsidiary but very beneficial result that it was possible to send fresh supplies to the forward troops, a valuable contributing factor to the maintenance of health and morale. As much as 50 tons per day of vegetables, fruit and eggs were sent forward in this way. Later, when the cultivated areas of Central Burma were reached, it was possible to make use of local resources and the availability here and in the Shan States was exploited to the full. In the case of Arakan, it was, of course, possible to send fresh supplies up by coaster.

356. I do not intend here to recapitulate the story of the loss of transport aircraft to China and the problems of the lengthening L. of C. It is enough to remember that the available lift was never as much as we wanted and that often it was sufficiently low as to constitute a major administrative crisis. Moreover, we could not plan with certainty on those we had, since the possibility of further withdrawals existed and had to be guarded against. Efforts, therefore, to increase the efficiency of the air supply system were continuous. But I would like to say at the outset that, in spite of these efforts, adequate supplies could not have been brought forward but for the courage and skill of the R.A.F., R.C.A.F. and U.S.A.A.F. squadrons, which often substantially exceeded the approved maximum sustained rates of flying effort, in spite of very hazardous routes over high mountains in often terrible weather.

357. The first major development during the period under report was the switch of an air supply base from Agartala to Chittagong on the 27th January, 1945, when No. 3 R.A.M.O. was moved across and reopened as No. 7. This was the first step in bringing the air bases forward to keep up with the advance of Fourteenth Army. Chittagong airfield had originally been designed for the operation of light

bombers, and considerable engineering effort was required to adapt the installation to take continuous traffic imposing much heavier loads. Nevertheless C. 46 aircraft started to operate on this route on the 2nd February. No. 7 R.A.M.O., incidentally had no Air Despatch Company allotted to it but, using pioneer labour only, achieved the very fine average of over 700 tons per day in April.

358. In February there occurred an expansion of the Army Air Transport Organization, which had existed since October, 1944. The existing system of air supply had clearly been stretched to the utmost, and would not bear the strain of future operations unless expanded. As a result of investigations, I decided to appoint a Commander, Combined Army Air Transport Organization (C.A.A.T.O.), responsible for the co-ordination and executive control of the entire Army aspect of air transport, and under the direct control of my Headquarters. Brigadier J.A. Dawson was appointed to this important command. In more detail, his responsibilities included the command and control of the existing R.A.M.Os. the co-ordination of demands from formations for the transport by air of personnel, supplies and equipment, and for the allocation of these demands to the appropriate R.A.M.Os. His duties also included giving advice and assistance to units who were preparing for air-transported operational rôles and keeping my Headquarters informed of the air transport and supply situation.

359. To ensure that this new organization worked smoothly, I established it alongside Headquarters, Combat Cargo Task Force (Brigadier-General F.W. Evans), which was the Allied Air Forces' organization in charge of all the transport aircraft in the theatre. Subsequent events showed that this arrangement was on the right lines and that C.A.A.T.O. had played a vital part in the operational successes achieved by Fourteenth Army, 15 Indian Corps and Northern Combat Area Command. The closest co-operation and liaison with the Air Force is essential at all levels for the efficient working of an air transport and supply system and in this I was particularly fortunate in having General G. Stratemeyer, Commanding General, Eastern Air Command, to work with. The harmonious relations established between us, and the close and friendly working of our respective staffs, did much to dissolve the difficulties which, on occasion, are bound to arise when one Service is largely dependent on another for all the essentials of its existence under adverse conditions of climate and terrain.

The Organization was thus as follows: —

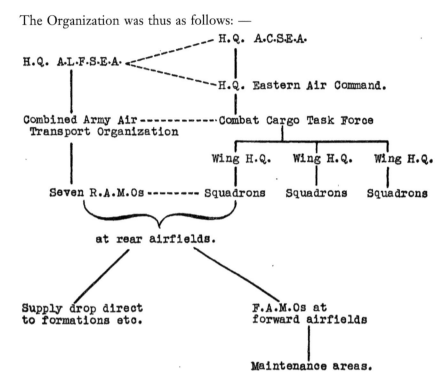

360. One thing is vital for an organization such as C.A.A.T.O., and that is first-class communications. Not only must the aircraft deliver the correct loads at the right places, but the system must be sufficiently flexible to allow of demands being changed at very short notice – for instance, ammunition may suddenly be required instead of petrol where unexpected opposition is met. It must be possible for demands from forward formations to be sent back at top speed so as to allow the proper sorting of these demands by C.A.A.T.O.'s staff and for the correct instructions to be sent out to the R.A.M.Os. Information must also be sent back to allow the correct briefing of pilots so that supplies are landed at the right airfield or dropped over the right dropping zone. The situation forward is a constantly changing one, and in the case of supply-dropping where units are in the jungle away from roads and tracks, the use of a central dropping zone is impracticable and deliveries have to be made to each brigade or unit.

It was in this matter of communications that C.A.A.T.O. was insufficiently well provided, and such mistakes as occurred were in the main attributable to this cause. Unfortunately Signals personnel and equipment were among the most serious shortages in the theatre and so it was not possible to bring C.A.A.T.O.'s communications up to the standard required.

361. As Fourteenth Army's advance progressed and the capture of Rangoon became likely, so the necessity for increasing the air supply lift and getting the air

supply bases forward became more pressing. The Imphal group of airfields was particularly uneconomical as not only were they the most distant, with a bad mountain crossing *en route*, but all stores sent from them were a charge on road transport from Manipur Road forward. This situation had been improved by the opening of the petrol pipeline on the 2nd March (see paragraph 332), but by this time the airfields were already too far behind to allow operation at economic ranges.

The original plans for Akyab and Ramree Advanced Bases were that all-weather airfields would be completed at Akyab by the 30th April for three transport squadrons, and at Kyaukpyu for the same number by the 15th May. These dates were, however, not nearly early enough to support Fourteenth Army's rapid advance and it became necessary to develop fair-weather airfields and to put them into operation simultaneously with the construction of the all-weather ones. Two squadrons of C.47 aircraft began supply operations from Akyab on the 20th March, with No. 1 R.A.M.O. which had been switched from Imphal, and a further two squadrons by the end of the month. Half a squadron operated from Kyaukpyu during April for the supply of troops in Arakan only. The all-weather airfields were in fact completed in both places in early May, when each base operated three squadrons of C.47 transport aircraft.

362. The extent of all this development and the effect of the increased number of aircraft we eventually received are shown in the tonnage figures. The table given in paragraph 352 showed a total average daily tonnage of 247. This average rose each month until in March, 1945, the figure of 1903 tons daily was reached. In April this daily average was slightly lower, being 1,845 tons. For comparison with the table for November, 1944, here is the distribution for April, 1945:-

Location	Squadrons	R.A.M.O.	Average tons/day	Remarks
Tulihal	435 R.C.A.F.	No. 6	247	
Comilla	238 R.A.F.	No. 3	21	R.A.M.O. opened 23rd April
	13, 14, 15 and 16			
Chittagong	U.S.A.A.F. (C.C.)	No. 7	733	
	2 U.S.A.A.F. (C.C.)			
Dohazari	4 U.S.A.A.F. (C.C.)	No. 4	171	
	3 U.S.A.A.F. (C.C.)			31 and 117 Sqns. Moved to
Hathazari	31 and 117 R.A.F.	No. 5	236	Ramree on 16th April.
	62, 194, and 267 R.A.F.			436 R.C.A.F. moved to
Akyab	436 R.C.A.F.	No. 1	393	Ramree on 16th April.
				R.A.M.O. opened 16th April
Ramree	436 R.C.A.F.	No. 2	44	(from Kangla).
		Seven		
Total	Fifteen Squadrons	R.A.M.Os.	1845 tons	

When considering these figures, however, it must not be imagined that the actual tonnage remained constant at about the average figure. On the contrary, on occasions very high peak performances were made when conditions were right, aircraft flying as many as five sorties. It was the need to handle these peaks, which had to compensate for other days when flying was bad, that really tested the supply organization and its capacity.

363. The development of air supply as outlined above made heavy demands on airfield engineer construction effort, both for the supply bases and for the forward landing grounds. That forward airfield construction more than kept pace with requirements is shown by the fact that the percentage of supplies dropped – as opposed to landed – decreased from 28% in November, 1944 to 14.6% in March 1945. Rear airfields for supply purposes required extensive development if high peak tonnage figures were to be achieved. It was found that the ideal to aim at was two strips each 2,300 yards long, complete with loading bays. Over a hundred aircraft on the ground may have to be catered for, flying up to five sorties daily. Airfield construction for transport as well as for tactical purposes will be dealt with in more detail later in this part of the Despatch.

364. Casualty evacuation was linked with the organization of air supply. The medical aspect will be dealt with later when the services under the control of the Adjutant-General's branch are considered. Here it is enough to note that casualties were evacuated from formations by light aircraft (L.5), piloted by U.S.A.A.F. and R.A.F. personnel, back to the forward airfields where there were Casualty Clearing Stations with the F.A.M.Os. – usually a distance of 30–50 miles. Such cases as required further evacuation were then carried by C. 47 transport aircraft to forward base hospitals which in turn were situated near the R.A.M.Os. The extent to which air evacuation was used is shown by the fact that in March 1945, 13,000 casualties were transported by air. In some sectors evacuation by road or air was for periods impossible, and the medical centres had to be entirely supplied by air dropping.

365. With the capture of Rangoon, the need for air supply by no means ceased. Our forces were scattered down the whole length of Burma and internal communications were still only fragmentary. Moreover the port itself had to be repaired and stocked, installations brought round from the other Ls. of C., and the land Ls. of C. northwards from Rangoon rehabilitated and developed. Although the period after the capture of Rangoon falls outside this Despatch, it should be noted that the supply of the forces in Central Burma in monsoon conditions presented considerable difficulties, and deliveries fell short of the tonnage required. Nevertheless, the capture of Rangoon was the beginning of the end of a system of supply which was nothing short of amazing, consisting as it did of a fantastic single overland route, costing immense resources in men and materials and paying very small dividends, while by far the greater part of the Army's requirements were brought in by air supply developed as never before.

Thus the plans for the quickest possible development of Rangoon Port were of prime importance. Some indication of how this problem was tackled is given in the next section.

SECTION XXIII (paras. 366–371)
PLANS FOR DEVELOPING RANGOON

Assembly of Force Commanders: The splitting of the reconnaissance party: The alternative convoy plan.

---

366. Experience in Africa and Europe had shown repeatedly the importance of really good planning and organization where the reopening of a captured port was concerned. In the case of Rangoon we were more than ever working against time, since the monsoon was almost on us and it was essential to relieve the air transport system of the heavy load it was carrying, as this load was being carried partly at the expense of aircraft serviceability.

367. The project for the reopening of Rangoon and the development of the Advanced Base was known as operation "Stanza." An administrative appreciation was prepared at my Headquarters and in March it was handed over to the Commander, No. 1 Area, South-East Asia Command, who had been designated for the Rangoon Advanced Base Area. The Advanced Base Commanders of all three Services together with essential staff had been assembled in Calcutta. It was agreed that planning should be co-ordinated by the Army, in the person of the Commander, No. 1 Area, as Rangoon was from the administrative angle predominantly the Army's concern.

368. When it was decided that a seaborne expedition would be put in to assist Fourteenth Army in their advance to Rangoon new complications arose. In all plans for the development of a port and advanced base it is essential that the reconnaissance party gets in immediately after the place is captured. But in this particular instance it was going to be impossible until a few days before the event to forecast whether Fourteenth Army or 15 Indian Corps would enter Rangoon first. There was a strong possibility that either formation might be held up short of the city itself while the other got in from the opposite direction, and that the occupation of the city by one would not necessarily open the way at once for the other. If the reconnaissance party was committed with what turned out to be the wrong formation, it might not be able to function during the first few vital days following the fall of the city, which would inevitably result in dislocation of the rehabilitation plans.

369. It was therefore decided to split the reconnaissance party into three groups. First there was the Road Party. This was the main reconnaissance party and consisted of such staff and administrative services as would be needed to carry out the detailed reconnaissance for depots, etc. Its task was to organize the opening of the port as soon as the first ships arrived. This party left Calcutta early in April and, travelling by road *via* Manipur Road and Imphal, succeeded in catching up 4 Corps in time to enter Rangoon with them from the north, after the link-up with 15 Indian Corps had been effected.

370. The second group of the reconnaissance party was the Sea Party. This was envisaged as the substitute for the Road Party, and its composition was sufficiently strong to enable it by itself, to carry out the same tasks. It was held in readiness to go in with one of 15 Indian Corps' convoys as soon as it was clear that the fall of the city was imminent. Finally, there was the Air Party, consisting of the three Service Advanced Base Commanders each with his senior staff officer. This party remained behind to complete the final details, and then was flown in as soon as the Rangoon airfield (Mingaladon) was clear.

371. The second main problem which arose was how advantage could be taken of an early fall of the city. If 15 Indian Corps met heavy opposition – and it had to be assumed that it would – build-up convoys, including the follow-up division would be required. If the city fell quickly or if it fell to Fourteenth Army, the most urgent requirements were all the units and stores for the quick development of the Advanced Base. It was therefore essential to have a Stanza (Advanced Base Development) convoy, containing the necessary transportation and engineer stores, together with the units, for the immediate reopening of Rangoon Port, ready to replace one of the later Dracula operational convoys, should it be found possible to reduce or defer the Dracula build-up. This naturally involved considerable manipulation of the shipping and stores concentration programmes; but this Stanza convoy was successfully prepared, and did in the event go in on D plus 21 in place of one of the later Dracula convoys.

SECTION XXIV (paras. 372–393)

AIRFIELD CONSTRUCTION

The organization of Air Forces: The airfield engineer organization: Work on Base airfields, airfields for air supply and the China lift: Forward airfield construction: Fourteenth Army's advance: Airfields in Arakan: The development of Akyab and Kyaukpyu.

---

372. The airfield construction work carried out under the control of my Headquarters was so extensive and varied that it deserves treatment in a section to itself. This operational commitment of the Army has proved to be a major factor, both strategic and administrative, in any theatre of war. In such an undeveloped theatre as South-East Asia, where air transport was used on an unprecedented scale the commitment was correspondingly even greater.

373. The presence in the theatre of both British, including Dominion, and United States Air Forces with widely varying functions resulted in a highly complicated organization. Until the end of November, 1944, Fourteenth Army was supported by 3 Tactical Air Force, and the Headquarters of both formations were at Comilla. When 15 Indian Corps was separated from Fourteenth Army and came under my direct command, the R.A.F. Groups with these formations (221 Group with Fourteenth Army, 224 Group with 15 Indian Corps), became in effect separate tactical air forces. At the same time 3 Tactical Air Force ceased to

exist as such, its operational echelon being merged into Headquarters, Eastern Air Command (which, as I have mentioned before, was an integrated operational Headquarters formed from Headquarters, U.S.A.A.F., India/Burma Theatre and elements from Air Command, South-East Asia) and its administrative echelon became Headquarters, R.A.F., Bengal /Burma.

374. The Strategic Air Force, with its Headquarters in Calcutta, operated the strategic bomber squadrons, some of which were based on airfields in the Allied Land Forces, South-East Asia area, for whose construction and maintenance my engineers were responsible. The air supply part of air operations was controlled by the Combat Cargo Task Force which was formed shortly after my arrival. The air transport service to China was operated by the U.S. Air Transport Command, but a considerable proportion of my Allied Land Forces, South-East Asia engineer resources was devoted to the construction of airfields and associated installations in North-East Assam. The ground operations of Northern Combat Area Command were supported by 10 U.S.A.A.F., and the airfield engineer works in this area were largely constructed by American engineer aviation battalions, although the Divisional engineers of 36 British Division provided their own light aircraft strips.

375. To meet the air forces organization described above, my Chief Engineer (Major-General K. Ray, seconded from the U.D.F.), working under the Engineer-in-Chief, South-East Asia Command, through the Deputy Engineer-in-Chief (Air), exercised technical control over the Deputy Chief Engineer, Fourteenth Army, and formed the link on airfield matters with Headquarters, Eastern Air Command and Combat Cargo Task Force. When I moved my Advanced Headquarters from Delhi to Barrackpore, the Deputy Engineer-in-Chief (Air) also moved there from Comilla, and the air elements of the Allied Land Forces, South-East Asia engineer staff came under his control. He worked with Headquarters, R.A.F. Bengal/Burma, which as I have stated above was the administrative echelon of the R.A.F. Headquarters. When the development of Akyab and Ramree airfields was undertaken, special engineer forces were formed for airfield development under the direct control of my Headquarters.

376. In describing the engineer work carried out I have divided work into various categories. First, the Base airfields for both strategic and tactical squadrons, next the transport airfields (excluding those for the China supply lift), then those built for the China lift, then some miscellaneous airfield work in the rear areas, and lastly and in greater detail, the forward airfield construction, including the development of the Advanced Bases at Akyab and Ramree.

377. Of the Base airfields, the bulk of those which were intended for the Strategical Air Force were sited in India, but thirteen bomber airfields had been constructed by the Chief Engineer, Fourteenth Army. Three of these were later transferred to the Engineer-in-Chief, India Command, and of the remaining ten, five were used by medium and light bombers during the period covered by this

Despatch, and the other five were converted for use by transport aircraft and fighters. During the early stages of Fourteenth Army and 15 Indian Corps' offensive, base airfields were used by tactical squadrons, fighters operating from Imphal and Palel, and also from the bomber fields at Kumbirgram, Chittagong, Chiringa, Cox's Bazaar and Comilla, which were adapted to meet fighter requirements.

378. Initially, the air supply lift for Fourteenth Army was flown from bomber airfields which had been converted for this purpose. The airfields used were Sylhet, Comilla, Fenny and Chittagong, and supplies were carried to the airfields in the Imphal Plain. The increase in the tonnage carried has already been described. All this had to be met by more maintenance, development and construction by the airfields engineers. The building of the advanced air bases will be described under forward airfield development. I will only add here that during the year ending the 31st March, 1945, 550,000 tons of supplies and stores had been carried by air to forward areas from airfields constructed by Allied Land Forces, South-East Asia engineers.

379. The American air lift to China reached gigantic proportions considering the difficulty of the route, and it has received world-wide publicity. What is not so generally realised and certainly received less publicity, is that the airfields in North-East Assam to support this traffic, were built almost entirely by British agency, first under the Chief Engineer, 11 Army Group, until November, 1944, and thereafter by the Chief Engineer, L. of C. Command. One United States engineer battalion assisted in the later stages. Owing to the diversity of the works, it is not practicable to give full details of the construction undertaken during the period covered by this Despatch, but the following table shows the situation at about the time I took over command in November, 1944, giving the work completed and the amount in hand as regards the eleven all-weather airfields in North-East Assam:

Description	*Completed*	*Under Construction*
Runways	13 miles	—
Taxi tracks	25 miles	7 miles
Aircraft standings	486	20
Aircraft parking aprons	37 acres	23 acres
Roads	80 miles	23 miles
Accommodation	33,106 men	—
Covered Storage	63 acres	4¼ acres

The effect of these works on the air supply lift to China is indicated by the fact that the lift was trebled between June, 1944, and March, 1945, as shown by the following figures.

	June 1944	*March* 1945
No. of completed sorties per month	3,702	11,347
Tons lifted to China	14,150	41,580

380. A considerable amount of other rear airfield work was undertaken in the L. of C. Command area, in addition to what has been mentioned in the preceding paragraphs. For example, twenty-one fair-weather satellite airfields had to be maintained. These had been out of action during the monsoon and subsequent drainage and repair work was heavy. There were local labour difficulties in Arakan where the small isolated Japanese air raids of the Autumn of 1944 had caused casualties. These raids had repercussions over a wide area and there was a marked reluctance by civil labour to work on airfields. Although I have not covered the whole field of rear airfield construction work, I hope I have said enough to show that it represented a very considerable engineer effort, requiring organization and a high peak rate of output.

381. In dealing with forward airfield construction, it is, I think, best to take the advance of Fourteenth Army first. The first group of four forward airfields, apart from the reconditioning of the strip at Tamu, were constructed near Kalemyo. These strips were all developed to operate transport aircraft as well as fighters; and were constructed by a Forward Airfield Engineer Group. The other axis of Fourteenth Army's advance, that of 19 Indian Division *via* Pinlebo and Wuntho, was at first covered by fighters operating at extreme range from the Imphal airfield group. Later, three Japanese airstrips in the Indaw oilfields area were developed. These, when captured, were found to be short and built to a very poor specification. Much work was required to render them adequate for the operations of our own aircraft.

382. For the main advance into Central Burma and southwards, the Shwebo group of airfields became of paramount importance. These were captured at the end of December, 1944. The group consisted of five Japanese airstrips which all gave considerable trouble in development. Owing to the enemy's denial measures, it was found quicker to develop the taxi-tracks as strips than to repair the runways. The volume of air traffic and the friable nature of the soil in this area made the dust problem acute, which shortage of water made is difficult to remedy. With the capture of Monywa in January a further group of four enemy airfields was developed. Little work was required as denial measures had been slight. A noticeable feature of these as of other Japanese airfields was the elaborate nature of the dispersal areas – a tribute to our air attacks. Another group lay near Myingyan, important because it was the southern terminal of the I.W.T. link from Kalewa. Here five airfields were developed, two of which were Japanese. The latter had been denied in the most effective way yet met by our engineers, nine inches of hand-packed stone having been spread over the surface.

383. In February 1945, four airfields were constructed to support 33 Corps' crossings of the Irrawaddy. These were sited at Sadaung, Ondaw (two) and Allagappa. The work was not only extensive and technically difficult owing to the soil, but much of it had to proceed under observed artillery fire. Meanwhile, 4 Corps was advancing down the Gangaw Valley towards Pakokku. The airfields

here were essential to the advance since the road could not carry the traffic required by a Corps of two divisions and a tank brigade. By analogy with the rail-head, from which the road traffic proceeds forward, airheads were constructed. One was constructed about halfway down the Gangaw Valley at Kan, with a subsidiary airfield at the top of the valley at Tilin, while another was made near the Irrawaddy at Sinthe. These airheads each consisted of two 2,000 yard airstrips and a 700 yard casualty evacuation strip, complete with unloading bays, taxi tracks, etc. The Tilin airfield had one 1,500 yard strip and a 700 yard casualty strip. These airfields held the fighters to cover the Irrawaddy crossing and in addition some 200 transport aircraft landed daily with supplies and stores. They were constructed in record time by the forward airfield engineers, assisted by Corps and Divisional engineers and infantry working parties. Sinthe is of partic-ular interest for two reasons. It was made operational in five days, and completed in ten, by a Forward Airfield Engineer Group whose motor transport had only had one day for maintenance while covering 2,300 miles from Cocanada on the Madras coast of India. The other is that to alleviate the bad dust conditions, a six mile ditch had to be bulldozed from the nearest sources to bring water to a channel between the airstrips, whence it could be pumped onto them.

384. Directly our forces had broken out of the bridgeheads, a group of six air-fields were constructed south of the river, while to the north, 19 Indian Division was supported from the reconditioned Japanese airfields at Singu and later at Mandalay. The siting of these airfields had to be in accordance with the tactical situation, which often increased the engineering difficulties. Most of them were built under fire. One of them, at Tada-U, had to be operational for C.46 aircraft in 48 hours, and the job was completed within this incredibly short space of time.

385. The capture of Meiktila gave us a group of five important Japanese airfields. Moreover, owing to the speed of our advance, the enemy's denial measures were comparatively ineffective. One airfield was in five hours made ready, under fire, to receive transport aircraft bringing reinforcements. By the irony of fate it was not the Japanese denial measures which caused us trouble, but the Japanese efforts to maintain the airfields in action. Bomb craters caused by our attacks had been so inexpertly filled in that when heavy rain fell, water penetrated to the subgrade to such an extent that some fields had to be abandoned.

386. For the final advance to Rangoon there were three well defined groups of airfields, sited respectively in the Pyinmana, Toungoo and Nyaunglebin areas. All consisted of light Japanese airfields damaged to varying degrees. In addition to rendering these operational, other fair-weather strips had to be constructed. The advance was so rapid that at times it outstripped the physical movement of the forward airfield engineers. An additional complication arose in that we were now in the season when heavy pre-monsoon storms had to be expected, and in fact some exceptionally heavy storms occurred. A special organization had to be adopted to meet these particular circumstances. An advanced reconnaissance

party of airfield engineers accompanied the armoured spearhead; the C.R.E. (Commander, Royal Engineers) followed as closely as possible with a forward echelon of two field companies and a mechanical equipment platoon; while with the following brigades came the rear echelon consisting of an engineer battalion and a Corps mechanical equipment platoon. Forward airfield engineers had to carry seven days' rations and petrol, owing to rapid changes between formations and the fact that they were usually ahead of the regular supply points. Army control was maintained by continuous visits by air, but was extremely difficult to keep up to date.

387. The great distances covered, and the leap-frogging of formations on a single-way road, with close convoy timings, imposed a great strain on the forward airfield engineers. On one occasion the convoy timings were so tight that the last grader took its final run over the last apron, and drove direct to the starting point with only a few minutes to spare. Loss of this timing would have delayed the group for twelve hours. Under these conditions, the opening of nine airstrips over a distance of 200 miles in eleven days must be accounted a magnificent achievement.

388. The forward airfield construction described in the preceding paragraphs amounts to nearly 60 airstrips built or reconditioned, apart from light aircraft strips, but it only takes into account the principal airfields. As I said in the description of Base airfield work, many more airfields were used at various times than those actually specified here.

389. Turning now to 15 Indian Corps, it will be remembered that support was provided by 224 Group, R.A.F., whose five tactical wings operated from the all-weather airfields from Cox's Bazaar northwards, and in the dry season from fourteen fair-weather strips to the south. After the 1944 monsoon the first task was to resuscitate these strips, which had been out of action during the rains, as soon as possible. Six of them had also to be lengthened by 600 yards (to 2,300 yards) to take P.47 fighters, and all the accommodation associated with the airfields required heavy repairs. The first of these fair-weather airstrips was ready on the 10th November and the last on Christmas Day, 1944.

390. Directly Akyab Island was occupied, work began on expanding the existing all-weather airfield so that it could accommodate three transport and three and a half tactical squadrons, with a target completion date of the15th May. At the same time, to meet the immediate and pressing needs of Fourteenth Army, a fair-weather transport field for two squadrons was constructed and opened on the 17th February. Two tactical strips were also made. Fourteenth Army's rapid progress, however, made further demands on the airfield development of Akyab. A second fair-weather transport strip was called for, and an advance on the completion date for the all-weather airfield, and finally an increase in the operational capacity of the latter was required. Despite many difficulties this programme of work was completed ahead of schedule. The works on Akyab Island were begun

by the Chief Engineer, 15 Indian Corps, but early in February, the responsibility was taken over by the commander of an Army Group Royal Engineers, working directly under my Chief Engineer.

391. After the capture of Kyaukpyu, on Ramree Island, the existing Japanese fair-weather airstrip was repaired by Divisional engineers, despite heavy denial measures by the enemy. Work was begun immediately on the advanced Air Supply Base, at Akyab, which included the construction of an all-weather airfield for three transport and three and a half tactical squadrons. These works were controlled by a Deputy Chief Engineer working directly under my Headquarters.

392. Apart from the transport airfields on Akyab and Ramree mentioned above, 15 Indian Corps engineers constructed nine fair-weather fields for the air supply of 81 and 82 (West African) Divisions in the Kaladan, and 25 Indian Divisional Engineers constructed one transport strip at Myebon. In addition 42 light aircraft strips were made during the Arakan operations.

393. This section does not pretend to be comprehensive. No mention has been made of the more technical problems, or the provision and transport of the many stores and materials which airfield work required, nor of the methods used to overcome natural and enemy-created difficulties. The principal airfields have been mentioned, and in the above account eighty-six strips, apart from light air-craft strips, have received notice, but there were others. This will give a fair indication of the extent of the task performed.

SECTION XXV (paras. 394–419)
ADJUTANT-GENERAL STAFF AND SERVICES MATTERS

Reinforcements: Organization matters: Leave, repatriation and release: Morale: Recovery of Allied prisoners of war: "Indian National Army": The work of the Medical Services: The work of the other services controlled by the Adjutant-General's Department of the Staff.

---

394. Before dealing with the services under the control of the Adjutant-General's staff, I will deal with the direct responsibilities of that staff itself; that is, provision of reinforcements, raising of units, leave, repatriation, release, morale, recovery of Allied prisoners of war and matters in connection with the Japanese sponsored "Indian National Army."

395. There were twelve Reinforcement Camps in the Allied Land Forces, South-East Asia area; six at Comilla, four at Gauhati, one at Chittagong and one, for 36 British Division while they were operating with Northern Combat Area Command, at Dibrugarh. Up till the end of November, 1944, the flow of rein-forcements through these camps was satisfactory, except in the case of British infantry. From December onwards, however, as the land L. of C. lengthened, the main reinforcement problem became one of movement rather than of provision, since the air L. of C. became the only practical means of transport. In December,

for example, although 10,618 reinforcements were received from India, the onward flow was limited to about 150 men per day, the total flown forward during the month being 4,641. This was solely due to shortage of aircraft and to the fact that other forms of transport were required for other purposes, including the lifting forward of men other than reinforcements. The numbers flown forward, however, steadily improved from February, 1945, onwards; in April, for example, 10,066 reinforcements were flown in to Fourteenth Army during the month, including 5,473 to 4 Corps in eight days to replace losses in the Meiktila fighting. But the intake of reinforcements from India Command, together with the men discharged fit from hospitals and returning leave details, continued to exceed the numbers which could be flown into Burma. In April, therefore, arrangements had to be made with India Command to restrict the flow of reinforcements until the congestion in Comilla could be reduced.

396. An innovation occurred in February, when I accepted into Allied Land Forces, South-East Asia 3,000 British infantry reinforcements direct from the ship for two months' training at the reinforcement camps at Comilla. This was done at the request of India Command, who were unable to cope with the sudden increase in reinforcements who had only received unit training in the United Kingdom. The majority of these men had been transferred from the Royal Navy, Royal Marines, and the Royal Air Force, and excellent material they proved.

397. Battle casualties caused a sharp increase in the demands for both British and Indian infantry reinforcements in March, particularly officers. India Command responded promptly, sending forward large drafts, some of which were drawn from British battalions employed in internal security and frontier defence rôles. These were augmented at the end of the month by a special draft of some thirty majors and captains who were flown to Allied Land Forces, South-East Asia from battalions in India at my urgent request.

398. I have already mentioned in various places in this Despatch the major changes in organization which took place and I do not propose to go into more detail except in regard to the formation of areas, etc., in L. of C. Command. The following figures, however, are of interest as indicating the amount that was done in this direction. Between the 12th November, 1944 and the 3rd May, 1945, the total number of units of all types raised was 753, reorganized 627, and disbanded 407. As regards L. of C. Command, its organization continued to expand as the liberation of Burma progressed. The Headquarters had been raised in November. In January and February, five additional L. of C. Sub-Areas were established in Burma. No. 505 District for North Burma and No. 1 Area, South-East Asia Command, for Rangoon, were raised in March. The H.Q. for 505 District moved into Shwebo early in April, while the move of No. 1 Area into Rangoon has already been described in Section XXIII of the Despatch. In April No. 2 Area, South-East Asia Command and No. 555 Sub-Area were raised in anticipation of the requirements of future operations.

399. Several new leave schemes were introduced during the period under report, in addition to the normal leave system already in force in the theatre. In November 1944, a scheme was started under which British Service personnel could be granted 28 days' leave in the United Kingdom, and, in the following month, this was extended to include British personnel of the Indian Army. In December, too, a scheme providing for 61 days' leave in the United Kingdom, in lieu of reversion to the Home Establishment on long service grounds, was introduced, eligibility being the same as for repatriation. In February, leave travel by air to the United Kingdom was started in cases where operational requirements demanded the quick return of the men concerned. This air travel was extended in March to apply to all leave schemes.

400. A scheme for the repatriation of Southern Rhodesian troops was approved in February, and in April a similar scheme came into force, whereby all East and West African other ranks with between two and a half and three years overseas service could either be repatriated or granted home leave.

401. In April a warning order was issued to formations that release would start any time after the 1st May. This order gave the phasing of Groups 1 to 11.

402. The outstanding factor affecting morale generally was that both British and Indian troops now felt a complete sense of mastery over the Japanese. It was this confidence, born of success in battle, that carried them on so triumphantly. Various other factors had their effects, differing with the nationality of the troops concerned.

403. In the case of British troops, the increased publicity given to the theatre was welcomed, but certain announcements by politicians and in the Press, were received with misgivings. The 28 days' home leave scheme, mentioned above, came in for considerable criticism, which was not in fact justified. The operational and transportation (shipping and aircraft) situations were such that unfortunately only a small proportion of those entitled could avail themselves of the scheme. Moreover, men due for repatriation, who had completed more than three years' overseas service, felt that they had a prior claim on the accommodation absorbed by the leave personnel who had a good deal less overseas service. The Earl of Munster's report was favourably received. The reduction in and final abolition of postal charges on letters was appreciated. The Government's post-war gratuity proposals had an unfavourable reception. The supply and quality of cigarettes was bad.

404. Although the morale of Indian troops was maintained at a very high level, the inefficiencies of the Indian postal system, the non-receipt of family allowances by relatives, and various examples of victimisation and petty extortion by village officials continued to worry the Indian soldier.

405. West African morale was good and the troops gave a good account of themselves in action. Repatriation and home leave became the main topic of interest of

the West African troops, but a clear statement of policy on the subject was still awaited when I relinquished command. The increase in expatriation allowance, and the extension of the free postal concession to West Africans, were appreciated.

406. The morale of the East African troops was good and the introduction of the home leave scheme was welcomed. Relations with Europeans, which had deteriorated somewhat in the middle of the period under report, improved again later.

407. During April, 1945, it was learnt that there were about 350 Allied prisoners of war in Rangoon gaol. Plans were immediately made for their evacuation in anticipation of the early capture of Rangoon. Actually the first prisoners to be released were a party of 350 British, Indians and Americans whom the Japanese were trying to march out of Burma (see Para. 255). This party was discovered near Pegu on the 30th April, having been hastily abandoned by the enemy on the approach of one of our armoured columns. From them it was learnt that there were some 600–700 prisoners, not fit to move, still in Rangoon gaol. These were liberated when we re-entered Rangoon on the 3rd May. The general condition of these prisoners of war was somewhat better than was expected, there being only some 50 stretcher cases. Their morale was high, despite the fact that they had been ill-treated and underfed for three years. All Allied prisoners of war were immediately evacuated by returning transport aircraft to Allied Land Forces, South-East Asia Advanced Base Hospitals at Comilla. After a week's recuperation, they were transferred to Base Hospitals in India.

408. As the Japanese retreat from Burma progressed, they left the "Indian National Army" behind, totalling about 16,000 strong. These formations surrendered as we approached, incidentally providing a useful labour force. The units of the I.N.A. were made up of Indians locally enlisted in Malaya and of prisoners of war captured by the Japanese. The prisoners of war joined the I.N.A. for various reasons. Some joined under duress, in the hope of escaping to India; some joined it honestly believing that by doing so they would be fighting for the freedom of India; some because they felt that the creation and presence of an Indian Army under Indian officers might prevent Japanese atrocities and cruelties when they entered India; others joined solely as followers of Subhas Chandra Bose, and still others joined in order to avoid the hardships of a prisoner of war's life. But all members of the organization were treated by us as prisoners of war until they had been interrogated in India and classified as "Black" or "White." This caused a serious administrative problem. Initially the rate at which we could evacuate them was limited by India's ability to receive them; later it was restricted by shortage of transport aircraft and shipping. Large numbers, therefore, had to be held forward, and we had to accept the burden of feeding and guarding them. There was a very strong feeling against these men among the members of the Indian Army and special precautions had to be taken to prevent clashes.

409. Turning to the services administered by the Adjutant-General's branch of the staff, it is impossible in this campaign to over emphasise the importance of the work of the medical services. As I have said elsewhere, without the modern developments of medical science, the campaign could not have been fought at all. The degree of success attained is shown in the figures that I will quote. From November, 1944, to April, 1945, both months inclusive, the number of casualties from sickness totalled 69,713, while battle casualties amounted to 17,693. Thus, during the period under report, the ratio of medical to battle casualties was 3.93 to one. Even during the periods of hardest fighting in February and March, the ratio only fell to 2.4 and 1.8 to one respectively. Nevertheless the sick rate during this same period was surprisingly low. In early March, for example, it was only 0.96 per 1,000 per day; in late April it was 1.42 per 1,000 per day, that is, about one-third of the rate in October, 1944.

Such low figures among troops fighting and working in an unhealthy tropical climate, in areas where malaria, dysentery, scrub typhus, small-pox and cholera are endemic, are in themselves a tribute to the medical services. They can be attributed in part to the more extensive use of comparatively new drugs, e.g., mepacrine and sulphaguanidine, and to that invaluable insecticide, D.D.T. But I would like to lay stress on the important part played by good discipline, particularly in regard to anti-malaria measures and hygiene. Without this discipline, modern medical science and the efforts of the officers of the medical services are largely ineffective.

410. The difficulties of surface communications in the theatre resulted in two particular lines of development, namely, the evacuation of casualties by air, and the necessity for forward treatment being carried out in light medical units, since hospitals could not be moved in. These factors produced the "Corps Medical Centres," which consisted of one (or two) Indian Malaria Forward Treatment Centres, and one (or two) Casualty Clearing Stations, with ancillary units, such as X-ray, laboratory, transfusion units, etc. Casualties from forward formations usually 30–50 miles distant, were carried to these Centres in light aircraft (L.5), piloted by U.S.A.A.F. and R.A.F. personnel. As a general rule, cases requiring more than three weeks' treatment were evacuated from these Centres by C.47 (Dakota) aircraft to forward base hospitals, but geography and climate imposed certain restrictions. In crossing the high mountain ranges often obscured by cloud, aircraft flew at 13,000–15,000 feet altitude, sometimes being forced up to 17,000 feet. Since oxygen was not available, this imposed limitations on the types of cases which could be evacuated. During the Irrawaddy crossings, for example, there was a sharp increase in the number of chest wounds. Such cases had to be retained in forward areas until convalescence was well established.

411. In Fourteenth Army, some 75 per cent. of medical cases were returned direct to units from the Corps Medical Centres. With regard to surgical cases, the establishment of these Centres also resulted in an immense saving of manpower

and suffering. Thorough and timely forward surgery was rendered possible, followed by rapid evacuation to base.

412. In the Arakan, the series of assault landings made amongst mangrove swamps, inland creeks and other ground unsuitable for advanced landing grounds, made early evacuation difficult. Hand-carriages, jeeps, assault landing craft and small river steamers had to be used as far as the advanced landing grounds, which prevented early evacuation of casualties to Casualty Clearing Stations. This disadvantage was partially offset by locating Mobile Surgical Units forward with Field Ambulances, to carry out emergency life-saving surgery.

413. In certain sectors, air and overland evacuation were alike impossible over long periods. A medical centre in the Tiddim area, for example, was supplied entirely by air-drop, and it held and treated a large number of wounded and sick, with excellent results.

414. There can be few campaigns in history, fought under such adverse conditions, in which the general health of large armies was maintained at such a high level. It must not be forgotten that the primary function of the medical services is officially defined as the maintenance of health and prevention of disease, a function which in popular esteem tends to get lost sight of or overshadowed by the glamour of their other duties in tending the sick and wounded.

415. Turning to the other services, our Provost resources were seriously strained during the period under review, and great difficulty was experienced in the provision of trained personnel and of certain items of stores, particularly traffic control and signal equipment, also of vehicles of the correct type. With the rapid advance over difficult terrain, and the opposed crossings of the Chindwin and Irrawaddy, the control of traffic became a major problem. It was largely solved by the use of light aircraft under the direction of the Assistant Provost Marshal. Communications between ground and air were successfully maintained and outstanding results were achieved.

416. The question of Welfare was one to which I devoted much time and thought. Its importance was great, particularly owing to the total lack of amenities or even civilization to be found in the majority of the operational areas. Furthermore, short leave was a greater rarity in this theatre than in others owing to the length of time it took to send parties to and from India. Its importance was great for the numerous Indian troops, but even more so for the British and African soldiers serving in a land other than their own.

Leave hostels and camps were established for all ranks at suitable centres in India, through the efforts of India Command and the numerous voluntary workers who helped to run them. Further, many residents in India extended the hospitality of their homes to both officers and other ranks. I should like here to pay tribute to all those who helped in these ways. Leave centres and clubs were planned for future establishment in Burma at such places as Maymyo, Mandalay and Rangoon, as were Amenity Store Depots which enabled troops whether British, Indian or African to purchase essential and other articles, which the country in which they were fighting could not supply. A great deal of welfare work was necessary in Rangoon; and careful forethought and planning was needed to ensure that sufficient personnel and equipment were brought in at once, by sea and air, to open several welfare centres within a few weeks of the capture of the city.

A large and increasing number of officers were employed by the Welfare Service, and results were continually more apparent. The introduction of the various women's services was both popular and successful, and the work done by the Women's Voluntary Service, the Women's Auxiliary Service (Burma) and by welfare workers of the First Aid Nursing Yeomanry was greatly appreciated by the troops of all the Allies.

Many philanthropic bodies sent their representatives to this theatre of war and did excellent work catering for the needs of the troops. Units of the Soldiers', Sailors', and Airmen's Families Association and of the Incorporated Soldiers' Sailors' and Airmen's Help Society looked after the troops' personal interests in connection with their family affairs in the United Kingdom. I would like to mention, in particular, the Y.W.C.A. without whose work it would have been impossible to bring many women helpers of other organizations concerned into Rangoon.

There was a steady increase in the number of artistes sent out by E.N.S.A. for "live" entertainment and the standard was improved. That many "Stars" came out, was usually the result of personal letters to them. The Faiye Dilhust Shabah organized by India Command provided live entertainment for Indian troops. The transport for entertainment parties, including air transport represented considerable effort. It was difficult to bring cinema shows up to the standard I should have liked, for many reasons. Indian films were provided for the Indian troops.

Radio distribution vans were of value in broadcasting music and records to isolated units. Broadcasting was supplied at first from Delhi and later from Radio SEAC, but unfortunately the supply of wireless sets failed by thousands to reach the entitlement figure fixed by the War Office.

An adequate supply of reading matter was of first importance. Daily news was catered for by the newspaper SEAC, whose paid sales exceeded 20,000 a day in Fourteenth Army alone. A weekly magazine "Phoenix" started publication in February. The first consignment of 11,300 copies of Sunday newspapers from the United Kingdom was flown in in the Spring of 1945, and was very popular, troops being able to read their home papers only 7 days after publication. Reading matter for Indian troops presented special difficulties owing to differences of language.

Of welfare equipment generally, sports gear was satisfactory as a great amount was made in India, but gramophones, wireless sets (as already mentioned) and musical instruments were always in short supply and were many thousands below the target figure laid down.

417. The work of registration and concentration of the graves of battle casualties was kept well up to date. The Graves Registration Service had the important task of tracing missing and deceased prisoners of war, and a start was made to clarify the situation regarding Rangoon gaol, in which many Allied prisoners were held captive.

418. Army Educational Corps personnel have been primarily concerned with the production of daily news-sheets including some in the vernacular, which have kept the troops informed about their own and other war fronts, and in touch with home news and developments. Tackling the important task of the primary education of Indian troops has, of course, only been possible when formations have been withdrawn from active operations. A start was also made on post-war education to assist the soldier in learning or re-learning trades for civil life.

419. Finally, I will add a note on the work of the Royal Army Pay Corps and its Indian equivalent. Their task has been no easy one. During the Burma campaign, neither banks nor treasuries were available, and all the cash required for the Forces had to be taken into the country. The bulk of this was flown in and distributed from forward airstrips. Frequently it was necessary to get the cash to units by air-drop. With my approval, and the concurrence of the Commander-in-Chief, India, the accounts of British other ranks serving in South-East Asia Command and India Command were transferred from Meerut to Fixed Centre Paymasters in the U.K. This should have greatly facilitated the accounting procedure connected with release and repatriation.

SECTION XXVI (paras. 420–440)
QUARTER-MASTER-GENERAL'S SERVICES MATTERS
Supplies: Ordnance Services: Electrical and Mechanical Engineers: Pioneers and Labour: Remounts and Veterinary Services: Postal, canteens and salvage: Major deficiencies of equipment.

420. I do not intend this to be in any way a technical report, nor that it should attempt to be complete. I will only mention a few matters which should be of general interest; many of the major aspects of administration affecting the Services, and their more outstanding achievements, have been referred to already.

421. A revised Field Service ration scale for Indian troops was introduced in November 1944. This was followed by a revised scale for British troops on the 1st March, 1945, and for African troops on the 1st May. These scales were not only of great calorific value but provided a more varied and palatable diet. Starting in November, 1944, 585 tons of frozen meat per month were delivered into Assam, Eastern Bengal and Arakan by nine aircraft sorties six days a week. A large proportion of British and African troops benefited from this scheme, though local distribution was still somewhat restricted by the full quota of insulated lorries not yet being available. From November also, 40 tons per month of frozen meat were

being shipped to Chittagong, where two 16 ton cold storage plants had just been installed, and six others were in course of erection. Rail delivery of frozen meat into Assam began in January, and the fly-in of this commodity could then be stopped. Rail delivery into Eastern Bengal also began directly the cold storage plants in that area were ready (15th February). A 3,000 ton refrigerated store ship arrived from the U.K. in February, and was located at Chittagong as a floating store. A 500 ton cold storage plant was also installed at this port in March.

The above arrangements greatly improved the situation as regards British and African troops. Meat issues to Indian troops were also increased, but not to the same extent. They rose from 2.87 issues per month in December to over eight in February. I should have liked to have improved on this figure, but several factors prevented further increase; the large number of Indian troops in the theatre compared with the available supply of goats, the apparent impossibility of increasing the supply of dehydrated meat from India, and, lastly, the religious susceptibilities of the Indian troops themselves.

422. Little opportunity has arisen so far in this Despatch to give any account of the work of the Ordnance services, and I will now remedy this omission. In November, 1944, the main Ordnance depots for the maintenance of the Allied forces were located as follows:- at Manipur Road, for the Northern L. of C, a Base Ordnance Depot and a Base Ammunition Depot, and at Chittagong for the Southern L. of C, similar depots. The position of these depots remained unchanged until February 1945, when instructions were issued for the switch of ordnance stores from Manipur Road to Chittagong, for the maintenance of Fourteenth Army and 15 Indian Corps from airfields in the Chittagong area. Large quantities of stores and ammunition were consequently transferred by rail to Chittagong, and also diverted to Chittagong from depots in India. All vehicles and heavy equipment still continued to be despatched through Manipur Road.

423. In March, two ammunition depots, each designed to support a Corps of two divisions, were switched from Manipur Road to Akyab and Ramree, and, from the 1st April, the ammunition supply of Fourteenth Army became dependent on these two depots. It was decided to close the Manipur Road Ordnance depot as soon as possible, in order to enable it to be reopened at Rangoon. To allow this, the formation of a Central Burma stockpile was begun at Myingyan. This was to consist of 15 days' reserve of certain essential ordnance stores. By early April, the Manipur Road Depot was considerably reduced and the Chittagong Depot assumed all responsibility for issues after the 15th. During this month no fewer than 7,800 vehicles were sent forward from Manipur Road to Fourteenth Army, to create the necessary reserve in Central Burma before the monsoon closed the road L. of C.

424. The following table shows the tonnages handled and vehicles issued from the main Depots on the Northern and Southern Ls. of C. in November 1944, and for comparison, April 1945.

Tonnages and Vehicles Handled

	M.T. Spares	Other Ordnance Stores	Ammunition	Vehicles
November, 1944-				
Northern L. of C.	1,100	6,200	4,000	1,325
Southern L. of C.	1,300	6,200	no record	450
April, 1945-				
Northern L. of C.	3,300*	7,500*	8,500*	7,900
Southern L. of C.	3,300	7,200	17,000	620

* Surplus tonnage backloaded to India.

425. The work of the Electrical and Mechanical Engineers has already been mentioned in the early parts of the Despatch. I would like to draw attention to a few miscellaneous points which carry valuable lessons for the future. Just before the crossing of the Irrawaddy, most formations concentrated their workshops forward. The necessity for workshop personnel being trained to defend themselves became immediately apparent. Japanese "jitter-parties" crossed the river every night, while other parties of enemy stragglers, often quite large, attacked our E.M.E. recovery parties; enemy patrols laid mines actually in our workshop areas.

426. When it was decided to fly 2 British Division out of Burma, arrangements were made to collect their vehicles. Unfortunately the lessons which should have been learnt from similar circumstances in the Kabaw Valley were forgotten, and again it was not appreciated that elaborate precautions are necessary to guard vehicle parks. The result was that several hundred vehicles were rendered temporarily useless within 24 hours of being collected because valuable parts were stolen; considerable repair resources had to be diverted to make them serviceable again.

427. Another lesson learnt during this period was that when a force is dependent on air supply, careful consideration must be given to the provision of heavy spares such as tank parts. A reserve of essential parts must be created as far forward as possible by the time the advance begins. There were occasions when heavy tank parts could not be brought in when required, because at the time the air lift needed was too great in proportion to their value.

428. Fourteenth Army took over 30,000 vehicles into Burma. Although the advance was over roads previously considered impassable for mechanical formations, only one sixth of these vehicles failed to reach their final destination. But the wear and tear was heavy; on an average, each vehicle passed through E.M.E. second or third line workshops once every three months. An additional load was placed on the E.M.E. by the long road L. of C. Replacement vehicles had to travel 600 miles from Manipur Road railhead to the Irrawaddy, and at least half the distance was over extremely bad roads. Nearly a third of these replacement vehicles required extensive repairs, and all of them required careful overhaul, before they could be issued to units.

429. It is not surprising, from what has been said so far of the enormous administrative effort which the Burma campaign entailed, that the labour force required was very considerable. As far as military labour was concerned, the Pioneer and Labour formations in the Allied Land Forces, South-East Asia area in November 1944 consisted of the following units:-

Type of Unit	Number of Units	Total working strength
Indian Pioneer Corps	234	71,872
Indian State Labour Units	59	42,100
Civil Pioneer Force Battalions	20	20,480
Assam Civil Porters Corps	11	10,560
Labour provided by the Indian Tea Association	—	78,796
Madras Labour Units	13	12,480
Ceylon Auxiliary Pioneer Corps	13	4,290
Italian Auxiliary Pioneer Corps	2 groups	1,520
5 (East African) Pioneer Corps	1	480
Total		242,578

This large force was mainly concentrated on the Northern L. of C. from Manipur Road to Imphal and southwards, and from Assam southwards down the Ledo Road with the United States forces. There were, however, also considerable numbers in the Chittagong area, and with the forward elements of Fourteenth Army.

430. By the end of April, 1945, the labour employed in Burma had reached the half-million mark, of which about half was unregimented civil labour. Some 53,000 of the regimented part of this labour force were employed on building and maintaining the Ledo Road to China. The Americans provided technical troops and recruited civilians, but organized military labour was commanded by Indian Pioneer Corps Group Commanders. There was a British Pioneer and Labour Staff on the increment with American H.Q., and the arrangement whereby the British provided the main labour force for the effort worked smoothly. The advance of Fourteenth Army entailed close support by Pioneer units, and there was a steady flow of Pioneer companies from the L. of C. into the Army area, especially during March, 1945. Civil Labour Control teams, composed of 150 officers who had received special training, were flown into Burma in March, and they were most successful in obtaining local civilians to work for the Army. At Mandalay and Shwebo in particular, the arrival of these teams to organize civil labour avoided the necessity of transporting large labour forces over the already strained L. of C. The labour aspect of the development of Rangoon was well handled. Pioneer companies and Civil Labour Control teams were included in the earliest convoys, and the result was that at no stage was the port development hindered by shortage of labour.

431. The work done by the Pioneers and other labour units was both strenuous and varied. Their many duties included the building of roads, railways and

airfields, and the handling of all military stores at docks, stations, depots and air-fields. Pioneer companies took part in all the amphibious "right hook" operations on the Arakan coast, and they went well forward portering with Fourteenth Army and 36 British Division. They formed, moreover, a vital part of the great air supply organization, providing the working parties at both the Rear and Forward Airfield Maintenance Organizations; in the case of 36 British Division, they were actually employed to collect the supplies dropped in the Divisional dropping zones.

432. One of the few decreases to be reported during the period of this Despatch is in animal transport. The decision in March to employ 5 and 17 Indian Divisions on a motor transport basis, as well as the fly-out of 2 British Division and later 36 British Division, entailed the progressive withdrawal of large numbers of animals. This involved a considerable change in the function of the Remount Service, Allied Land Forces, South-East Asia, which was designed to hold animal reinforcements at basic wastage figures. Large numbers of animals were collected and returned to India, while, of complete units, it was found possible to withdraw five Animal Transport companies and five Field Ambulance troops to India in April.

On the veterinary side, the only contagious disease of major importance which occurred among animals was Epizootic Lymphangitis. Energetic control measures were taken and although cases were fairly numerous, the disease did not interfere with operations. Successful results were obtained from plastic surgical operations, which enabled animals suffering from saddle injuries to be quickly taken into work again with special saddle fittings.

433. The efficient working of the field postal system is a very important factor in the maintenance of morale. In December 1944, exceptionally heavy Christmas mails were distributed without delay; a large number of low medical category British soldiers being lent to the Base Post Office to meet the abnormal pressure of work. In January, a daily fly-in of all classes of mail from Imphal to Fourteenth Army units was introduced, and, from the experience gained, it was decided to allot special aircraft for mail conveyance, flying two sorties per day. Mail deliveries which would have taken many days by road were thus accomplished in one – an improvement in service which was much appreciated. Free postage conces-sions were introduced early in February 1945, and concessional rates for parcels in March, which afforded substantial reductions as compared with the old rates.

434. I am glad to be able to report an improvement in the Canteen Services during the period of this Despatch, which can be judged by the fact that the sales increased from about 2¼ million rupees in November 1944 to 5½ million in April 1945. This increase is greatly out of proportion to the increase in troops and was due to the opening of more canteens and the importation of a wider range of goods for sale. There was, however, throughout the campaign a serious shortage of both cigarettes and beer. In March 1945, for example, when opera-tions were at their height, the fighting soldier had to be content with a meagre allowance of 100 cigarettes and three bottles of beer per month.

435. The problem of disposal of salvage was difficult in this theatre. The policy was to concentrate on the recovery of serviceable or semi-serviceable articles (capable of re-issue as far forward as possible) and to discourage the collection of scrap, which, even when it could be transported, was difficult to sell. In January 1945, the Salvage service assumed responsibility for breaking down vehicles written off by Ordnance, which by then had risen to many thousands, at the rate of 2,000 per month. Engines and batteries were removed and returned through Ordnance channels, as were a large number of serviceable spares of other natures, including 21,600 tyres. Other important salvage operations included the back-loading of 218,700 parachutes and 180,300 petrol and oil containers, both items which were in great demand. Over 15,000 tons of material were salvaged between November 1944 and April 1945, inclusive; the estimated value of which exceeded £1,150,000.

436. Finally, no account of administrative matters in this campaign would be completed without a brief mention of deficiencies in equipment. These were inevitably many since the European theatre obviously had to have priority. In many cases lack of equipment was partially overcome by the ingenuity and impro-visation of base and field units, and I therefore propose to confine my remarks to the most serious deficiencies.

437. When I assumed command in November 1944 the vehicle situation had become extremely serious. This was due to four causes. Firstly, provision action in the past had been inadequate; secondly, there had been very heavy wastage during the battles of the preceding summer; thirdly, the need to equip newly raised transport companies to support the coming offensive; fourthly, the diffi-culty of procuring vehicles of lend-lease origin, bids for which had to include full operational justification and were very carefully screened by the American authorities in India and Washington.

I had a close examination carried out and ordered that future estimated pro-duction should be allocated in detail only to essential projects. As a result it was found that, provided production and movement kept up to expectation, all essen-tial commitments could be met except for specialist vehicles, especially break-down lorries, the need for which was increasing owing to extended Ls. of C. and rough roads and terrain.

The responsibility for equipping units prior to moving them into my area rested with India Command. But the industrial capacity of India was stretched to the limit and many units arrived deficient, or equipped with worn out vehicles. This was a constant source of anxiety and I directed that a pool of Allied Land Forces, South-East Asia vehicles should be held in Calcutta, from which the requirements of units could be met as they passed through. This system worked well and had it not been initiated many units would have gone forward badly equipped, and it would have been impossible to re-equip 2 British and 26 Indian Divisions for the Dracula operation at such short notice.

438. It became apparent early in 1945 that the restriction of tyre imports to India on account of the world shortage of rubber would seriously affect the production of new vehicles unless considerable economies were at once effected. Tyres in short supply were those required for the 3-ton 4×4 lorry and the 15-cwt. 4×4 truck.[3] Reduction in the output of these vehicles would have had the most serious repercussions at a time when the increasing mobility of operations called for the greatest possible supply of these types. Immediate measures of economy, salvage, repair and control of issues were taken, with the result that demands on India were progressively and markedly decreased. Some idea of the effort needed to achieve this result may be gained from the fact that, in four months, no fewer than 97,200 covers and 51,700 tubes were backloaded for reconditioning.

439. During March, complaints were received from Fourteenth Army regarding the unsatisfactory condition of replacement tank engines that had been reconditioned in Base Workshops in India. This situation was aggravated by the fact that we could not await the delivery of new engines which were on order from America. No fewer than 101 Grant, 47 Stuart and 68 Sherman engines had to be delivered early in April, to refit the two tank brigades for their drive on Rangoon. The majority of these engines were in the west of India, and it was obvious that they could not now be issued without overhaul and test. By agreement with India Command, a senior R.E.M.E. officer was flown to Kirkee to supervise and accelerate the tests. By means of special rail, sea and air transport arrangements, combined with the fortunate arrival of some Sherman engines from America, the demand was met in full and in time.

440. The supply of 25-pr. H.E. ammunition caused anxiety early in 1945, since 500,000 rounds had had to be backloaded from India for the European theatre. Fortunately stocks in my depots were high at that time and supply for the succeeding months was met by backloading from Ceylon, giving priority in manufacture to the reconditioning of existing stocks and by speeding up indigenous production.

   The only other serious ammunition shortage was in 3.7-in. A.A. H.E., fuze 117. This was due to the increasingly extensive use of these guns in a ground rôle. The heavy ammunition expenditure thus incurred was only met by using up all existing stocks in India, and by greatly increasing provision action.

SECTION XXVII (paras. 441–447)
CIVIL AFFAIRS STAFF (BURMA)

The separation of Civil Affairs Staff (Burma) and H.Q. Allied Land Forces, South-East Asia; The transport problem: Stores for Civil Affairs: The necessity for integration of Civil Affairs and Military Staffs.

---

441. It is possible that no country suffered more extensively from the destruction of war than Burma. Twice has the area which constitutes the heart of the whole country's life and economy been fought over, and between these periods of

fighting it was subject to a sterile and damaging occupation. As Commander-in-Chief, therefore, my responsibility for restoring civil life behind the battle area by means of Military Government was a heavy one.

442. When my Advanced Headquarters moved from Delhi to Barrackpore at the end of November, 1944, the shortage of accommodation at the new site made it necessary to leave the Civil Affairs Staff behind. This proved most unfortunate, even though Civil Affairs interests were represented at my Headquarters by a senior officer. For a very heavy burden was thrown on the former, particularly with regard to transport, workshops, signals, and the operation of railway and inland water transport, just at a moment when the Army was seriously short of these services for its own operational needs. It was not until the Chief Civil Affairs Officer and his staff rejoined my Headquarters in March, 1945, that integration began and developed to mutual advantage. The Civil Affairs Staff is a military organization and an integral part of the Staff as a whole and can only function properly as such. This fact is sometimes lost sight of both by the military Staff proper and the Civil Affairs Staff themselves. If this close integration does not exist, Civil Affairs cannot be expected to plan adequately, nor to produce their own requirements, with the result that the Army in the end is compelled to take on commitments which it has not foreseen and is not equipped to perform.

443. Without attempting to give a full account of the rehabilitation and organization of Burma after its progressive recapture, I intend to give some account of a few aspects of the subject. How this responsibility increased with our advance is shown by the fact that in November, 1944, we had 66 Civil Affairs officers operating in Burma. In May, 1945, we had 1,915. We were at first desperately short of experienced men for this work, and what was eventually accomplished in 1945 under the leadership of Major-General H.E. Rance reflected the greatest credit on all concerned.

444. The provision of transport for civil relief purposes was a matter of difficulty. Since no special provision had been made by the United Kingdom against Civil Affairs (Burma) demand for a total of about 7,000 vehicles, all their essential requirements had to be provided out of Army stocks. By the beginning of May, 1945, some 1,900 new vehicles, the maximum that could be spared, had been allocated for this purpose. This transport was organized into three groups. No. 1 Transport Group had one company operating in Arakan, one in the Fourteenth Army sector, forward of Mandalay, and one earmarked for Rangoon. No. 2 Group had a company working in Northern Combat Area Command, where two more companies were being raised. No. 3 Group had a company on the Manipur Road – Imphal run, while new companies were being raised at Toungoo and Myingyan. Nevertheless, with only five companies actually in operation at the end of the period, the relief supplies handled between November, 1944, and May, 1945, totalled over 13,000 tons.

445. While the Civil Affairs stores tonnage was small, Civil Affairs Staff (Burma) were allotted a tonnage on the L. of C. and sent it forward under their own arrangements. As larger areas of Burma were liberated, a new system was introduced, with effect from the 1st February, 1945, whereby all Civil Affairs Staff (Burma) stores were demanded and called forward through military channels. The internal movement of Civil Affairs stores, especially in North Burma, presented several problems, owing to the paucity of communications and the shortage of transport. The communication system developed for the supply of the advancing armies did not correspond with that required to deal with civil needs. Thus it was only possible, initially, to distribute a very bare minimum of relief stores. A transport company was raised to assist in bringing the Civil Affairs stores from Manipur Road to Imphal, and from Imphal essential stores for North Burma were carried in transport aircraft, at an average rate of 75 tons per day.

446. During the period under report, demands for essential relief stores for the whole of Burma were placed by S.A.C.S.E.A. on India Command, to cover six months' military occupation. Estimated requirements included stores in the following categories: food, agricultural implements, medical and veterinary requirements, hospital equipment, stores and equipment for refugee camps, household goods, soap, clothing, footwear and newsprint. To tide over the inevitable delay before the arrival of these stores, a special urgent demand was placed for certain essential commodities. This special demand included food, and also sufficient stores for the immediate equipment of 21 hospitals and 73 dispensaries.

447. The demands mentioned in the previous paragraph, to cover six months' military occupation, could not be met wholly from India's resources. India Command accepted certain items and indented on the United Kingdom for the balance, where the War Office was already taking advance procurement action. To assist the War Office in selecting goods, the Principal Commercial Officer of the Civil Affairs Staff was sent to England, with the task of preparing specifications for such commodities as were available, and accepting alternatives when necessary. By early May, the position with regard to these stores demands was satisfactory. India's quota of wheat had been increased to enable her to supply flour and atta, and she was also supplying the majority of the other food items required. Other stores which India had arranged to supply included 850,000 lbs. of soap and 35,000,000 yards of cloth. Medical stores had already been shipped from the U.K. The results achieved on the medical side deserve special note. The number of hospital beds opened increased from 400 in November, 1944, to about 3,000 by May, 1945, and in addition, a large number of local dispensaries had been installed all over the country.

SECTION XXVIII (paras. 448–451)
CONCLUSIONS ON ADMINISTRATION

General conclusion: The vital necessity for air supply: The importance of Akyab and Kyaukpyu: The importance of the capture of Rangoon.

---

448. As I stated at the beginning of this part of the Despatch I have gone into the administrative aspects of this campaign in considerable detail, and what I have said should suffice to show the tremendous complexity of the problem and the difficulties involved; the need for the most careful administrative planning, improvisation and energy, and how magnificently all requirements were met by all ranks throughout Allied Land Forces, South-East Asia ; and finally the success that was achieved without which the speed and the scope of the operations would not have been possible.

The main conclusions that I reach from this administrative survey are three-fold; the vital necessity of air supply; the importance of Akyab and Kyaukpyu; the importance of the capture of Rangoon.

449. Because we had to enter Burma by the "back door" the capacity of the undeveloped land Ls. of C. were totally insufficient to maintain the large modern army that was necessary to defeat the Japanese. The minimum requirements of Fourteenth Army averaged some 2,000 tons per day. The maximum tonnage that could possibly be carried on the Northern L. of C. into Central Burma, despite the tremendous amount of equipment, material and energy that was expended in its development, was only 700 tons a day. The balance, therefore, could only be brought in by air, and this fact shows quite clearly that the maintenance of operations at the scale finally achieved would have been quite impossible without air supply. This air supply was used on a scale greater than in any other theatre of war. Its success was due to the splendid integration, co-operation and energy of the air forces concerned and the various ground organizations, all of which started from scratch with very little previous experience. This success has un-doubtedly been one of the features of the campaign.

450. The capture of Akyab and Kyaukpyu and the rapid development of their ports and airfields were vital to the successful conclusion of the campaign, namely, the capture of Rangoon. It was only from the airfields at these two places that transport aircraft, operating at maximum economic range, could reach our forward troops in the railway corridor and the Irrawaddy Valley. Thus, although the operations of Fourteenth Army were inevitably the more spectacular, their triumph could not have been achieved without the success of the operations carried out by 15 Indian Corps in Arakan.

451. The capture of Rangoon, prior to the monsoon, was of great administrative importance. Not only did it cut the Japanese mainline of supply into Burma, but it was the first step to enabling me to maintain Fourteenth Army by sea, thereby releasing the bulk of air transport (now required for essential rest and refit for

future operations) and gradually liquidating that expensive administrative route, the Northern L. of C. The Air and Northern Ls. of C. would have been hard put to it alone to have maintained our forces in Burma during the monsoon.

In addition the capture of Rangoon enabled me to build up an advanced base from which future sea, land and airborne operations could be mounted and maintained.

PART III
SECTION XXIX (paras. 452–465)
ACKNOWLEDGMENTS

The Soldiers; Indian, Gurkha, British, American, African and Chinese: Fourteenth Army: 15 Indian Corps: The Navy: The Air Forces: Northern Combat Area Command: India Command: The Army Air Transport Organization: General Sir William Slim: Lieut-General Sir Philip Christison: H.Q. Allied Land Forces, South-East Asia.

---

452. At the conclusion of an outstandingly successful campaign, it is impossible to pay adequate tribute everywhere it is deserved, since so many have contributed towards the combined achievement.

Many Commanders and formations have been specifically mentioned in the first two parts of this Despatch. I therefore propose to confine my appreciation here to the few, whose outstanding claims will be sincerely acknowledged by the many, to whom space does not allow me to pay individual tribute.

453. First and foremost should be acknowledged the debt which is owed to the fighting soldiers, Indian, Gurkha, British, American, African and Chinese.

By far the greatest part of the fighting units in my Command were from the Indian Army. I had already had experience of the excellence of the Indian formations in Africa and Italy, but the campaign in Burma above all showed their versatility and ability to assimilate new ideas and technique, qualities perhaps less expected than the valour which we have come to take for granted. The development of which the Indian soldier has proved capable is one of the most remarkable features of the war, and no praise is too high for those who by command and training have produced this development. The Indian Armoured Corps came into their own for the first time. They fought magnificently, and their gunnery was excellent; their maintenance – without which armoured formations can achieve little – was first class under the exacting test of the dash for Rangoon. The Indian Field Regiments fully lived up to the high standard of the Indian Army. The Sappers and Miners Engineer Battalions, Signallers, R.I.A.S.C. and all the other arms and services did sterling work under often extremely hard conditions. Nevertheless, the heaviest burden fell on the infantryman, more so in this campaign than most, and it is the Indian and Gurkha infantryman, who mastered and conquered a fanatical enemy, that I should like to single out for special praise.

The appalling climatic and topographical conditions under which the campaign was fought were perhaps even sterner tests for the British troops than they were for the troops drawn from India, Africa and Nepal. But despite this the British soldier proved once again that he is second to none. The doggedness which will not allow reverse to become final defeat, his genius for improvisation and his adaptability to constantly changing conditions were all demonstrated. Separated by hundreds of miles, and for many long years, from all contact with the civilization which had hitherto been an integral part of his life and outlook, he nevertheless remained cheerful, undaunted and determined to inflict upon the enemy the defeat which he now knew lay within his power to accomplish. And especially it was the infantryman again, his hardships more often than not increased by the lack of numbers in his platoon and company, who bore the chief burden. The British who served in Burma have indeed deserved well of their country.

There were very few American soldiers under my command, and these were withdrawn before the battle for Central Burma and the dash for Rangoon. Nevertheless, the Mars Brigade fought with conspicuous success in difficult country in the operations which led to the re-opening of the Burma Road. It was a matter of great regret to me that I was not able to retain this formation in the Command longer.

The African soldier was making history. For the first time divisions from East and West Africa were fighting as complete formations with the British Commonwealth forces. They showed outstanding ability to endure terrible conditions of terrain and climate, and to operate with limited resources and slender communications with the outside world.

The Chinese were well trained and good fighters. They inflicted many defeats on the Japanese in Northern Combat Area Command before they were finally withdrawn, after they had reached Lashio.

454. Having praised the fighting man himself, I will next say a few words about the great formations which won the battles, Fourteenth Army and 15 Indian Corps.

The great battles fought in 1944 in Arakan, and at Kohima and Imphal under the leadership of General Sir George Giffard laid the groundwork for our subsequent achievement. In those battles of annihilation, Fourteenth Army and 15 Indian Corps found their souls, and, whilst redeeming the days of adversity of 1942 and 1943, they destroyed a great part of the Japanese army.

455. After these decisive successes, Fourteenth Army pressed on with the pursuit of the withdrawing enemy throughout the monsoon season. By its close the enemy were back at the Chindwin, and the offensive to gain a hold in the dry belt of Central Burma was launched, with the object of bringing the enemy to decisive battle. Following an advance which gave the Japanese no time to recover their balance, the wide Irrawaddy River – a most formidable military obstacle – was

forced at four opposed crossings, and bridgeheads held against fierce counter-attacks.

Then followed the brilliant Meiktila battle in which the enemy was out-manoeuvred, out-fought and so severely mauled that never again was General Kimura able to regroup his forces so as to fight as an army. This success was exploited in the dash to capture Rangoon with mechanised columns and armour, re-inforced and maintained by air transport. In any theatre such an exploitation of success would be noteworthy; in the peculiar and difficult conditions of the Burma war, it was a brilliant feat.

These are achievements of which any army should be proud; an excellent plan triumphantly executed. The troops displayed outstanding endurance against severe physical difficulties and fought magnificently. The versatility and all-round efficiency of the army was fully displayed in the later stages, when, after many months of success in the jungle, it won decisive victories in open and mobile fighting.

456. 15 Indian Corps deserves separate mention. The Arakan was an extraordinarily difficult terrain, with its wide tidal chaungs, huge areas of mangrove swamp and jungle which often stretched without a break from the mountains inland to the sea itself. Improvisation and initiative were the order of the day. It was a remarkable feat to establish in the short time available both fair- and all-weather airfields and supply bases at Akyab and Ramree. On these depended both the ability of Fourteenth Army to make its final dash for Rangoon and the safety of that army's supplies if the monsoon came before Rangoon was reached. Finally it was 15 Indian Corps which mounted the very hazardous operation for the capture of Rangoon by the "sea gate," and by its successful accomplishment, to open the port at least fourteen valuable days earlier than would otherwise have been possible.

The operations of 15 Indian Corps and Fourteenth Army were inter-dependent and only by the combination of these geographically separated campaigns was the reconquest of Burma made possible.

457. This campaign was above all a combined operation, in which command of the sea and air was vital to the land battle. The destruction of the Japanese armies, and therefore the main responsibility for the success or failure of the campaign, fell to the Army's lot. But since we were compelled to do this by the worst natural line of approach, and against the grain of the country, we were forced to depend heavily on the sea and air for our supply lines. The Royal Navy and Royal Indian Navy protected and kept open the one, while the Royal Air Force and U.S. Army Air Force dominated the other. The Army's debt to the other Services is large.

458. Under Admiral Sir Arthur Power, Commander-in-Chief, East Indies Fleet, the Royal Navy and Royal Indian Navy played an outstanding part throughout the campaign. I wish to express to him the Army's gratitude and admiration for the gallantry, enterprise and seamanship displayed by all ranks and ratings

under his command. The series of combined operations leap-frogging down the Arakan coast were carried out with limited resources, against the hazards of an exceptionally treacherous and intricate shore. I should like to pay a special tribute to those men of the Royal Indian Navy who manned the landing craft. It was appropriate that the final assault of all – that of Rangoon – should also have been the highest test of seamanship and skill, since both the weather and the navigational problems were exceptionally severe.

459. Air power was a vital element and dominating factor in our strategy. The resources were never able to meet the demands without exacting the utmost from both man and machine. The achievements of the Air Forces, both those of the British Empire and those of the United States' were of the highest order and our success is due in great part to their efforts. To Air-Marshal Sir Guy Garrod and Air-Marshal Sir Keith Park, his successor in command, I would like to express the Army's gratitude and admiration for the gallantry and devotion to duty of all ranks under their command.

In particular, I would like to pay tribute to General Stratemeyer, the Commanding General of Eastern Air Command, who had control of the tactical air battle and of all the aircraft taking part in it. While Air Command, South-East Asia was at Kandy, near the Supreme Commander, Eastern Air Command was close beside my Advanced Headquarters at Barrackpore, 2,000 miles away. Inevitably I spent most of my time here, and the co-operation between General Stratemeyer's staff and my own was both continuous and successful, and Eastern Air Command provided us with invariable assistance and unfailing support.

I cannot speak too highly of the work done by the squadrons which swept the Japanese from the skies, disrupted their land communications, and provided our troops with close fire support which was all the more valuable owing to the restricted amount of artillery available.

Air transport was used on a scale hitherto uprecedented in modern war. In the administrative part of this Despatch the tonnages handled daily are recorded, but to get the true measure of the effort, it should be remembered that the air-crews who delivered the goods often made three or four journeys a day over hazardous jungle country, often flying in appalling conditions of weather; many casualties were caused by these fearful conditions, but the risks were unflinchingly faced. The ground crews worked unceasingly by day and night in the open, sometimes in torrential rain, to keep the aircraft in commission and to enable the very high rates of service to be maintained.

460. I should like to pay tribute to the allied army forces, American and Chinese, which operated under Lieutenant-General Dan. I. Sultan. Although they did not take part in the later phases of the conquest of Burma they accomplished the politically important task of opening the Ledo/Burma Road to China. Particularly I thank General Sultan for his loyalty and whole-hearted co-operation throughout the campaign. I also pay tribute to General Sun Li Jen and General Liao Yo Hsiang for the way in which they inspired and led their forces.

461. On behalf of my own staff, and of the whole of the Allied Land Forces, South-East Asia, I should like to express our gratitude to His Excellency General (now Field-Marshal) Sir Claude Auchinleck and the staffs, troops and workers of the India Base for their unfailing and whole-hearted support throughout our operations. Since India was our base, the immense administrative task of supplying and maintaining our forces fell on India Command. The speed at which the campaign moved meant many alterations and our requirements sometimes necessarily came at short notice. Despite the difficulties which India's transportation system imposes, they never let us down.

462. To single out any branch of the Army for particular mention would be invidious, when all contributed so notably to the common victory. Their achievements have, I hope been made clear already in the Despatch. I will, however, mention the Army organization created to deal with the problems of air supply, the Army Air Transport Organization, commanded by Brigadier J.A. Dawson, since it was new and achieved such striking results. This is a field in which all have much still to learn. But enormous credit is due to this pioneer organization, not only for its solid achievements, but for the speed with which it improvised fresh methods and strove constantly to improve the technique of air-dropping. This method of supply will, I am sure, be greatly developed in the future, and the work of A.A.T.O. will have laid valuable foundations.

463. Just as Fourteenth Army's success was an outstanding feat of arms by the fighting soldier, so it was a personal triumph for its Commander, Lieutenant-General (now Field-Marshal) Sir William Slim. Throughout the campaign he led his Army magnificently. His is the credit for the planning and execution of the battle in Central Burma which finally defeated the Japanese armies. Having early secured the initiative, he forced General Kimura to conform to his strategy until he was driven out of Rangoon. He made an excellent plan, and pushed it resolutely through.

464. Lieutenant-General Sir Philip Christison commanded 15 Indian Corps in Arakan in an independent rôle, directly under H.Q., Allied Land Forces. His planning, in conjunction with Rear-Admiral Martin and Air Vice-Marshal the Earl of Bandon, of a series of intricate combined operations, worked smoothly and well, and were a model of inter-Service co-operation. His personality and drive were an inspiration to his troops and played an important part in the success of his command.

465. Finally, I would like to place on record the splendid work done by my own staff officers, NCOs, and men at H.Q., Allied Land Forces. In particular I bring to notice the work of Major-General G.P. Walsh, my Chief of General Staff and of Major-General E.M. Bastyan, my Major-General-in-Charge, Administration. During the period on which I am reporting, they carried out a great measure of reorganization of their respective divisions of the staff and carried very heavy responsibilities. I cannot speak too highly of the work of these officers and their

staffs, and I consider that the success achieved by my forces was to a great extent made possible by the work and ability of these two officers.

APPENDIX A

27 Feb. 45.

ALLIED LAND FORCES SOUTH EAST ASIA
OPERATION INSTRUCTION No. 12.

To:- Lieut-General SIR WILLIAM SLIM, K.C.B., C.B.E., D.S.O.,
   General Officer Commanding-in-Chief, Fourteenth Army.
Lieut-General DAN I. SULTAN, Commanding General,
   Northern Combat Area Command.
Lieut-General Sir PHILIP CHRISTISON, K.B.E., C.B., M.C.
   General Officer Commanding, 15 Indian Corps.
Ref. Maps: Survey of India ¼″ to 1 mile.

OBJECT
1. To capture Rangoon before the monsoon.

APPRECIATION
2. The battle for Mandalay is approaching its climax and large forces of the enemy are now concentrated in that area.

Fourteenth Army are attacking them from the north and are also encircling them from the west.

The Japanese intention is clearly to fight it out. This is borne out by the movements westwards of certain forces now east of the Irrawaddy.

The battle for Mandalay will therefore be slow; it will probably be grim; its outcome will nevertheless be certain.

3. To achieve our object it is first necessary to destroy the Japanese forces now in the Mandalay area.

This requires a concentrated effort by Fourteenth Army and N.C.A.C., both directed towards this common aim.

Only by this means shall we be able to capture Rangoon before the monsoon.

4. The withdrawal of formations of 15 Indian Corps must continue as planned.
  TASKS

5. *Fourteenth Army*
  (*a*) Will destroy the Japanese forces now facing them in the Mandalay area.
  (*b*) Will seize Rangoon before the monsoon.

6. *N.C.A.C.*
  (*a*) Will secure with all speed the general area Kyaukme SS 90 – Lashio.
  (*b*) Will then turn S.W. to assist in the destruction of the enemy forces in the Mandalay area.
  (*c*) After the battle of Mandalay, will exploit towards Loilem.

7. 15 *Indian Corps*
   (*a*) In general:-
     (i) Will contain the maximum number of enemy forces with the resources at their disposal.
     (ii) Operations will be developed so as not to call on air supply for maintenance.
   (*b*) In particular:-
     (i) Will destroy enemy forces in the An area.
     (ii) Will operate towards Prome, as far as resources permit, from a bridgehead in the Taungup area.

8. This Operation Instruction supersedes all previous Operation Instructions.

ACKNOWLEDGE.

> Signed: OLIVER LEESE.
> Lieutenant-General,
> Commander-in-Chief,
> Allied Land Forces, S.E.A.

APPENDIX B.
JAPANESE FORMATIONS IN BURMA AT THE BEGINNING OF MAY, 1945, WITH ESTIMATED STRENGTHS.
(A) – WEST OF RAILWAY CORRIDOR.
28th Army.

54 Division	5,500
55 Division (less 144 Regt. and portion Divisional troops)	4,800
72 Independent Mixed Brigade	1,600
153 Regiment, 49 Division	500
	12,400
Non-Divisional troops	4,800
Air (ground) troops	500
Naval (shore-based) troops	500
	18,200

(B) – EAST OF RAILWAY CORRIDOR, INCLUDING TENASSERIM COAST.
15th and 33rd Armies.

4 and 16 Regts., 2 Division	1,000
15 Division	3,000
18 Division	2,900
31 Division	4,000
33 Division	2,500
49 Division (less 153 Regt.)	1,500

53 Division	2,500
144 Regt., 55 Division (plus proportion Divisional troops)	2,500
56 Division	3,500
24 Independent Mixed Brigade	3,000
	26,400
Non-Divisional troops	29,000
Air (ground) troops	1,500
Naval (shore-based) troops	2,000
	58,900

CONTENTS

INTRODUCTION

PART I. NARRATIVE OF OPERATIONS

SECTION I (paras. 2–18). THE SITUATION ON TAKING OVER COMMAND.

Location of my HQ: Constitution of the command: Note on the topography and climate of Burma: The task: Strategic plans already in existence: The new directive.

SECTION II (paras. 19–27). THE OPERATIONAL SITUATION IN NOVEMBER.

The failure of the Japanese invasion of Spring, 1944: The importance of the 1944 monsoon operations: The state of the enemy, his strength and dispositions: Relative strengths: Our assets of sea and air power: Air supply.

SECTION III (paras. 28–49). OPERATIONS IN DECEMBER.

The abandonment of the airborne operation: The decision to advance on a two Corps front: 33 Corps operations to the capture of Shwebo: 4 Corps operations: Operations by Northern Combat Area Command: The capture of Bhamo: Note on operations in Arakan.

SECTION IV (paras. 50–69). THE READJUSTMENT OF PLANS IN DECEMBER.

The diversion of resources to China and its adverse effects: The enemy's dispositions: The poor quality of Intelligence about the enemy: Fourteenth Army's plan for the battle of the Mandalay plain: Comments on the plan.

SECTION V (paras. 70–91). THE IRRAWADDY CROSSINGS.

The establishment of 19 Indian Division's bridgeheads: The advance of 33 Corps up to the river: The bringing forward of 17 Indian Division: The plan for the crossings: Operations in 19 Indian Division's bridgehead: The four main crossings described: Progress by Northern Combat Area Command.

SECTION VI (paras. 92–101). THE SITUATION IN FEBRUARY.
A.L.F.S.E.A. Operation Instruction of the 27th February 1945: The change in scope of the Burma operations: The Japanese plans for a counter-offensive: Operations to enlarge our bridgeheads: The Northern Combat Area Command front.

SECTION VII (paras. 102–117). THE BATTLE FOR MANDALAY.
The importance of Meiktila: The capture of Meiktila and its effect on the Japanese plans: The capture of Mandalay: The Japanese counter-offensive to retake Meiktila.

SECTION VIII (paras. 118–130). THE CLEARING OF THE MANDALAY PLAIN.
The end of operations by Northern Combat Area Command: The opening of the road to Meiktila: The capture of Kyaukse: The clearing of Ava and Sagaing: The Japanese decision to withdraw: The shortage of transport aircraft: The achievements of 33 Corps.

SECTION IX (paras. 131–158). OPERATIONS IN ARAKAN.
General remarks: Topography: 15 Indian Corps' plan: The Divisional plans: Opening stages of the offensive: The advance to Foul Point: Operations inland and in the Kaladan Valley.

SECTION X (paras. 159–185). CAPTURE OF AKYAB AND SUBSEQUENT EXPLOITATION.
Modified plans for the capture of Akyab: The enemy's withdrawal: The Myebon and Kangaw operations: The battle for Myohaung: Operations of the West African Divisions.

SECTION XI (paras. 186–211). THE EXTENSION OF THE ARAKAN CAMPAIGN.
Reasons for the extension of the campaign: The capture of Ramree and Cheduba: New instructions to the Commander, 15 Indian Corps: The new plan and its subsequent modification: The withdrawal of 25 Indian Division: The Letpan landing: Occupation of Taungup.

SECTION XII (paras. 212–227). PLANS FOR THE CAPTURE OF RANGOON.
The situation in Central Burma at the end of March: General Slim's plan for the drive south: The decision to go for Rangoon by sea: Reasons for this decision: Directive issued by the Supreme Allied Commander on the 17th April.

SECTION XIII (paras. 228–256). FOURTEENTH ARMY'S DRIVE SOUTH.
The regrouping phase: Fighting in the Irrawaddy Valley: The capture of Prome: 4 Corps' axis: Successive captures of Pyawbwe, Pyinmana and Toungoo: Japanese plans to defend Pegu: The advance to Pegu: Capture of Pegu.

SECTION XTV (paras. 257–265). THE CAPTURE OF RANGOON.
The plan for the seaborne operation against Rangoon: The airborne operation:
Rangoon discovered virtually abandoned: The link-up with Fourteenth Army.

SECTION XV (paras. 266–274). THE NEW SITUATION.
Opening of a new phase: Internal Security situation: Tactical situation after
capture of Rangoon: The administrative situation and the effect on future
plans.

SECTION XVI (paras. 275–281). OPERATIONS IN MAY.
New orders issued by General Slim: Arakan operations: 4 Corps operations:
33 Corps operations: Note on guerilla organizations.

SECTION XVII (paras. 282–291). THE FINAL BATTLES.
Reorganization of the Allied Land Forces: Formation and tasks of Twelfth
Army: Operations in the Irrawaddy Valley: The Lower Sittang Battle: The
Battle of the Break-out: Conclusion of operations.

SECTION XVIII (paras. 292–301). PLANS FOR MALAYA.
Joint Planning Staff Paper of the 23rd February 45: Operations Roger, Zipper
and Mailfist: Cancellation of Roger: D-Day for Zipper: Zipper appreciation
and plan.

PART II. ADMINISTRATION

SECTION XIX (paras. 302–310). THE MAINTENANCE PROBLEM.
The Northern, Southern and Air Lines of Communication generally: The size
of the problem.

SECTION XX (paras. 311–334). THE DEVELOPMENT OF THE
NORTHERN LINE OF COMMUNICATION.
Formation of L. of C. Command: Supply routes to the Advanced bases: The
Assam Railways: The problem of replacement vehicles: The development of
the Chindwin I.W.T. link: Changes in the organization of the L. of C.:
Changes in the organization of Supply and Transport: Further changes in the
organization of the L. of C.: The development of the Burma Railways: Petrol
distribution: Some statistics.

SECTION XXI (paras. 335–350). THE DEVELOPMENT OF THE
SOUTHERN LINE OF COMMUNICATION.
Development of Chittagong and the smaller Arakan ports: I.W.T. projects:
Development of Akyab and Kyaukpyu: The final stages in Arakan.

SECTION XXII (paras. 351–365). THE DEVELOPMENT OF THE
AIR LINES OF COMMUNICATION.
The air supply situation in November, 1944: The organization of F.A.M.Os.
and R.A.M.Os.: The opening of the Chittagong air base: Formation and
organization of C.A.A.T.O.: The switch to Akyab and Ramree Advanced Bases:
The air supply situation in April, 1945: Airfield construction: Casualty
evacuation: Situation after the capture of Rangoon.

Notes

1. Documents captured after our offensive opened in the middle of December showed that the Japanese intended to hold forward as long as possible, but that their main line was to be the Kaladan River from, and including, Akyab and Kyauktaw.

2. Operations in Burma and North-East India from the 16th November 1943, to the 22nd June, 1944.

3. A 4 × 4 lorry or truck is one in which the driving power is transmitted to all four wheels.

Index

(1) Index of Persons

(2) Index of Naval, Military and Air Force Units